尾田栄一郎

Ten years have passed since I first began my days of battle with the boys. Boys who were 10 when this manga started are now 20. They're probably hairy in the you-know-what. Let me be clear though, I mean the armpits. Well, this is getting a bit too long. (I mean the manga, not the pit hair.) There are still many things that I want to draw about, so whether you're a smooth boy or a hairy boy, I hope you'll stick around and enjoy the ride.

   —Eiichiro Oda, 2007

iichiro Oda began his manga career at the age of 17, when his one-shot cowboy manga **Wanted!** won second place in the coveted Tezuka manga awards. Oda went on to work as an assistant to some of the biggest manga artists in the industry, including Nobuhiro Watsuki, before winning the Hop Step Award for new artists. His pirate adventure **One Piece**, which debuted in **Weekly Shonen Jump** in 1997, quickly became one of the most popular manga in Japan.

ONE PIECE VOL. 45
WATER SEVEN PART 14

SHONEN JUMP Manga Edition

STORY AND ART BY EIICHIRO ODA

English Adaptation/Jake Forbes
Translation/Labaaman, HC Language Solutions, Inc.
Touch-up Art & Lettering/Primary Graphix
Design/Sean Lee
Supervising Editor/Yuki Murashige
Editor/Alexis Kirsch

Printed in the U.S.A.

Published by VIZ Media, LLC
P.O. Box 77010
San Francisco, CA 94107

12
First printing, May 2010
Twelfth printing, December 2021

viz.com

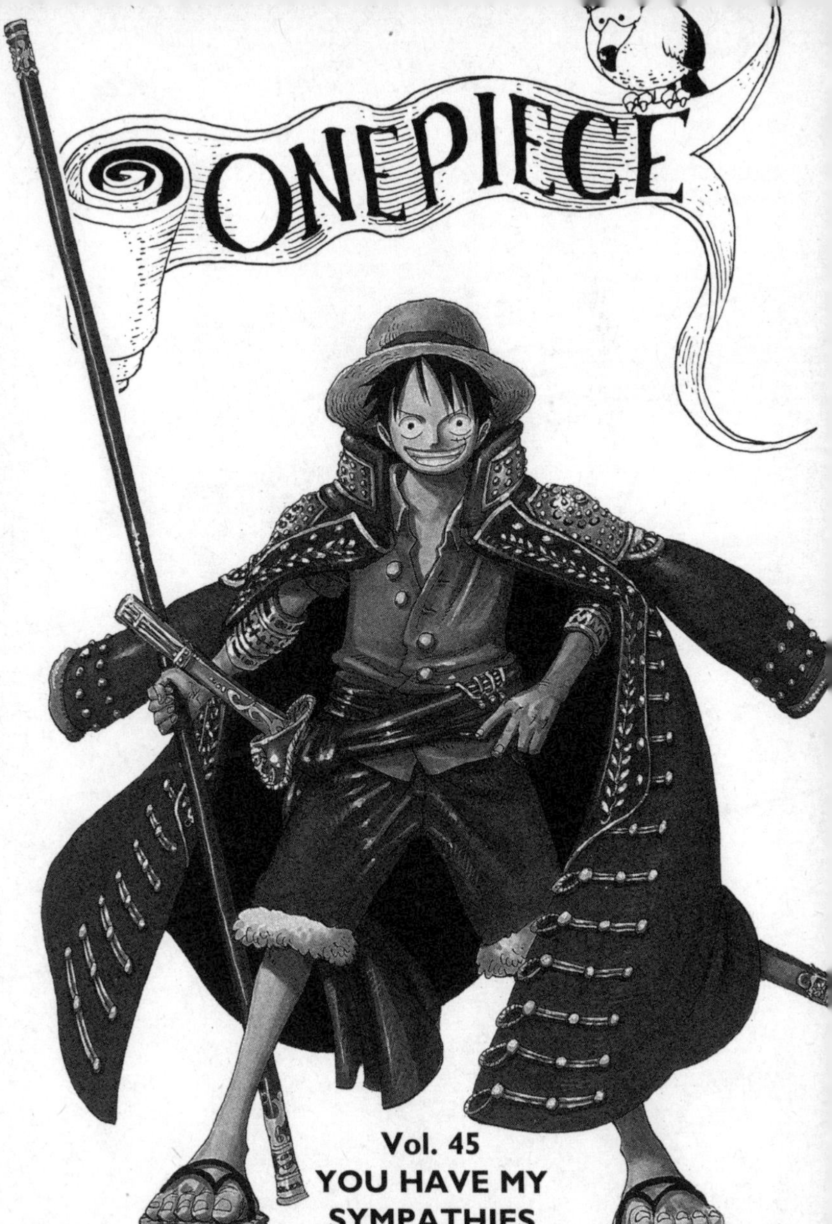
ONE PIECE

Vol. 45
YOU HAVE MY SYMPATHIES

STORY AND ART BY
EIICHIRO ODA

The Franky Family

Professional ship dismantlers, they moonlight as bounty hunters.

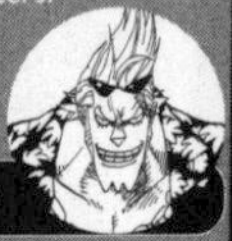

The master builder and an apprentice of Tom, the legendary shipwright.

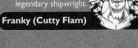

Franky (Cutty Flam)

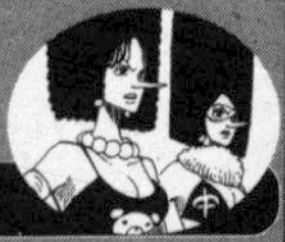

The Square Sisters

Kiwi & Mozu

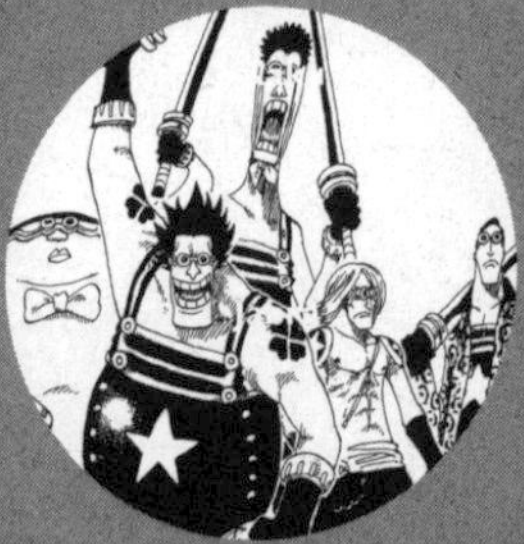

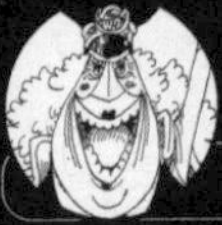

Formerly the beautiful secretary of Tom's Workers. Now stationmaster of Shift Station.

Kokoro

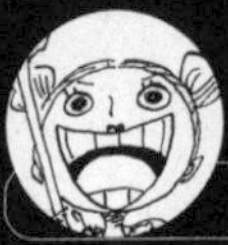

Kokoro's granddaughter.

Chimney

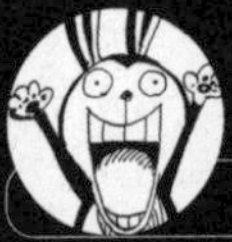

A cat (but actually a rabbit)

Gonbe

The Straw Hats

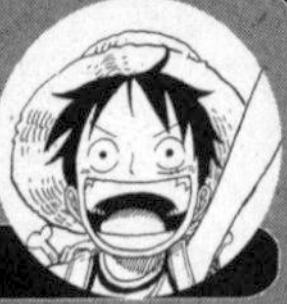

Boundlessly optimistic and able to stretch like rubber, he is determined to become King of the Pirates.

Monkey D. Luffy

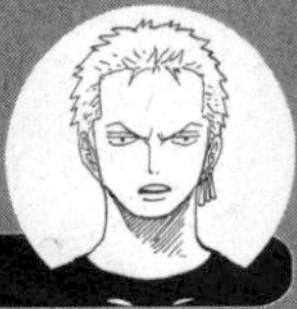

A former bounty hunter and master of the "three-sword" style. He aspires to be the world's greatest swordsman.

Roronoa Zolo

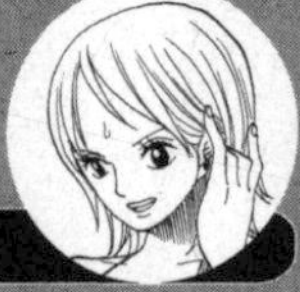

A thief who specializes in robbing pirates. Nami hates pirates, but Luffy convinced her to be his navigator.

Nami

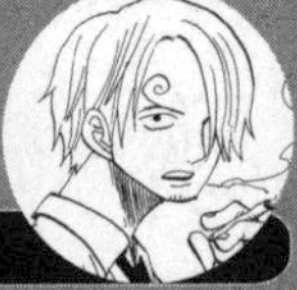

The bighearted cook (and ladies' man) whose dream is to find the legendary sea, the "All Blue."

Sanji

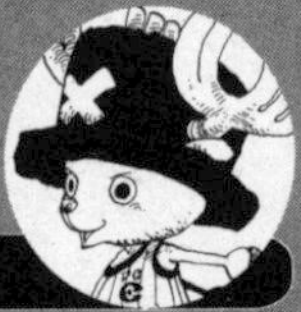

A blue-nosed man-reindeer and the ship's doctor.

Tony Tony Chopper

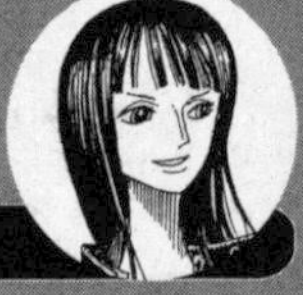

A mysterious woman in search of the Ponegliff on which true history is recorded.

Nico Robin

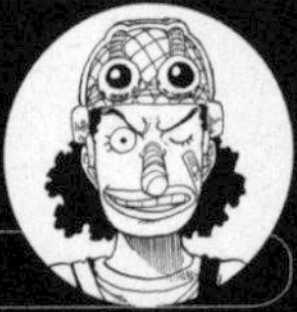

A village boy with a talent for telling tall tales. His father, Yasopp, is a member of Shanks's crew.

Usopp

Monkey D. Luffy started out as just a kid with a dream—to become the greatest pirate in history! Stirred by the tales of pirate "Red-Haired" Shanks, Luffy vowed to become a pirate himself. That was before the enchanted Devil Fruit gave Luffy the power to stretch like rubber, at the cost of being unable to swim—a serious handicap for an aspiring sea dog. Undeterred, Luffy set out to sea and recruited some crewmates—master swordsman Zolo; treasure-hunting thief Nami; lying sharpshooter Usopp; the high-kicking chef Sanji; Chopper, the walkin' talkin' reindeer doctor; and the latest addition, Nico Robin, an archaeologist with a powerful physique!

After many adventures, Luffy and his crew travel to Water Seven, the city of shipwrights. Their goal: to find a shipwright to join their crew and to get a new ship, since their old ship, the *Merry Go*, is badly damaged. Usopp is angry at the decision to find a new ship and leaves the crew, only to reappear in disguise as the Sniper King. Then suddenly, Robin leaves the crew as well, captured by the secret government organization CP9!
CP9's mission is to recover the blueprints for the ancient super weapon Pluton. To do this, CP9 needs the shipwright Franky, who possesses the blueprints, and Robin, the only living person capable of deciphering the ancient writings. With Franky and Robin in tow, CP9 sets out for the government's special judicial island, Enies Lobby.

Luffy and his crew go after CP9, and, after an epic battle, they save Robin and Franky from the evil government agents. But they are too late to prevent CP9 from initiating a Buster Call, a massive artillery assault that will wipe out all life on Enies Lobby! In the nick of time, the pirates manage to escape the doomed island on their old ship, the *Merry Go*. After performing this last service for them, the *Merry Go* falls apart. The heroes bid farewell to their trusted ship as it sinks to the bottom of the sea...

Galley-La Company

A top shipbuilding company. They are purveyors to the World Government.

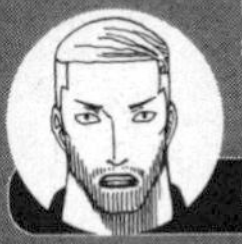

Mayor of Water Seven and president of Galley-La Company. Also one of Tom's apprentices.

Iceberg

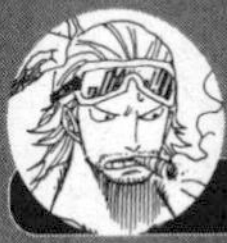

Rigging and Mast Foreman

Paulie

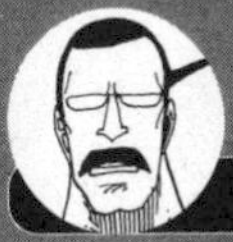

Pitch, Blacksmithing and Block-and-Tackle Foreman

Peepley Lulu

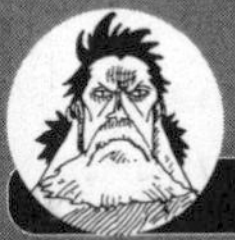

Cabinetry, Caulking and Flag-Making Foreman

Tilestone

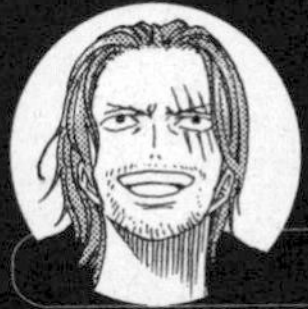

A pirate that Luffy idolizes. Shanks gave Luffy his trademark straw hat.

"Red-Haired" Shanks

Vol. 45
You Have My Sympathies

CONTENTS

Chapter 431: FIST OF LOVE

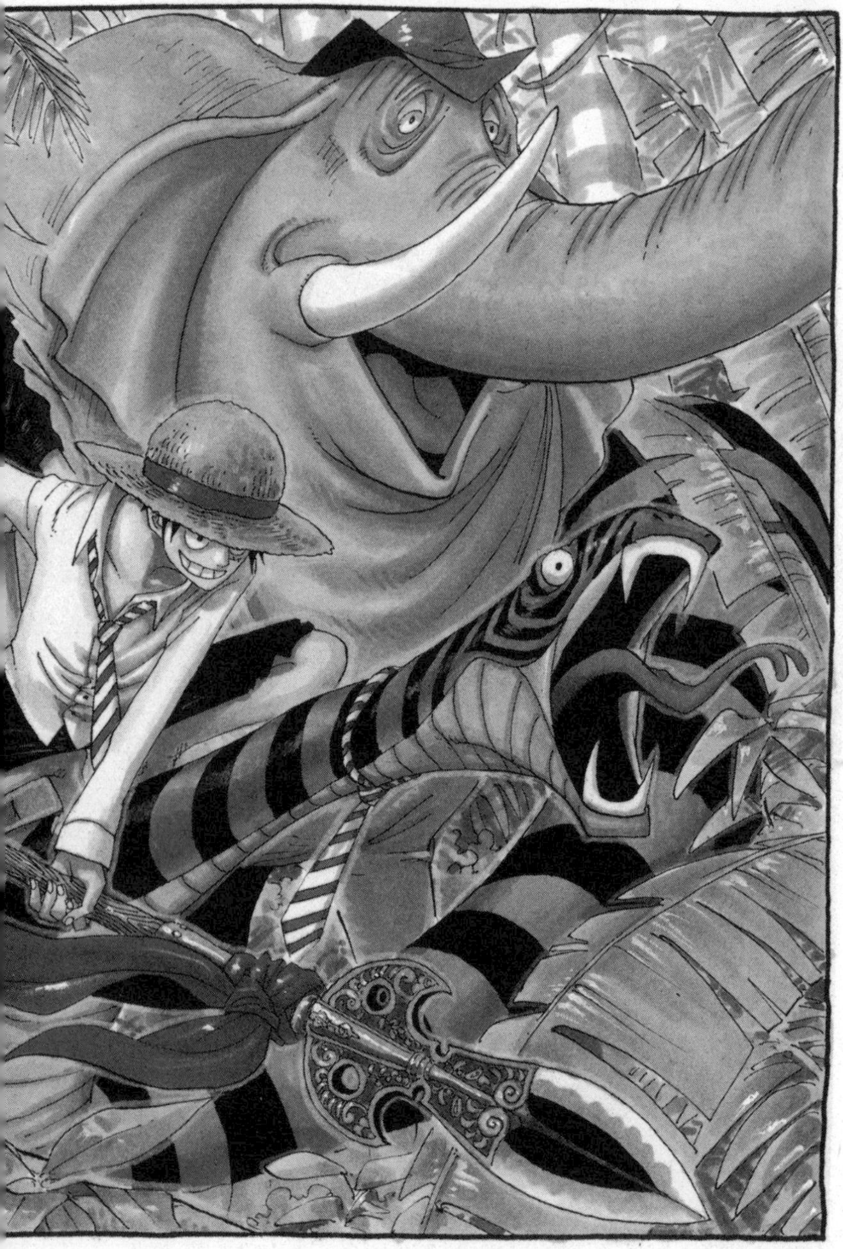

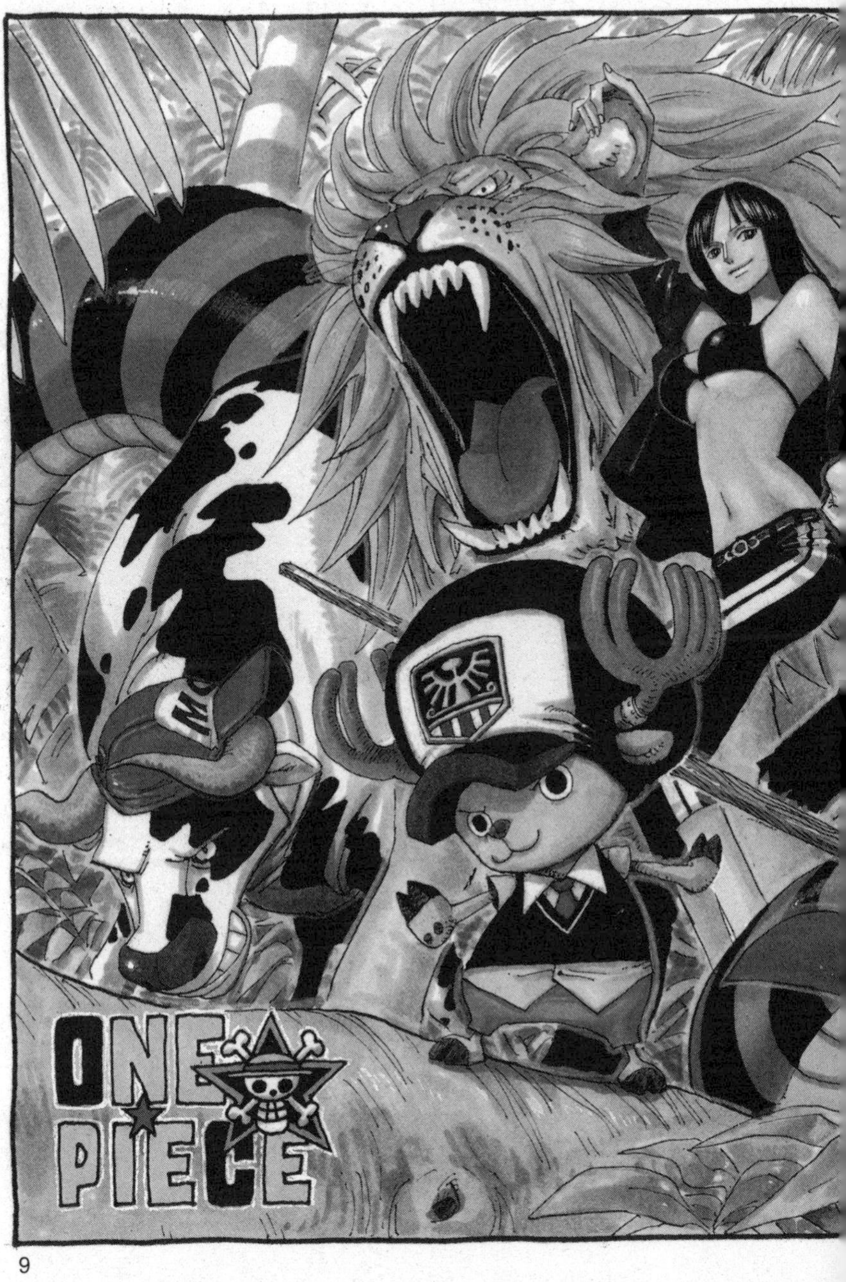
ONE PIECE

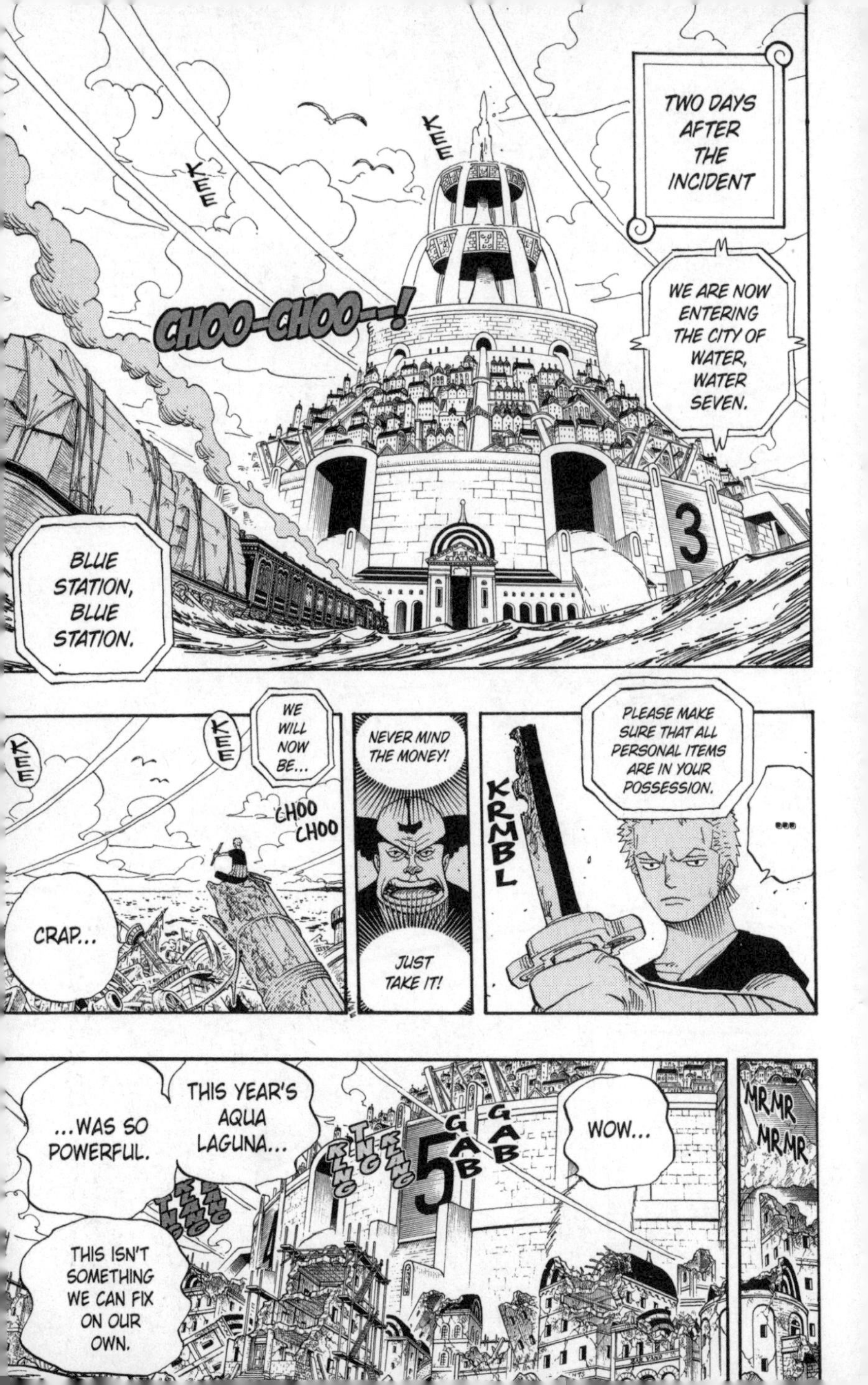
TWO DAYS AFTER THE INCIDENT
KEE
WE ARE NOW ENTERING THE CITY OF WATER, WATER SEVEN.
KEE
CHOO-CHOO--!
3
BLUE STATION, BLUE STATION.
PLEASE MAKE SURE THAT ALL PERSONAL ITEMS ARE IN YOUR POSSESSION.
...
KRMBL
NEVER MIND THE MONEY!
JUST TAKE IT!
WE WILL NOW BE...
KEE
KEE
CHOO CHOO
CRAP...
MRMR MRMR
WOW...
GAB GAB
5
THIS YEAR'S AQUA LAGUNA...
...WAS SO POWERFUL.
THIS ISN'T SOMETHING WE CAN FIX ON OUR OWN.

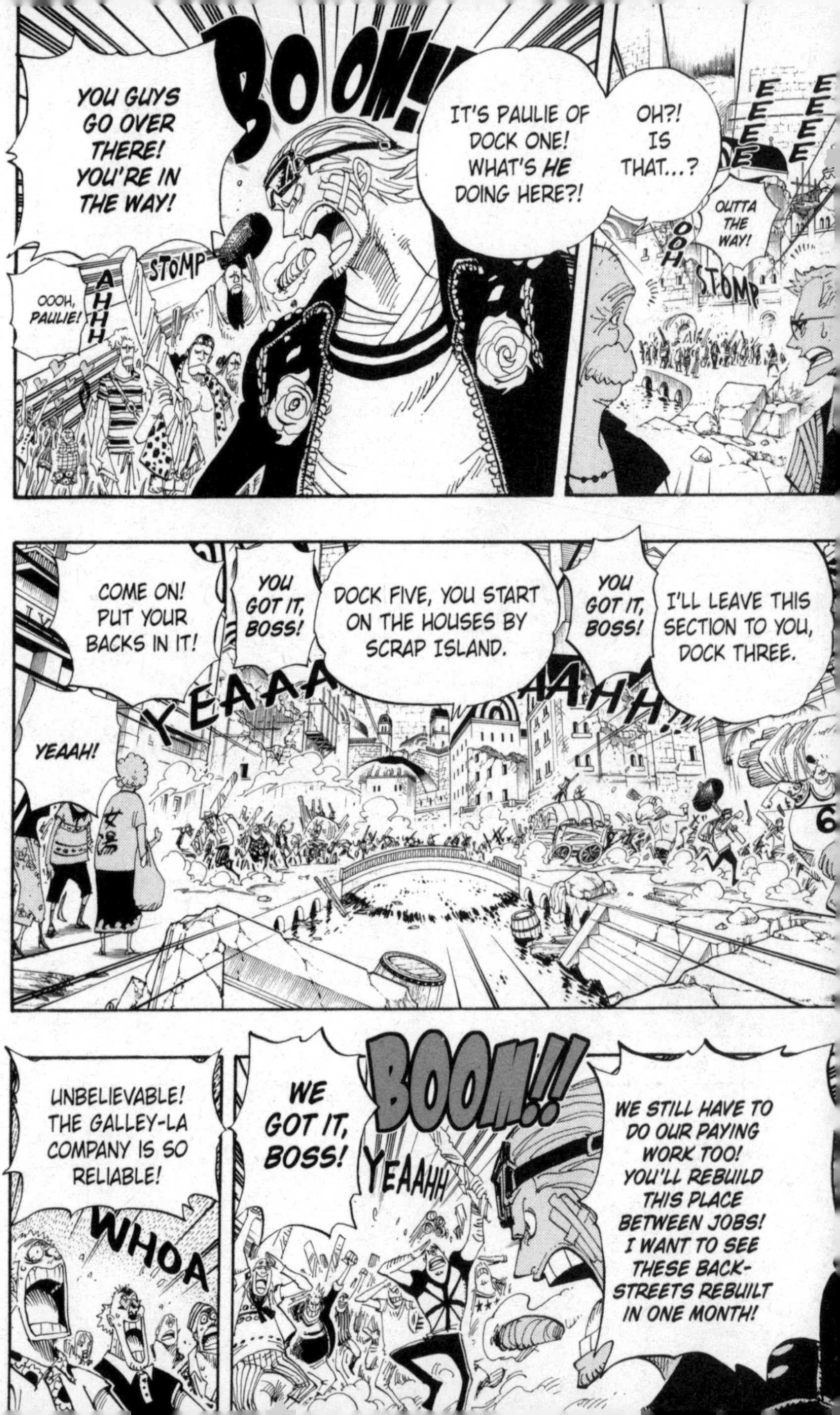
OH?! IS THAT...?
IT'S PAULIE OF DOCK ONE! WHAT'S HE DOING HERE?!
EEEEE EEEE
OUTTA THE WAY!
OOOH
STOMP
BOOM!!
YOU GUYS GO OVER THERE! YOU'RE IN THE WAY!
STOMP
AHHHH
OOOH, PAULIE!
I'LL LEAVE THIS SECTION TO YOU, DOCK THREE.
YOU GOT IT, BOSS!
DOCK FIVE, YOU START ON THE HOUSES BY SCRAP ISLAND.
YOU GOT IT, BOSS!
COME ON! PUT YOUR BACKS IN IT!
YEAAAAAHH!!
YEAAH!
BOOM!!
WE STILL HAVE TO DO OUR PAYING WORK TOO! YOU'LL REBUILD THIS PLACE BETWEEN JOBS! I WANT TO SEE THESE BACK-STREETS REBUILT IN ONE MONTH!
WE GOT IT, BOSS!
YEAAHH
UNBELIEVABLE! THE GALLEY-LA COMPANY IS SO RELIABLE!
WHOA

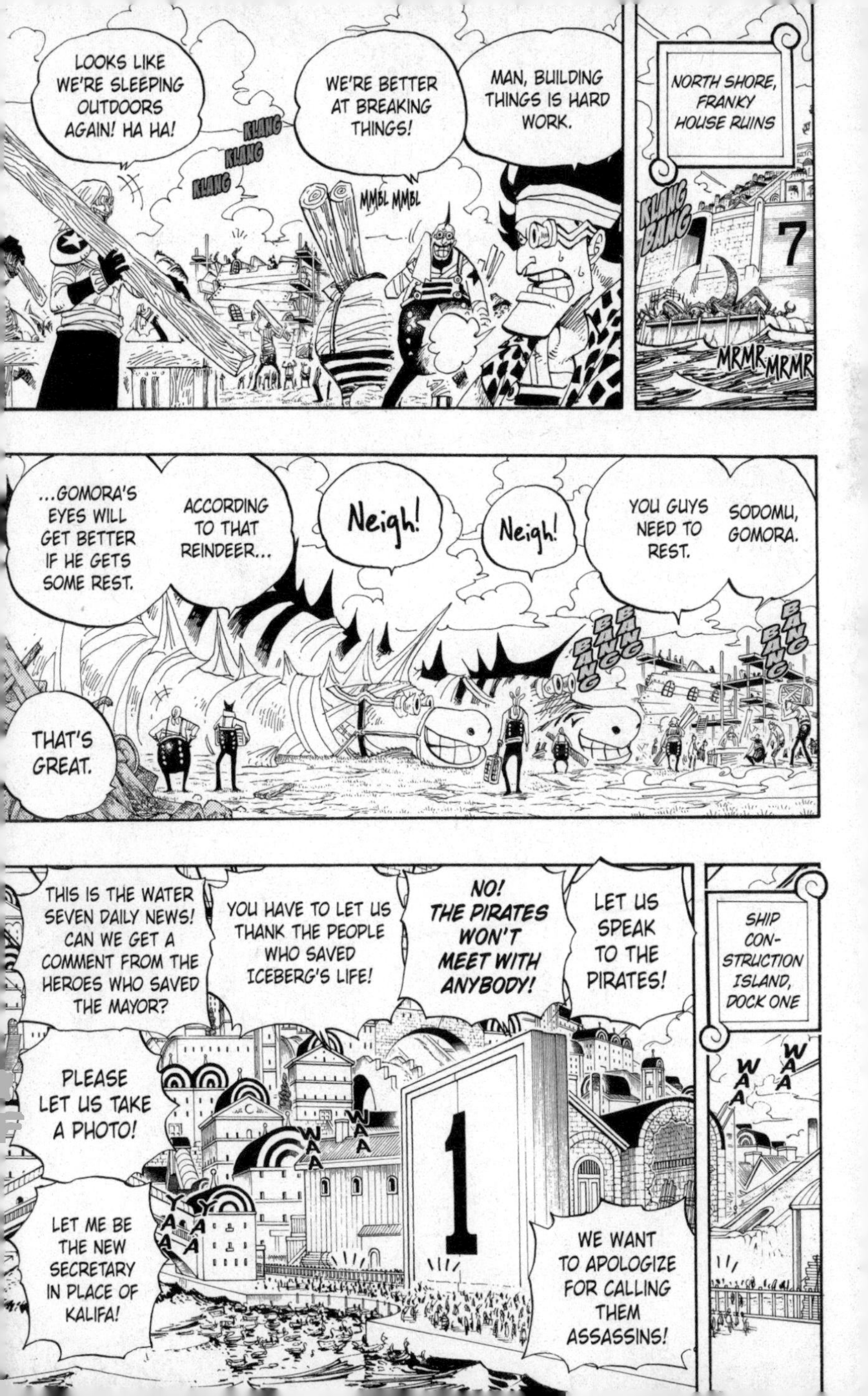
NORTH SHORE, FRANKY HOUSE RUINS
KLANG BANG
7
MRMR MRMR
MAN, BUILDING THINGS IS HARD WORK.
WE'RE BETTER AT BREAKING THINGS!
MMBL MMBL
KLANG KLANG KLANG
LOOKS LIKE WE'RE SLEEPING OUTDOORS AGAIN! HA HA!
SODOMU, GOMORA.
YOU GUYS NEED TO REST.
BANG
BANG BANG
Neigh!
Neigh!
ACCORDING TO THAT REINDEER...
...GOMORA'S EYES WILL GET BETTER IF HE GETS SOME REST.
THAT'S GREAT.
SHIP CON-STRUCTION ISLAND, DOCK ONE
WAA WAA
LET US SPEAK TO THE PIRATES!
NO! THE PIRATES WON'T MEET WITH ANYBODY!
YOU HAVE TO LET US THANK THE PEOPLE WHO SAVED ICEBERG'S LIFE!
THIS IS THE WATER SEVEN DAILY NEWS! CAN WE GET A COMMENT FROM THE HEROES WHO SAVED THE MAYOR?
WAA WAA
1
WE WANT TO APOLOGIZE FOR CALLING THEM ASSASSINS!
PLEASE LET US TAKE A PHOTO!
YAA YAA
LET ME BE THE NEW SECRETARY IN PLACE OF KALIFA!

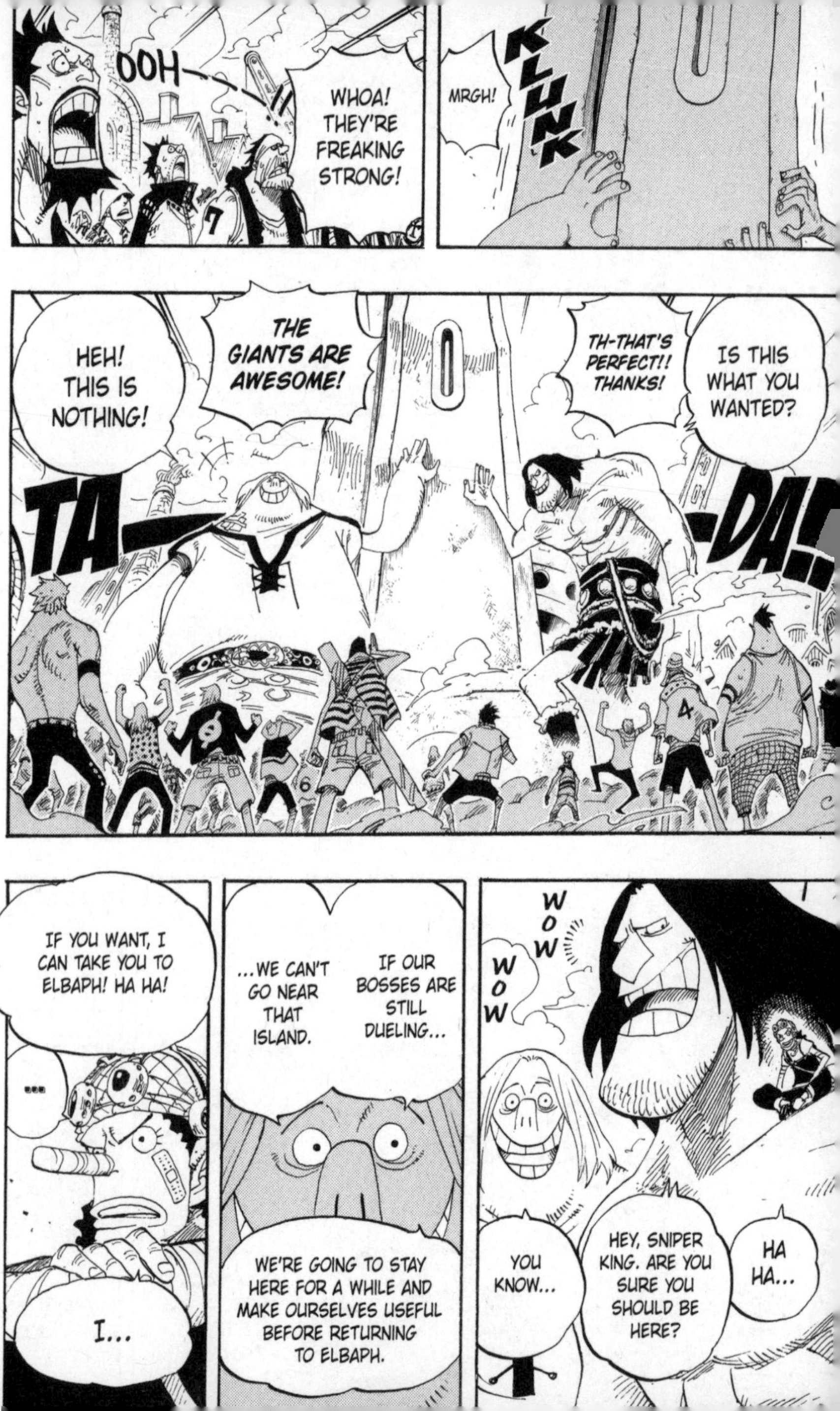
MRGH!
KLUNK
OOH
WHOA! THEY'RE FREAKING STRONG!
TA—DA!!
IS THIS WHAT YOU WANTED?
TH-THAT'S PERFECT!! THANKS!
THE GIANTS ARE AWESOME!
HEH! THIS IS NOTHING!
WOW
WOW
HA HA...
HEY, SNIPER KING. ARE YOU SURE YOU SHOULD BE HERE?
YOU KNOW...
IF OUR BOSSES ARE STILL DUELING...
...WE CAN'T GO NEAR THAT ISLAND.
WE'RE GOING TO STAY HERE FOR A WHILE AND MAKE OURSELVES USEFUL BEFORE RETURNING TO ELBAPH.
IF YOU WANT, I CAN TAKE YOU TO ELBAPH! HA HA!
...
I...

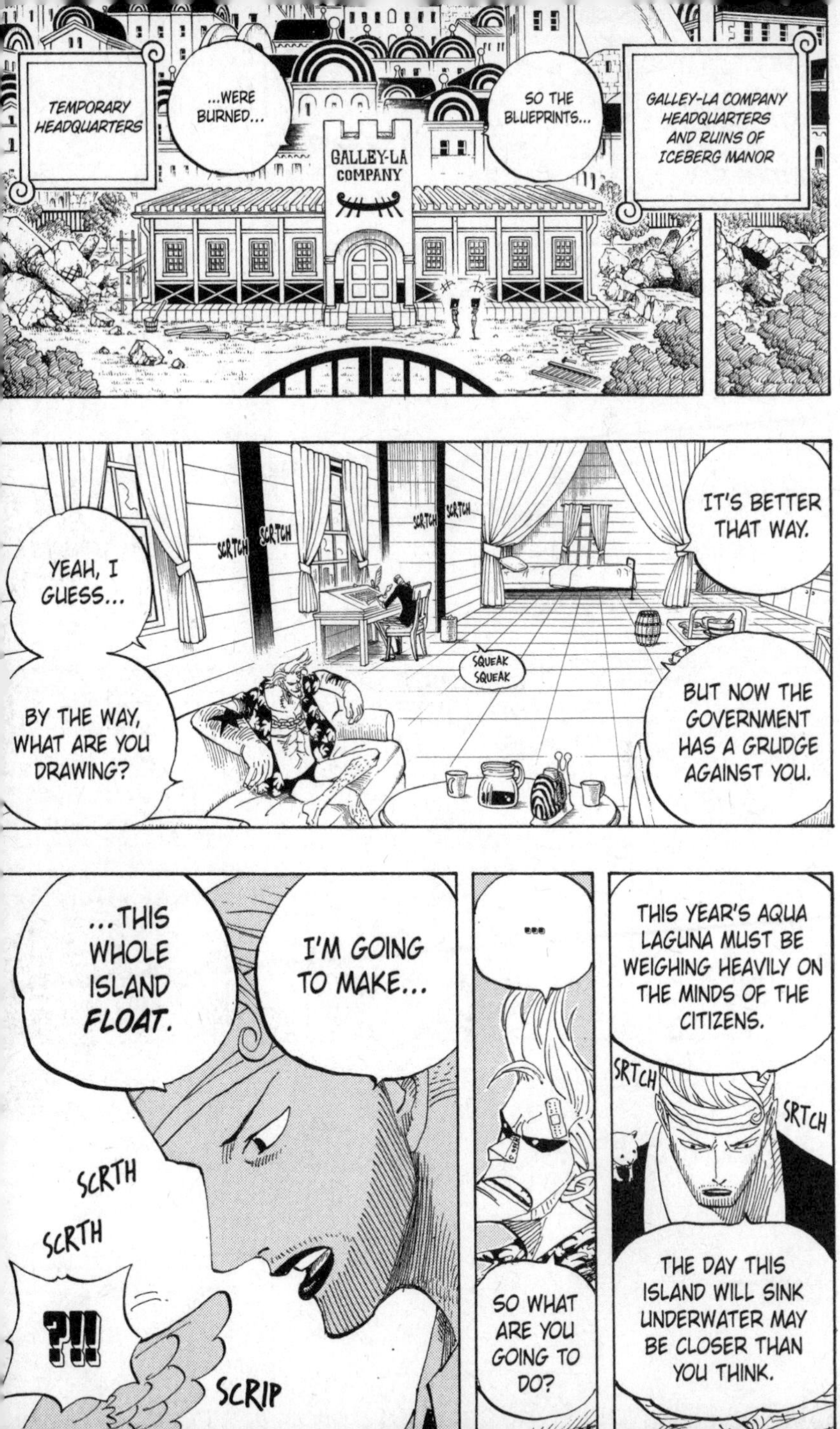
GALLEY-LA COMPANY HEADQUARTERS AND RUINS OF ICEBERG MANOR
SO THE BLUEPRINTS...
...WERE BURNED...
TEMPORARY HEADQUARTERS
GALLEY-LA COMPANY
IT'S BETTER THAT WAY.
BUT NOW THE GOVERNMENT HAS A GRUDGE AGAINST YOU.
SCRTCH SCRTCH
SCRTCH SCRTCH
SQUEAK SQUEAK
YEAH, I GUESS...
BY THE WAY, WHAT ARE YOU DRAWING?
THIS YEAR'S AQUA LAGUNA MUST BE WEIGHING HEAVILY ON THE MINDS OF THE CITIZENS.
SRTCH
SRTCH
THE DAY THIS ISLAND WILL SINK UNDERWATER MAY BE CLOSER THAN YOU THINK.
...
SO WHAT ARE YOU GOING TO DO?
I'M GOING TO MAKE...
...THIS WHOLE ISLAND FLOAT.
SCRTH
SCRTH
?!!
SCRIP

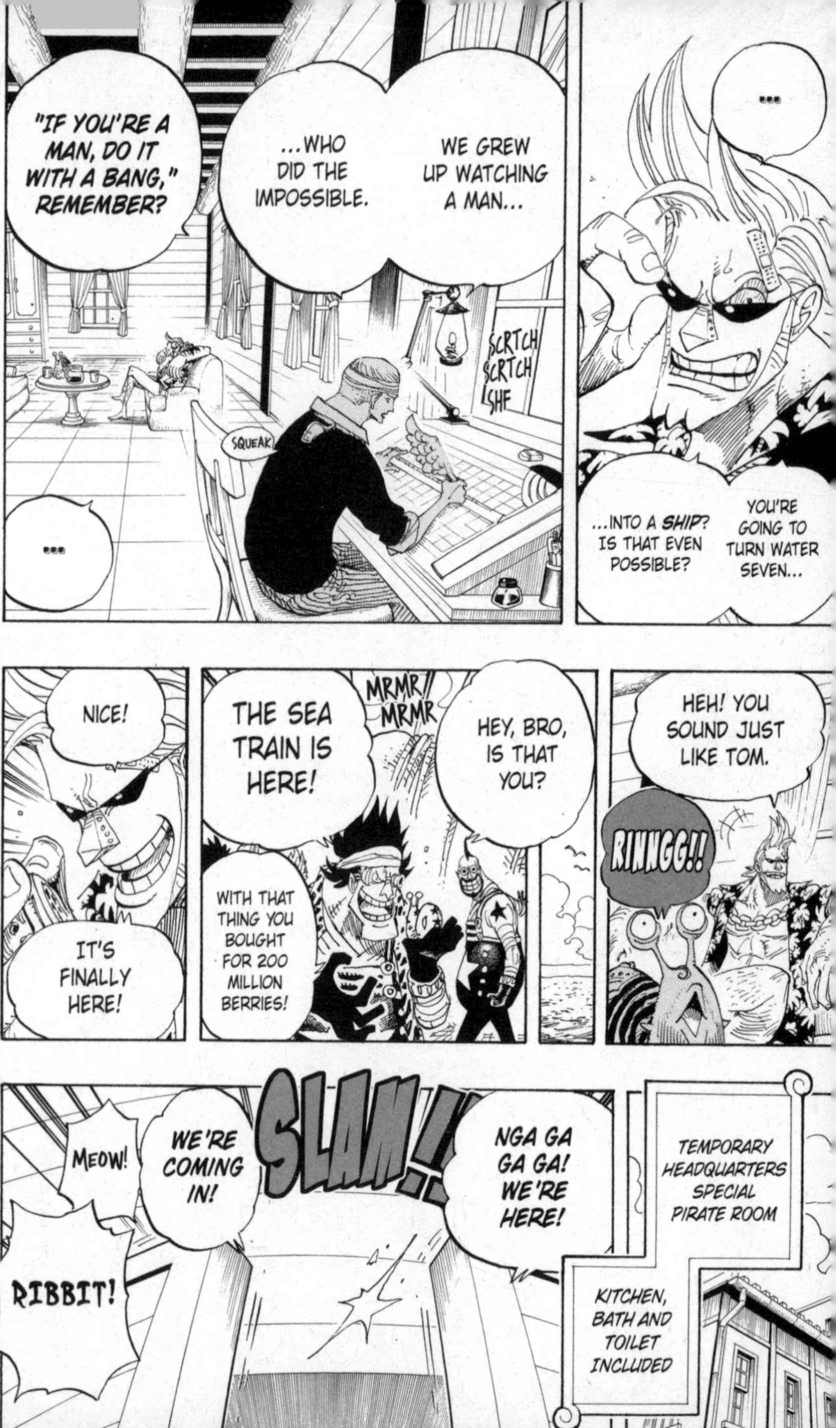
...
YOU'RE GOING TO TURN WATER SEVEN...
...INTO A *SHIP*? IS THAT EVEN POSSIBLE?
WE GREW UP WATCHING A MAN...
...WHO DID THE IMPOSSIBLE.
SCRTCH SCRTCH SHF
"IF YOU'RE A MAN, DO IT WITH A BANG," REMEMBER?
SQUEAK
...
HEH! YOU SOUND JUST LIKE TOM.
RINNGG!!
HEY, BRO, IS THAT YOU?
MRMR MRMR
THE SEA TRAIN IS HERE!
WITH THAT THING YOU BOUGHT FOR 200 MILLION BERRIES!
NICE!
IT'S FINALLY HERE!
TEMPORARY HEADQUARTERS SPECIAL PIRATE ROOM
KITCHEN, BATH AND TOILET INCLUDED
NGA GA GA GA! WE'RE HERE!
SLAM!!
WE'RE COMING IN!
MEOW!
RIBBIT!

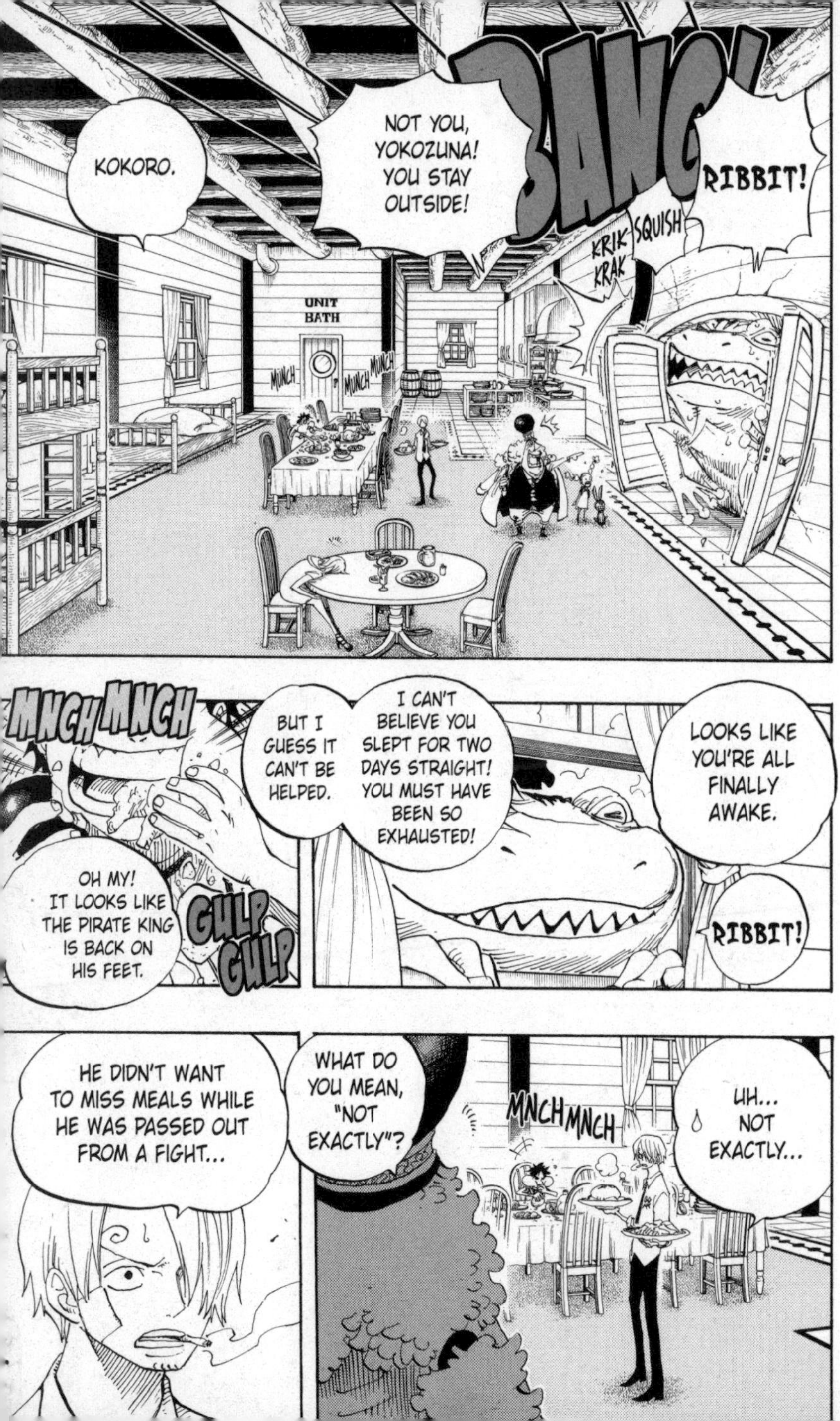
BANG'
RIBBIT!
SQUISH
KRIK KRAK
NOT YOU, YOKOZUNA! YOU STAY OUTSIDE!
KOKORO.
UNIT BATH
MUNCH MUNCH MUNCH
LOOKS LIKE YOU'RE ALL FINALLY AWAKE.
I CAN'T BELIEVE YOU SLEPT FOR TWO DAYS STRAIGHT! YOU MUST HAVE BEEN SO EXHAUSTED!
BUT I GUESS IT CAN'T BE HELPED.
RIBBIT!
MNCH MNCH
OH MY! IT LOOKS LIKE THE PIRATE KING IS BACK ON HIS FEET.
GULP GULP
UH... NOT EXACTLY...
MNCH MNCH
WHAT DO YOU MEAN, "NOT EXACTLY"?
HE DIDN'T WANT TO MISS MEALS WHILE HE WAS PASSED OUT FROM A FIGHT...

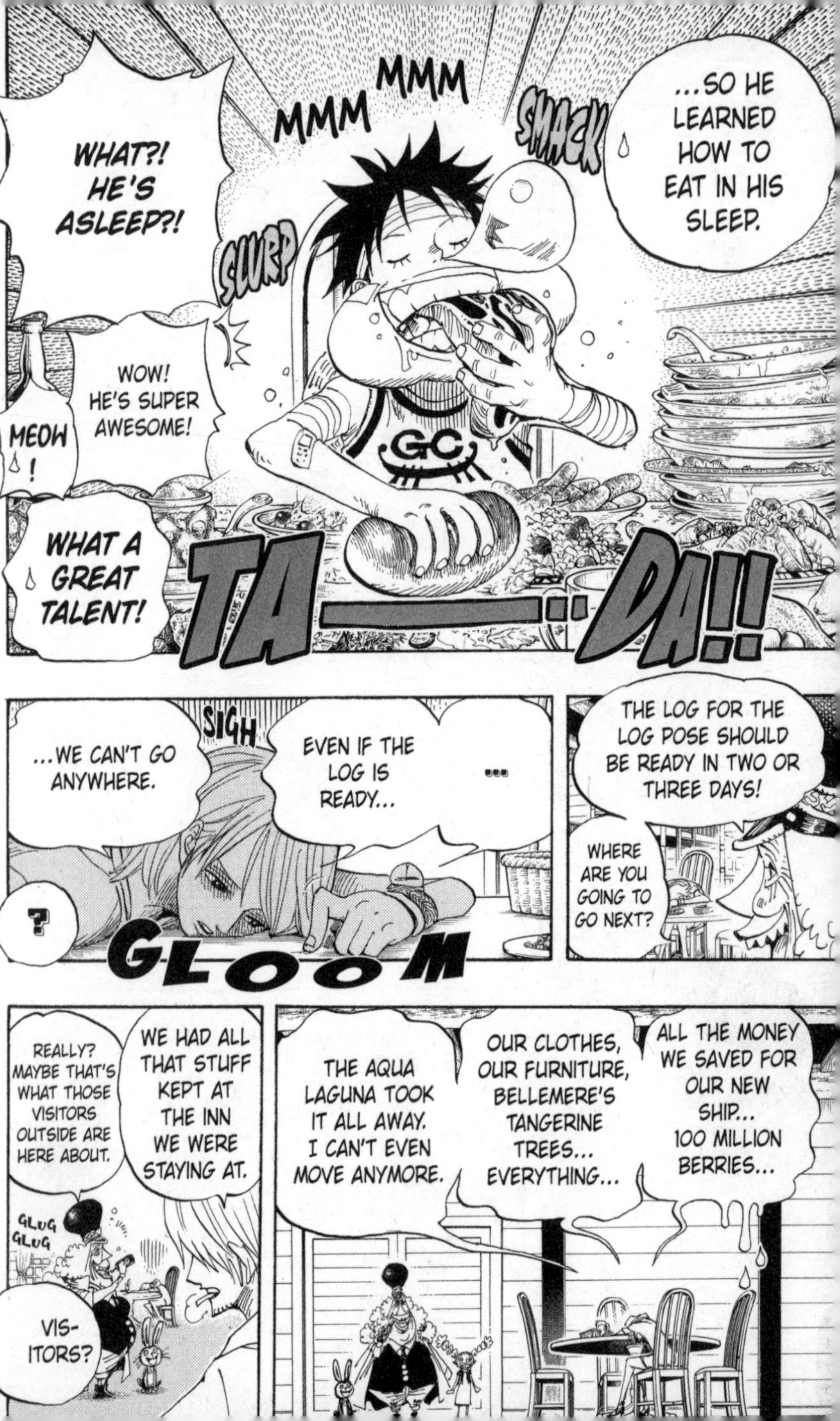
...SO HE LEARNED HOW TO EAT IN HIS SLEEP.
SMACK
MMM MMM
SLURP
WHAT?! HE'S ASLEEP?!
WOW! HE'S SUPER AWESOME!
MEOW!
WHAT A GREAT TALENT!
TA———DA!!
THE LOG FOR THE LOG POSE SHOULD BE READY IN TWO OR THREE DAYS!
WHERE ARE YOU GOING TO GO NEXT?
EVEN IF THE LOG IS READY...
...
SIGH
...WE CAN'T GO ANYWHERE.
?
GLOOM
ALL THE MONEY WE SAVED FOR OUR NEW SHIP... 100 MILLION BERRIES...
OUR CLOTHES, OUR FURNITURE, BELLEMERE'S TANGERINE TREES... EVERYTHING...
THE AQUA LAGUNA TOOK IT ALL AWAY. I CAN'T EVEN MOVE ANYMORE.
WE HAD ALL THAT STUFF KEPT AT THE INN WE WERE STAYING AT.
REALLY? MAYBE THAT'S WHAT THOSE VISITORS OUTSIDE ARE HERE ABOUT.
GLUG GLUG
VIS-ITORS?

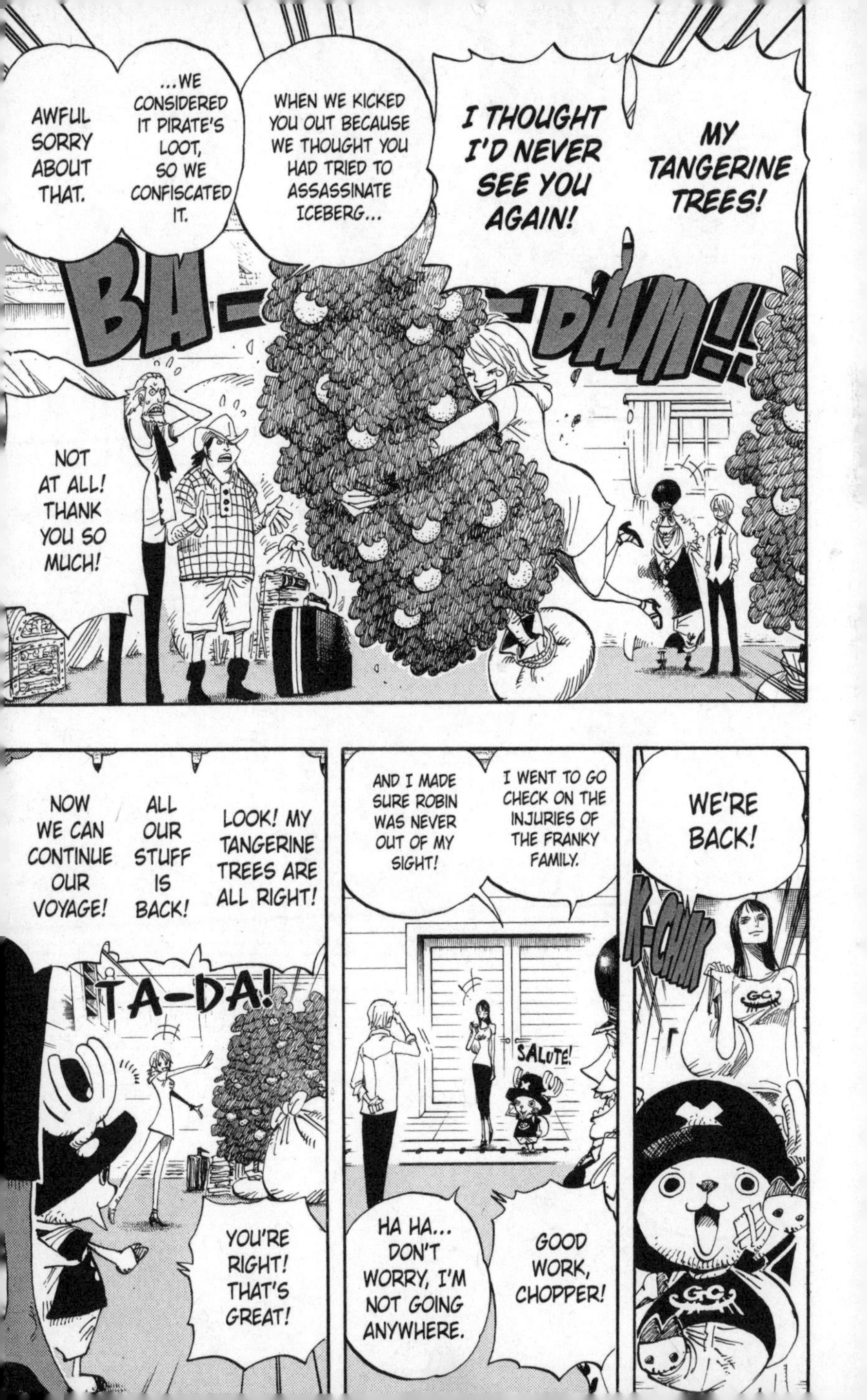
MY TANGERINE TREES!
I THOUGHT I'D NEVER SEE YOU AGAIN!
WHEN WE KICKED YOU OUT BECAUSE WE THOUGHT YOU HAD TRIED TO ASSASSINATE ICEBERG...
...WE CONSIDERED IT PIRATE'S LOOT, SO WE CONFISCATED IT.
AWFUL SORRY ABOUT THAT.
BA— —DAM!!
NOT AT ALL! THANK YOU SO MUCH!
WE'RE BACK!
K-CHAK
I WENT TO GO CHECK ON THE INJURIES OF THE FRANKY FAMILY.
AND I MADE SURE ROBIN WAS NEVER OUT OF MY SIGHT!
SALUTE!
GOOD WORK, CHOPPER!
HA HA... DON'T WORRY, I'M NOT GOING ANYWHERE.
LOOK! MY TANGERINE TREES ARE ALL RIGHT!
ALL OUR STUFF IS BACK!
NOW WE CAN CONTINUE OUR VOYAGE!
TA-DA!
YOU'RE RIGHT! THAT'S GREAT!

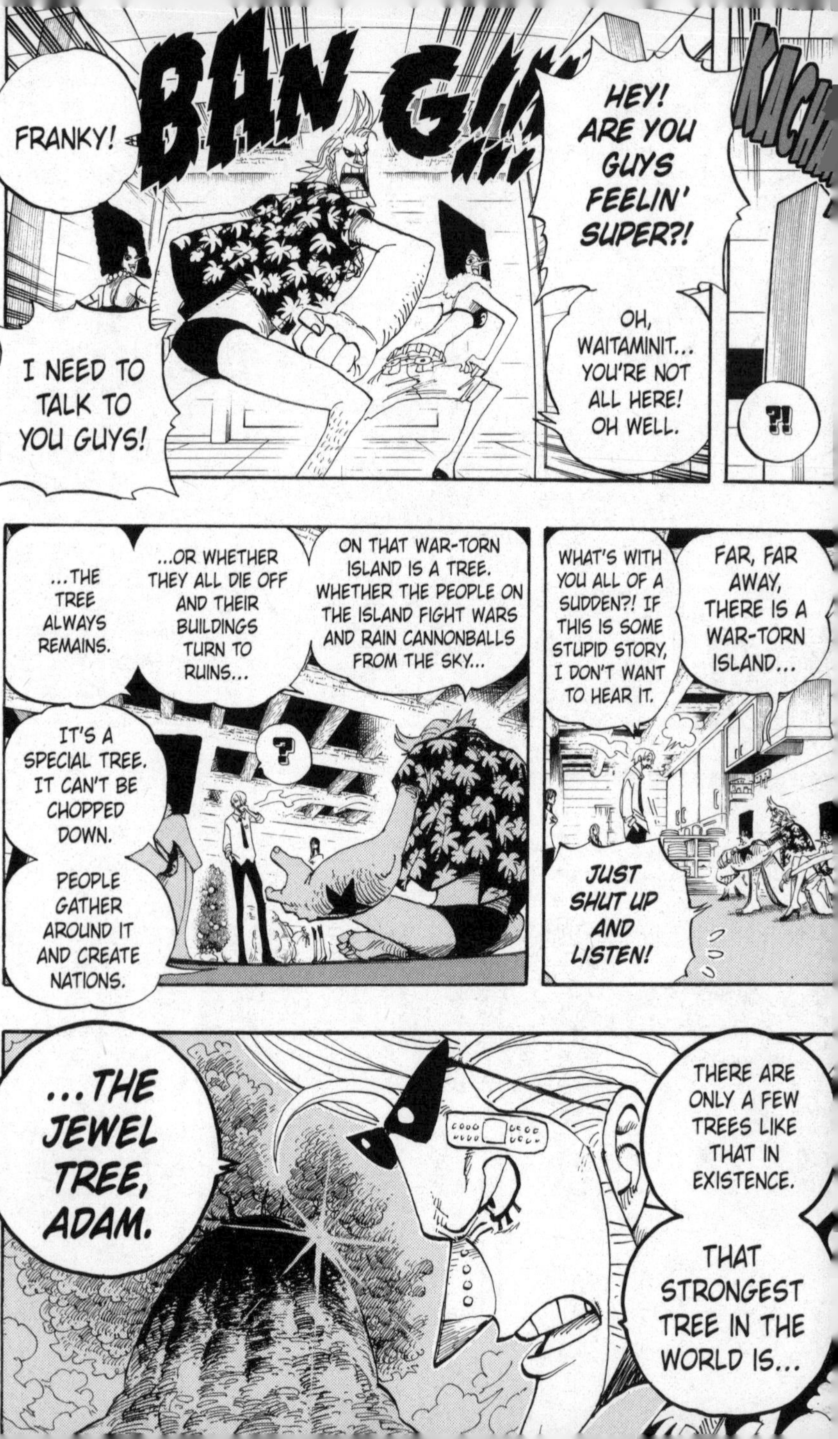
KACH
?!
HEY! ARE YOU GUYS FEELIN' SUPER?!
OH, WAITAMINIT... YOU'RE NOT ALL HERE! OH WELL.
BANG!!
FRANKY!
I NEED TO TALK TO YOU GUYS!
FAR, FAR AWAY, THERE IS A WAR-TORN ISLAND...
WHAT'S WITH YOU ALL OF A SUDDEN?! IF THIS IS SOME STUPID STORY, I DON'T WANT TO HEAR IT.
JUST SHUT UP AND LISTEN!
ON THAT WAR-TORN ISLAND IS A TREE. WHETHER THE PEOPLE ON THE ISLAND FIGHT WARS AND RAIN CANNONBALLS FROM THE SKY...
...OR WHETHER THEY ALL DIE OFF AND THEIR BUILDINGS TURN TO RUINS...
...THE TREE ALWAYS REMAINS.
?
IT'S A SPECIAL TREE. IT CAN'T BE CHOPPED DOWN.
PEOPLE GATHER AROUND IT AND CREATE NATIONS.
THERE ARE ONLY A FEW TREES LIKE THAT IN EXISTENCE.
THAT STRONGEST TREE IN THE WORLD IS...
...THE JEWEL TREE, ADAM.

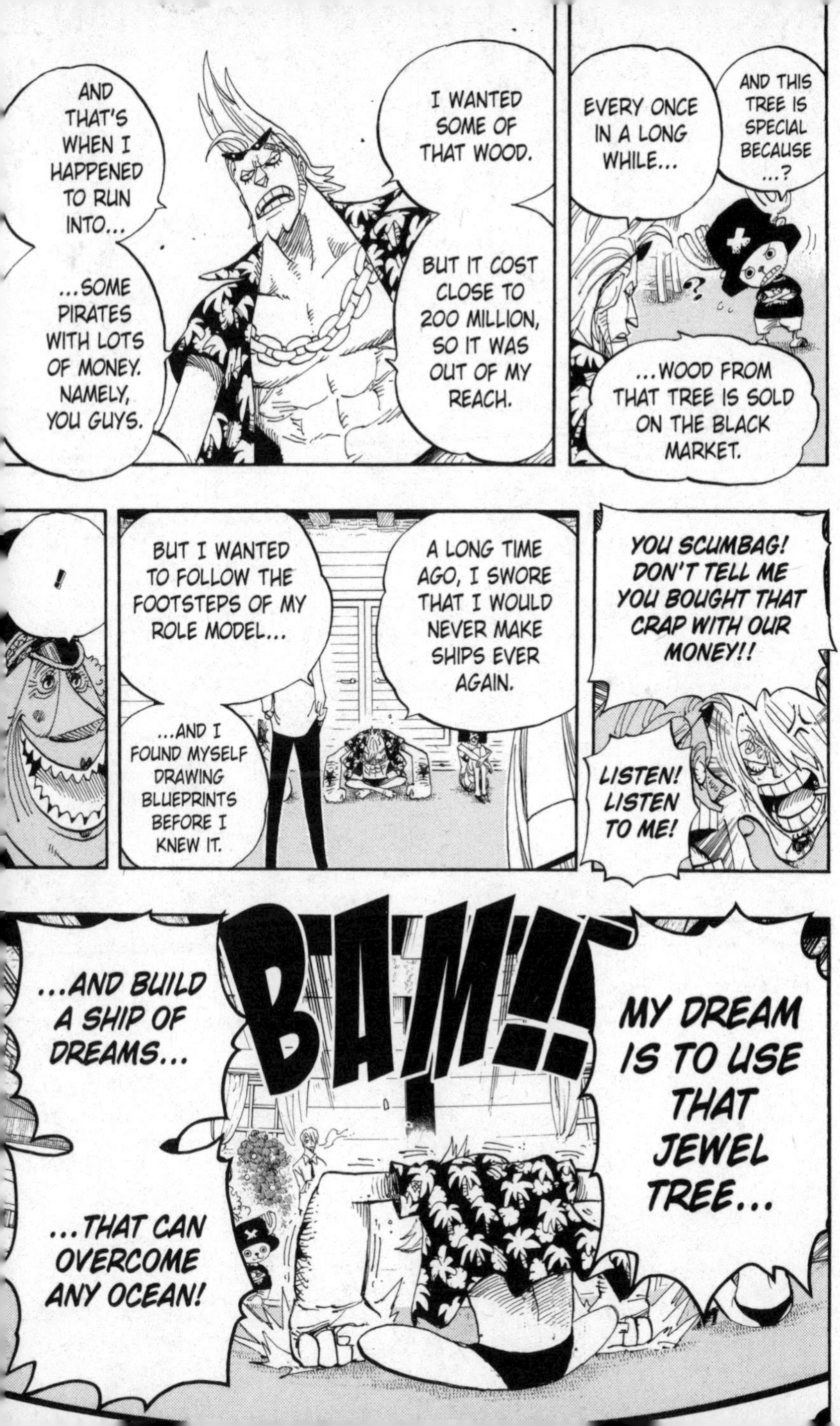
AND THIS TREE IS SPECIAL BECAUSE ...?
EVERY ONCE IN A LONG WHILE...
...WOOD FROM THAT TREE IS SOLD ON THE BLACK MARKET.
I WANTED SOME OF THAT WOOD.
BUT IT COST CLOSE TO 200 MILLION, SO IT WAS OUT OF MY REACH.
AND THAT'S WHEN I HAPPENED TO RUN INTO...
...SOME PIRATES WITH LOTS OF MONEY. NAMELY, YOU GUYS.
YOU SCUMBAG! DON'T TELL ME YOU BOUGHT THAT CRAP WITH OUR MONEY!!
LISTEN! LISTEN TO ME!
A LONG TIME AGO, I SWORE THAT I WOULD NEVER MAKE SHIPS EVER AGAIN.
BUT I WANTED TO FOLLOW THE FOOTSTEPS OF MY ROLE MODEL...
...AND I FOUND MYSELF DRAWING BLUEPRINTS BEFORE I KNEW IT.
!
MY DREAM IS TO USE THAT JEWEL TREE...
BAM!!
...AND BUILD A SHIP OF DREAMS...
...THAT CAN OVERCOME ANY OCEAN!

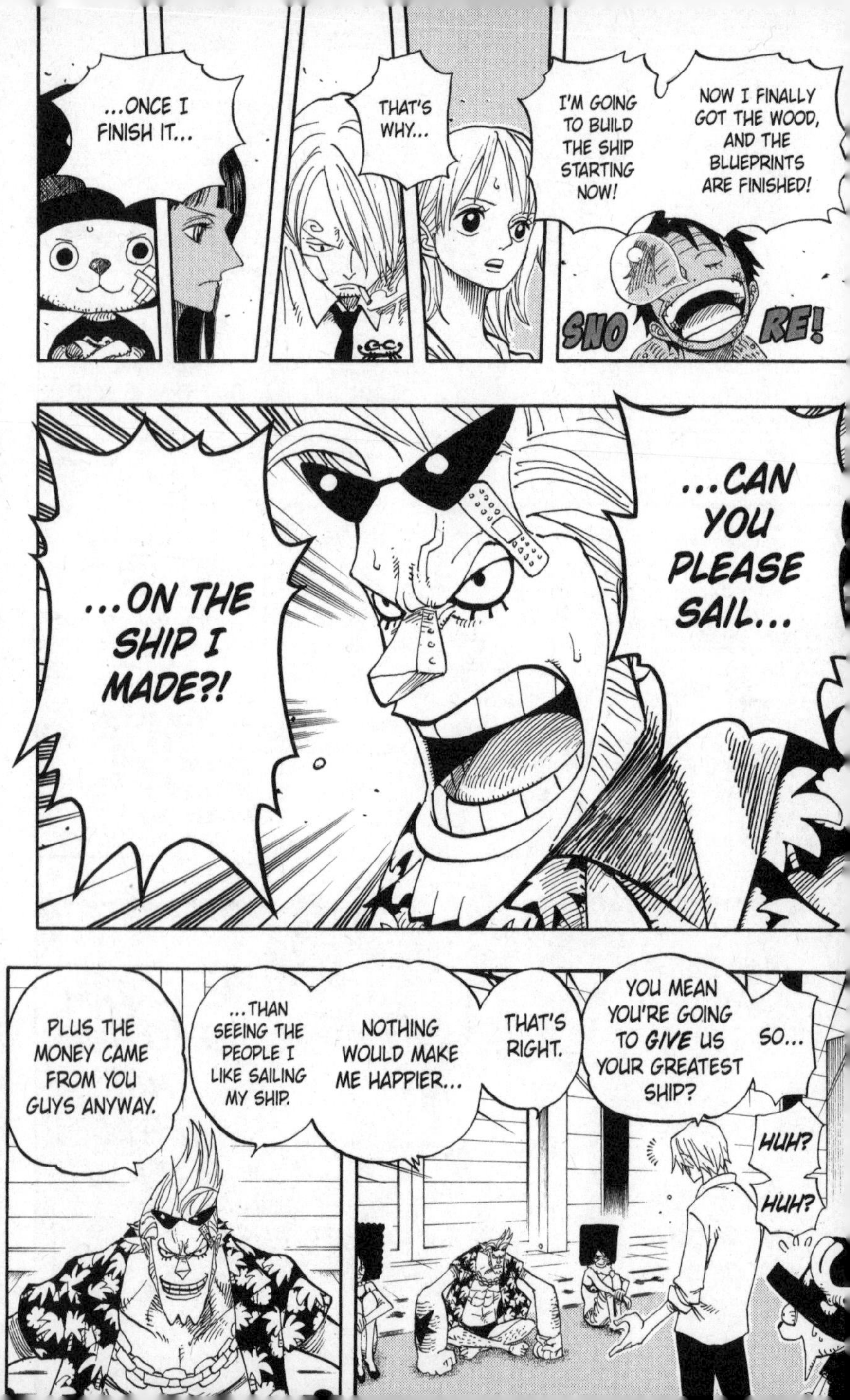
NOW I FINALLY GOT THE WOOD, AND THE BLUEPRINTS ARE FINISHED!
I'M GOING TO BUILD THE SHIP STARTING NOW!
SNO RE!
THAT'S WHY...
...ONCE I FINISH IT...
...CAN YOU PLEASE SAIL...
...ON THE SHIP I MADE?!
SO...
YOU MEAN YOU'RE GOING TO *GIVE* US YOUR GREATEST SHIP?
HUH?
HUH?
THAT'S RIGHT.
NOTHING WOULD MAKE ME HAPPIER...
...THAN SEEING THE PEOPLE I LIKE SAILING MY SHIP.
PLUS THE MONEY CAME FROM YOU GUYS ANYWAY.

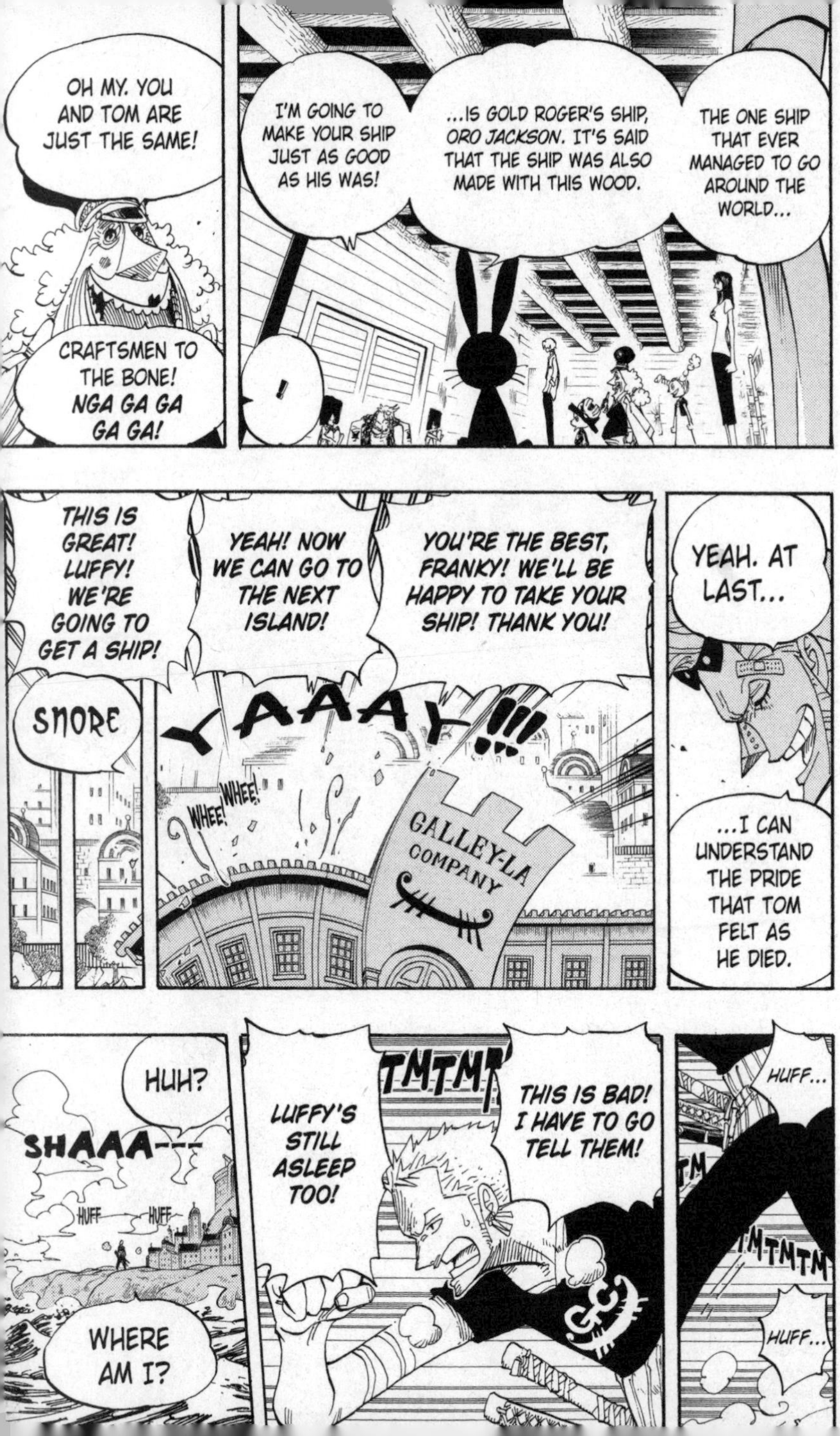
THE ONE SHIP THAT EVER MANAGED TO GO AROUND THE WORLD...
...IS GOLD ROGER'S SHIP, ORO JACKSON. IT'S SAID THAT THE SHIP WAS ALSO MADE WITH THIS WOOD.
I'M GOING TO MAKE YOUR SHIP JUST AS GOOD AS HIS WAS!
!
OH MY. YOU AND TOM ARE JUST THE SAME!
CRAFTSMEN TO THE BONE! NGA GA GA GA GA!
YEAH. AT LAST...
...I CAN UNDERSTAND THE PRIDE THAT TOM FELT AS HE DIED.
YOU'RE THE BEST, FRANKY! WE'LL BE HAPPY TO TAKE YOUR SHIP! THANK YOU!
YEAH! NOW WE CAN GO TO THE NEXT ISLAND!
THIS IS GREAT! LUFFY! WE'RE GOING TO GET A SHIP!
YAAAY!!!
WHEE!
WHEE!
GALLEY-LA COMPANY
SNORE
HUFF...
TM
TMTMTM
HUFF...
TMTMT
THIS IS BAD! I HAVE TO GO TELL THEM!
LUFFY'S STILL ASLEEP TOO!
HUH?
SHAAA---
HUFF
HUFF
WHERE AM I?

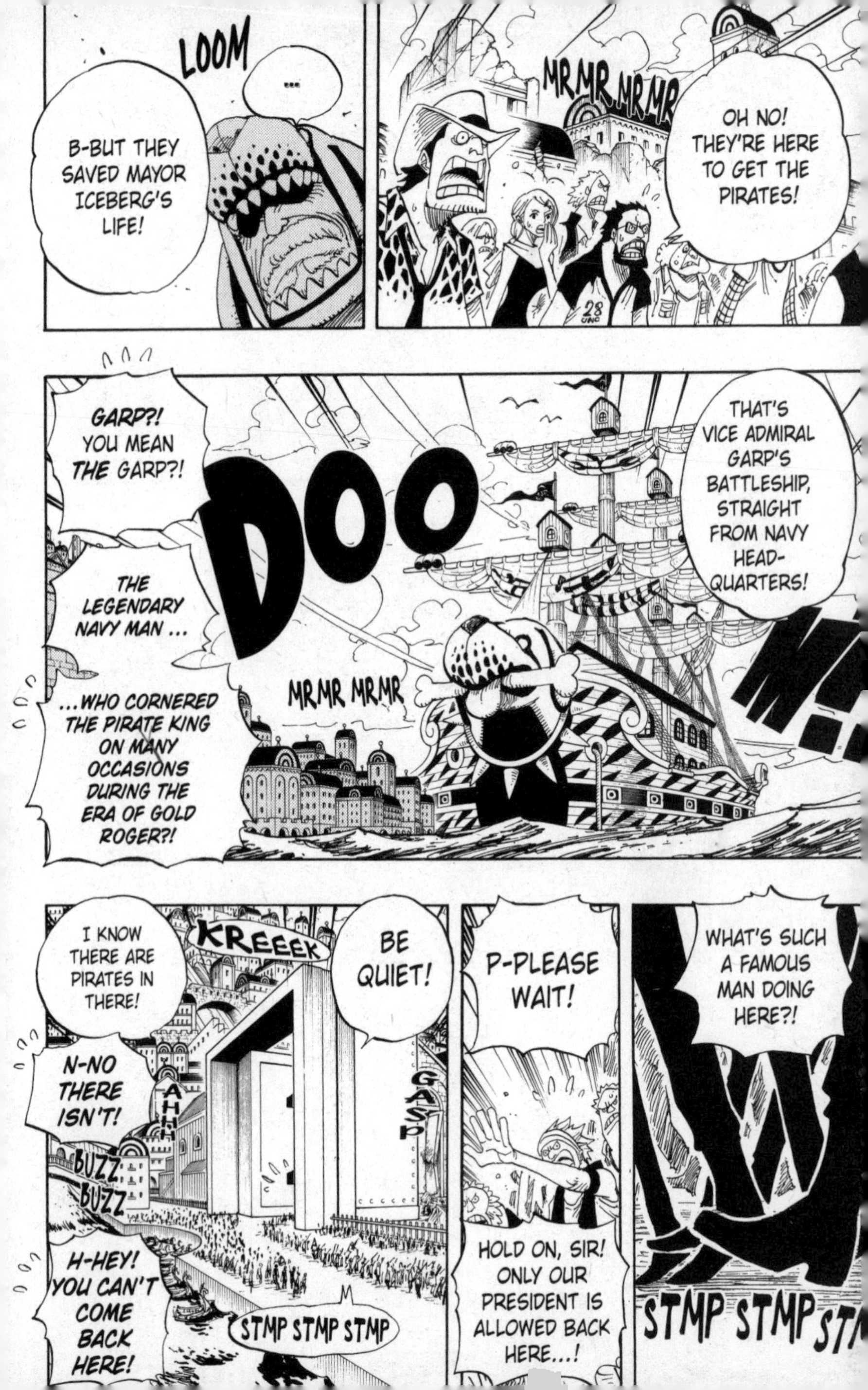
MRMR MRMR
OH NO! THEY'RE HERE TO GET THE PIRATES!
...
LOOM
B-BUT THEY SAVED MAYOR ICEBERG'S LIFE!
THAT'S VICE ADMIRAL GARP'S BATTLESHIP, STRAIGHT FROM NAVY HEAD-QUARTERS!
DOO
GARP?! YOU MEAN THE GARP?!
THE LEGENDARY NAVY MAN ...
MRMR MRMR
...WHO CORNERED THE PIRATE KING ON MANY OCCASIONS DURING THE ERA OF GOLD ROGER?!
WHAT'S SUCH A FAMOUS MAN DOING HERE?!
STMP STMP
P-PLEASE WAIT!
HOLD ON, SIR! ONLY OUR PRESIDENT IS ALLOWED BACK HERE...!
BE QUIET!
KREEEK
I KNOW THERE ARE PIRATES IN THERE!
GASP
N-NO THERE ISN'T!
AHHH
BUZZ BUZZ
H-HEY! YOU CAN'T COME BACK HERE!
STMP STMP STMP

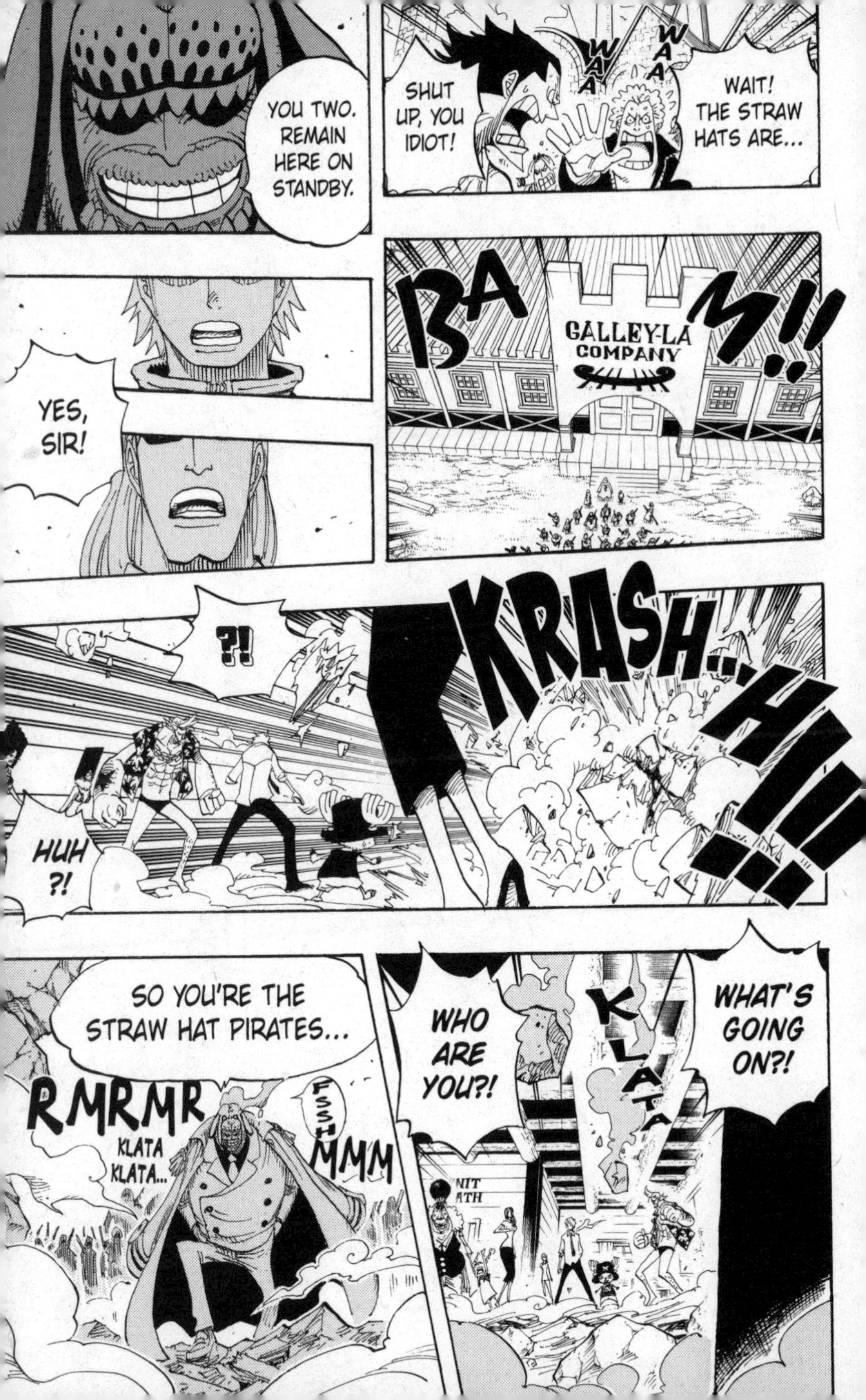
WAIT! THE STRAW HATS ARE...
WAA WAA
SHUT UP, YOU IDIOT!
YOU TWO. REMAIN HERE ON STANDBY.
BAM!!
GALLEY-LA COMPANY
YES, SIR!
KRASH...H!!!
?!
HUH ?!
WHAT'S GOING ON?!
KLATA
WHO ARE YOU?!
SO YOU'RE THE STRAW HAT PIRATES...
FSSH
MMM
RMRMR
KLATA KLATA...

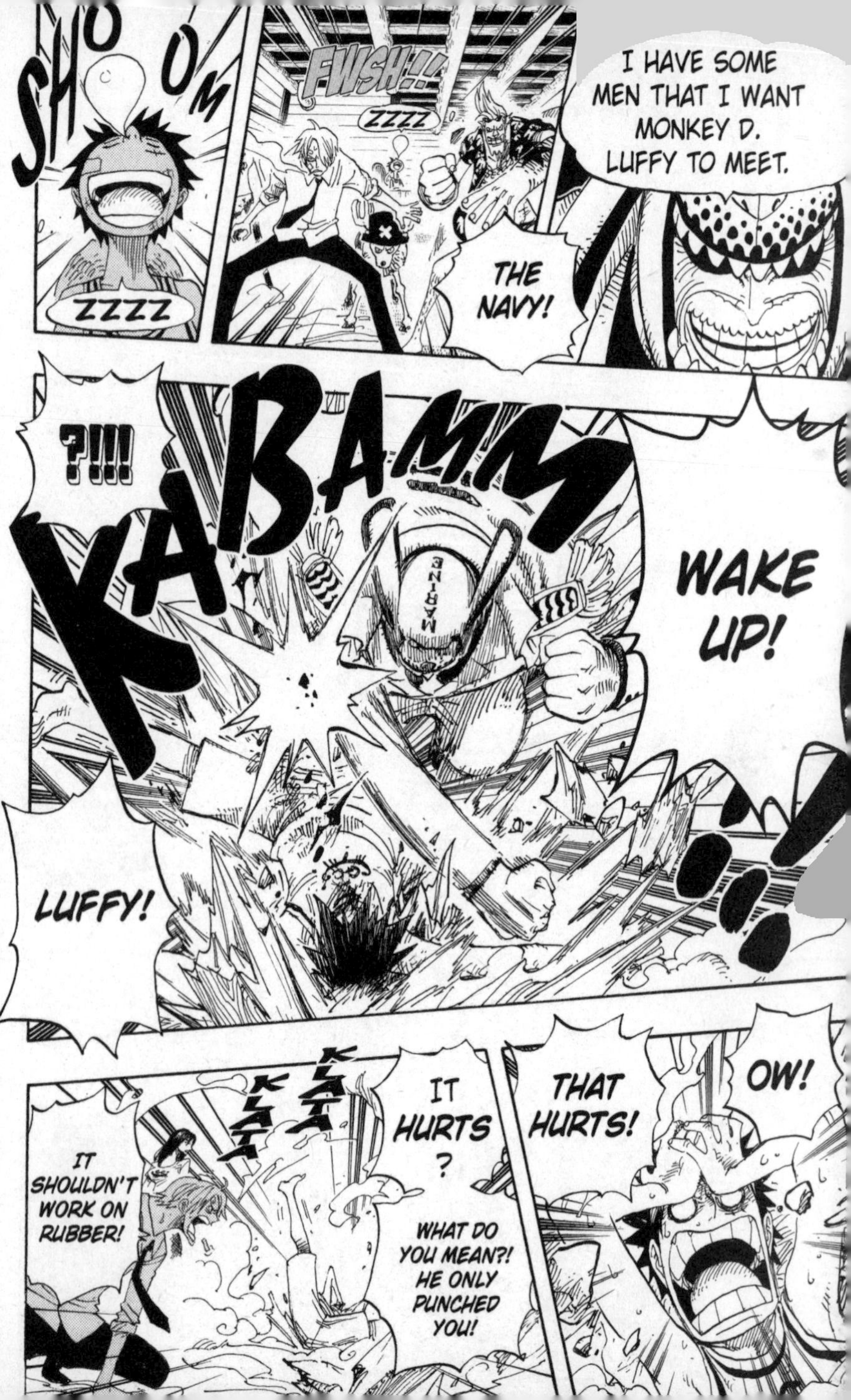
I HAVE SOME MEN THAT I WANT MONKEY D. LUFFY TO MEET.
FWSH!!!
ZZZZ
THE NAVY!
SHOOM
ZZZZ
WAKE UP!
KABAMM
?!!!
LUFFY!
OW!
THAT HURTS!
IT HURTS?
WHAT DO YOU MEAN?! HE ONLY PUNCHED YOU!
KLATA
KLATA
IT SHOULDN'T WORK ON RUBBER!

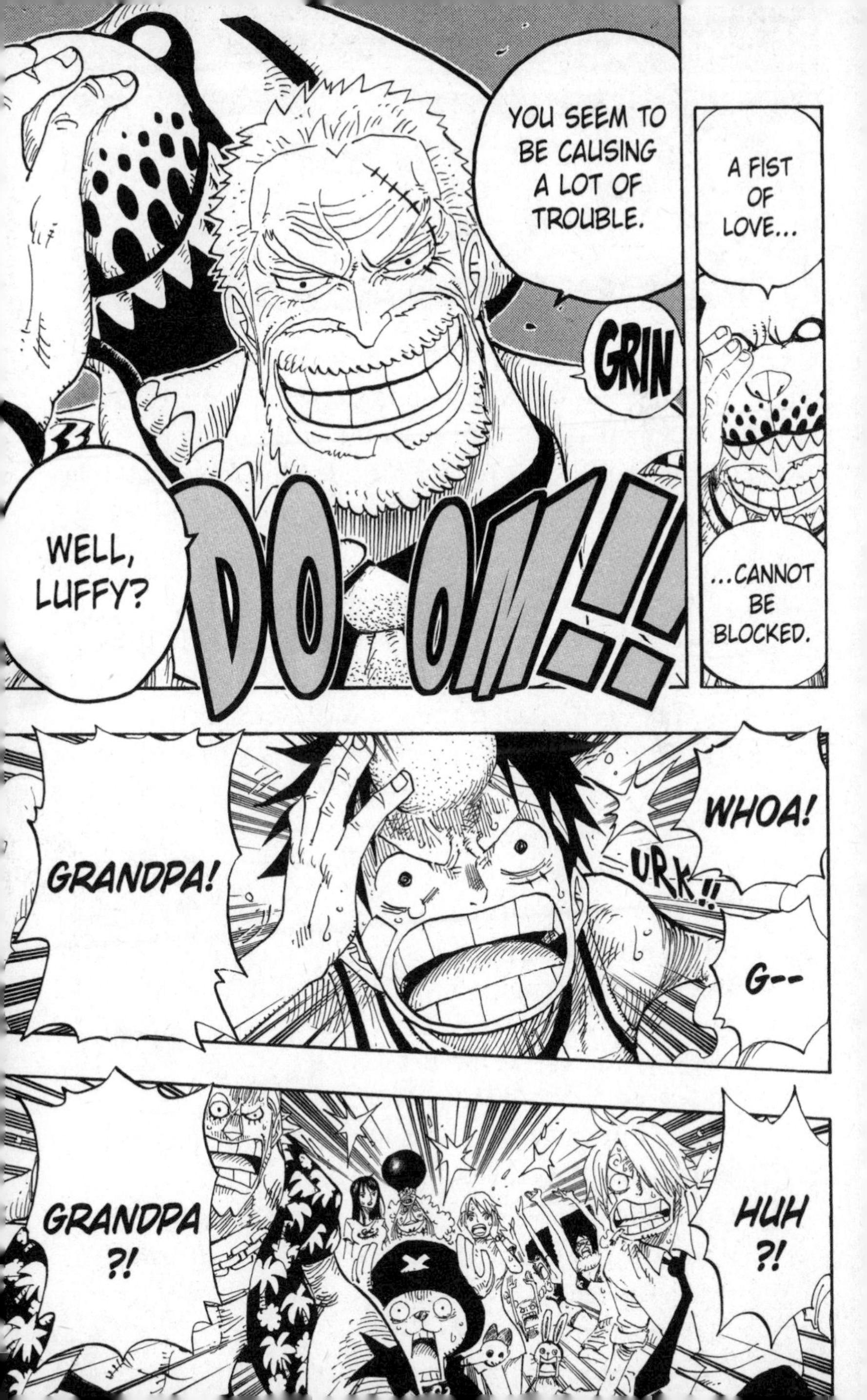
A FIST OF LOVE...
...CANNOT BE BLOCKED.
YOU SEEM TO BE CAUSING A LOT OF TROUBLE.
GRIN
DO-OM!!
WELL, LUFFY?
WHOA!
URK!!
G--
GRANDPA!
HUH ?!
GRANDPA ?!

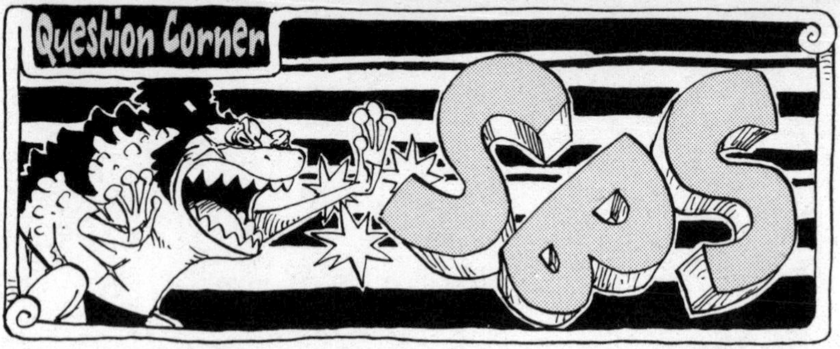
Question Corner
SBS

Reader: Oda Sensei! You haven't announced the title at the beginning of the Question Corner recently. But rest assured! As the captain of the "title call out team," let me request that you say the title while imitating Inoki eating a banana while pretending to be a gorilla! Go!
--White Bear

Oda: Uho! Uho! Hello all, uho! Munch, uho! How are you doing, uho?! One, uho! Two, uho! Three, uho! The Question, uho! Munch, Corner! Uho! Munch, Uho! Let's star...uho! I can't do this!! Let me do it normally, uho!
.........................Okay, on to the questions.

Q: Odacchi, when you eat sweet potatoes, do you do a Coup de Boo too? --Modai

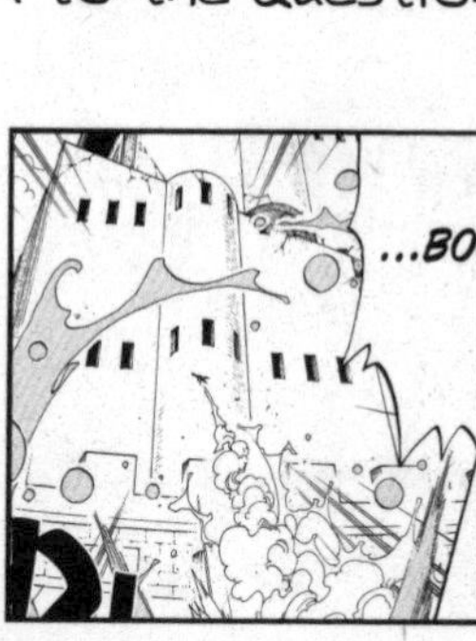
...BO

A: Yes, I do. The other day I ate sweet potatoes, and I flew all the way to New York with my Coup de Boo. I was "Coup de Boo Man in New York." Then I ate some more sweet potatoes and flew all the way back home.

Q: Odacchi! Out of the Six Powers, I want "Iron Body" the most. You can make any part of your body hard, right? Though wouldn't it be awful if "that" part didn't get hard? --Majin Moomin

A: I don't understand what you're getting at.

Chapter 432:
JACK-IN-THE-BOX

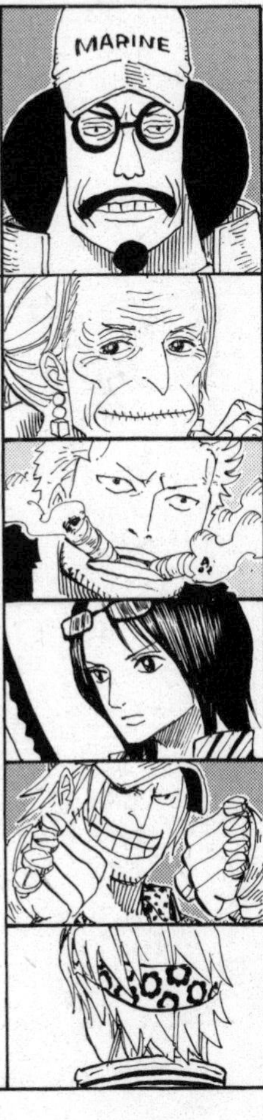
MARINE

MARINE

NAVY HQ RANKINGS

(WORLD GOVERNMENT)
COMMANDER IN CHIEF

Rank	Category
FLEET ADMIRAL (HEAD OF THE NAVY)	NAVY OFFICERS
ADMIRAL (GOVERNOR-GENERAL)	NAVY OFFICERS
VICE ADMIRAL, REAR ADMIRAL, COMMODORE	NAVY OFFICERS
CAPTAIN, COMMANDER, LIEUTENANT COMMANDER	NAVY OFFICERS
LIEUTENANT, LIEUTENANT JR. GRADE, ENSIGN	NAVY OFFICERS
WARRANT OFFICER	NAVY SOLDIERS
MASTER CHIEF PETTY OFFICER, CHIEF PETTY OFFICER, PETTY OFFICER	NAVY SOLDIERS
SEAMAN, SEAMAN APPRENTICE, SEAMAN RECRUIT	NAVY SOLDIERS
CHORE BOY	NAVY SOLDIERS

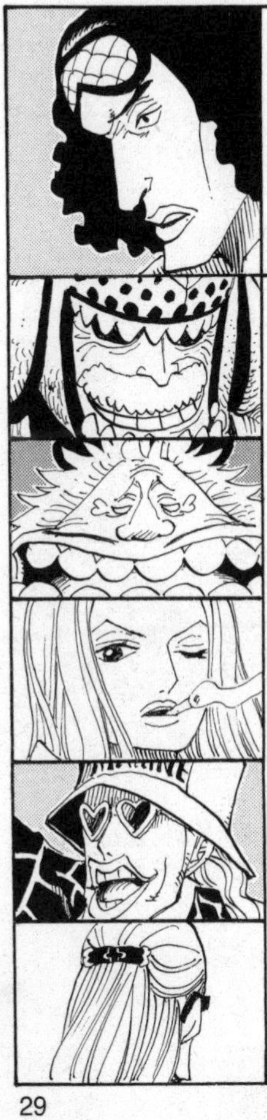

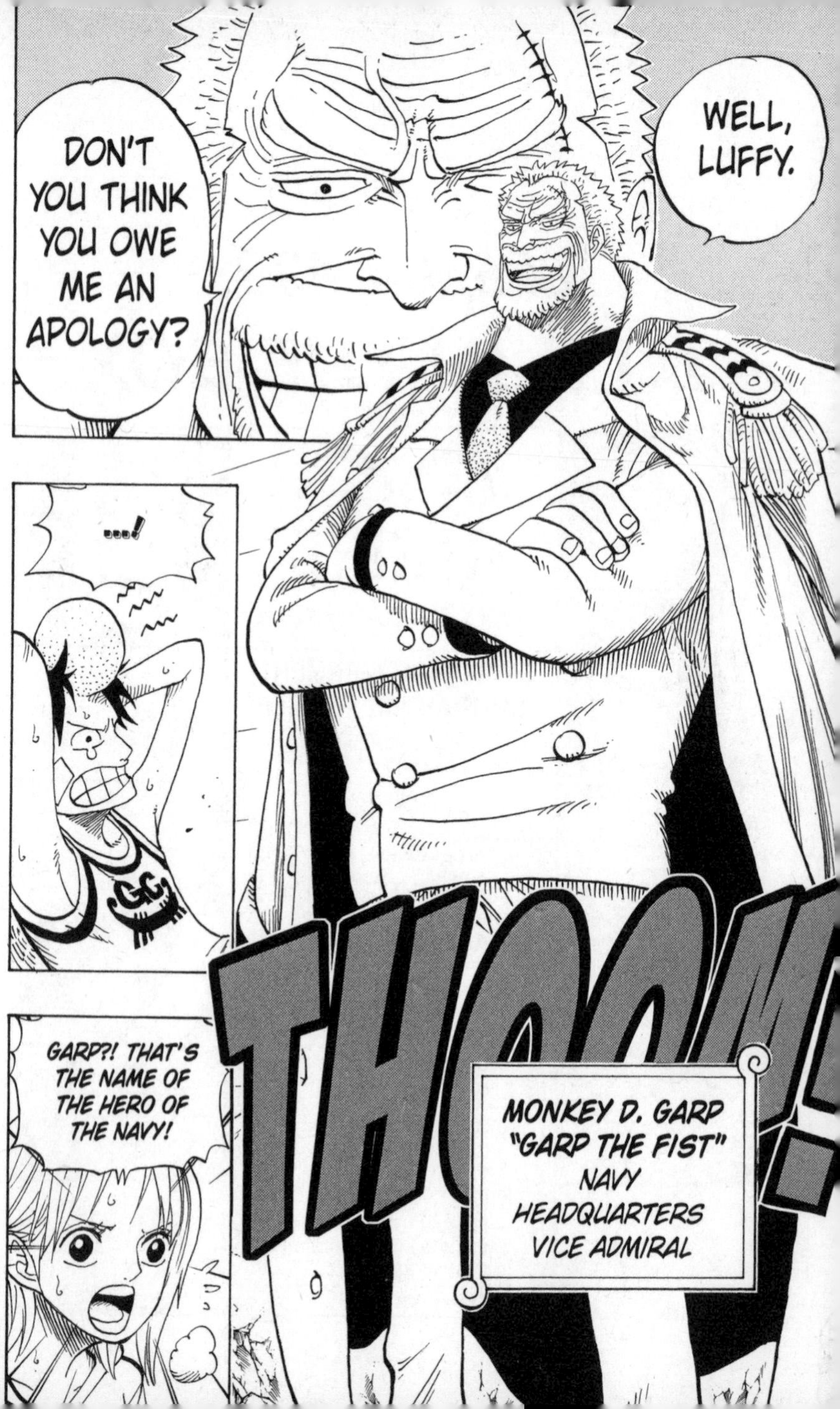
WELL, LUFFY.
THOOM!
MONKEY D. GARP
"GARP THE FIST"
NAVY
HEADQUARTERS
VICE ADMIRAL
DON'T YOU THINK YOU OWE ME AN APOLOGY?
...!
GARP?! THAT'S THE NAME OF THE HERO OF THE NAVY!

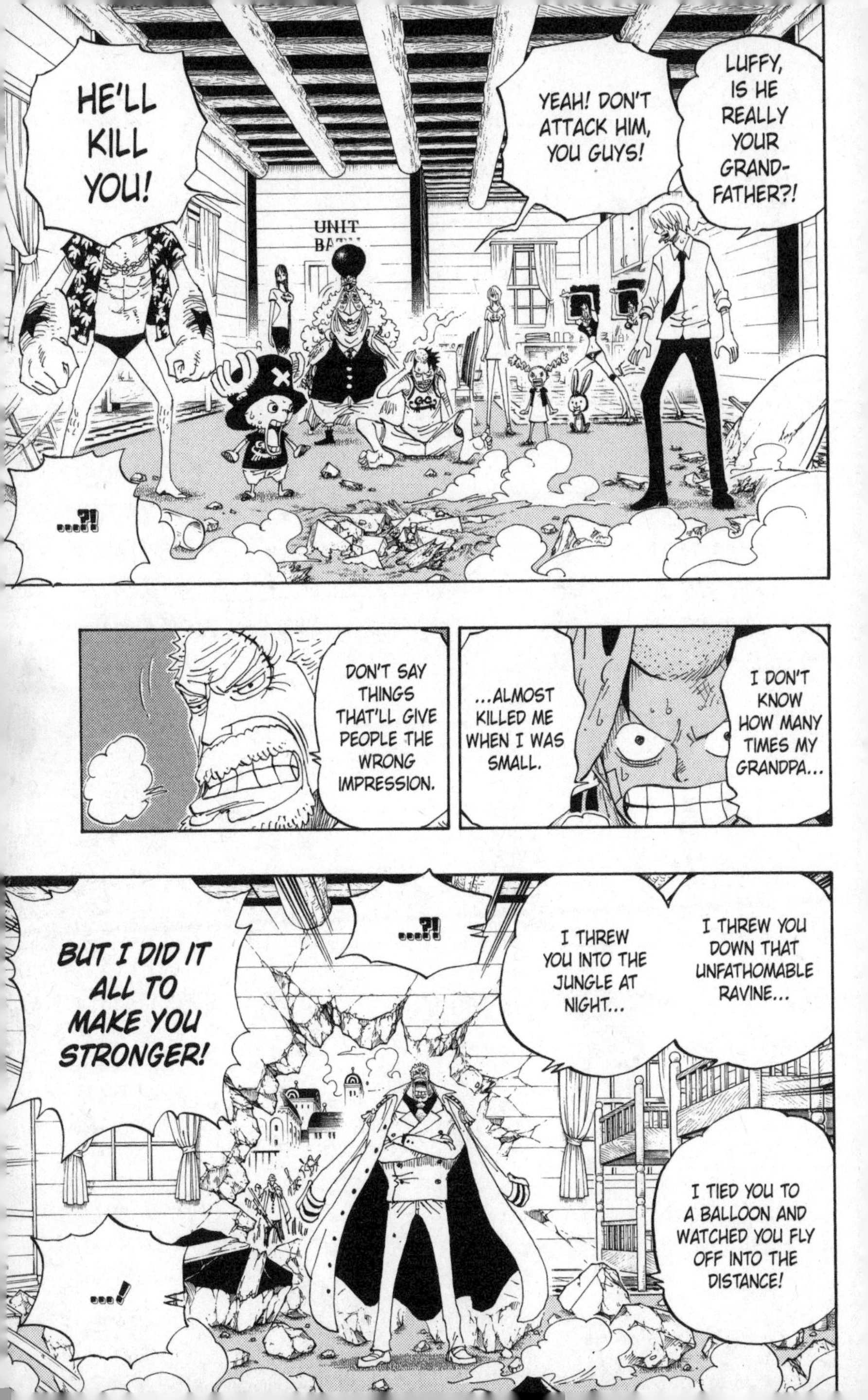
LUFFY, IS HE REALLY YOUR GRAND-FATHER?!
YEAH! DON'T ATTACK HIM, YOU GUYS!
HE'LL KILL YOU!
...?!
I DON'T KNOW HOW MANY TIMES MY GRANDPA...
...ALMOST KILLED ME WHEN I WAS SMALL.
DON'T SAY THINGS THAT'LL GIVE PEOPLE THE WRONG IMPRESSION.
I THREW YOU DOWN THAT UNFATHOMABLE RAVINE...
I THREW YOU INTO THE JUNGLE AT NIGHT...
...?!
I TIED YOU TO A BALLOON AND WATCHED YOU FLY OFF INTO THE DISTANCE!
BUT I DID IT ALL TO MAKE YOU STRONGER!
...!

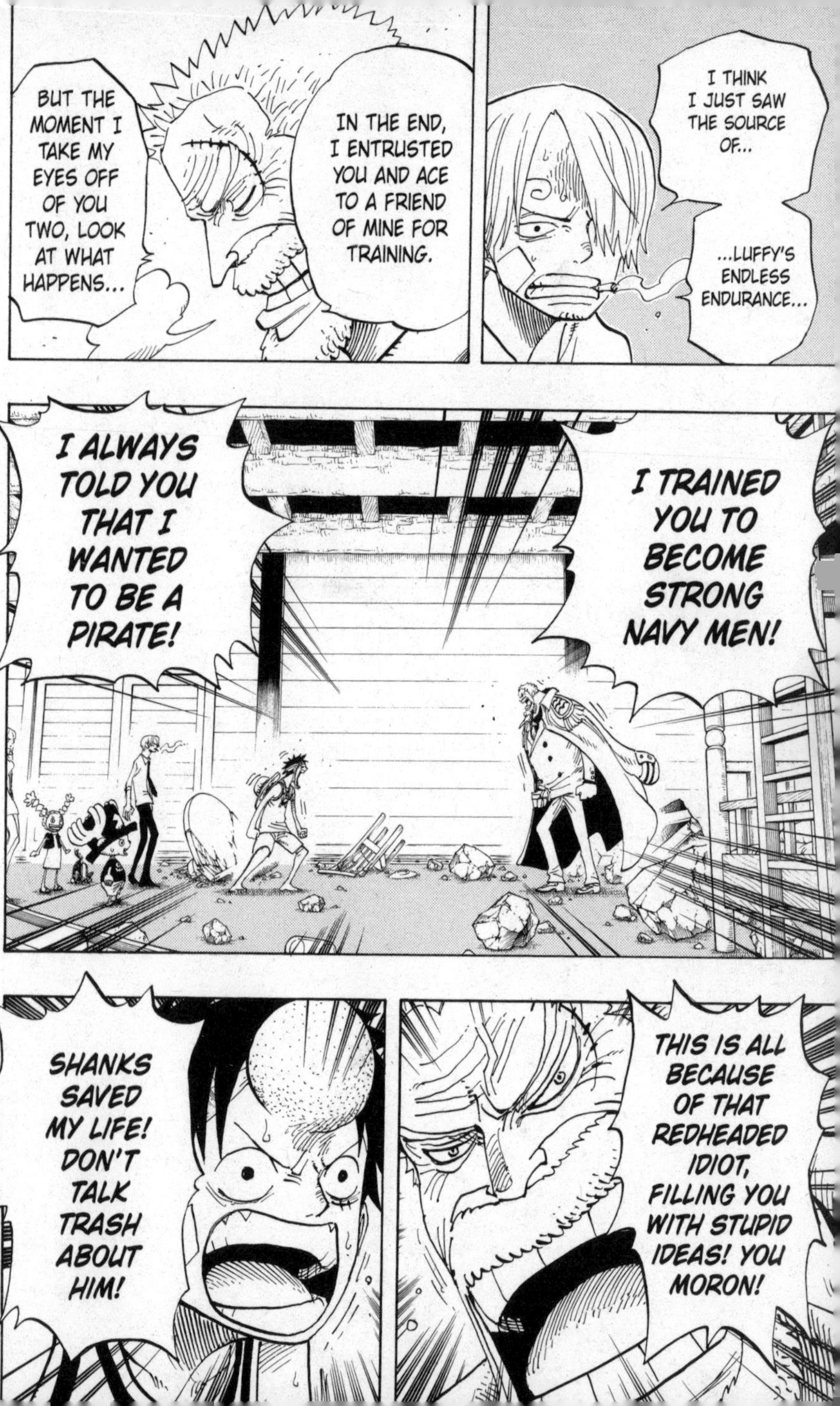
I THINK I JUST SAW THE SOURCE OF...
...LUFFY'S ENDLESS ENDURANCE...
IN THE END, I ENTRUSTED YOU AND ACE TO A FRIEND OF MINE FOR TRAINING.
BUT THE MOMENT I TAKE MY EYES OFF OF YOU TWO, LOOK AT WHAT HAPPENS...
I TRAINED YOU TO BECOME STRONG NAVY MEN!
I ALWAYS TOLD YOU THAT I WANTED TO BE A PIRATE!
THIS IS ALL BECAUSE OF THAT REDHEADED IDIOT, FILLING YOU WITH STUPID IDEAS! YOU MORON!
SHANKS SAVED MY LIFE! DON'T TALK TRASH ABOUT HIM!

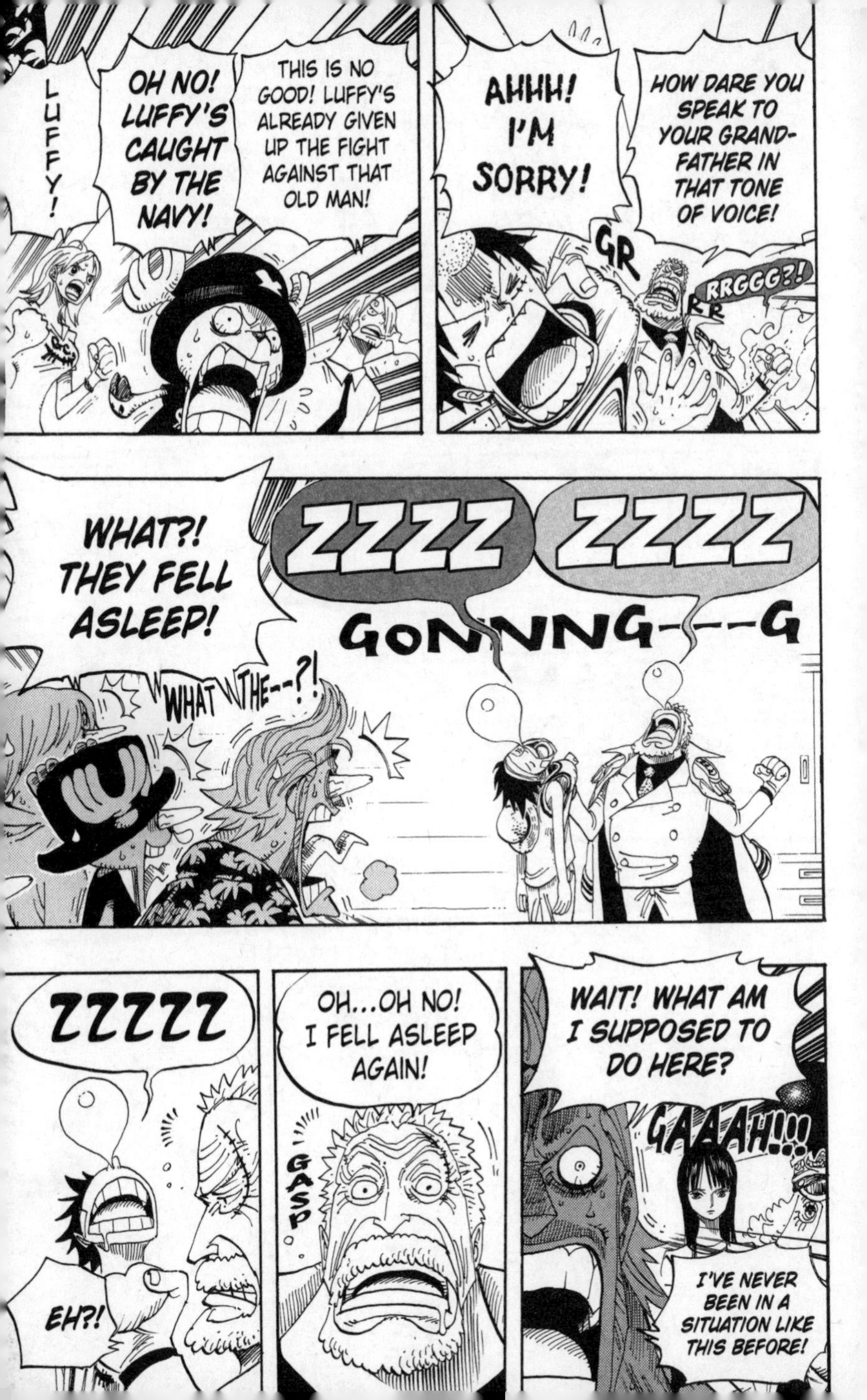
HOW DARE YOU SPEAK TO YOUR GRAND-FATHER IN THAT TONE OF VOICE!
AHHH! I'M SORRY!
GR
RRGGG?!
RR
THIS IS NO GOOD! LUFFY'S ALREADY GIVEN UP THE FIGHT AGAINST THAT OLD MAN!
OH NO! LUFFY'S CAUGHT BY THE NAVY!
LUFFY!
ZZZZ
ZZZZ
GONNNG---G
WHAT?! THEY FELL ASLEEP!
WHAT THE--?!
WAIT! WHAT AM I SUPPOSED TO DO HERE?
GAAAH!!!
I'VE NEVER BEEN IN A SITUATION LIKE THIS BEFORE!
OH...OH NO! I FELL ASLEEP AGAIN!
GASP
ZZZZZ
EH?!

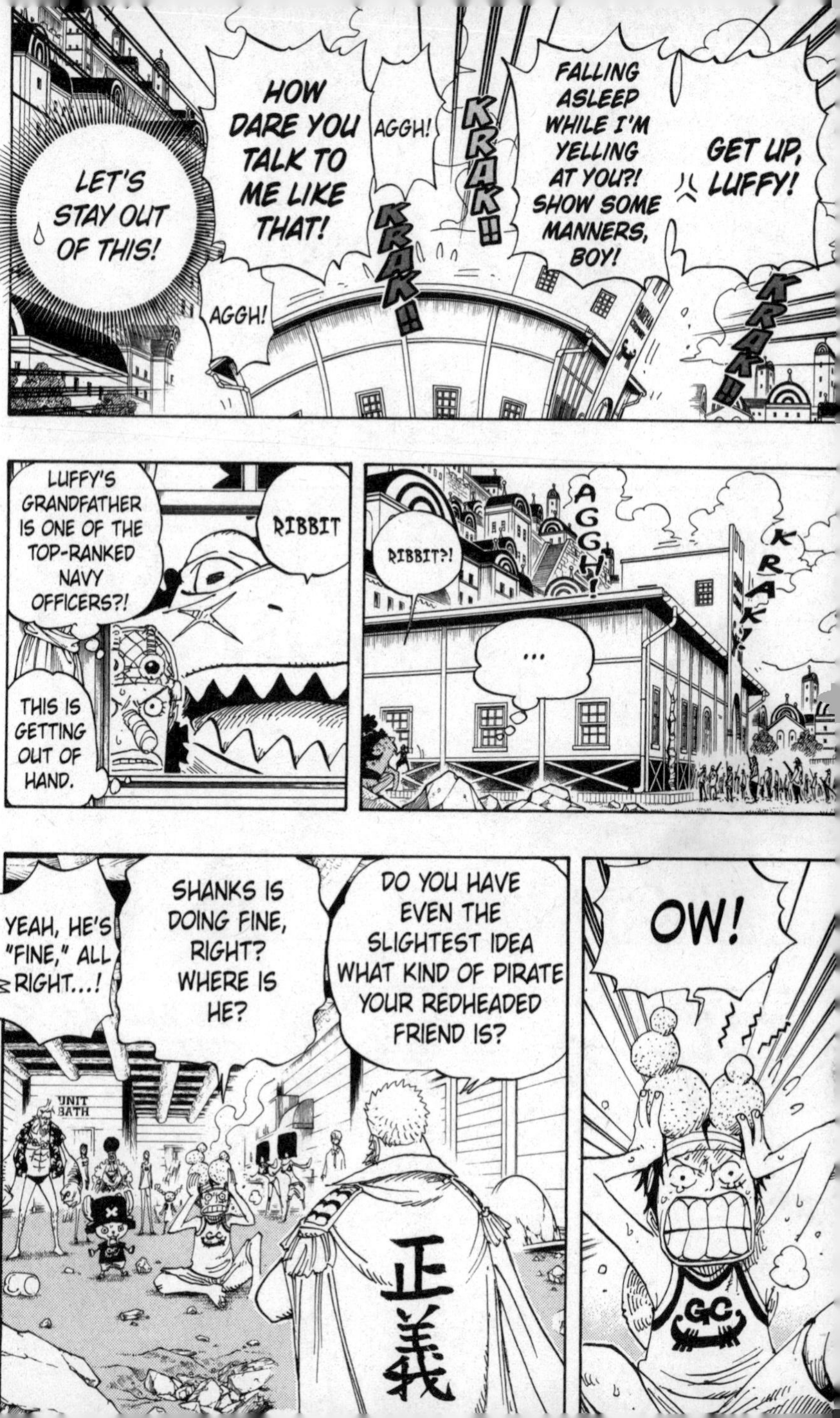
GET UP, LUFFY!
KRAK!!
FALLING ASLEEP WHILE I'M YELLING AT YOU?! SHOW SOME MANNERS, BOY!
KRAK!!
AGGH!
KRAK!!
HOW DARE YOU TALK TO ME LIKE THAT!
AGGH!
LET'S STAY OUT OF THIS!
AGGH!
KRAK!
RIBBIT?!
...
RIBBIT
LUFFY'S GRANDFATHER IS ONE OF THE TOP-RANKED NAVY OFFICERS?!
THIS IS GETTING OUT OF HAND.
OW!
DO YOU HAVE EVEN THE SLIGHTEST IDEA WHAT KIND OF PIRATE YOUR REDHEADED FRIEND IS?
正義
SHANKS IS DOING FINE, RIGHT? WHERE IS HE?
YEAH, HE'S "FINE," ALL RIGHT...!
UNIT BATH

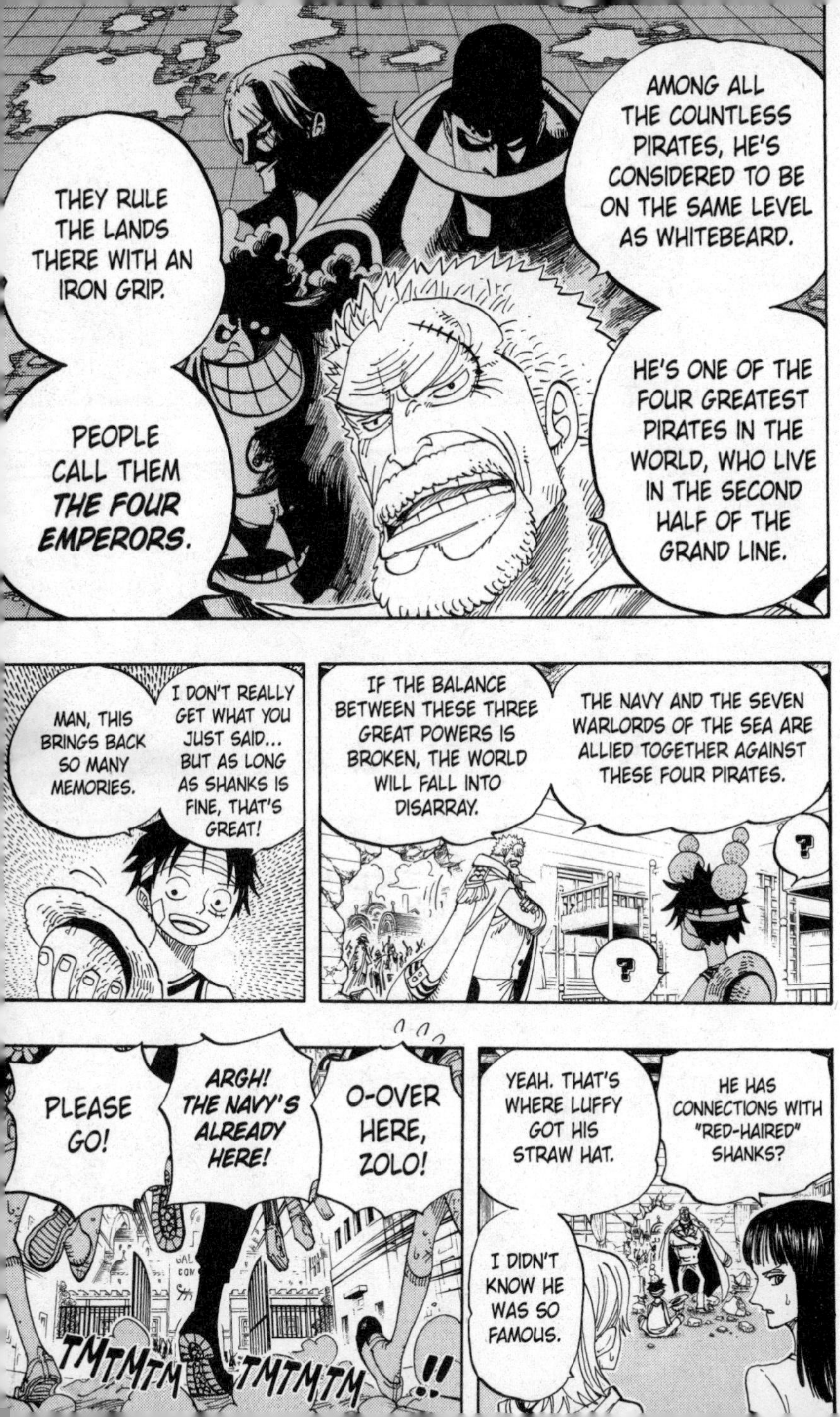
AMONG ALL THE COUNTLESS PIRATES, HE'S CONSIDERED TO BE ON THE SAME LEVEL AS WHITEBEARD.
HE'S ONE OF THE FOUR GREATEST PIRATES IN THE WORLD, WHO LIVE IN THE SECOND HALF OF THE GRAND LINE.
THEY RULE THE LANDS THERE WITH AN IRON GRIP.
PEOPLE CALL THEM *THE FOUR EMPERORS*.
THE NAVY AND THE SEVEN WARLORDS OF THE SEA ARE ALLIED TOGETHER AGAINST THESE FOUR PIRATES.
IF THE BALANCE BETWEEN THESE THREE GREAT POWERS IS BROKEN, THE WORLD WILL FALL INTO DISARRAY.
?
?
I DON'T REALLY GET WHAT YOU JUST SAID... BUT AS LONG AS SHANKS IS FINE, THAT'S GREAT!
MAN, THIS BRINGS BACK SO MANY MEMORIES.
HE HAS CONNECTIONS WITH "RED-HAIRED" SHANKS?
YEAH. THAT'S WHERE LUFFY GOT HIS STRAW HAT.
I DIDN'T KNOW HE WAS SO FAMOUS.
O-OVER HERE, ZOLO!
ARGH! THE NAVY'S ALREADY HERE!
PLEASE GO!
TMTMTM
TMTMTM
!!

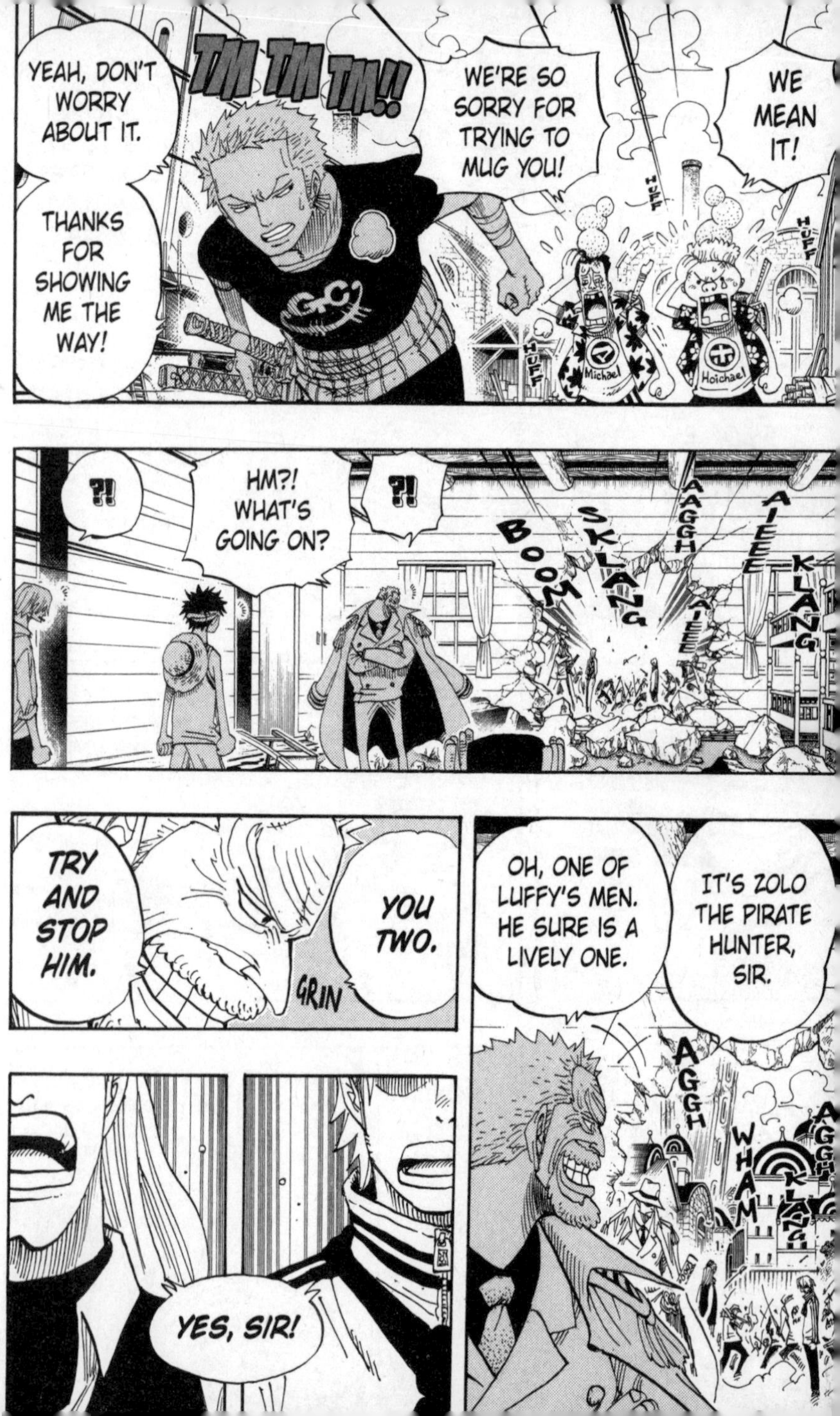
WE MEAN IT!
WE'RE SO SORRY FOR TRYING TO MUG YOU!
HUFF
HUFF
TM TM TM!!
YEAH, DON'T WORRY ABOUT IT.
THANKS FOR SHOWING ME THE WAY!
HUFF
Michael
Hoichael
KLANG
AIEEE
AAGGH
AIEEE
SKLANG
BOOM
?!
HM?! WHAT'S GOING ON?
?!
IT'S ZOLO THE PIRATE HUNTER, SIR.
OH, ONE OF LUFFY'S MEN. HE SURE IS A LIVELY ONE.
AGGH
KLANG
WHAM
AGGH
YOU TWO.
TRY AND STOP HIM.
GRIN
YES, SIR!

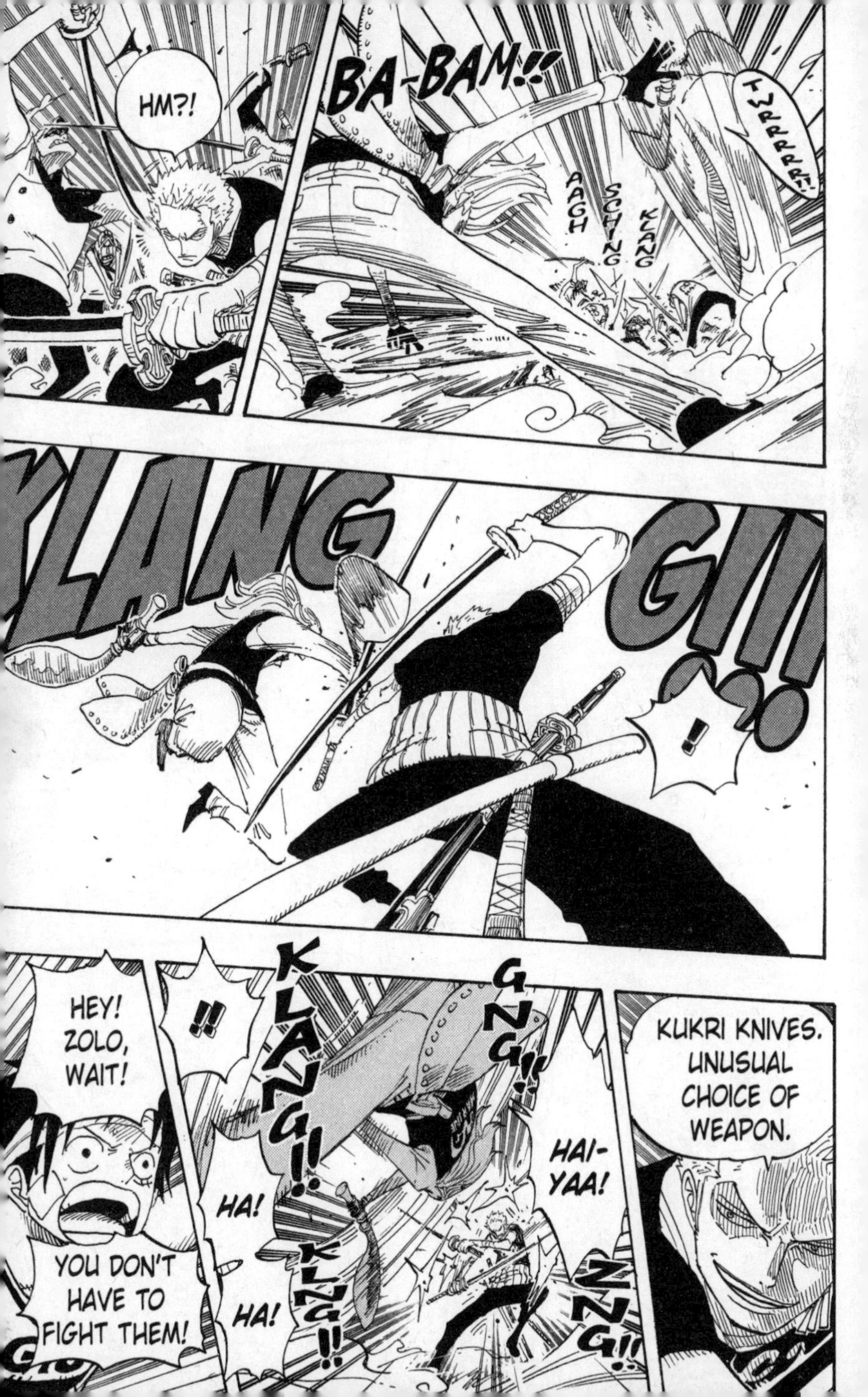

TWRRRRR!!
BA-BAM!!
KLANG
SCHING
AAGH
HM?!
!
KLANG
KUKRI KNIVES. UNUSUAL CHOICE OF WEAPON.
GNG!!
KLANG!!
HAI-YAA!
HA!
ZNG!!
KLNG!!
HA!
!!
HEY! ZOLO, WAIT!
YOU DON'T HAVE TO FIGHT THEM!

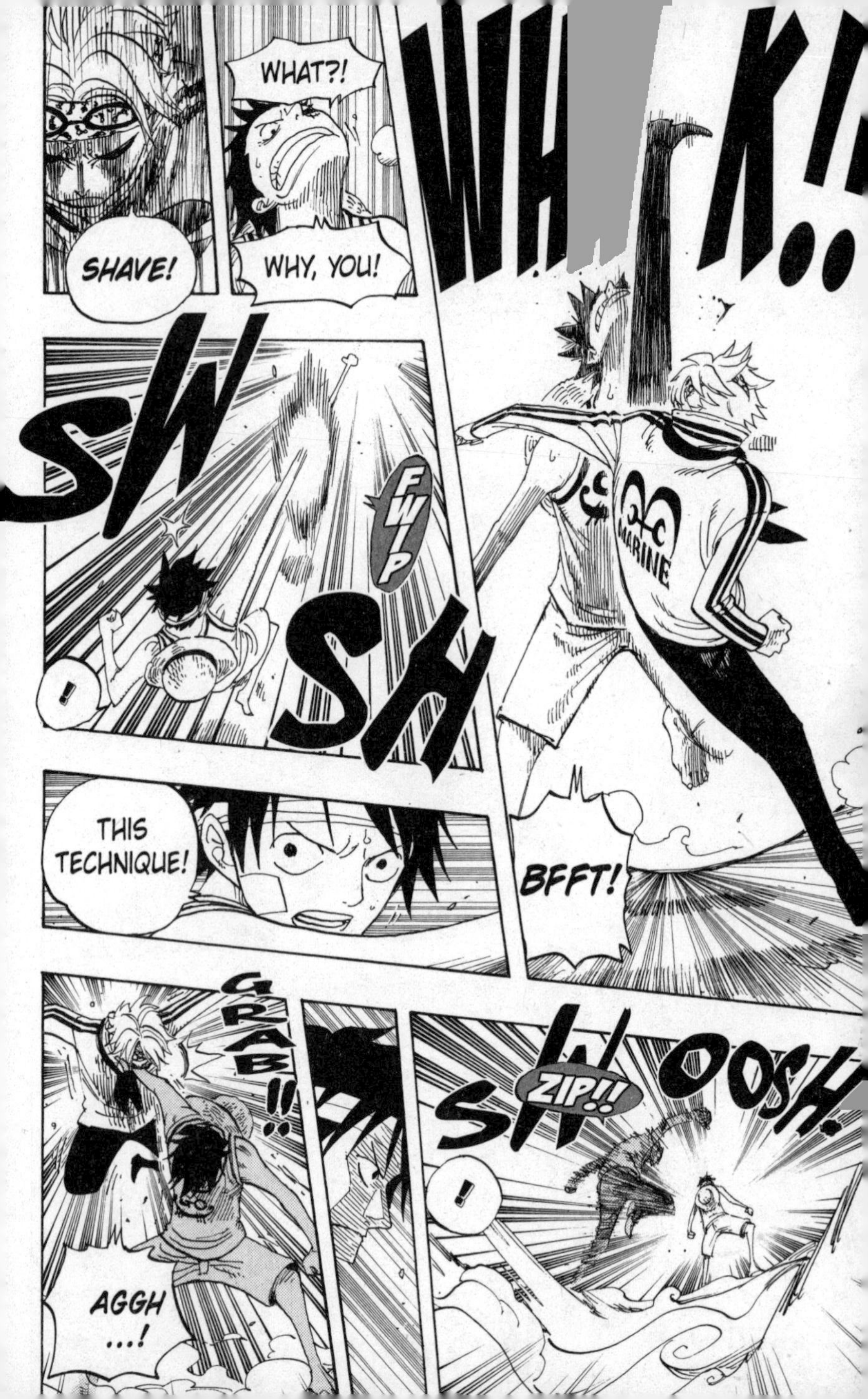
WH K!!
BFFT!
WHAT?!
WHY, YOU!
SHAVE!
SW
FWIP
SH
!
THIS TECHNIQUE!
SWOOSH!
ZIP!!
!
GRAB!!
AGGH ...!

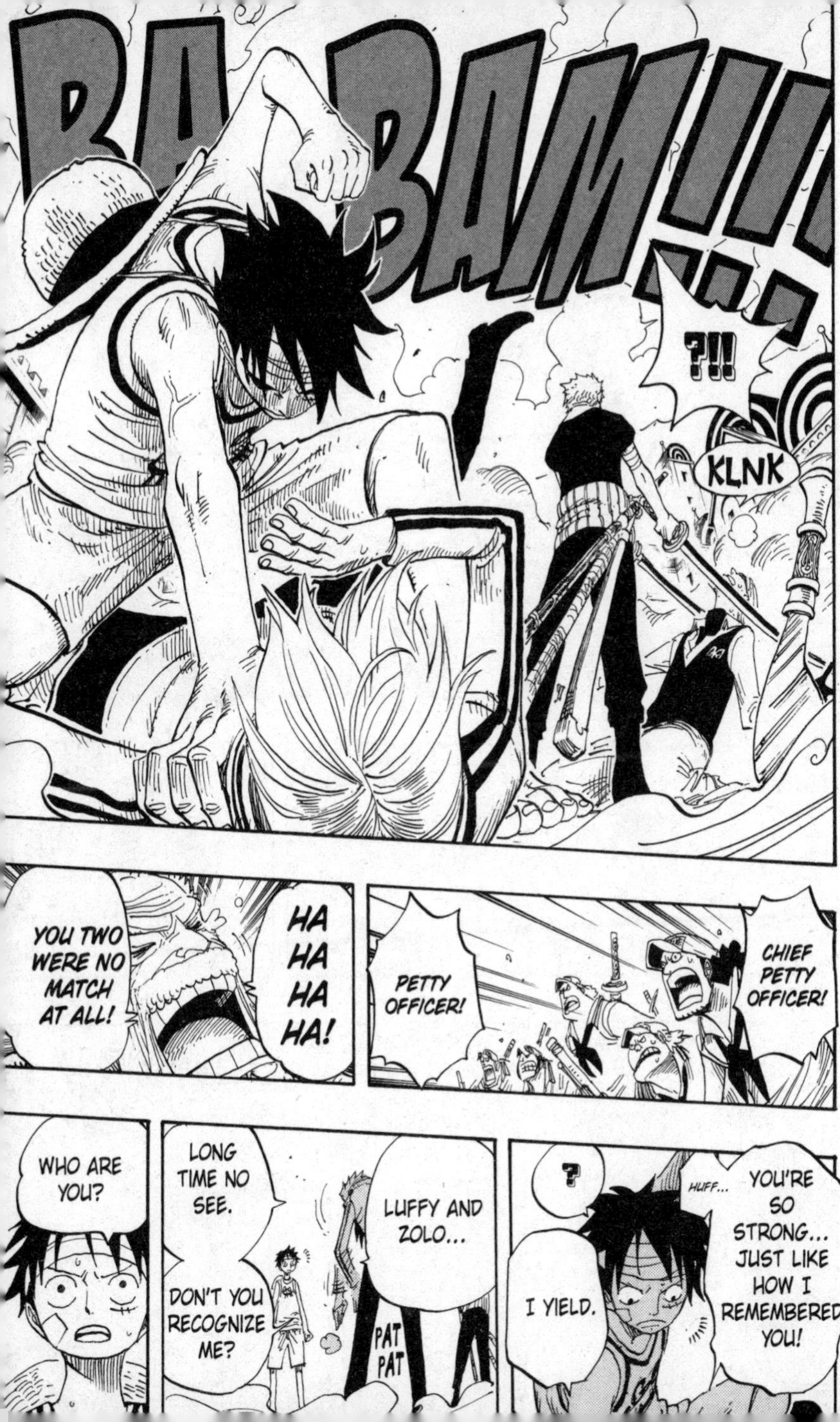
BA-BAM!!!
?!!
KLNK
CHIEF PETTY OFFICER!
PETTY OFFICER!
HA HA HA HA!
YOU TWO WERE NO MATCH AT ALL!
HUFF...
YOU'RE SO STRONG... JUST LIKE HOW I REMEMBERED YOU!
?
I YIELD.
LUFFY AND ZOLO...
LONG TIME NO SEE.
DON'T YOU RECOGNIZE ME?
PAT PAT
WHO ARE YOU?

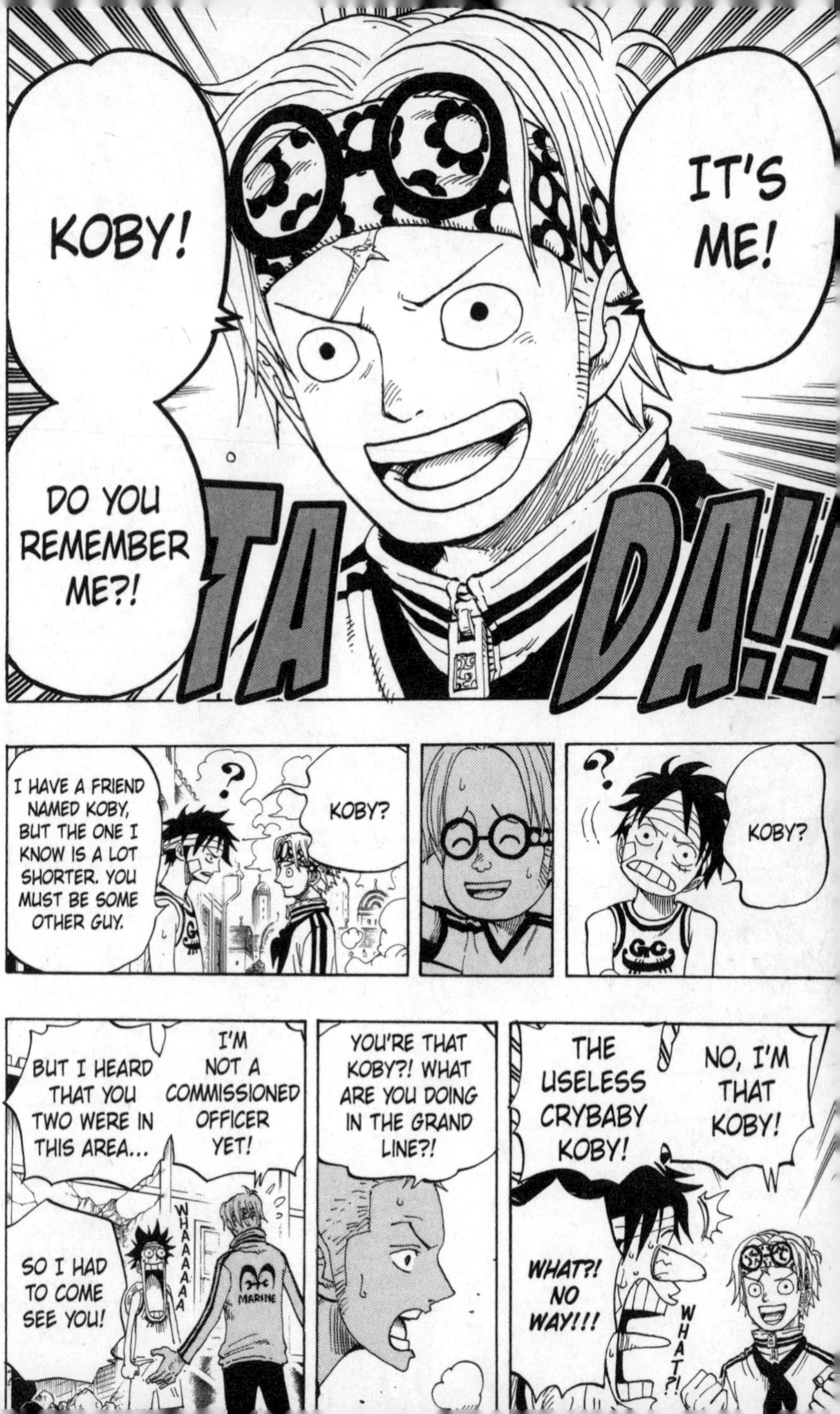
IT'S ME!
KOBY!
DO YOU REMEMBER ME?!
TA DA!!
KOBY?
KOBY?
I HAVE A FRIEND NAMED KOBY, BUT THE ONE I KNOW IS A LOT SHORTER. YOU MUST BE SOME OTHER GUY.
NO, I'M THAT KOBY!
THE USELESS CRYBABY KOBY!
WHAT?! NO WAY!!!
WHAT?!
YOU'RE THAT KOBY?! WHAT ARE YOU DOING IN THE GRAND LINE?!
I'M NOT A COMMISSIONED OFFICER YET!
BUT I HEARD THAT YOU TWO WERE IN THIS AREA...
WHAAAAAA
SO I HAD TO COME SEE YOU!
MARINE

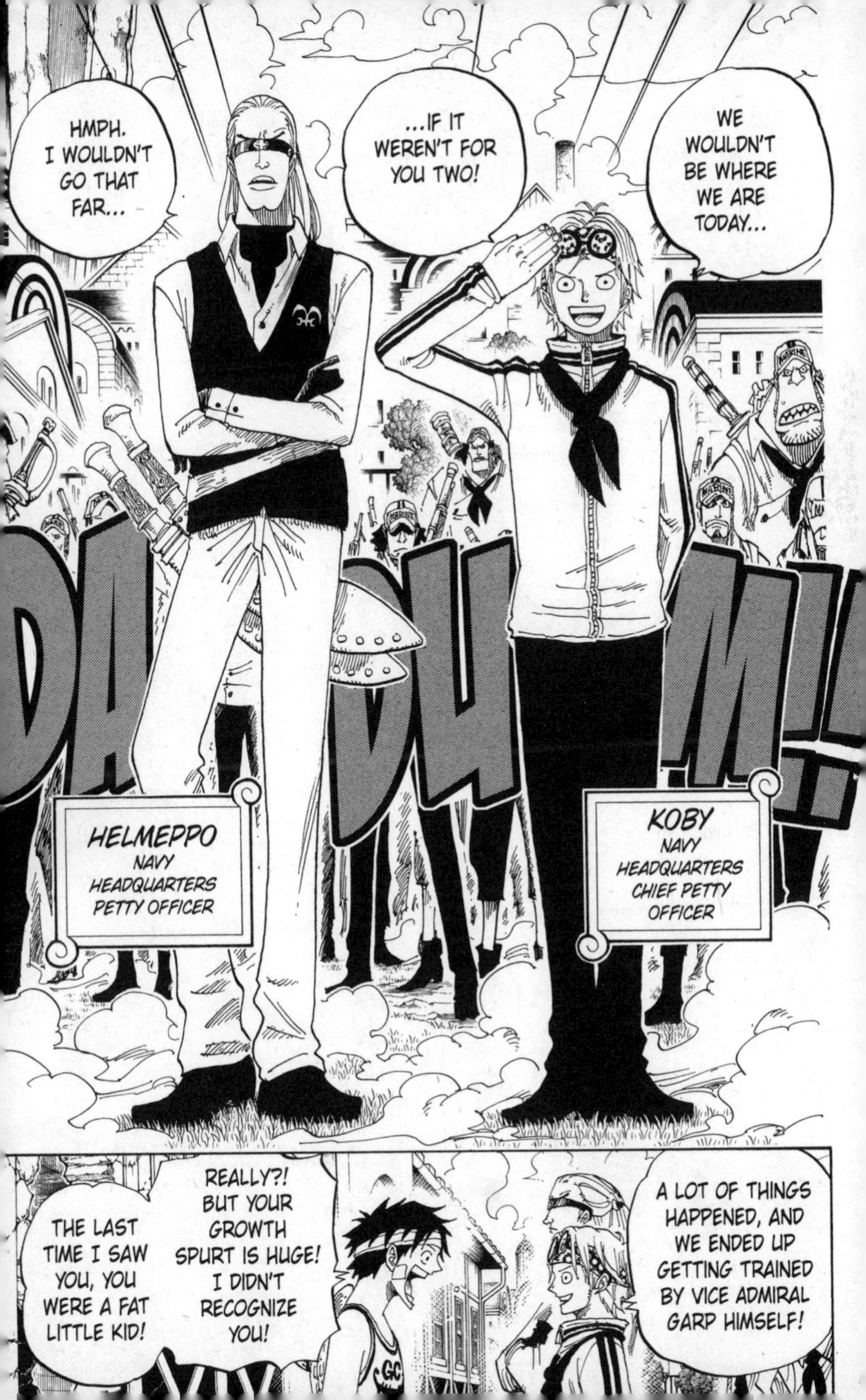
WE WOULDN'T BE WHERE WE ARE TODAY...
...IF IT WEREN'T FOR YOU TWO!
HMPH. I WOULDN'T GO THAT FAR...
DADUM!!
KOBY
NAVY HEADQUARTERS CHIEF PETTY OFFICER
HELMEPPO
NAVY HEADQUARTERS PETTY OFFICER
A LOT OF THINGS HAPPENED, AND WE ENDED UP GETTING TRAINED BY VICE ADMIRAL GARP HIMSELF!
REALLY?! BUT YOUR GROWTH SPURT IS HUGE! I DIDN'T RECOGNIZE YOU!
THE LAST TIME I SAW YOU, YOU WERE A FAT LITTLE KID!

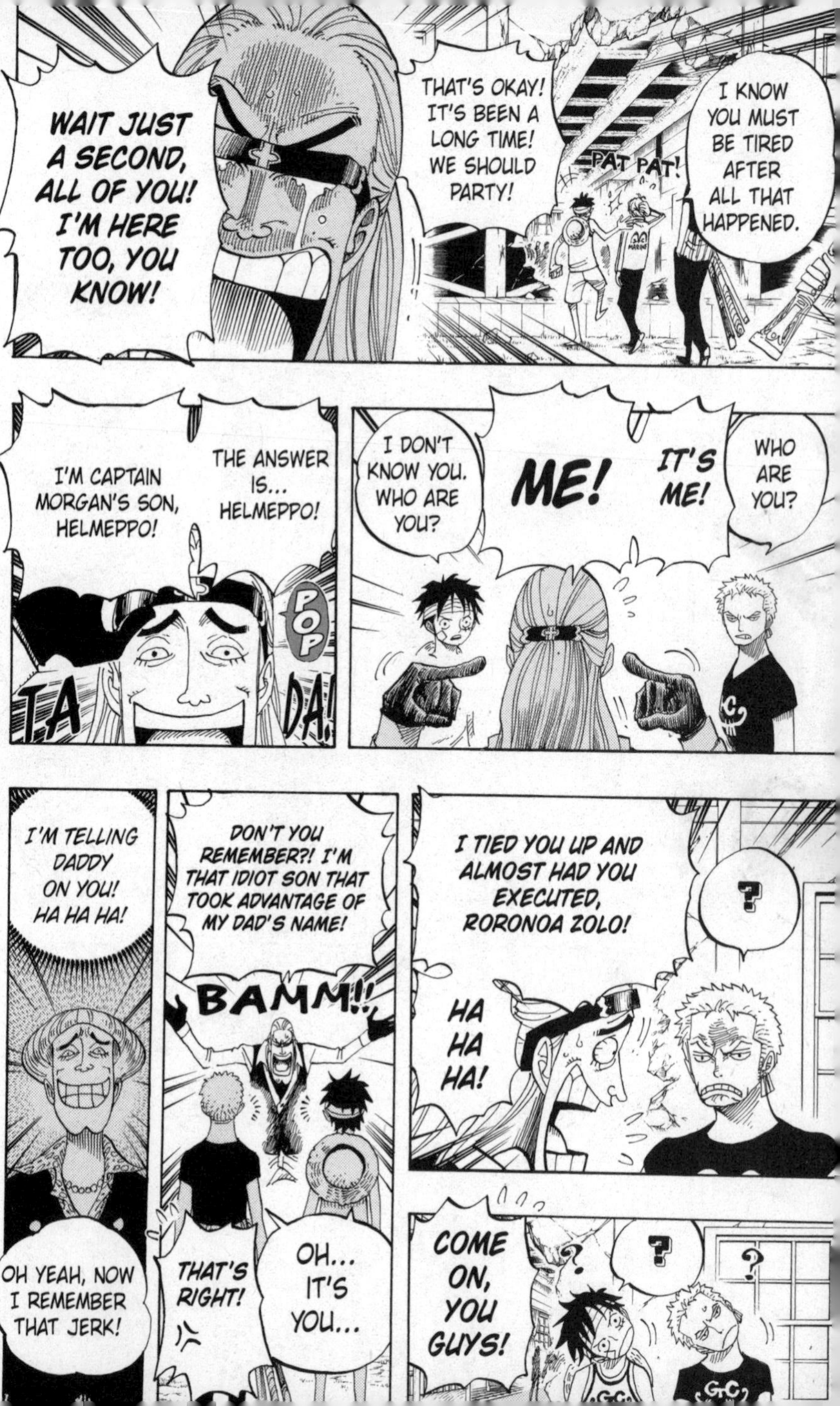
I KNOW YOU MUST BE TIRED AFTER ALL THAT HAPPENED.
THAT'S OKAY! IT'S BEEN A LONG TIME! WE SHOULD PARTY!
PAT PAT!
WAIT JUST A SECOND, ALL OF YOU! I'M HERE TOO, YOU KNOW!
WHO ARE YOU?
IT'S ME!
ME!
I DON'T KNOW YOU. WHO ARE YOU?
THE ANSWER IS... HELMEPPO!
I'M CAPTAIN MORGAN'S SON, HELMEPPO!
POP
TA DA!
I TIED YOU UP AND ALMOST HAD YOU EXECUTED, RORONOA ZOLO!
HA HA HA!
COME ON, YOU GUYS!
DON'T YOU REMEMBER?! I'M THAT IDIOT SON THAT TOOK ADVANTAGE OF MY DAD'S NAME!
BAMM!!
OH... IT'S YOU...
THAT'S RIGHT!
I'M TELLING DADDY ON YOU! HA HA HA!
OH YEAH, NOW I REMEMBER THAT JERK!

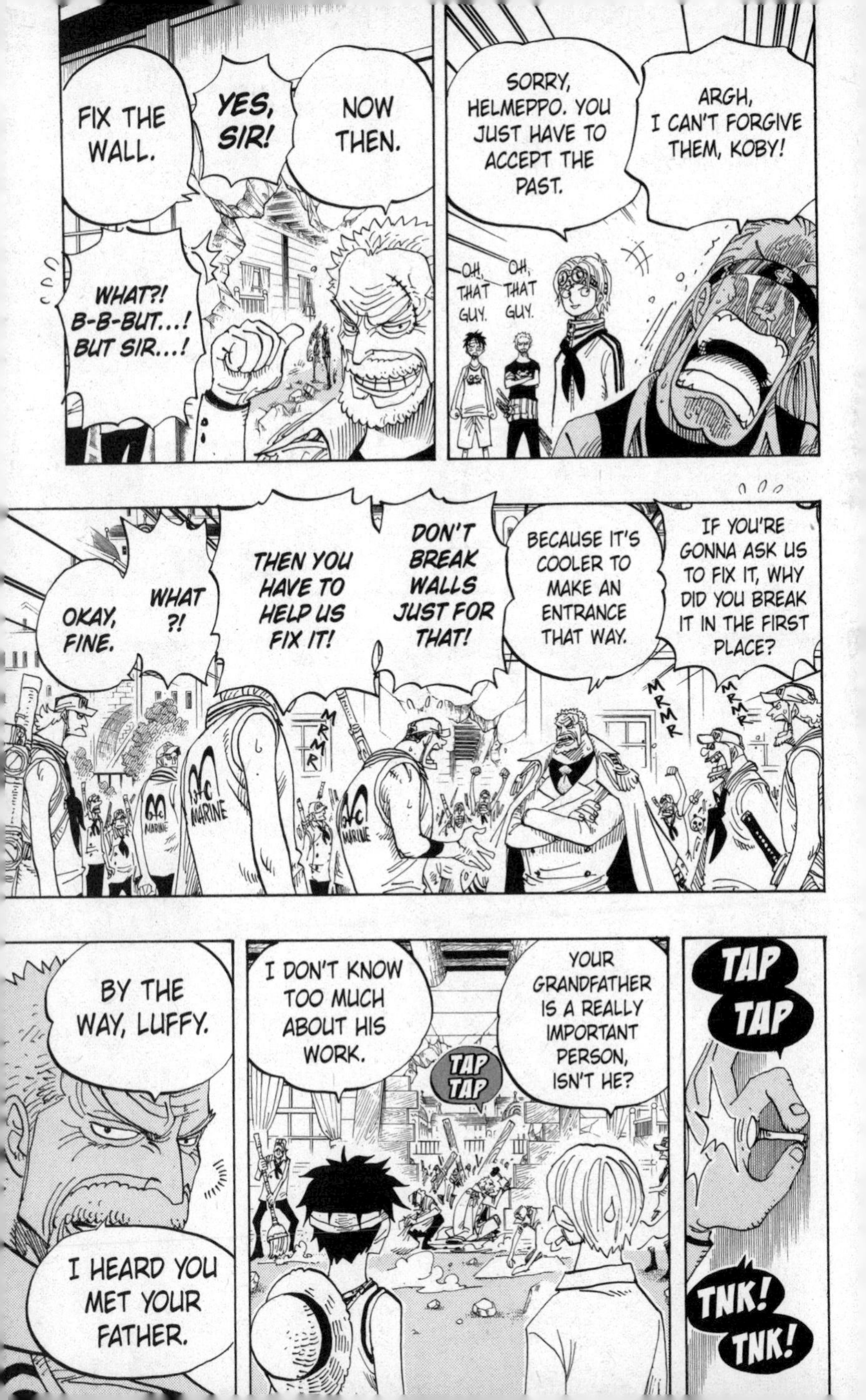
ARGH, I CAN'T FORGIVE THEM, KOBY!
SORRY, HELMEPPO. YOU JUST HAVE TO ACCEPT THE PAST.
OH, THAT GUY.
OH, THAT GUY.
NOW THEN.
YES, SIR!
FIX THE WALL.
WHAT?! B-B-BUT...! BUT SIR...!
IF YOU'RE GONNA ASK US TO FIX IT, WHY DID YOU BREAK IT IN THE FIRST PLACE?
MRMR
BECAUSE IT'S COOLER TO MAKE AN ENTRANCE THAT WAY.
MRMR
DON'T BREAK WALLS JUST FOR THAT!
MRMR
THEN YOU HAVE TO HELP US FIX IT!
WHAT?!
OKAY, FINE.
TAP TAP
TNK! TNK!
YOUR GRANDFATHER IS A REALLY IMPORTANT PERSON, ISN'T HE?
TAP TAP
I DON'T KNOW TOO MUCH ABOUT HIS WORK.
BY THE WAY, LUFFY.
I HEARD YOU MET YOUR FATHER.

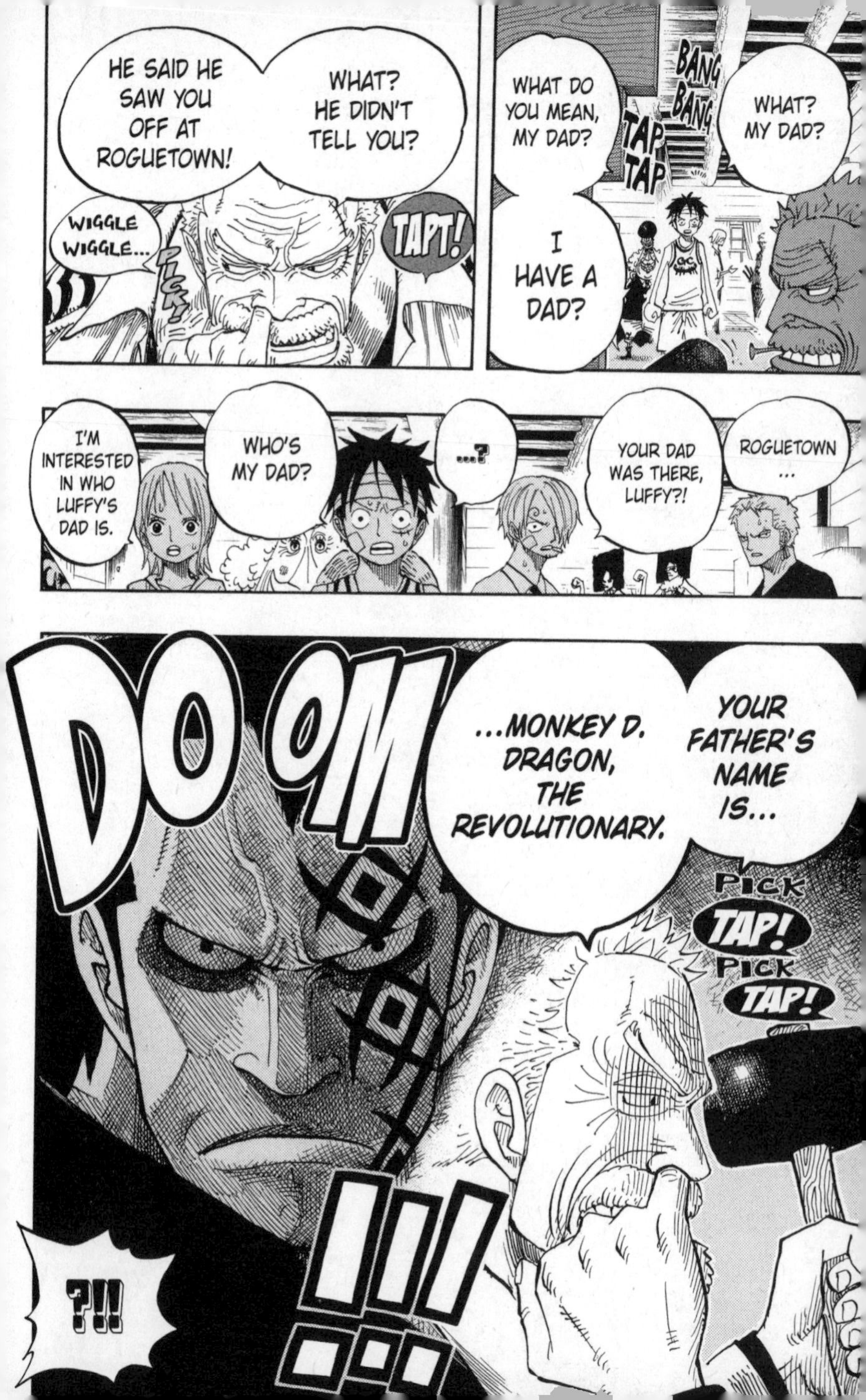
BANG BANG
WHAT? MY DAD?
WHAT DO YOU MEAN, MY DAD?
TAP TAP
I HAVE A DAD?
WHAT? HE DIDN'T TELL YOU?
HE SAID HE SAW YOU OFF AT ROGUETOWN!
TAPT!
PICK!
WIGGLE WIGGLE...
ROGUETOWN...
YOUR DAD WAS THERE, LUFFY?!
...?
WHO'S MY DAD?
I'M INTERESTED IN WHO LUFFY'S DAD IS.
YOUR FATHER'S NAME IS...
...MONKEY D. DRAGON, THE REVOLUTIONARY.
PICK
TAP!
PICK
TAP!
DOOM
!!!...
?!!

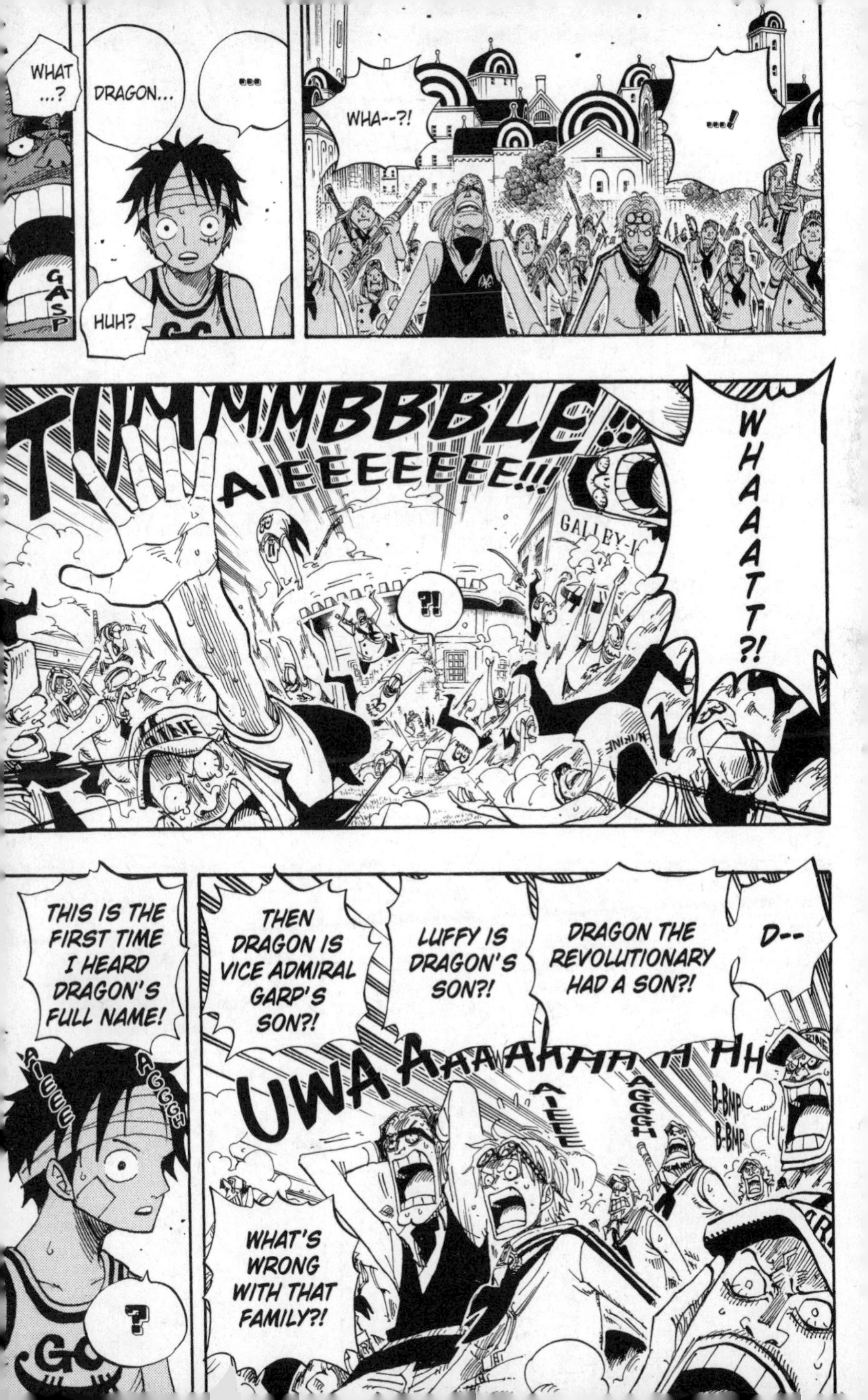

...!
WHA--?!
...
DRAGON...
HUH?
WHAT ...?
GASP
WHAAAATT?!
TUMMMBBBLE!!
AIEEEEEEEE!!!
GALLEY-1
?!
D--
DRAGON THE REVOLUTIONARY HAD A SON?!
LUFFY IS DRAGON'S SON?!
THEN DRAGON IS VICE ADMIRAL GARP'S SON?!
UWAAAAHHHHHH
AIEEE
AGGGH
B-BMP B-BMP
WHAT'S WRONG WITH THAT FAMILY?!
THIS IS THE FIRST TIME I HEARD DRAGON'S FULL NAME!
AIEEE
AGGGH
?

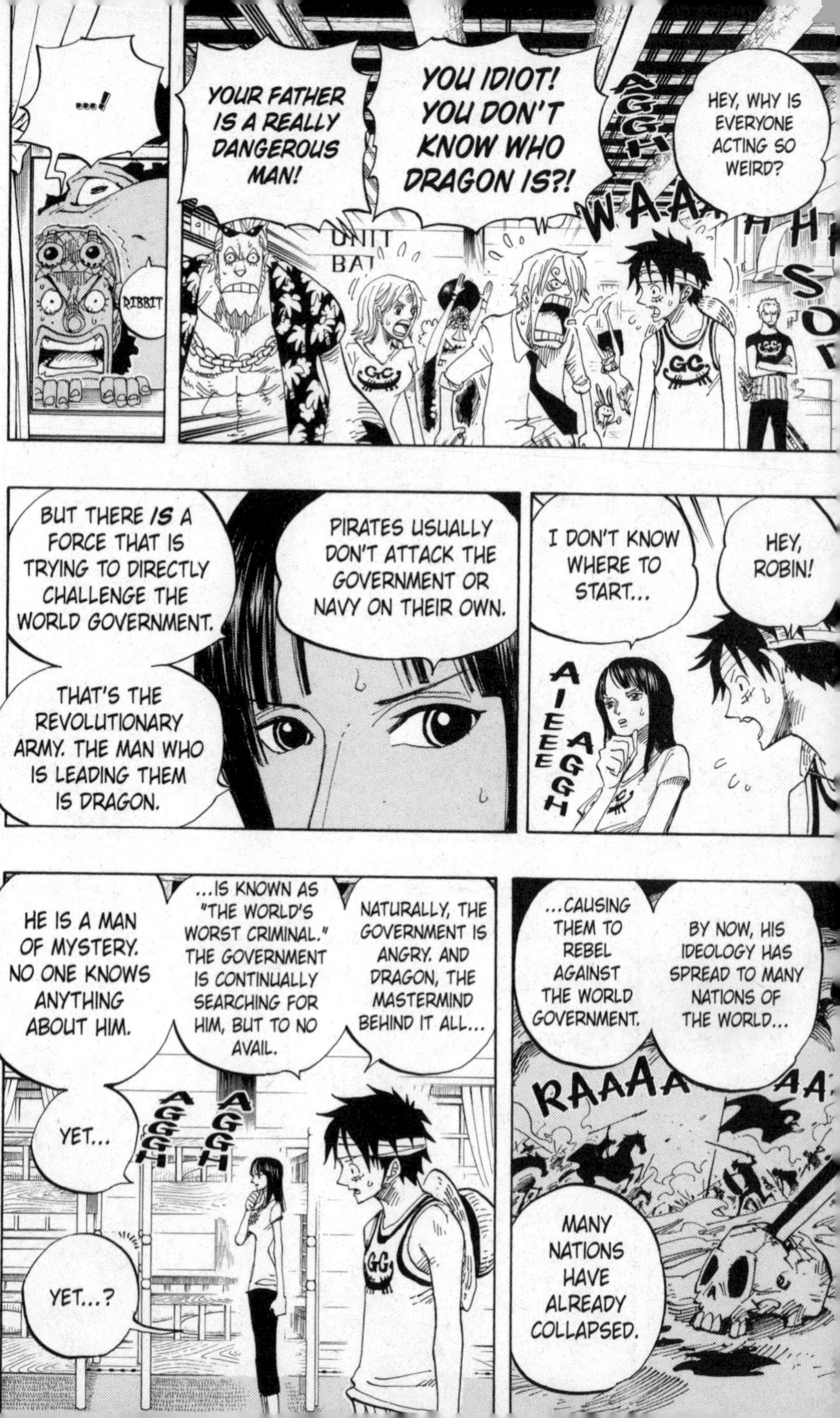
HEY, WHY IS EVERYONE ACTING SO WEIRD?
AGGH
WAAAHH
YOU IDIOT! YOU DON'T KNOW WHO DRAGON IS?!
YOUR FATHER IS A REALLY DANGEROUS MAN!
...!
RIBBIT
HEY, ROBIN!
I DON'T KNOW WHERE TO START...
AIEEE
AGGH
PIRATES USUALLY DON'T ATTACK THE GOVERNMENT OR NAVY ON THEIR OWN.
BUT THERE *IS* A FORCE THAT IS TRYING TO DIRECTLY CHALLENGE THE WORLD GOVERNMENT.
THAT'S THE REVOLUTIONARY ARMY. THE MAN WHO IS LEADING THEM IS DRAGON.
BY NOW, HIS IDEOLOGY HAS SPREAD TO MANY NATIONS OF THE WORLD...
...CAUSING THEM TO REBEL AGAINST THE WORLD GOVERNMENT.
RAAAA
AA
MANY NATIONS HAVE ALREADY COLLAPSED.
NATURALLY, THE GOVERNMENT IS ANGRY. AND DRAGON, THE MASTERMIND BEHIND IT ALL...
...IS KNOWN AS "THE WORLD'S WORST CRIMINAL." THE GOVERNMENT IS CONTINUALLY SEARCHING FOR HIM, BUT TO NO AVAIL.
HE IS A MAN OF MYSTERY. NO ONE KNOWS ANYTHING ABOUT HIM.
YET...
AGGGH
AGGH
YET...?

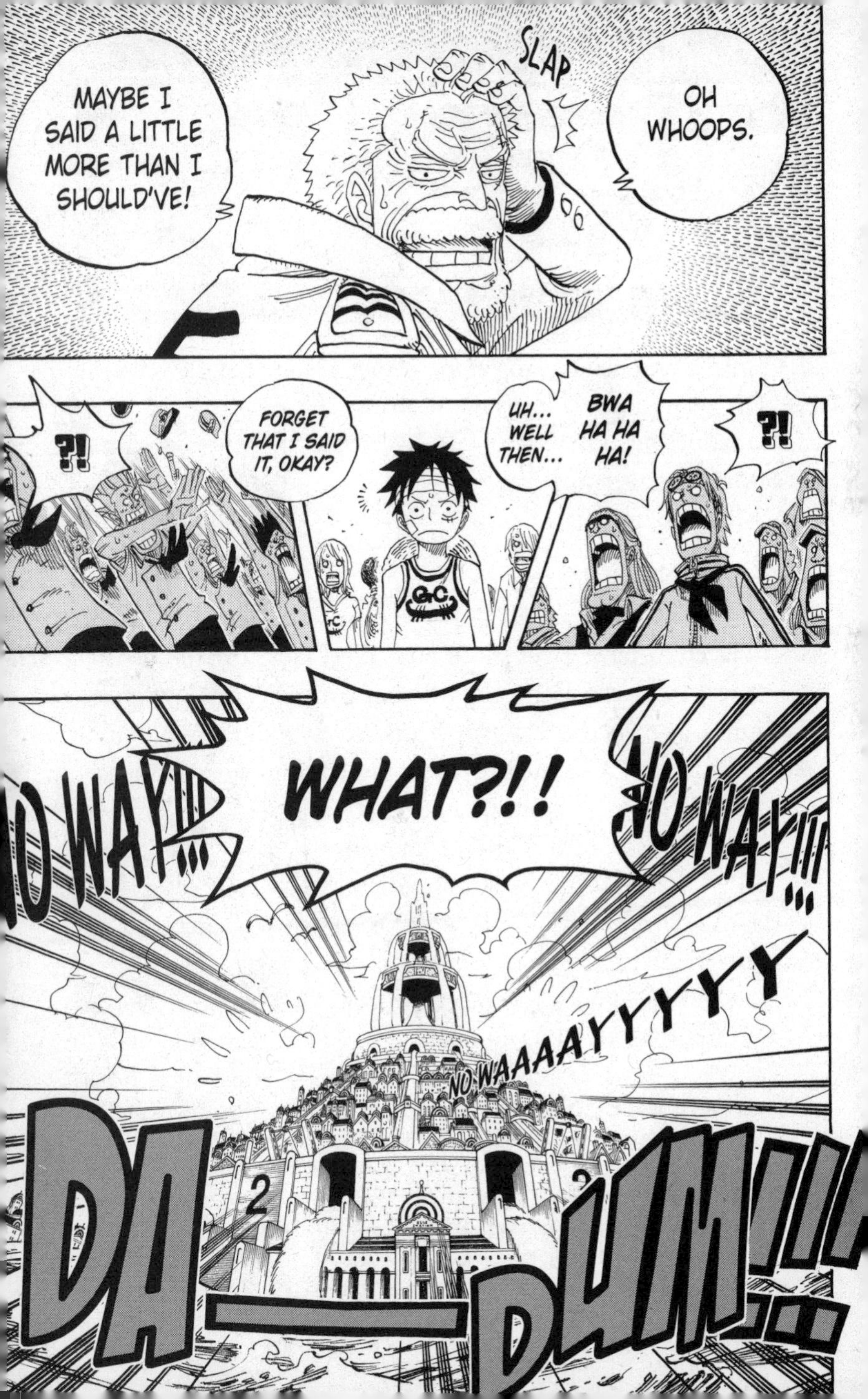
OH WHOOPS.
SLAP
MAYBE I SAID A LITTLE MORE THAN I SHOULD'VE!
?!
BWA HA HA HA!
UH... WELL THEN...
FORGET THAT I SAID IT, OKAY?
?!
NO WAY!!!
WHAT?!!
NO WAY!!!
NO WAAAAYYYYY
DA—DUM!!!

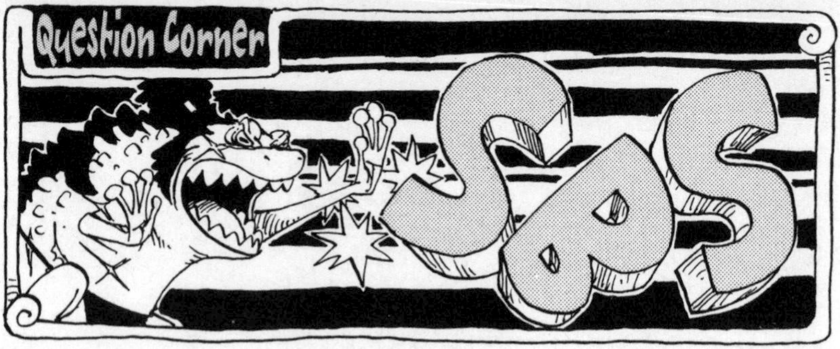
Question Corner
SBS

Q: Clang! Clang clang clang clang clang! Clang clang! Oda Sensei! Did you get Kumadori's name from the kumadori stage makeup worn by kabuki actors? Answer me!

--Shou-kun

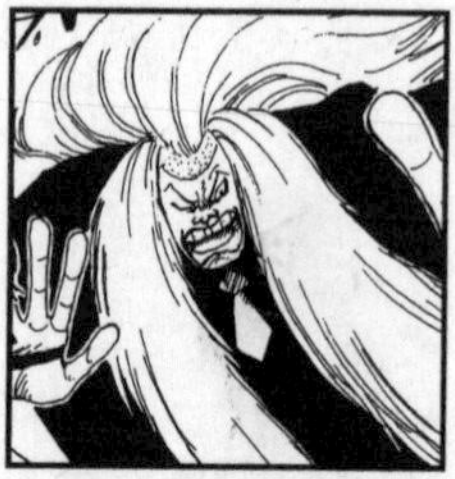

A: That's right. I used it as is.

Q: Odacchi! I have a question! Hey! Hey! Hey! In volume 44, page 148, panel 5, the guy that has dynamite equipped on him! I-i-i-i-is this Ryotsu? Kankichi Ryotsu from Kochira Katsushika-ku Kameari Koen-mae Hashutsujo? ("This is the police box in front of Kameari Park in Katsushika Ward") I knew it! Why?! Why?! Why?! Why is he there?! Is it his brother? Or what is it? Did he change jobs from being a cop to a Navy man? What's going on?! If you don't answer me, I'll call you out on sexual harassment!

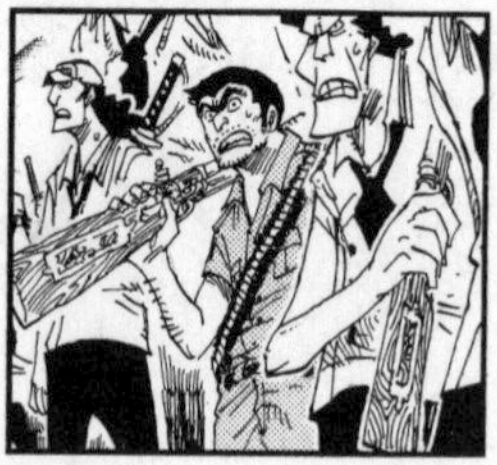

--The Touch Boss

A: I received a lot of letters asking about this. You're right, this is the famous Ryo-san from the manga Kochikame! 2006 was the 30th anniversary of Kochikame, which started in 1976. There was a call for celebration that year, so all the current Weekly Shonen Jump manga hid Ryo-san in one issue and had the readers try to find him. This project, in which all the Jump artists participated, was possible only due to the popularity of Kochikame and its creator, Mr. Akimoto. Thirty years of Kochikame--that's amazing! Congratulations!

Chapter 433:

THE NAME OF THAT SEA

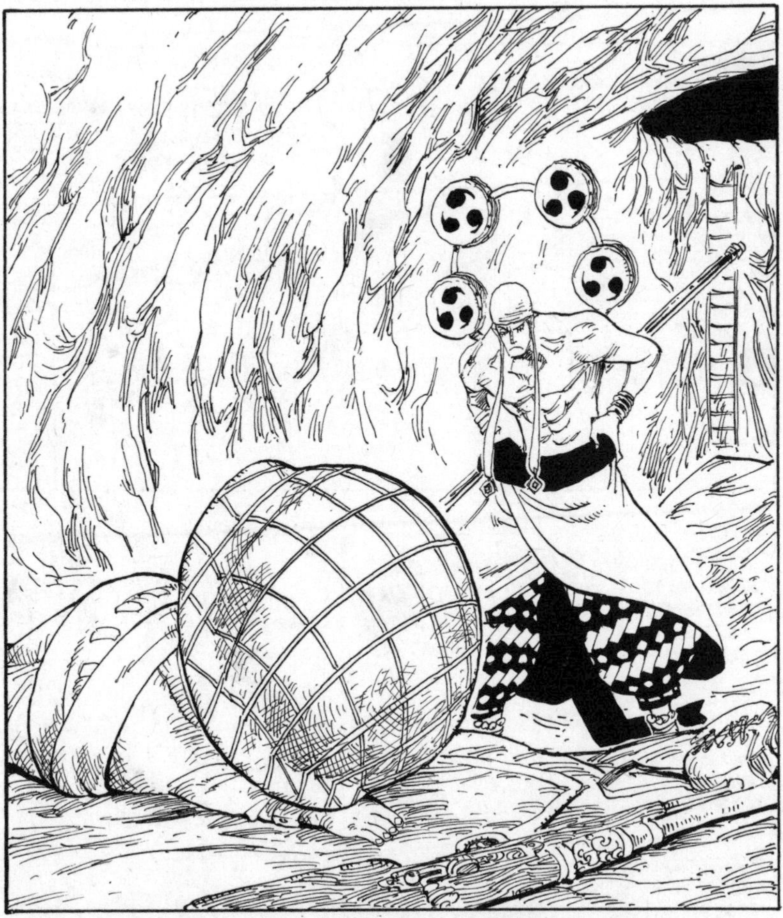

ENERU'S GREAT SPACE MISSION, VOL. 4:
"THERE'S SOMEBODY IN THE HOLE"

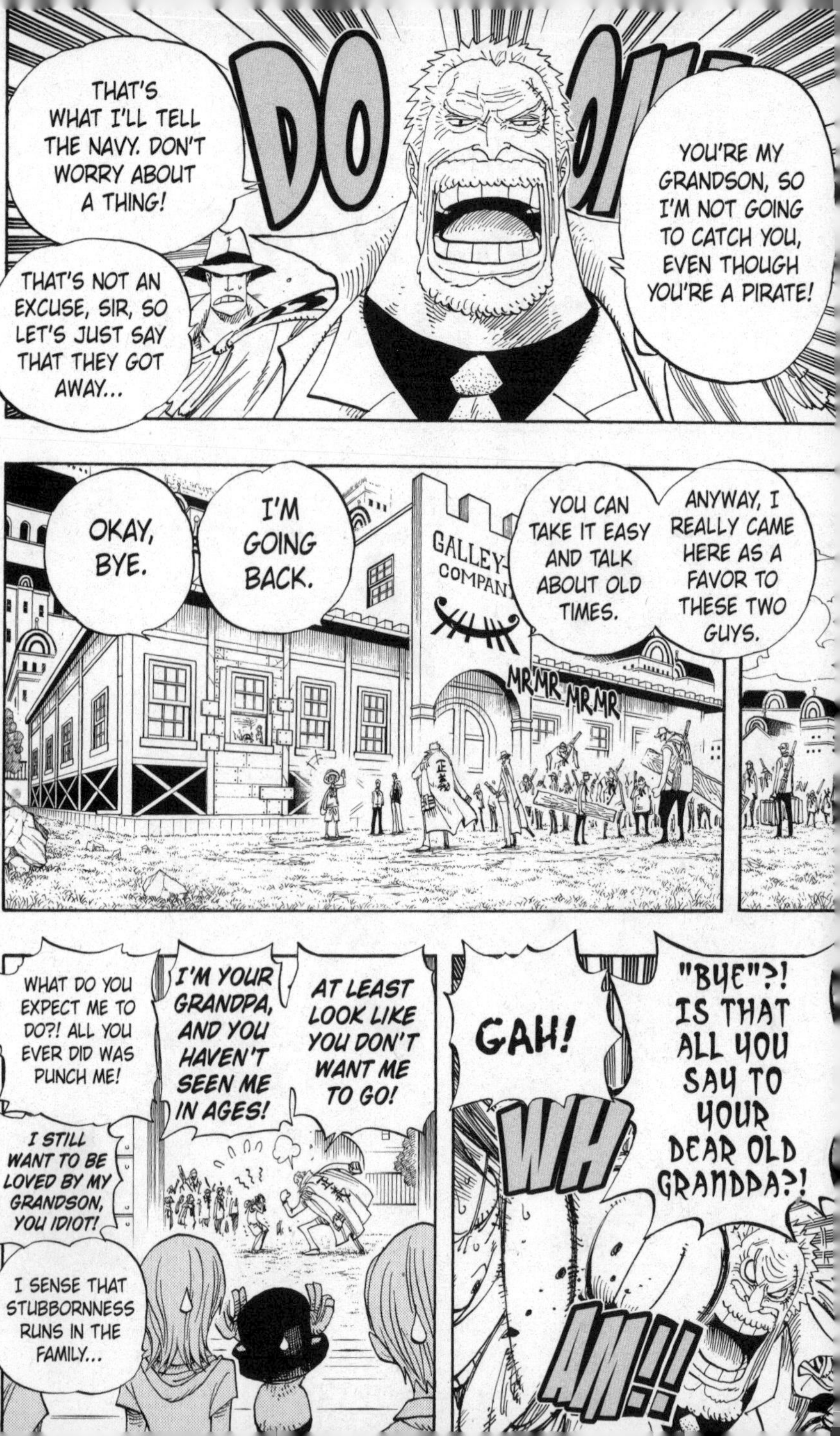
YOU'RE MY GRANDSON, SO I'M NOT GOING TO CATCH YOU, EVEN THOUGH YOU'RE A PIRATE!
DO
THAT'S WHAT I'LL TELL THE NAVY. DON'T WORRY ABOUT A THING!
THAT'S NOT AN EXCUSE, SIR, SO LET'S JUST SAY THAT THEY GOT AWAY...
ANYWAY, I REALLY CAME HERE AS A FAVOR TO THESE TWO GUYS.
YOU CAN TAKE IT EASY AND TALK ABOUT OLD TIMES.
GALLEY- COMPANY
I'M GOING BACK.
OKAY, BYE.
MR MR MR MR
"BYE"?! IS THAT ALL YOU SAY TO YOUR DEAR OLD GRANDPA?!
GAH!
WH
AM!!
AT LEAST LOOK LIKE YOU DON'T WANT ME TO GO!
I'M YOUR GRANDPA, AND YOU HAVEN'T SEEN ME IN AGES!
WHAT DO YOU EXPECT ME TO DO?! ALL YOU EVER DID WAS PUNCH ME!
I STILL WANT TO BE LOVED BY MY GRANDSON, YOU IDIOT!
I SENSE THAT STUBBORNNESS RUNS IN THE FAMILY...

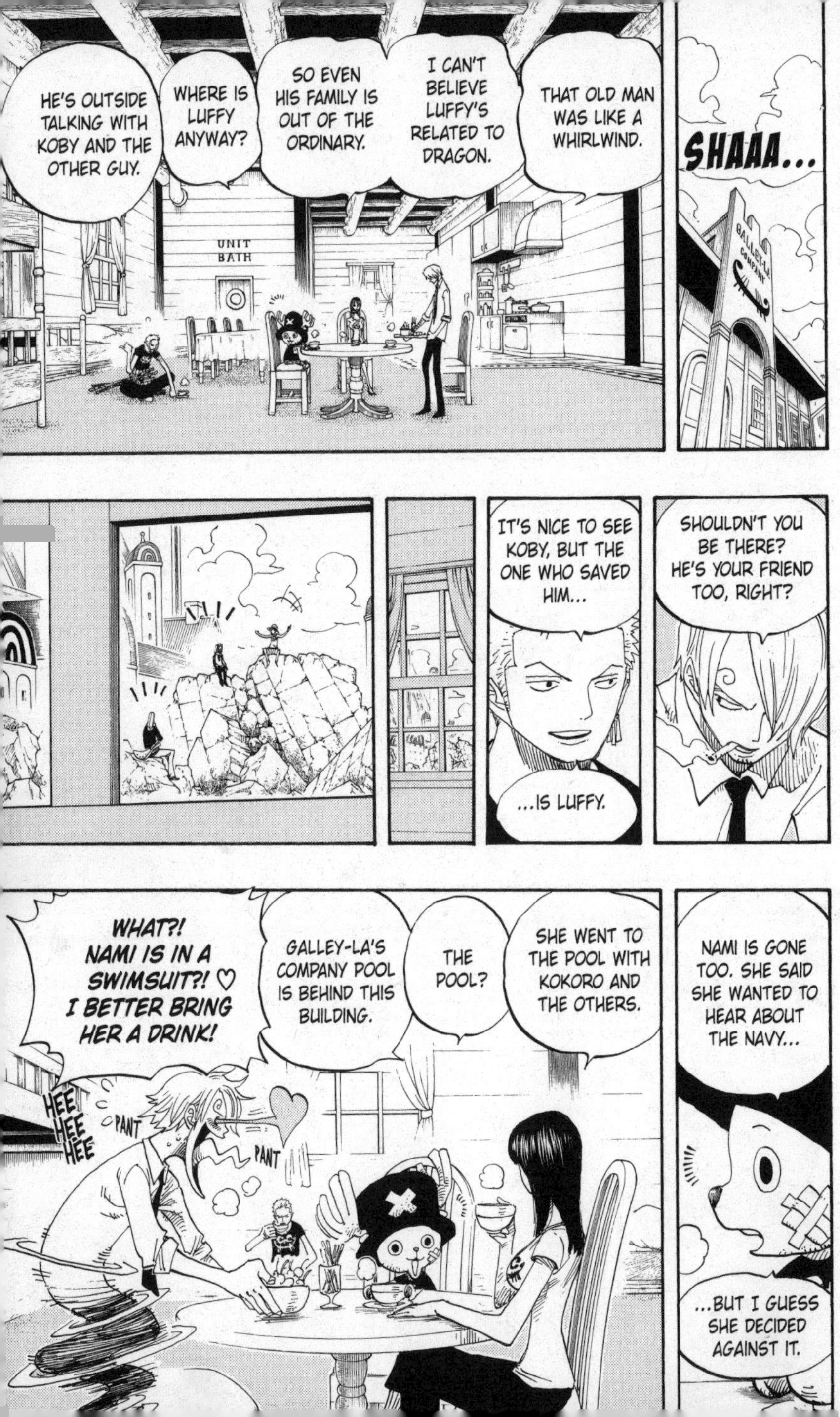
SHAAA...
THAT OLD MAN WAS LIKE A WHIRLWIND.
I CAN'T BELIEVE LUFFY'S RELATED TO DRAGON.
SO EVEN HIS FAMILY IS OUT OF THE ORDINARY.
WHERE IS LUFFY ANYWAY?
HE'S OUTSIDE TALKING WITH KOBY AND THE OTHER GUY.
UNIT BATH
SHOULDN'T YOU BE THERE? HE'S YOUR FRIEND TOO, RIGHT?
IT'S NICE TO SEE KOBY, BUT THE ONE WHO SAVED HIM...
...IS LUFFY.
NAMI IS GONE TOO. SHE SAID SHE WANTED TO HEAR ABOUT THE NAVY...
...BUT I GUESS SHE DECIDED AGAINST IT.
SHE WENT TO THE POOL WITH KOKORO AND THE OTHERS.
THE POOL?
GALLEY-LA'S COMPANY POOL IS BEHIND THIS BUILDING.
WHAT?! NAMI IS IN A SWIMSUIT?! ♡ I BETTER BRING HER A DRINK!
HEE HEE HEE
PANT
PANT

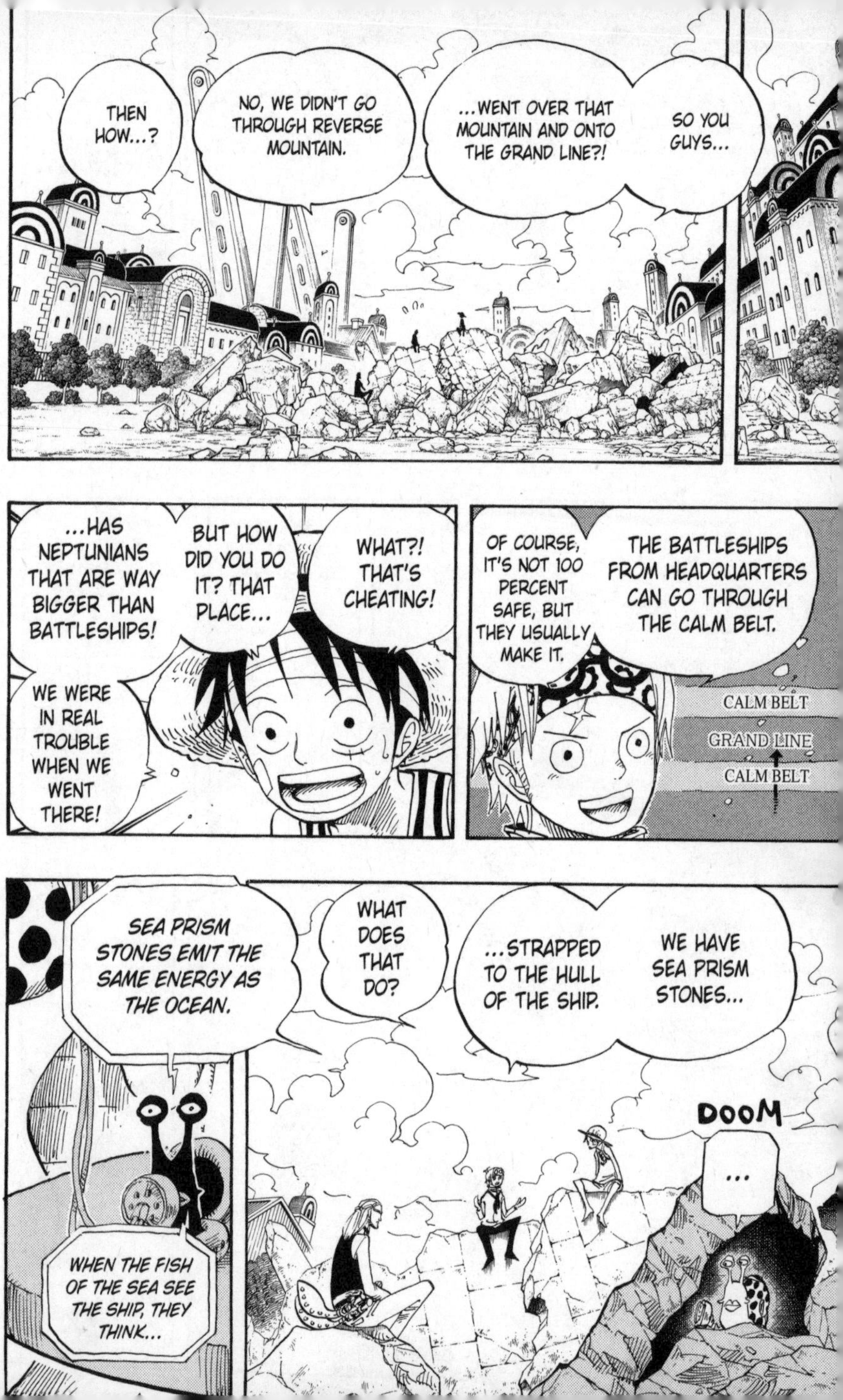
SO YOU GUYS...
...WENT OVER THAT MOUNTAIN AND ONTO THE GRAND LINE?!
NO, WE DIDN'T GO THROUGH REVERSE MOUNTAIN.
THEN HOW...?
THE BATTLESHIPS FROM HEADQUARTERS CAN GO THROUGH THE CALM BELT.
OF COURSE, IT'S NOT 100 PERCENT SAFE, BUT THEY USUALLY MAKE IT.
CALM BELT
GRAND LINE
CALM BELT
WHAT?! THAT'S CHEATING!
BUT HOW DID YOU DO IT? THAT PLACE...
...HAS NEPTUNIANS THAT ARE WAY BIGGER THAN BATTLESHIPS!
WE WERE IN REAL TROUBLE WHEN WE WENT THERE!
WE HAVE SEA PRISM STONES...
...STRAPPED TO THE HULL OF THE SHIP.
WHAT DOES THAT DO?
DOOM
...
SEA PRISM STONES EMIT THE SAME ENERGY AS THE OCEAN.
WHEN THE FISH OF THE SEA SEE THE SHIP, THEY THINK...

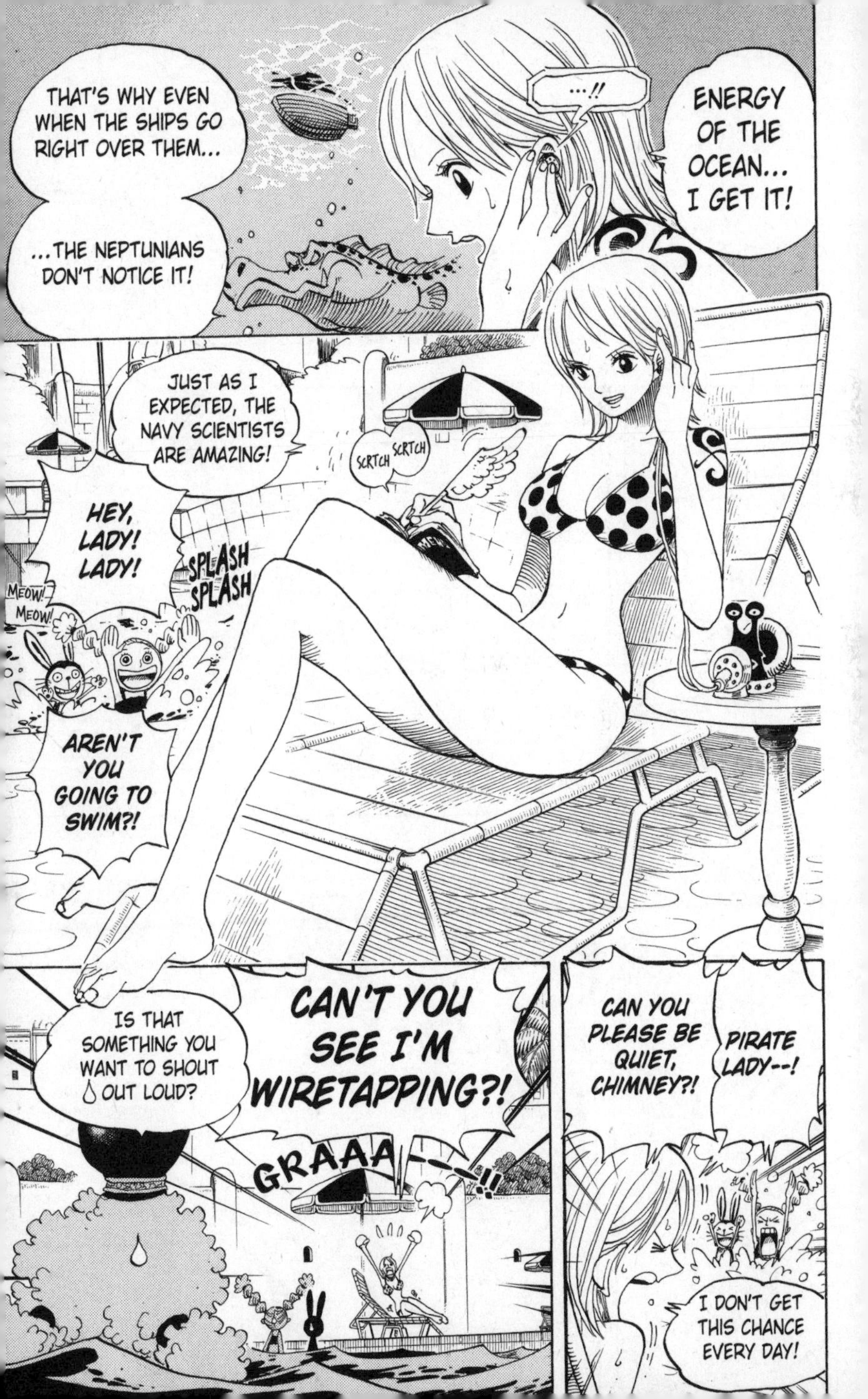
ENERGY OF THE OCEAN... I GET IT!
...!!
THAT'S WHY EVEN WHEN THE SHIPS GO RIGHT OVER THEM...
...THE NEPTUNIANS DON'T NOTICE IT!
JUST AS I EXPECTED, THE NAVY SCIENTISTS ARE AMAZING!
SCRTCH SCRTCH
SPLASH SPLASH
HEY, LADY! LADY!
MEOW! MEOW!
AREN'T YOU GOING TO SWIM?!
PIRATE LADY--!
CAN YOU PLEASE BE QUIET, CHIMNEY?!
I DON'T GET THIS CHANCE EVERY DAY!
CAN'T YOU SEE I'M WIRETAPPING?!
IS THAT SOMETHING YOU WANT TO SHOUT OUT LOUD?
GRAAAA---!!

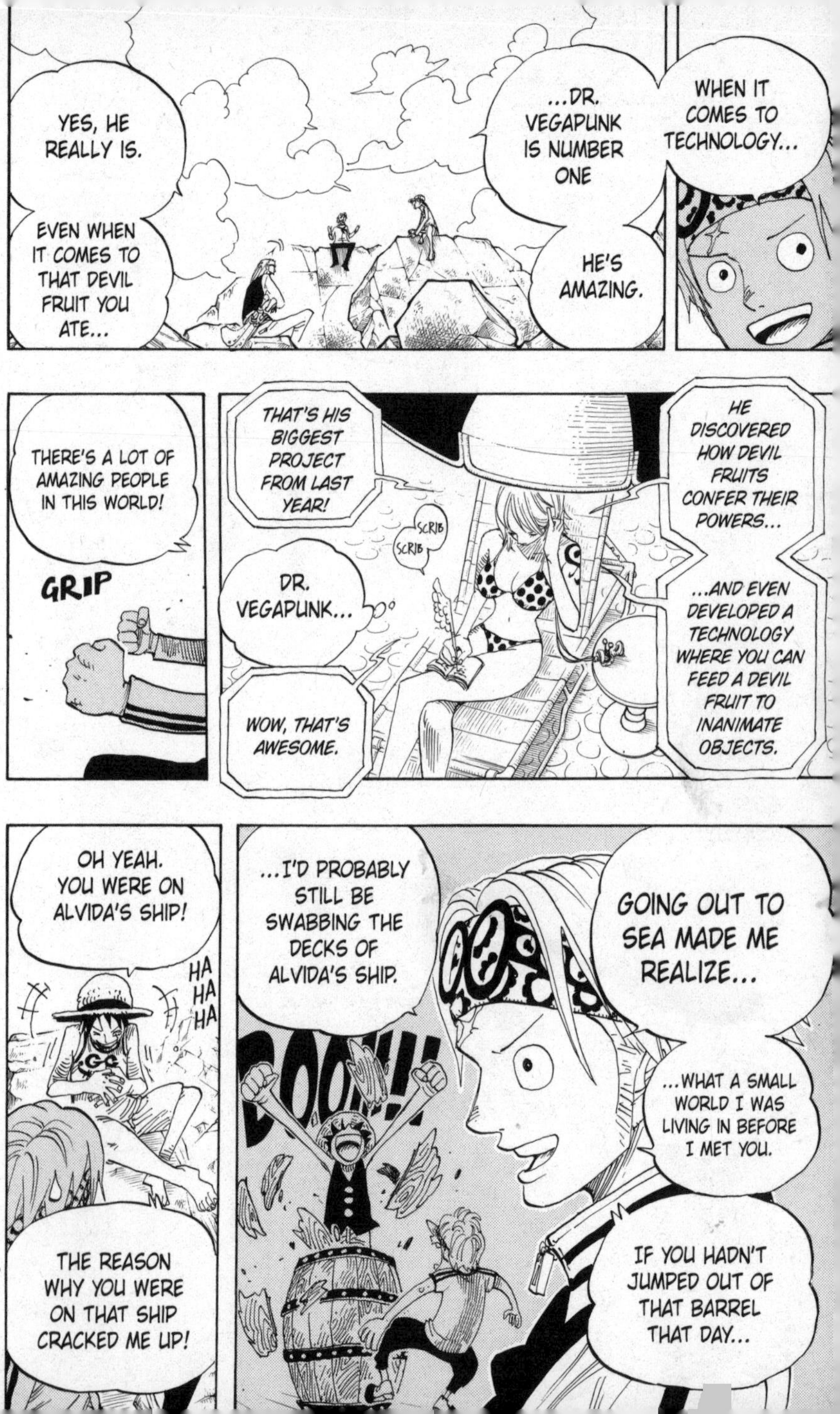
WHEN IT COMES TO TECHNOLOGY...
...DR. VEGAPUNK IS NUMBER ONE
HE'S AMAZING.
YES, HE REALLY IS.
EVEN WHEN IT COMES TO THAT DEVIL FRUIT YOU ATE...
HE DISCOVERED HOW DEVIL FRUITS CONFER THEIR POWERS...
...AND EVEN DEVELOPED A TECHNOLOGY WHERE YOU CAN FEED A DEVIL FRUIT TO INANIMATE OBJECTS.
THAT'S HIS BIGGEST PROJECT FROM LAST YEAR!
SCRIB SCRIB
DR. VEGAPUNK...
WOW, THAT'S AWESOME.
THERE'S A LOT OF AMAZING PEOPLE IN THIS WORLD!
GRIP
GOING OUT TO SEA MADE ME REALIZE...
...WHAT A SMALL WORLD I WAS LIVING IN BEFORE I MET YOU.
IF YOU HADN'T JUMPED OUT OF THAT BARREL THAT DAY...
...I'D PROBABLY STILL BE SWABBING THE DECKS OF ALVIDA'S SHIP.
OH YEAH. YOU WERE ON ALVIDA'S SHIP!
HA HA HA
THE REASON WHY YOU WERE ON THAT SHIP CRACKED ME UP!

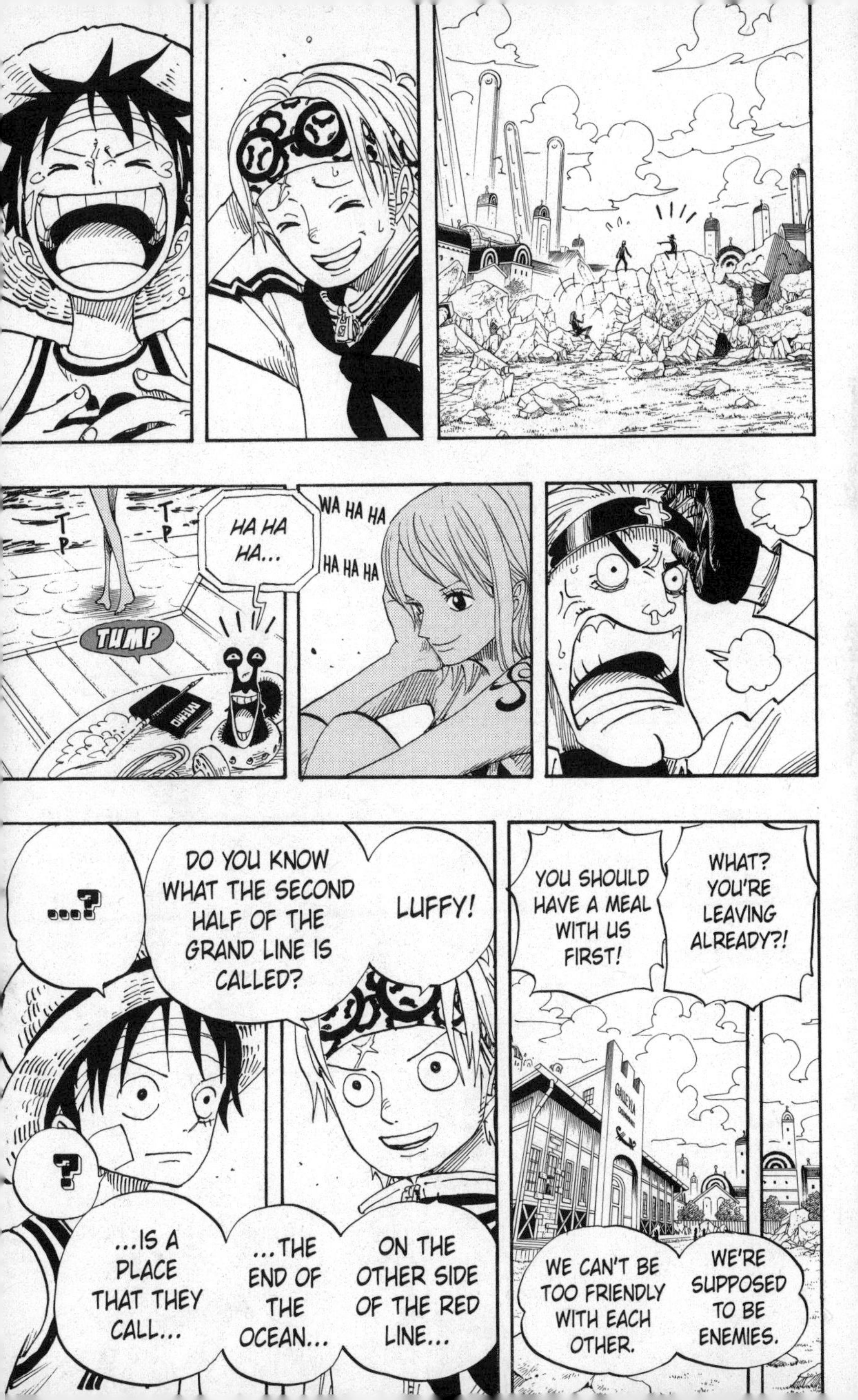
WA HA HA
HA HA HA
TP
TP
HA HA HA...
TUMP
MEMO
WHAT? YOU'RE LEAVING ALREADY?!
YOU SHOULD HAVE A MEAL WITH US FIRST!
WE'RE SUPPOSED TO BE ENEMIES.
WE CAN'T BE TOO FRIENDLY WITH EACH OTHER.
LUFFY!
DO YOU KNOW WHAT THE SECOND HALF OF THE GRAND LINE IS CALLED?
...?
?
ON THE OTHER SIDE OF THE RED LINE...
...THE END OF THE OCEAN...
...IS A PLACE THAT THEY CALL...

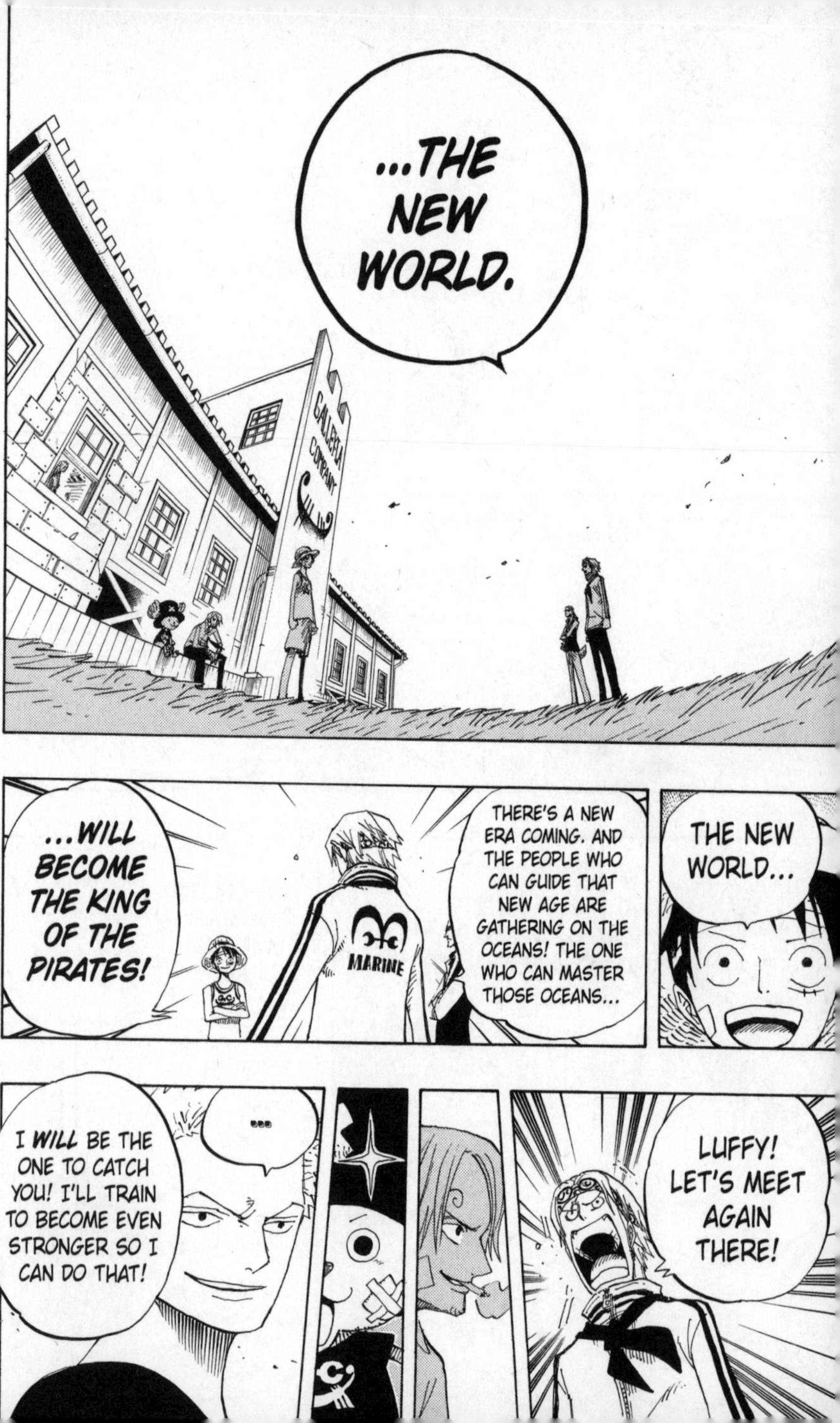
...THE NEW WORLD.
GALLEY-LA COMPANY
THE NEW WORLD...
THERE'S A NEW ERA COMING. AND THE PEOPLE WHO CAN GUIDE THAT NEW AGE ARE GATHERING ON THE OCEANS! THE ONE WHO CAN MASTER THOSE OCEANS...
MARINE
...WILL BECOME THE KING OF THE PIRATES!
LUFFY! LET'S MEET AGAIN THERE!
...
I WILL BE THE ONE TO CATCH YOU! I'LL TRAIN TO BECOME EVEN STRONGER SO I CAN DO THAT!

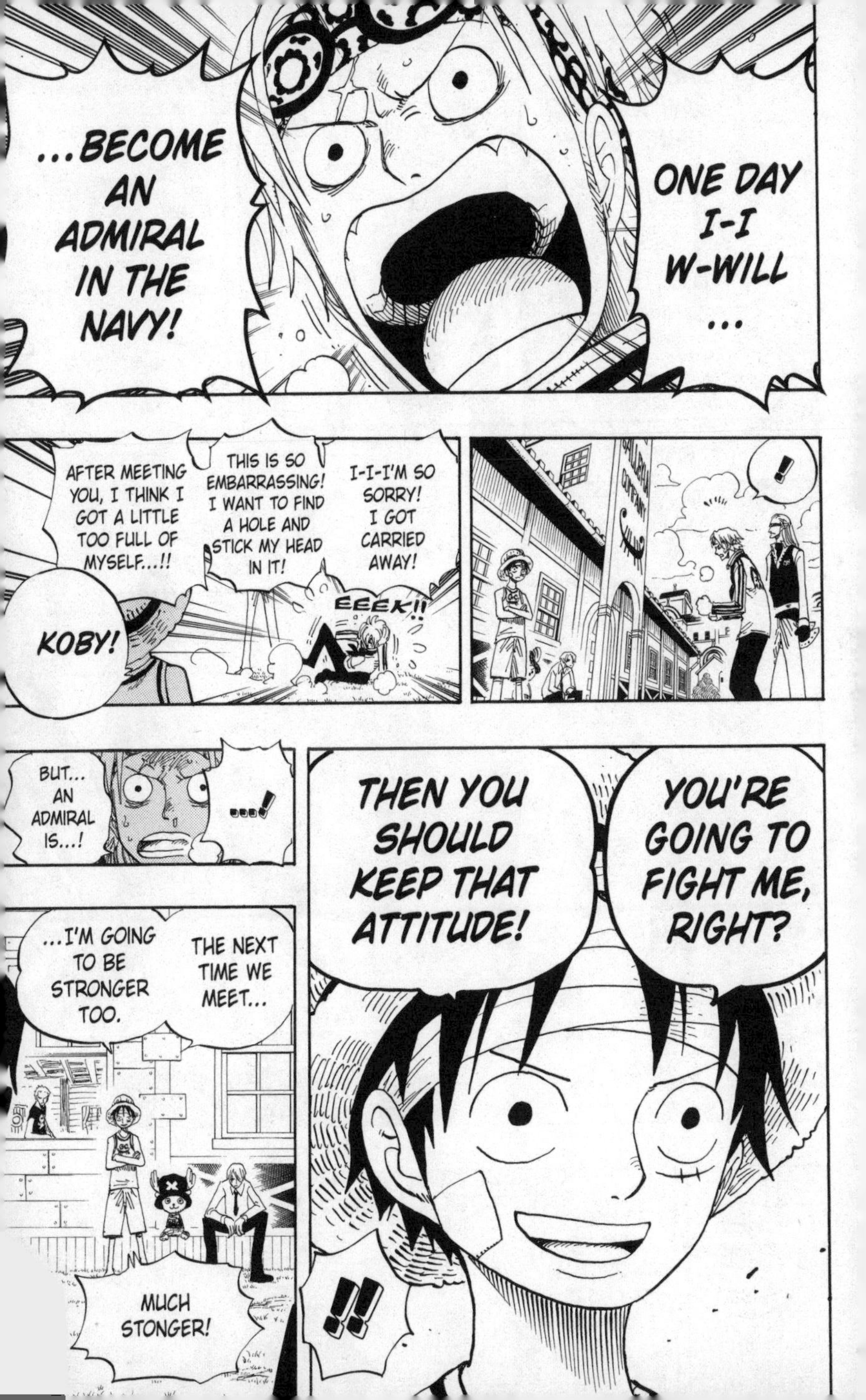
ONE DAY I-I W-WILL ...
...BECOME AN ADMIRAL IN THE NAVY!
!
I-I-I'M SO SORRY! I GOT CARRIED AWAY!
THIS IS SO EMBARRASSING! I WANT TO FIND A HOLE AND STICK MY HEAD IN IT!
AFTER MEETING YOU, I THINK I GOT A LITTLE TOO FULL OF MYSELF...!!
EEEK!!
KOBY!
YOU'RE GOING TO FIGHT ME, RIGHT?
THEN YOU SHOULD KEEP THAT ATTITUDE!
!!
...!
BUT... AN ADMIRAL IS...!
THE NEXT TIME WE MEET...
...I'M GOING TO BE STRONGER TOO.
MUCH STONGER!

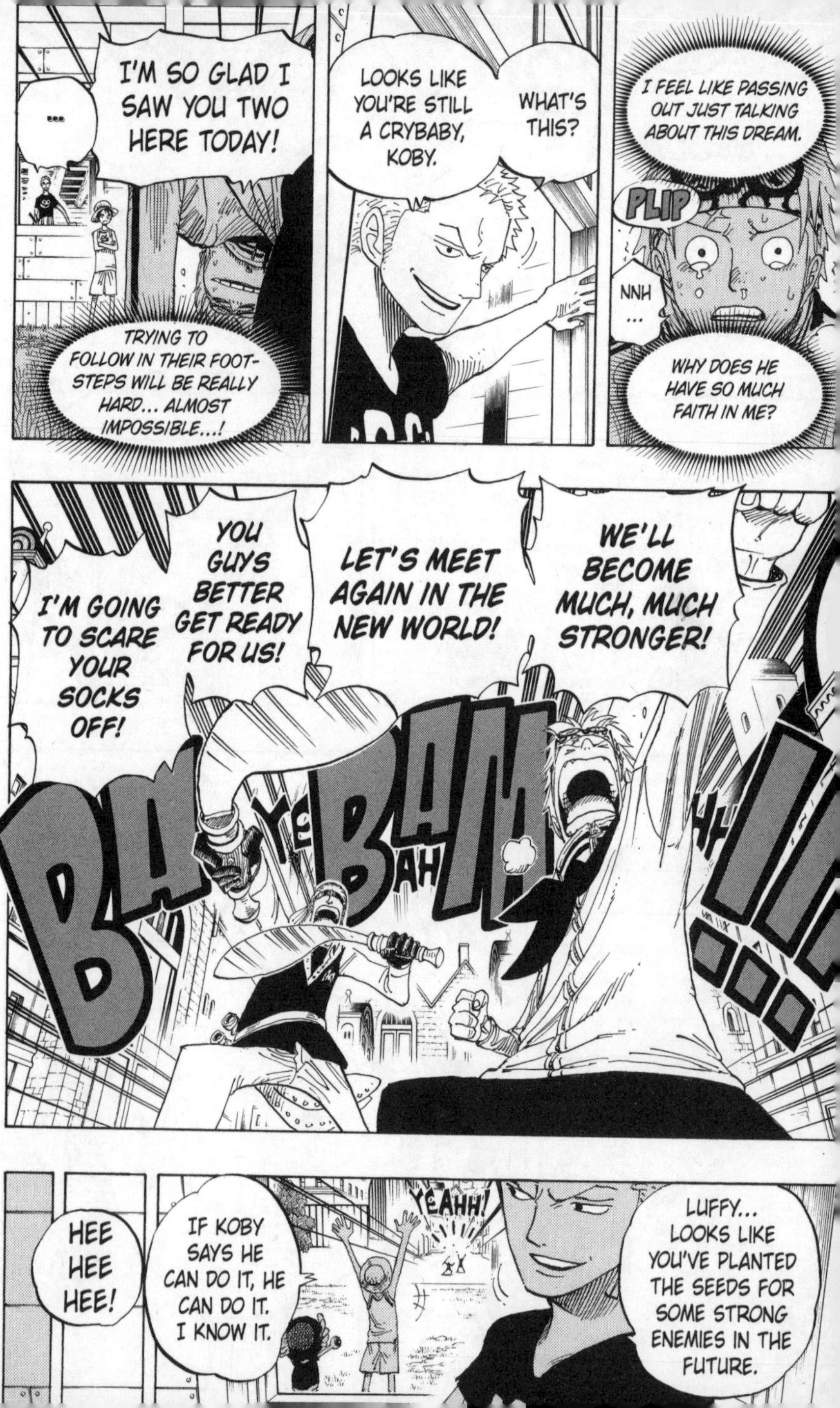
I FEEL LIKE PASSING OUT JUST TALKING ABOUT THIS DREAM.
PLIP
NNH ...
WHY DOES HE HAVE SO MUCH FAITH IN ME?
WHAT'S THIS?
LOOKS LIKE YOU'RE STILL A CRYBABY, KOBY.
I'M SO GLAD I SAW YOU TWO HERE TODAY!
...
TRYING TO FOLLOW IN THEIR FOOT-STEPS WILL BE REALLY HARD... ALMOST IMPOSSIBLE...!
WE'LL BECOME MUCH, MUCH STRONGER!
LET'S MEET AGAIN IN THE NEW WORLD!
YOU GUYS BETTER GET READY FOR US!
I'M GOING TO SCARE YOUR SOCKS OFF!
LUFFY... LOOKS LIKE YOU'VE PLANTED THE SEEDS FOR SOME STRONG ENEMIES IN THE FUTURE.
YEAHH!
IF KOBY SAYS HE CAN DO IT, HE CAN DO IT. I KNOW IT.
HEE HEE HEE!

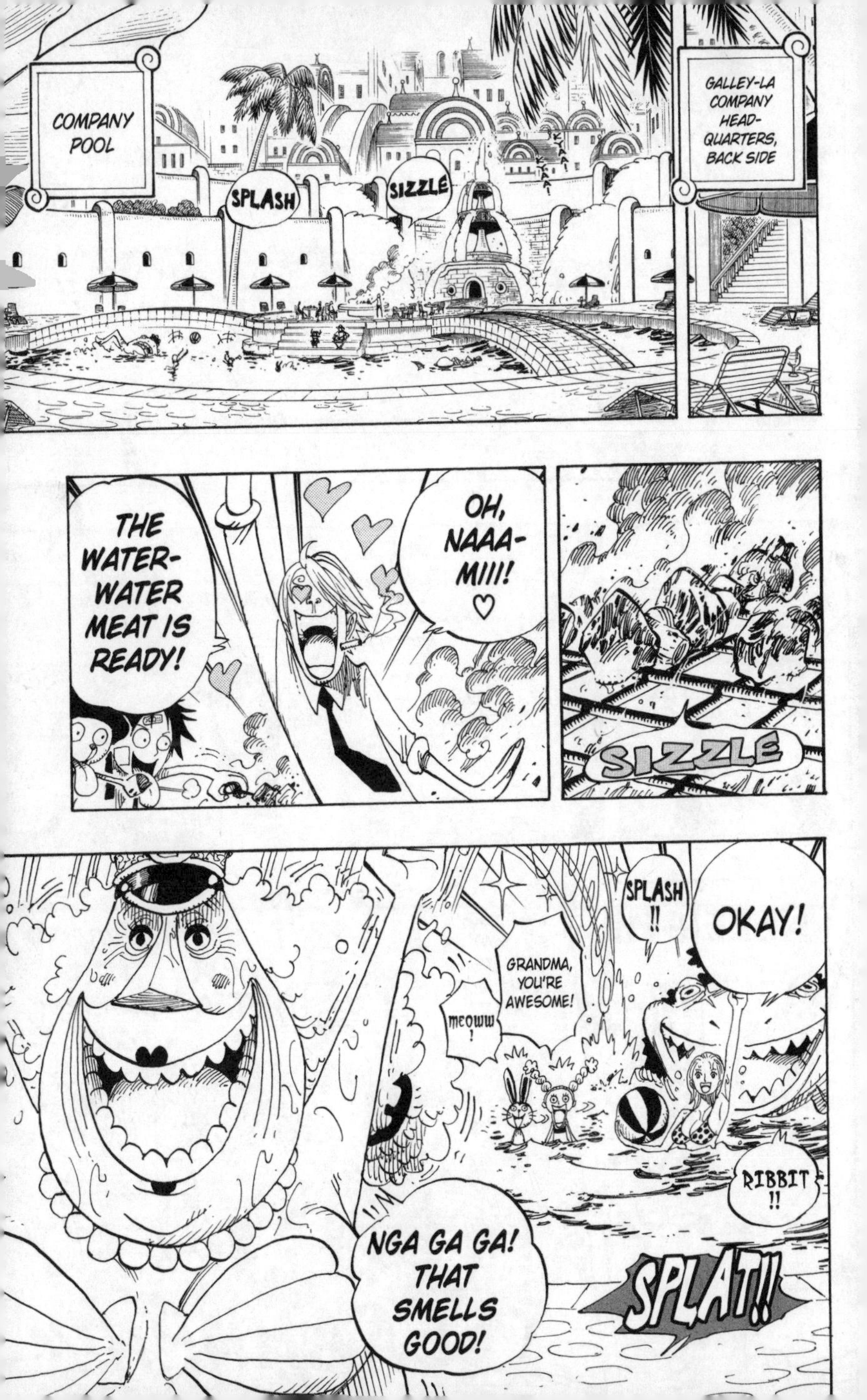
GALLEY-LA COMPANY HEAD-QUARTERS, BACK SIDE
COMPANY POOL
SIZZLE
SPLASH
SIZZLE
OH, NAAA-MI!!! ♡
THE WATER-WATER MEAT IS READY!
OKAY!
SPLASH!!
GRANDMA, YOU'RE AWESOME!
MEOWW!
RIBBIT!!
SPLAT!!
NGA GA GA! THAT SMELLS GOOD!

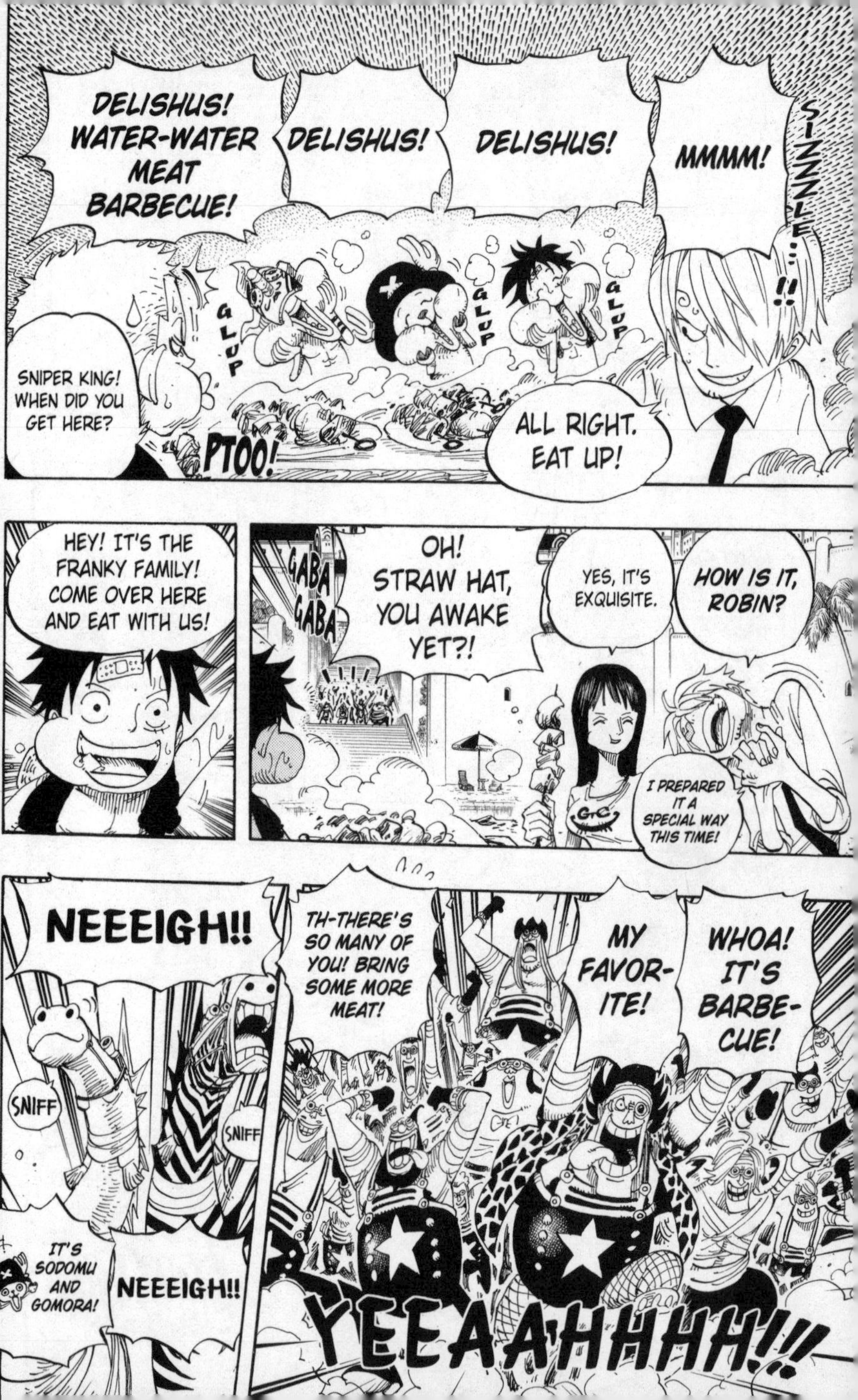
MMMM!
SIZZZZLE...!!
DELISHUS!
DELISHUS!
DELISHUS! WATER-WATER MEAT BARBECUE!
GLUP
GLUP
GLUP
ALL RIGHT. EAT UP!
SNIPER KING! WHEN DID YOU GET HERE?
PTOO!
HOW IS IT, ROBIN?
YES, IT'S EXQUISITE.
I PREPARED IT A SPECIAL WAY THIS TIME!
OH! STRAW HAT, YOU AWAKE YET?!
GABA GABA
HEY! IT'S THE FRANKY FAMILY! COME OVER HERE AND EAT WITH US!
WHOA! IT'S BARBE-CUE!
MY FAVOR-ITE!
TH-THERE'S SO MANY OF YOU! BRING SOME MORE MEAT!
YEEAAHHHH!!!
NEEEIGH!!
SNIFF
SNIFF
NEEEIGH!!
IT'S SODOMU AND GOMORA!

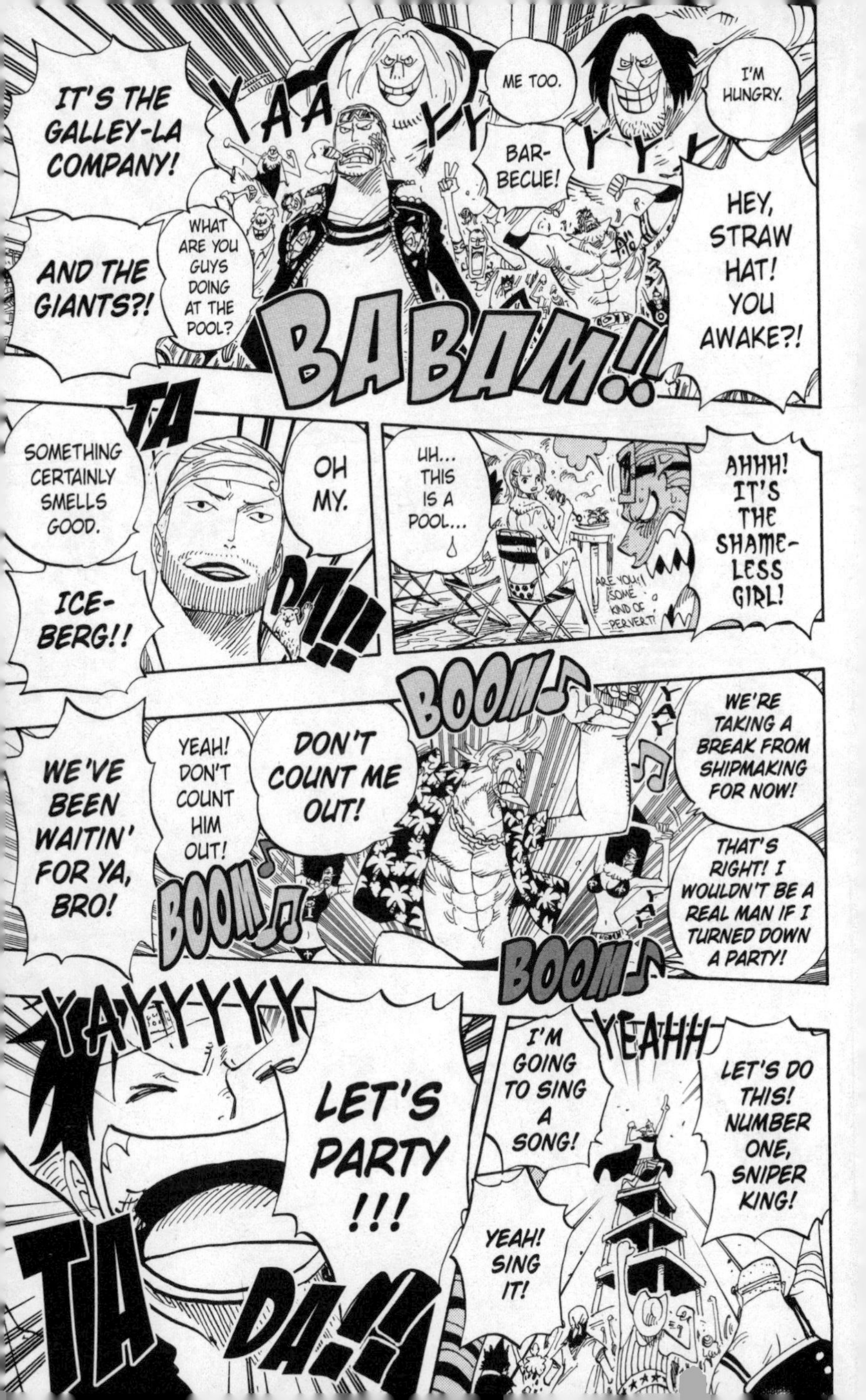
I'M HUNGRY.
ME TOO.
YAAYYYYYY
HEY, STRAW HAT! YOU AWAKE?!
BAR-BECUE!
IT'S THE GALLEY-LA COMPANY!
WHAT ARE YOU GUYS DOING AT THE POOL?
AND THE GIANTS?!
BABAM!!
AHHH! IT'S THE SHAME-LESS GIRL!
ARE YOU SOME KIND OF PERVERT?!
UH... THIS IS A POOL...
OH MY.
TA
SOMETHING CERTAINLY SMELLS GOOD.
DA!!!
ICE-BERG!!
BOOM
YAY
WE'RE TAKING A BREAK FROM SHIPMAKING FOR NOW!
THAT'S RIGHT! I WOULDN'T BE A REAL MAN IF I TURNED DOWN A PARTY!
YAY
BOOM
DON'T COUNT ME OUT!
YEAH! DON'T COUNT HIM OUT!
WE'VE BEEN WAITIN' FOR YA, BRO!
BOOM
YEAHH
LET'S DO THIS! NUMBER ONE, SNIPER KING!
I'M GOING TO SING A SONG!
YEAH! SING IT!
YAYYYYY
LET'S PARTY!!!
TA
DA!!

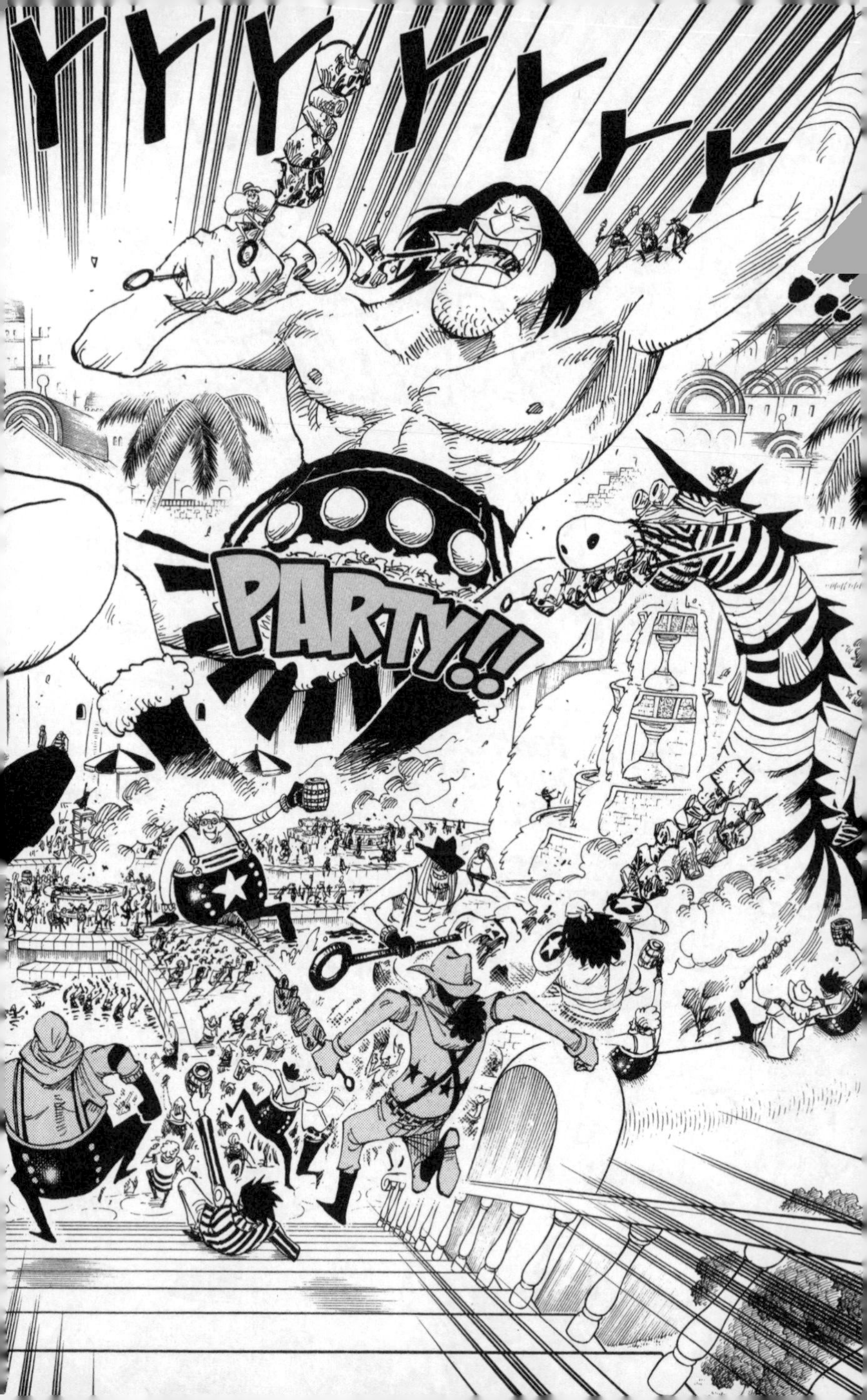

YYYYYYYYY
PARTY!!

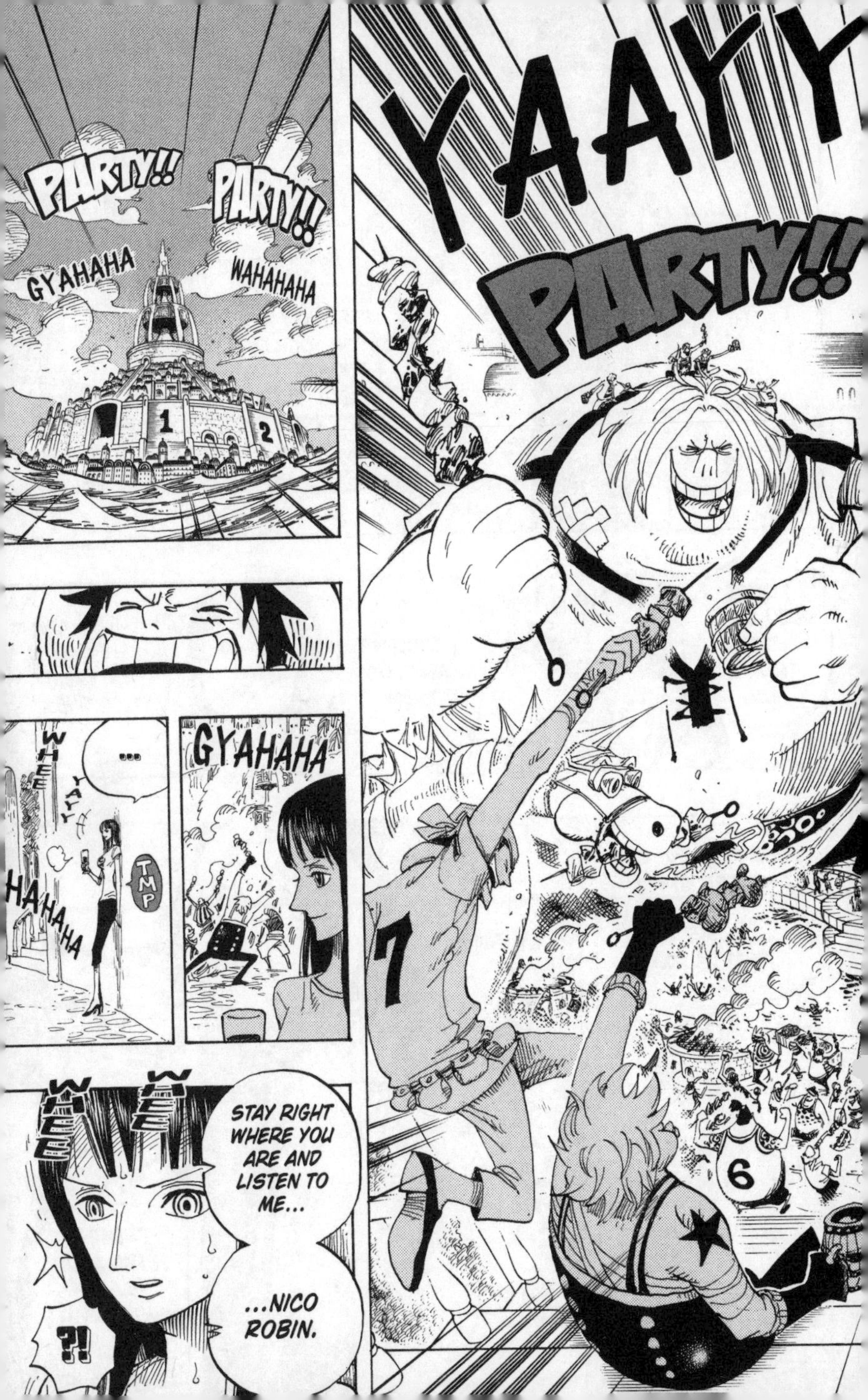
YAAYY
PARTY!!
PARTY!!
PARTY!!
WAHAHAHA
GYAHAHA
GYAHAHA
...
YAYY
WHEE
TMP
HAHAHAHA
WHEE
WHEE
STAY RIGHT WHERE YOU ARE AND LISTEN TO ME...
...NICO ROBIN.
?!

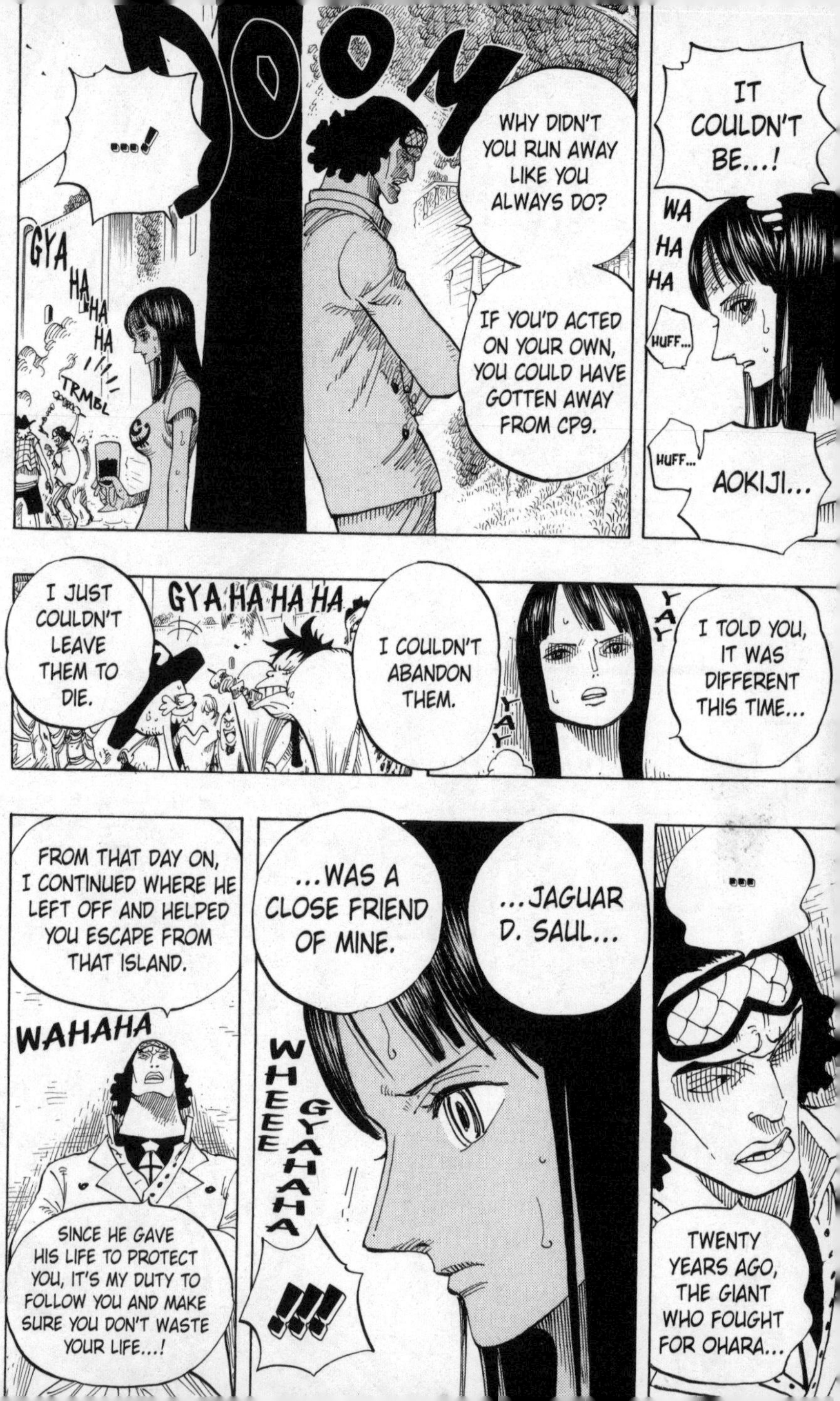
IT COULDN'T BE...!
WA HA HA
HUFF...
HUFF...
AOKIJI...
WHY DIDN'T YOU RUN AWAY LIKE YOU ALWAYS DO?
IF YOU'D ACTED ON YOUR OWN, YOU COULD HAVE GOTTEN AWAY FROM CP9.
DOOM
...!
GYA HA HA HA HA
TRMBL
YAY
I TOLD YOU, IT WAS DIFFERENT THIS TIME...
YAY
I COULDN'T ABANDON THEM.
GYA HA HA HA
I JUST COULDN'T LEAVE THEM TO DIE.
...
TWENTY YEARS AGO, THE GIANT WHO FOUGHT FOR OHARA...
...JAGUAR D. SAUL...
...WAS A CLOSE FRIEND OF MINE.
WHEEE
GYAHAHAHA
!!!
FROM THAT DAY ON, I CONTINUED WHERE HE LEFT OFF AND HELPED YOU ESCAPE FROM THAT ISLAND.
WAHAHA
SINCE HE GAVE HIS LIFE TO PROTECT YOU, IT'S MY DUTY TO FOLLOW YOU AND MAKE SURE YOU DON'T WASTE YOUR LIFE...!

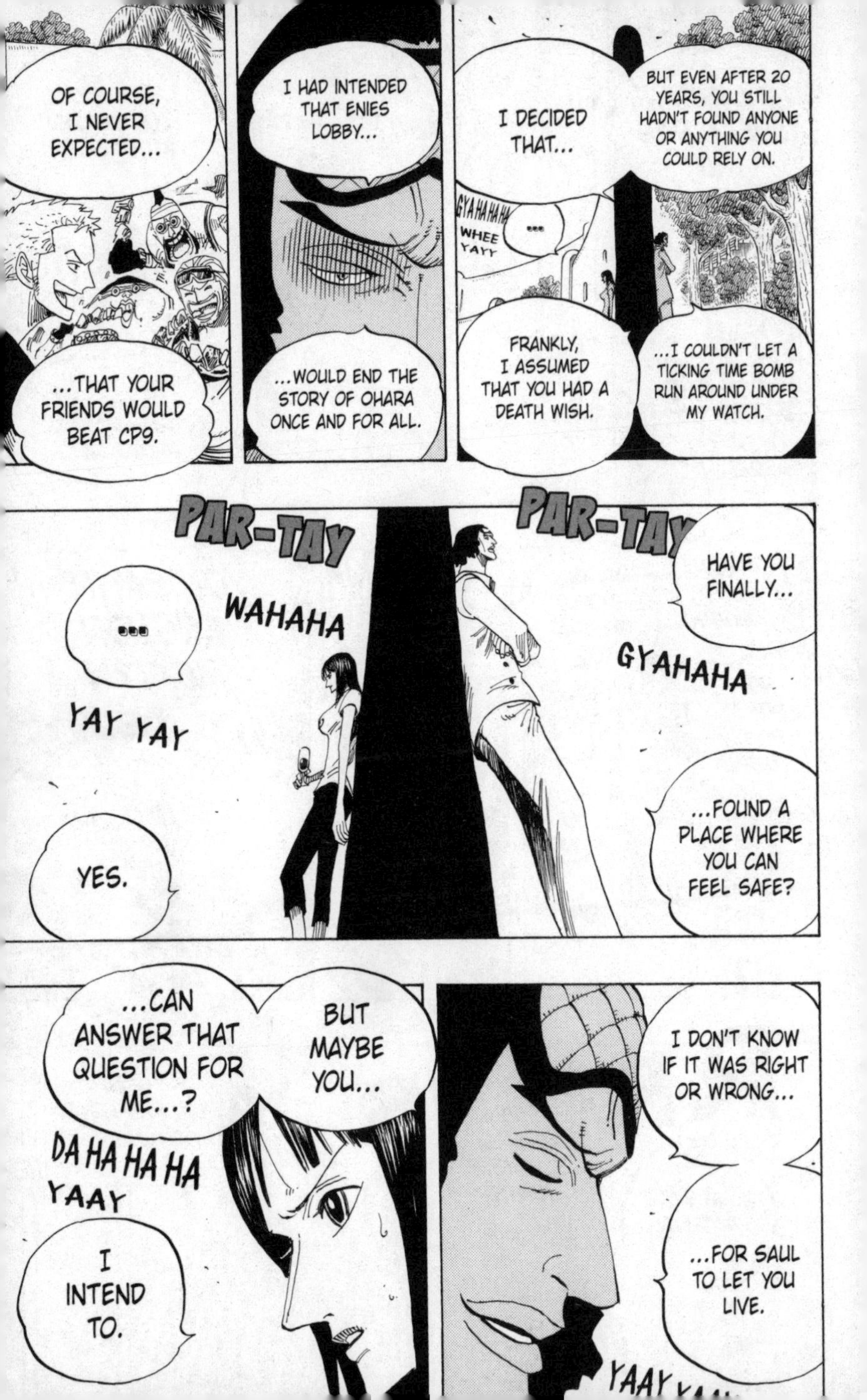
BUT EVEN AFTER 20 YEARS, YOU STILL HADN'T FOUND ANYONE OR ANYTHING YOU COULD RELY ON.
I DECIDED THAT...
GYAHAHAHA
WHEE
YAYY
...
...I COULDN'T LET A TICKING TIME BOMB RUN AROUND UNDER MY WATCH.
FRANKLY, I ASSUMED THAT YOU HAD A DEATH WISH.
I HAD INTENDED THAT ENIES LOBBY...
...WOULD END THE STORY OF OHARA ONCE AND FOR ALL.
OF COURSE, I NEVER EXPECTED...
...THAT YOUR FRIENDS WOULD BEAT CP9.
PAR-TAY
HAVE YOU FINALLY...
GYAHAHA
...FOUND A PLACE WHERE YOU CAN FEEL SAFE?
PAR-TAY
WAHAHA
...
YAY YAY
YES.
I DON'T KNOW IF IT WAS RIGHT OR WRONG...
...FOR SAUL TO LET YOU LIVE.
YAAY
BUT MAYBE YOU...
...CAN ANSWER THAT QUESTION FOR ME...?
DA HA HA HA
YAAY
I INTEND TO.

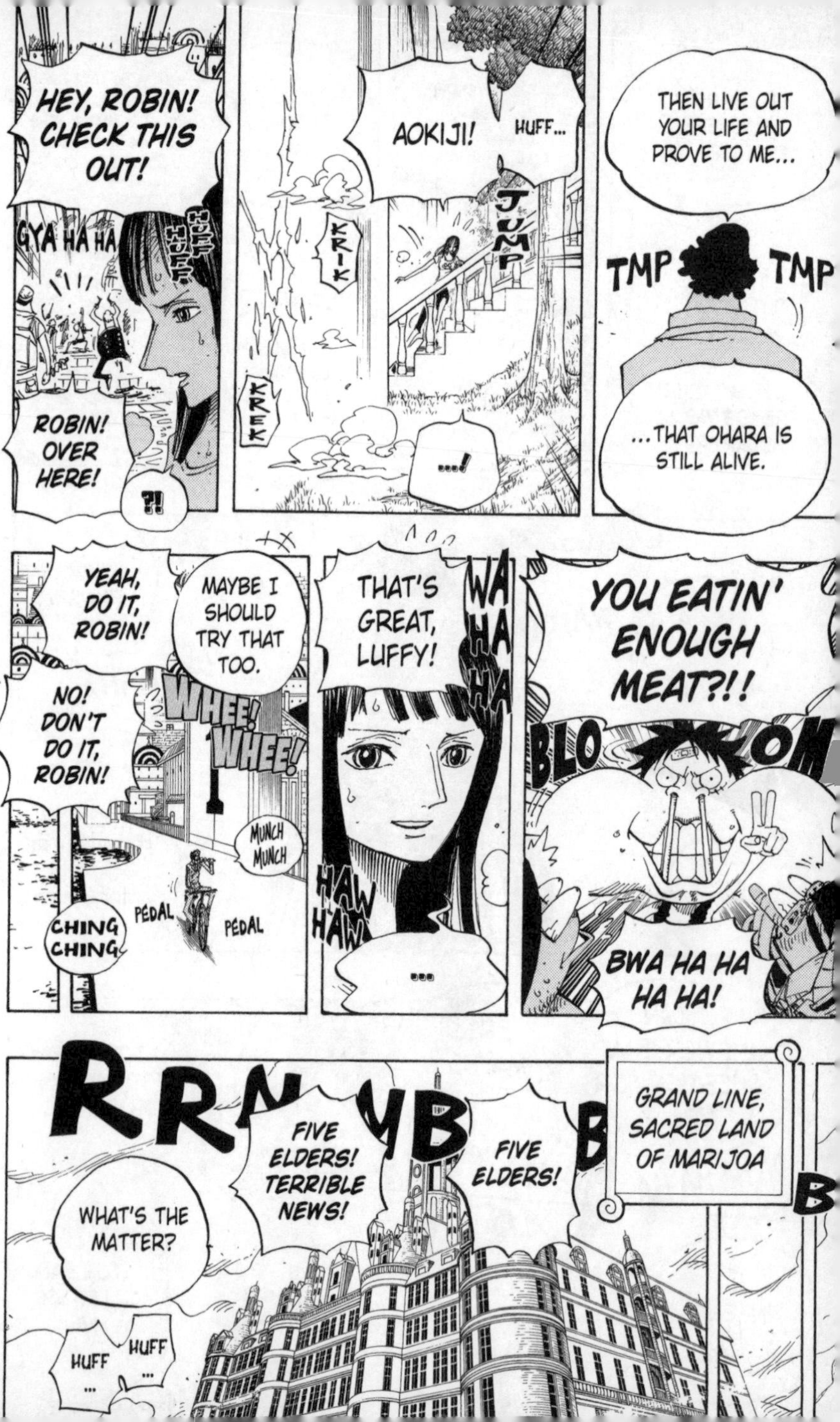
THEN LIVE OUT YOUR LIFE AND PROVE TO ME...
TMP TMP
...THAT OHARA IS STILL ALIVE.
AOKIJI!
HUFF...
JUMP
KRIK
KREK
...!
HEY, ROBIN! CHECK THIS OUT!
HUFF HUFF
GYA HA HA
ROBIN! OVER HERE!
?!
YOU EATIN' ENOUGH MEAT?!!
BWA HA HA HA HA!
THAT'S GREAT, LUFFY!
WA HA HA HA
HAW HAW
...
YEAH, DO IT, ROBIN!
MAYBE I SHOULD TRY THAT TOO.
NO! DON'T DO IT, ROBIN!
WHEE! WHEE!
MUNCH MUNCH
PEDAL PEDAL
CHING CHING
GRAND LINE, SACRED LAND OF MARIJOA
FIVE ELDERS!
FIVE ELDERS! TERRIBLE NEWS!
WHAT'S THE MATTER?
HUFF... HUFF...

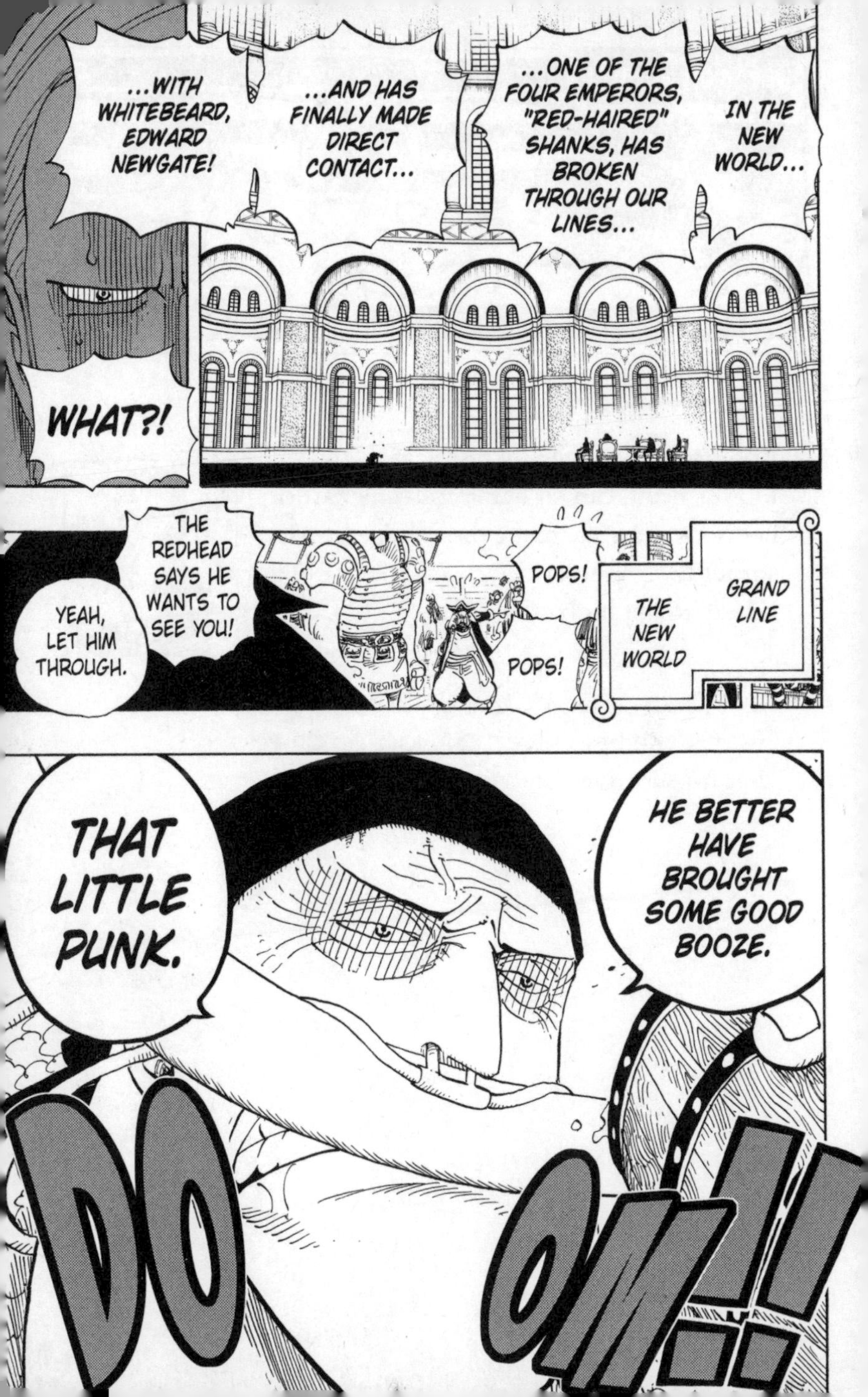
IN THE NEW WORLD...
...ONE OF THE FOUR EMPERORS, "RED-HAIRED" SHANKS, HAS BROKEN THROUGH OUR LINES...
...AND HAS FINALLY MADE DIRECT CONTACT...
...WITH WHITEBEARD, EDWARD NEWGATE!
WHAT?!
GRAND LINE
THE NEW WORLD
POPS!
POPS!
THE REDHEAD SAYS HE WANTS TO SEE YOU!
YEAH, LET HIM THROUGH.
HE BETTER HAVE BROUGHT SOME GOOD BOOZE.
THAT LITTLE PUNK.
DOON!!

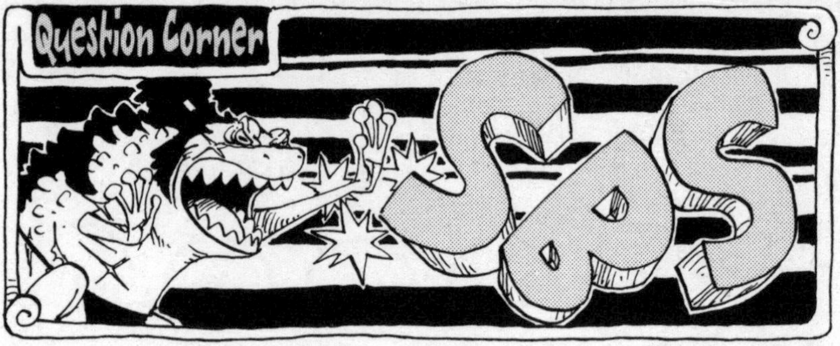
Question Corner
SBS

Q: Robin's Devil Fruit ability, the Flower-Flower Fruit, can let her sprout any part of her body. Can she make those huge breasts sprout too? "Areola Fleur!" (Said like Robin.) I'd like to get hit by that...

--Ero-Ero Fruit User

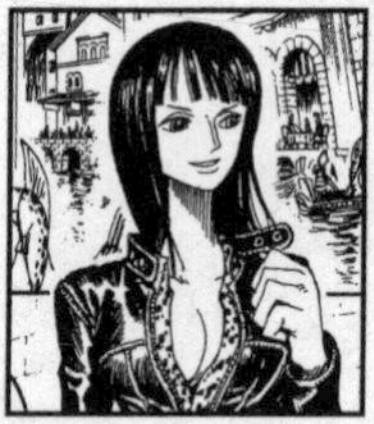

A: "Un Fleur," "Dos Fleurs," "Areola Fleur." That's pretty clever of you. Stop it!
But I'm sure she can do it! ♡

Chapter 434:
WHITEBEARD AND RED-HAIR

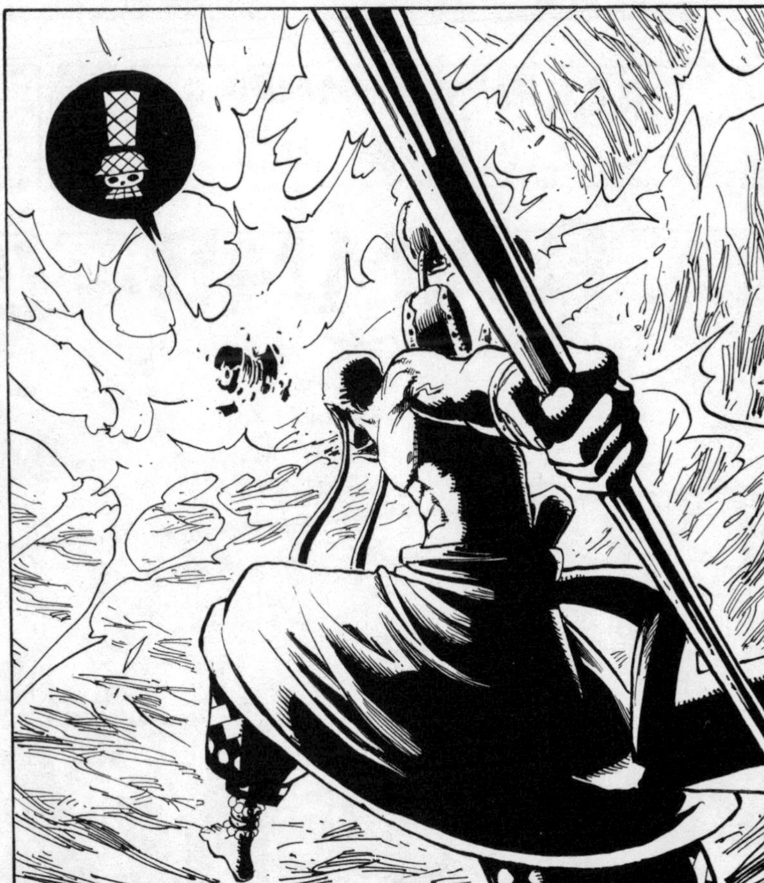
!

ENERU'S GREAT SPACE MISSION, VOL. 5:
"SHOOT FIRST, ASK QUESTIONS LATER"

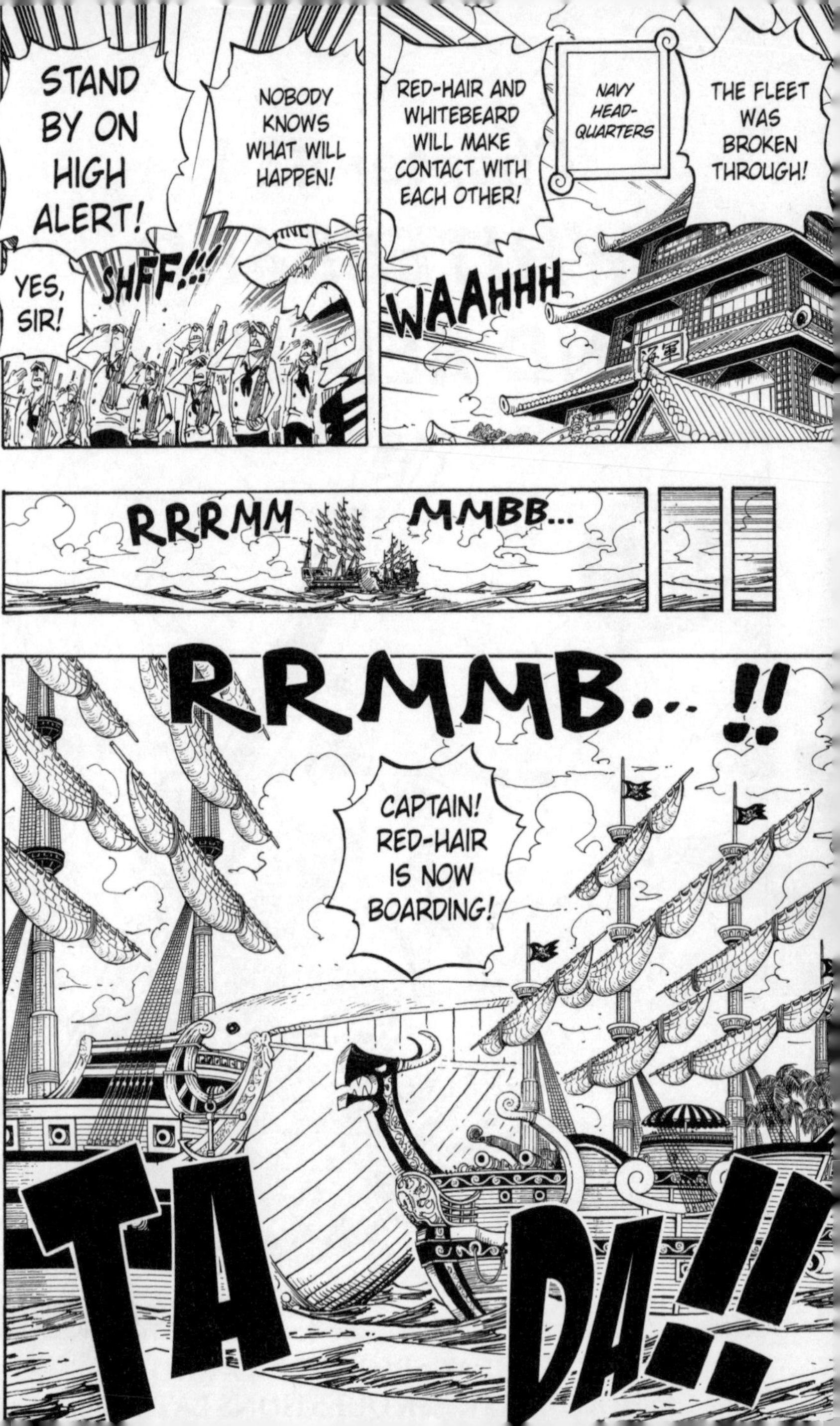
NAVY HEAD-QUARTERS
THE FLEET WAS BROKEN THROUGH!
RED-HAIR AND WHITEBEARD WILL MAKE CONTACT WITH EACH OTHER!
WAAHHH
NOBODY KNOWS WHAT WILL HAPPEN!
STAND BY ON HIGH ALERT!
SHFF!!!
YES, SIR!
RRRMM MMBB...
RRMMB...!!
CAPTAIN! RED-HAIR IS NOW BOARDING!
TA DA!!

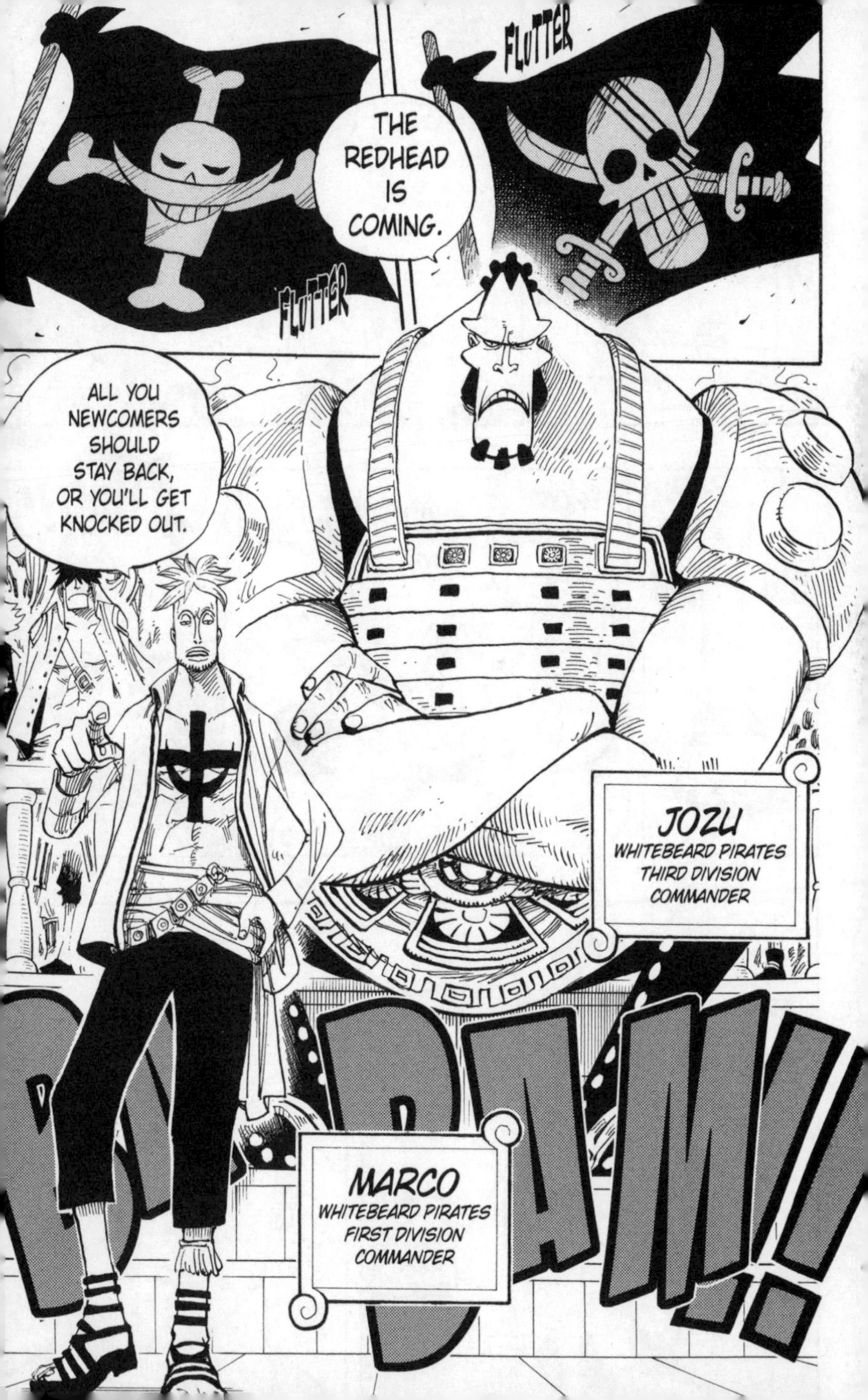
FLUTTER
FLUTTER
THE REDHEAD IS COMING.
ALL YOU NEWCOMERS SHOULD STAY BACK, OR YOU'LL GET KNOCKED OUT.
JOZU
WHITEBEARD PIRATES THIRD DIVISION COMMANDER
MARCO
WHITEBEARD PIRATES FIRST DIVISION COMMANDER

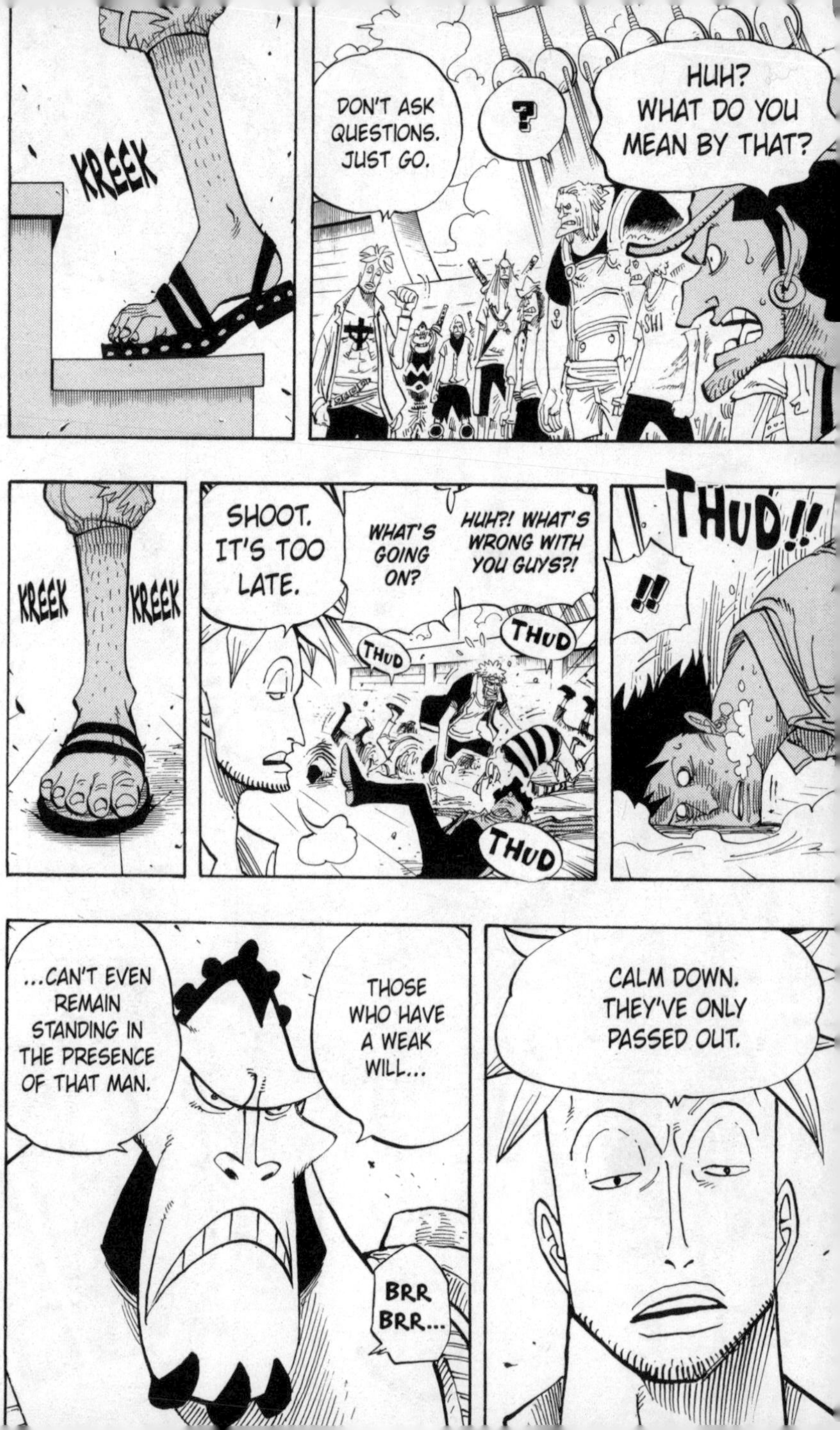
HUH? WHAT DO YOU MEAN BY THAT?
?
DON'T ASK QUESTIONS. JUST GO.
KREEK
THUD!!
!!
HUH?! WHAT'S WRONG WITH YOU GUYS?!
WHAT'S GOING ON?
SHOOT. IT'S TOO LATE.
THUD
THUD
THUD
KREEK
KREEK
CALM DOWN. THEY'VE ONLY PASSED OUT.
THOSE WHO HAVE A WEAK WILL...
...CAN'T EVEN REMAIN STANDING IN THE PRESENCE OF THAT MAN.
BRR BRR...

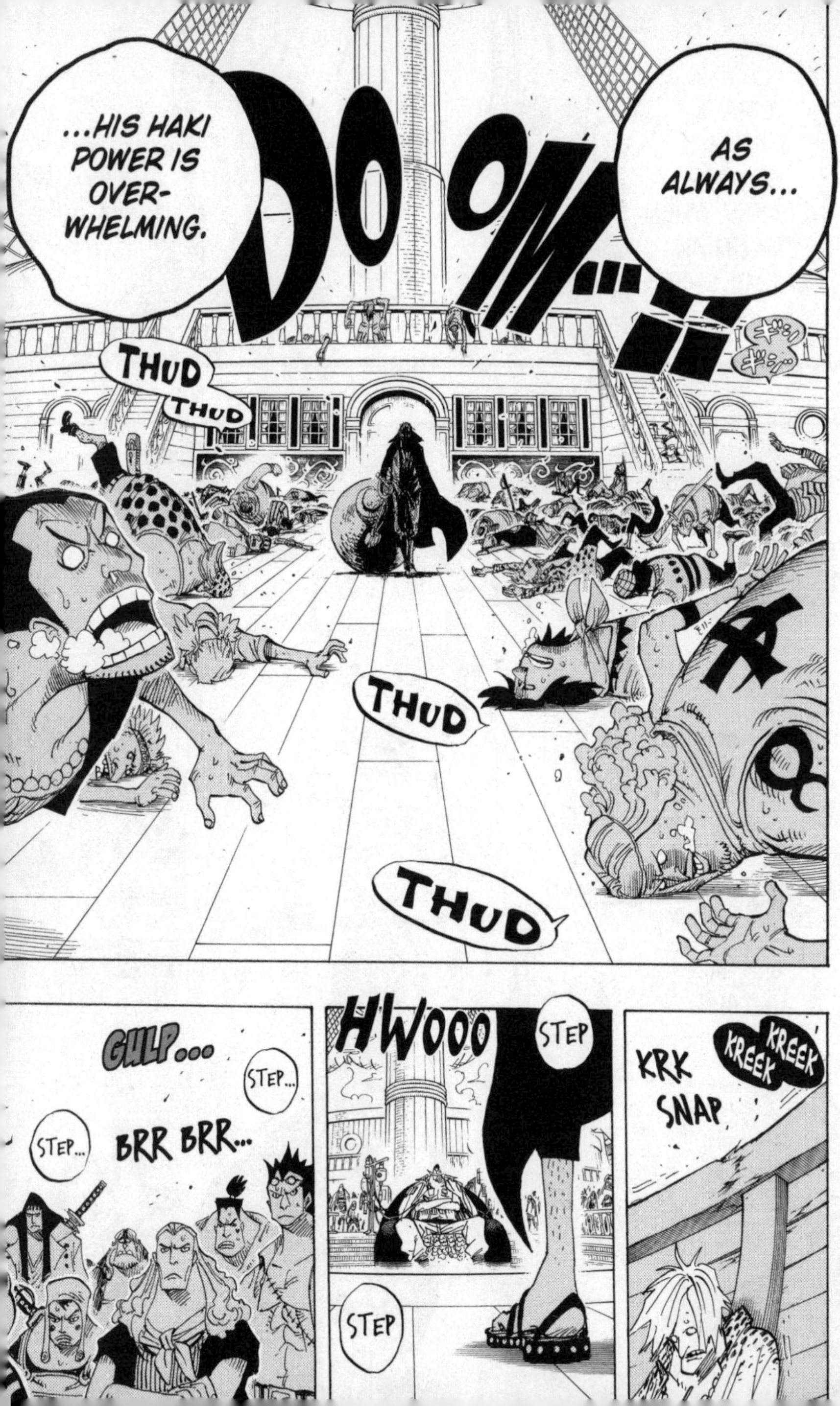
AS ALWAYS...
...HIS HAKI POWER IS OVER-WHELMING.
DOOM...!!
THUD
THUD
THUD
THUD
KREEK KREEK
KRK SNAP
HWOOO
STEP
STEP
STEP...
STEP...
GULP...
BRR BRR...

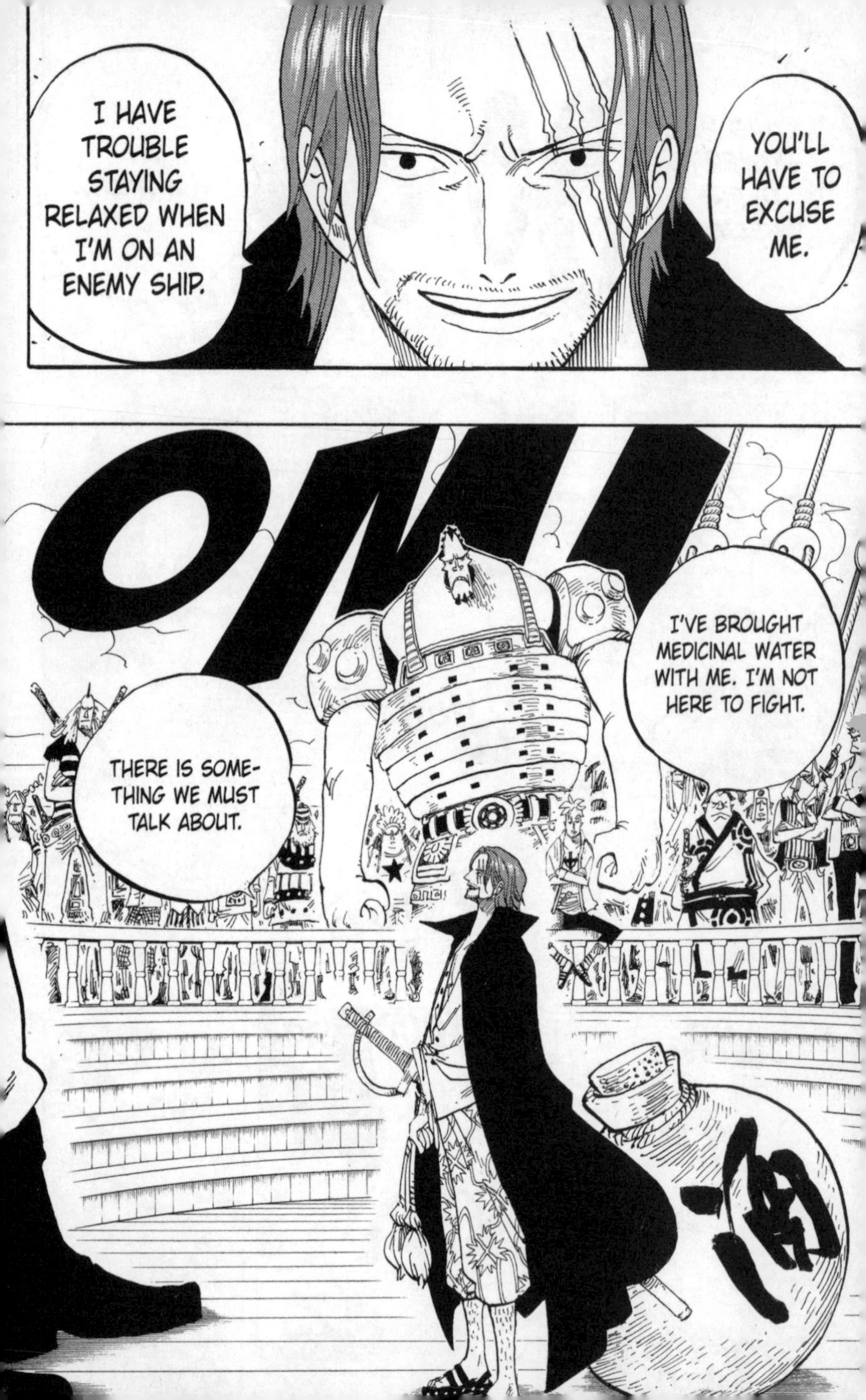
YOU'LL HAVE TO EXCUSE ME.
I HAVE TROUBLE STAYING RELAXED WHEN I'M ON AN ENEMY SHIP.
I'VE BROUGHT MEDICINAL WATER WITH ME. I'M NOT HERE TO FIGHT.
THERE IS SOME-THING WE MUST TALK ABOUT.

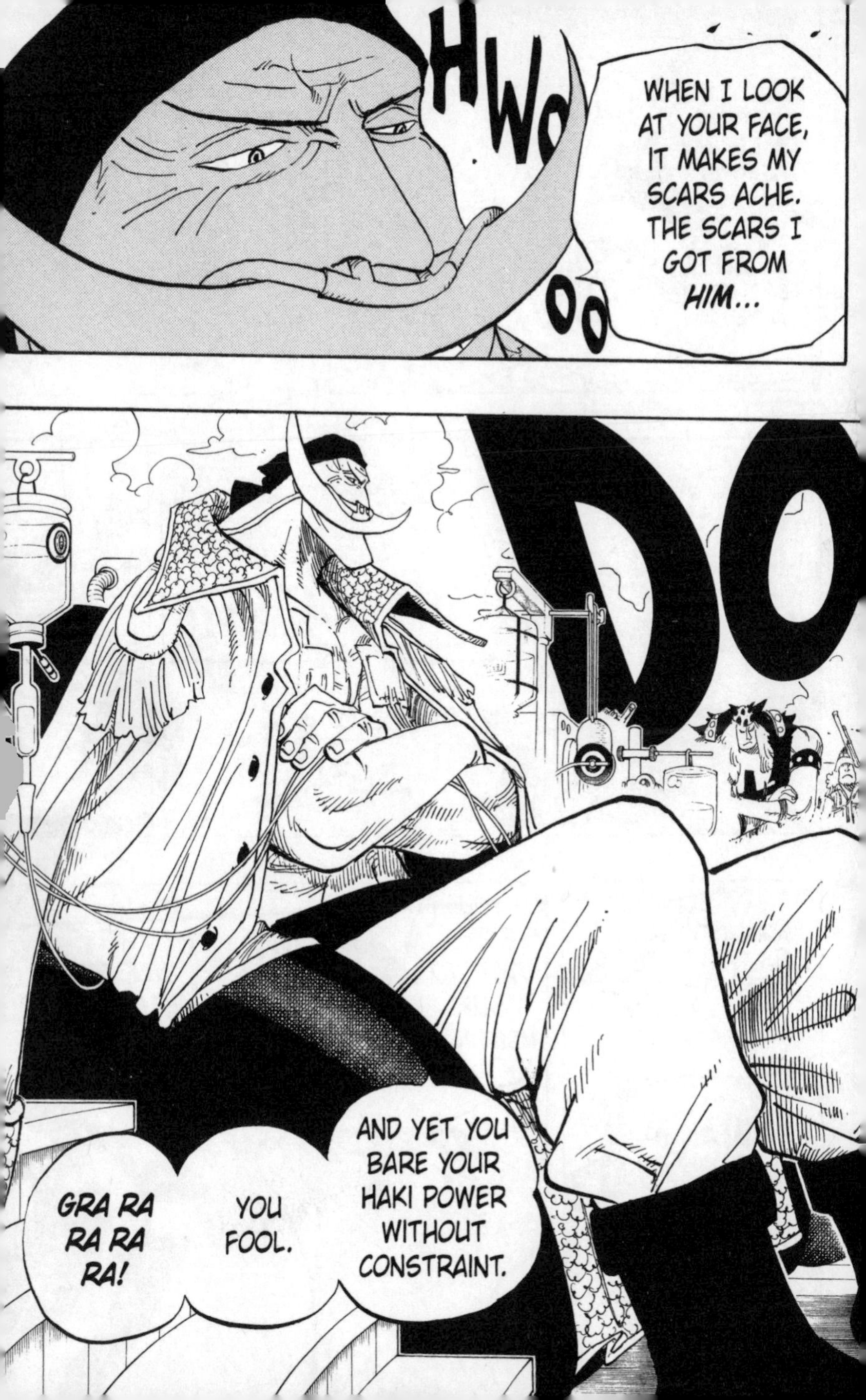
WHOOO
WHEN I LOOK AT YOUR FACE, IT MAKES MY SCARS ACHE. THE SCARS I GOT FROM *HIM*...
DO
AND YET YOU BARE YOUR HAKI POWER WITHOUT CONSTRAINT.
YOU FOOL.
GRA RA RA RA RA!

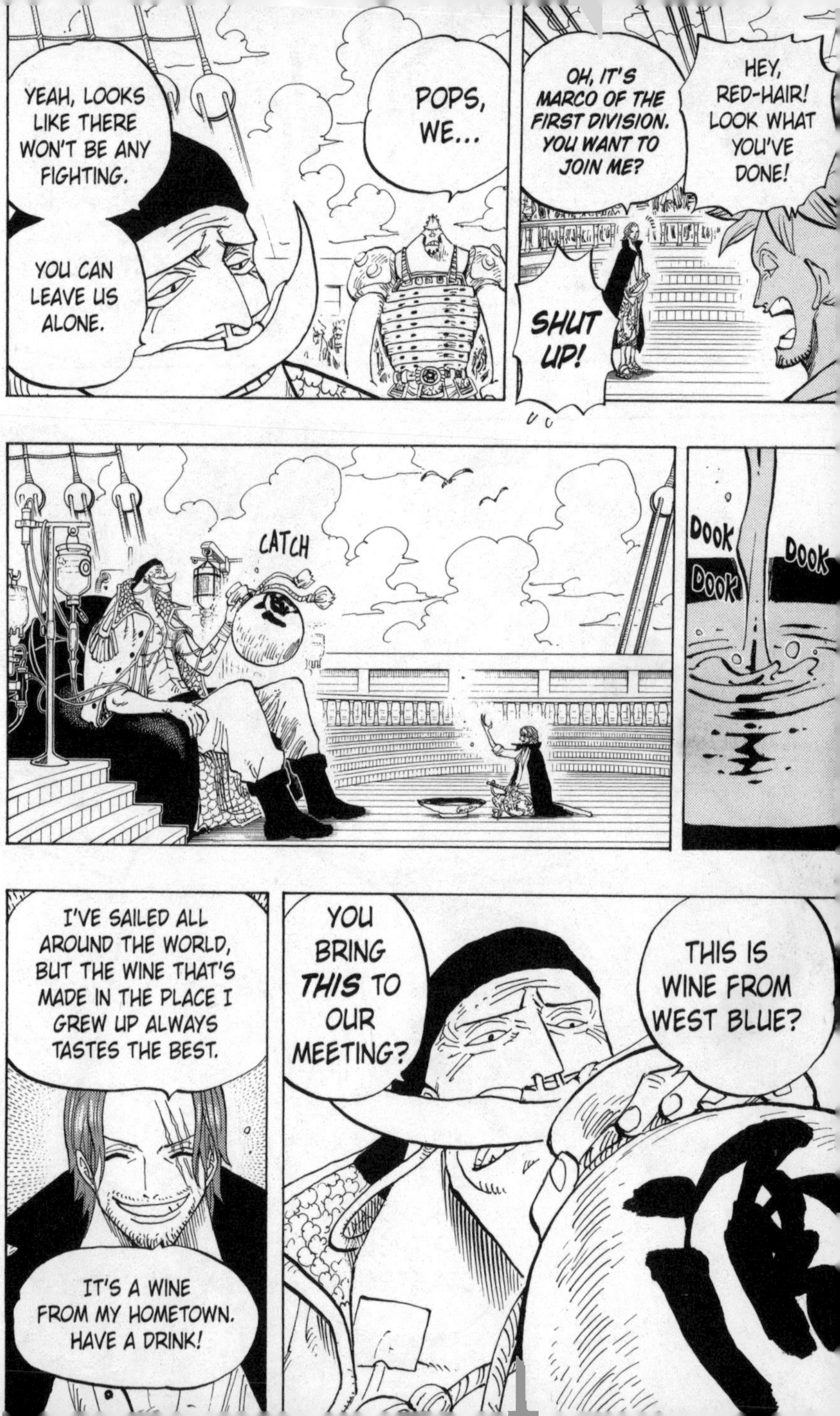
HEY, RED-HAIR! LOOK WHAT YOU'VE DONE!
OH, IT'S MARCO OF THE FIRST DIVISION. YOU WANT TO JOIN ME?
SHUT UP!
POPS, WE...
YEAH, LOOKS LIKE THERE WON'T BE ANY FIGHTING.
YOU CAN LEAVE US ALONE.
DOOK
DOOK
DOOK
CATCH
THIS IS WINE FROM WEST BLUE?
YOU BRING THIS TO OUR MEETING?
I'VE SAILED ALL AROUND THE WORLD, BUT THE WINE THAT'S MADE IN THE PLACE I GREW UP ALWAYS TASTES THE BEST.
IT'S A WINE FROM MY HOMETOWN. HAVE A DRINK!

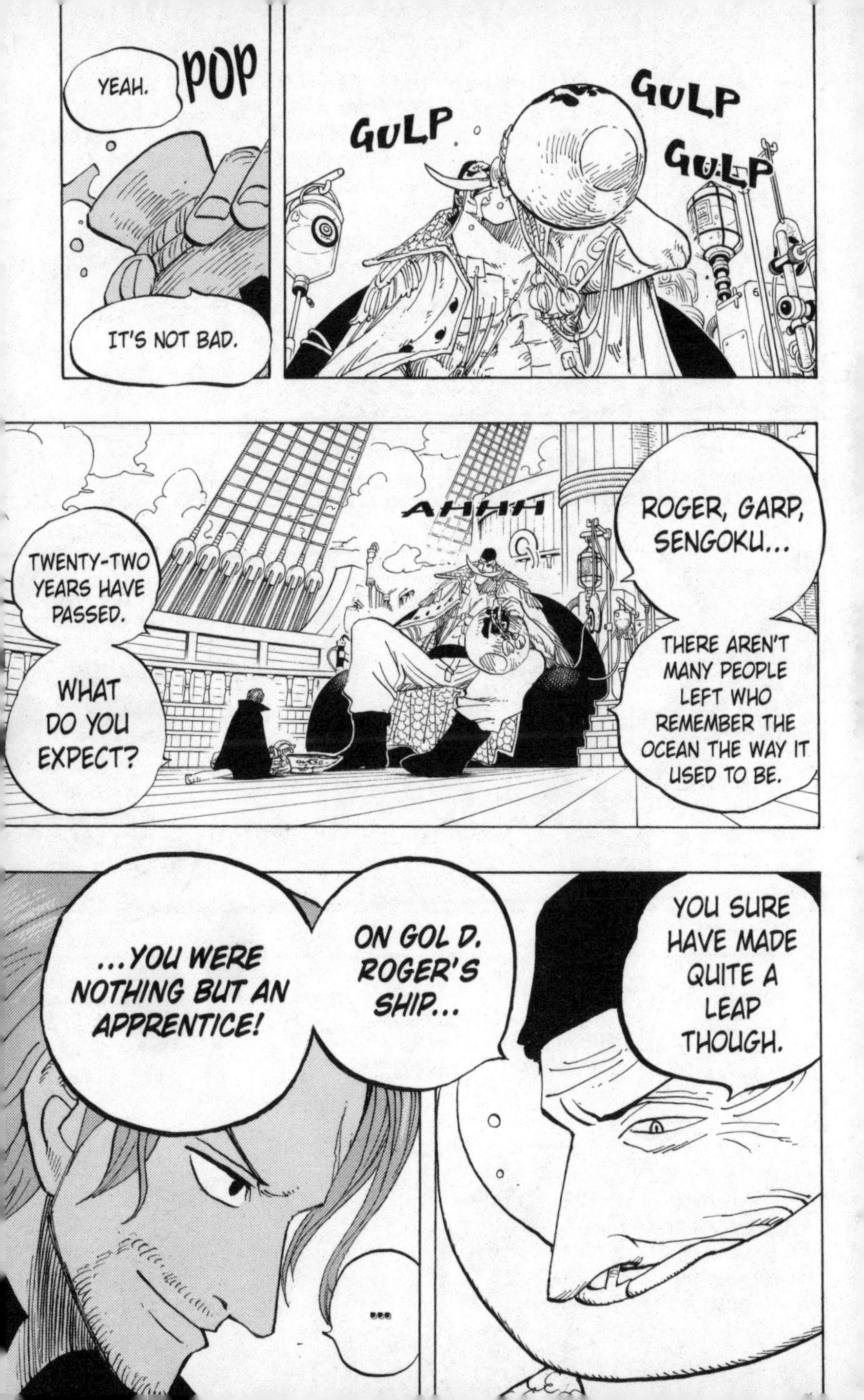
GULP
GULP
GULP
YEAH.
POP
IT'S NOT BAD.
ROGER, GARP, SENGOKU...
THERE AREN'T MANY PEOPLE LEFT WHO REMEMBER THE OCEAN THE WAY IT USED TO BE.
AHHH
TWENTY-TWO YEARS HAVE PASSED.
WHAT DO YOU EXPECT?
YOU SURE HAVE MADE QUITE A LEAP THOUGH.
ON GOL D. ROGER'S SHIP...
...YOU WERE NOTHING BUT AN APPRENTICE!
...

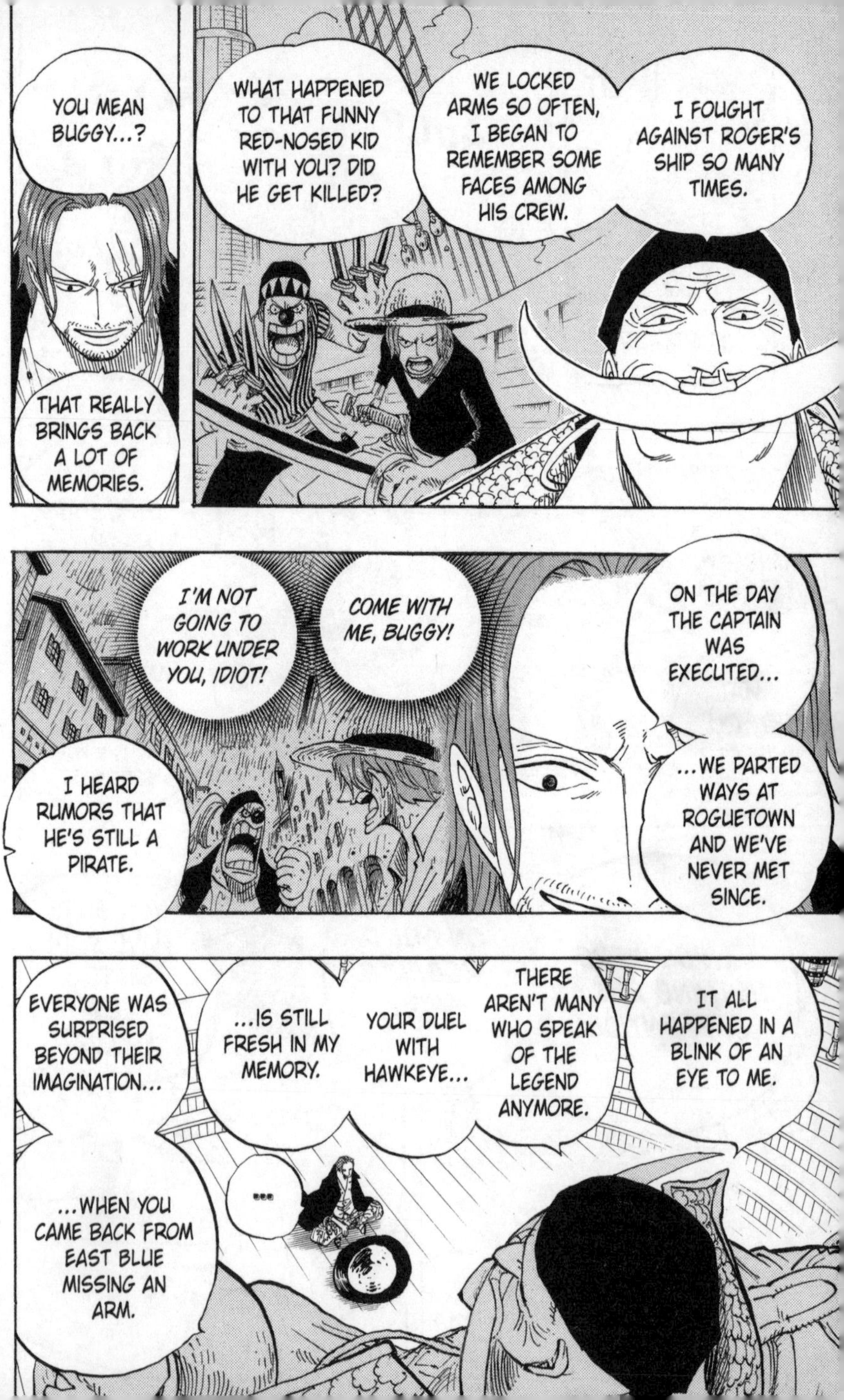
I FOUGHT AGAINST ROGER'S SHIP SO MANY TIMES.
WE LOCKED ARMS SO OFTEN, I BEGAN TO REMEMBER SOME FACES AMONG HIS CREW.
WHAT HAPPENED TO THAT FUNNY RED-NOSED KID WITH YOU? DID HE GET KILLED?
YOU MEAN BUGGY...?
THAT REALLY BRINGS BACK A LOT OF MEMORIES.
ON THE DAY THE CAPTAIN WAS EXECUTED...
COME WITH ME, BUGGY!
I'M NOT GOING TO WORK UNDER YOU, IDIOT!
...WE PARTED WAYS AT ROGUETOWN AND WE'VE NEVER MET SINCE.
I HEARD RUMORS THAT HE'S STILL A PIRATE.
IT ALL HAPPENED IN A BLINK OF AN EYE TO ME.
THERE AREN'T MANY WHO SPEAK OF THE LEGEND ANYMORE.
YOUR DUEL WITH HAWKEYE...
...IS STILL FRESH IN MY MEMORY.
EVERYONE WAS SURPRISED BEYOND THEIR IMAGINATION...
...WHEN YOU CAME BACK FROM EAST BLUE MISSING AN ARM.
...

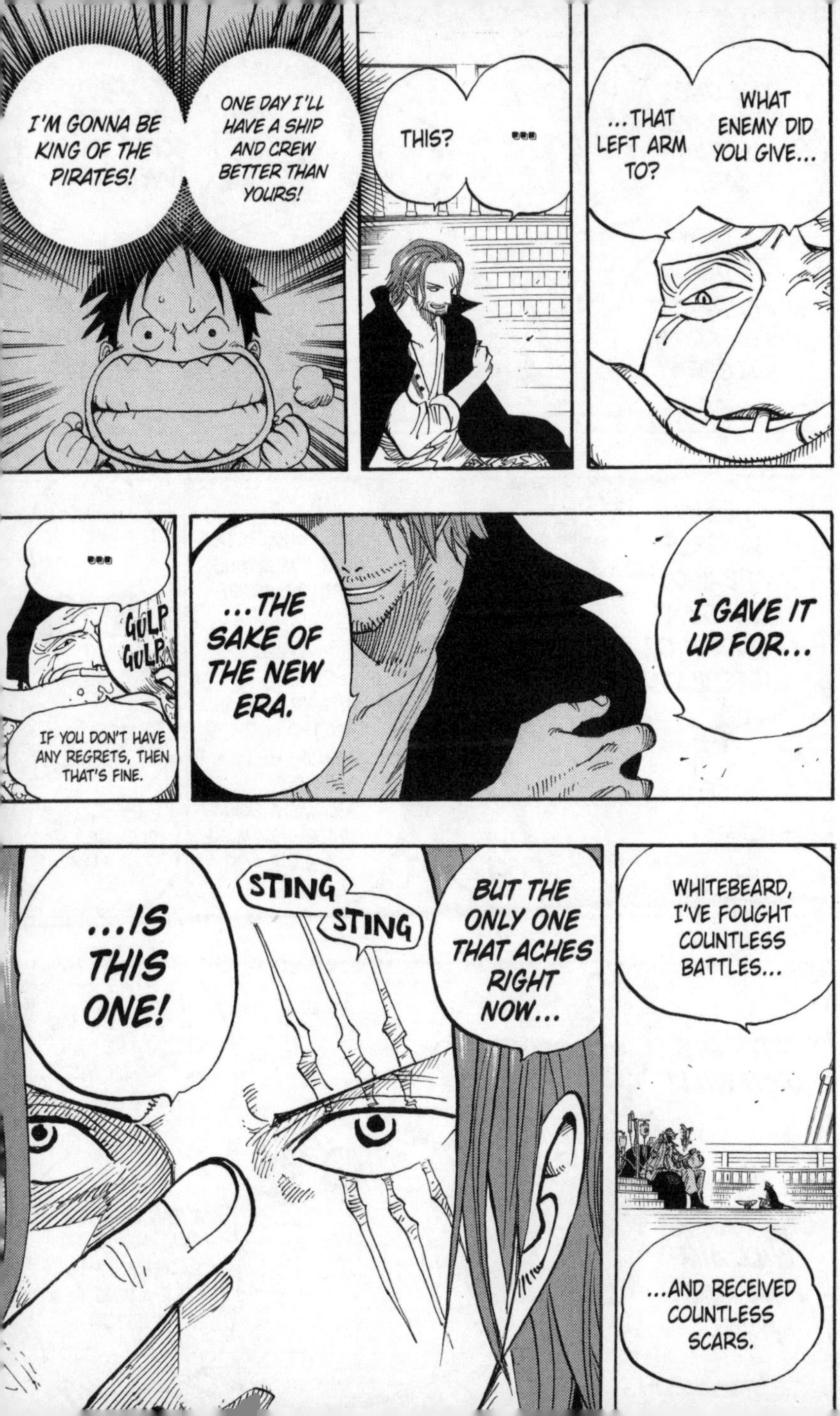

WHAT ENEMY DID YOU GIVE...
...THAT LEFT ARM TO?
...
THIS?
ONE DAY I'LL HAVE A SHIP AND CREW BETTER THAN YOURS!
I'M GONNA BE KING OF THE PIRATES!
I GAVE IT UP FOR...
...THE SAKE OF THE NEW ERA.
...
GULP GULP
IF YOU DON'T HAVE ANY REGRETS, THEN THAT'S FINE.
WHITEBEARD, I'VE FOUGHT COUNTLESS BATTLES...
...AND RECEIVED COUNTLESS SCARS.
BUT THE ONLY ONE THAT ACHES RIGHT NOW...
STING
STING
...IS THIS ONE!

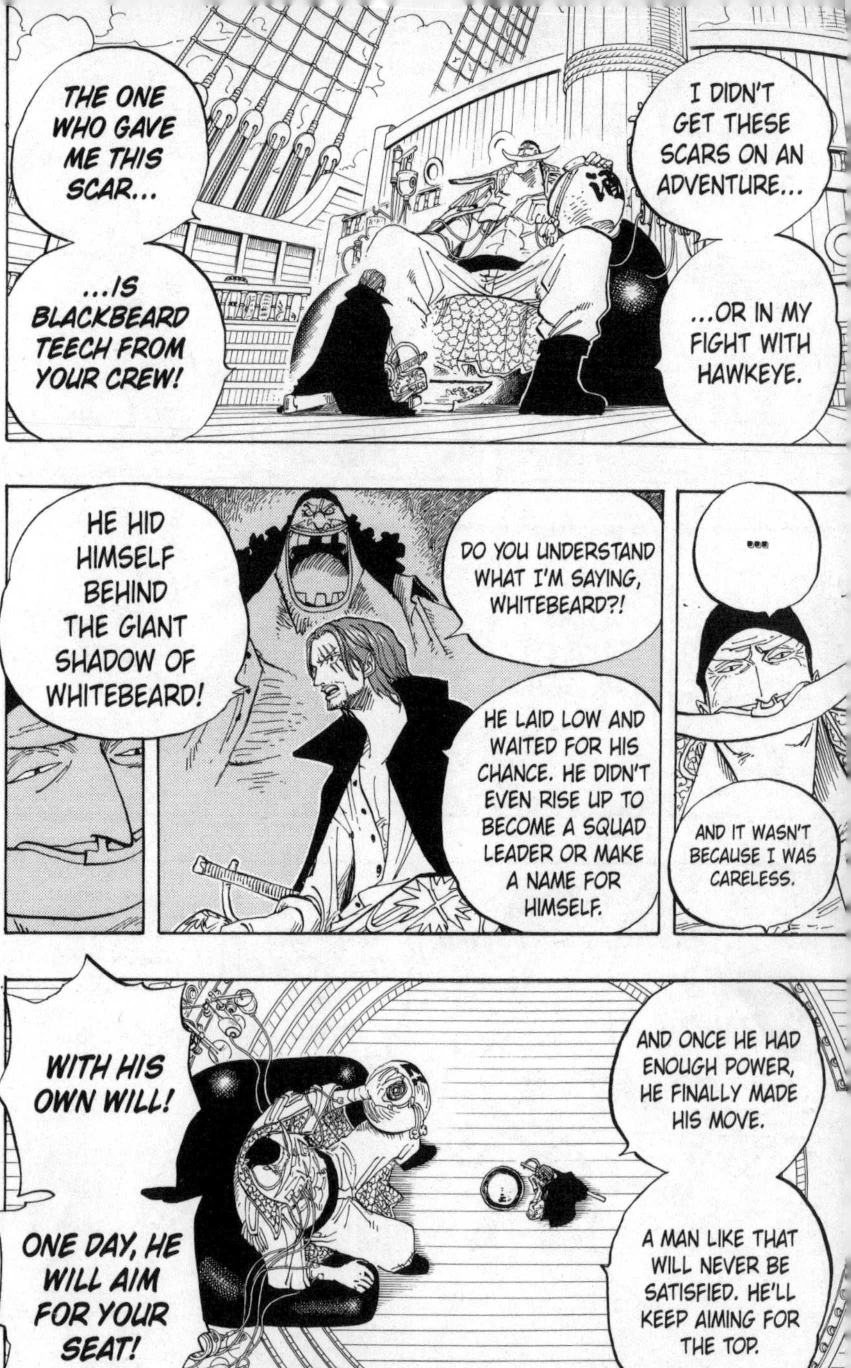
I DIDN'T GET THESE SCARS ON AN ADVENTURE...
...OR IN MY FIGHT WITH HAWKEYE.
THE ONE WHO GAVE ME THIS SCAR...
...IS BLACKBEARD TEECH FROM YOUR CREW!
...
AND IT WASN'T BECAUSE I WAS CARELESS.
DO YOU UNDERSTAND WHAT I'M SAYING, WHITEBEARD?!
HE LAID LOW AND WAITED FOR HIS CHANCE. HE DIDN'T EVEN RISE UP TO BECOME A SQUAD LEADER OR MAKE A NAME FOR HIMSELF.
HE HID HIMSELF BEHIND THE GIANT SHADOW OF WHITEBEARD!
AND ONCE HE HAD ENOUGH POWER, HE FINALLY MADE HIS MOVE.
A MAN LIKE THAT WILL NEVER BE SATISFIED. HE'LL KEEP AIMING FOR THE TOP.
WITH HIS OWN WILL!
ONE DAY, HE WILL AIM FOR YOUR SEAT!

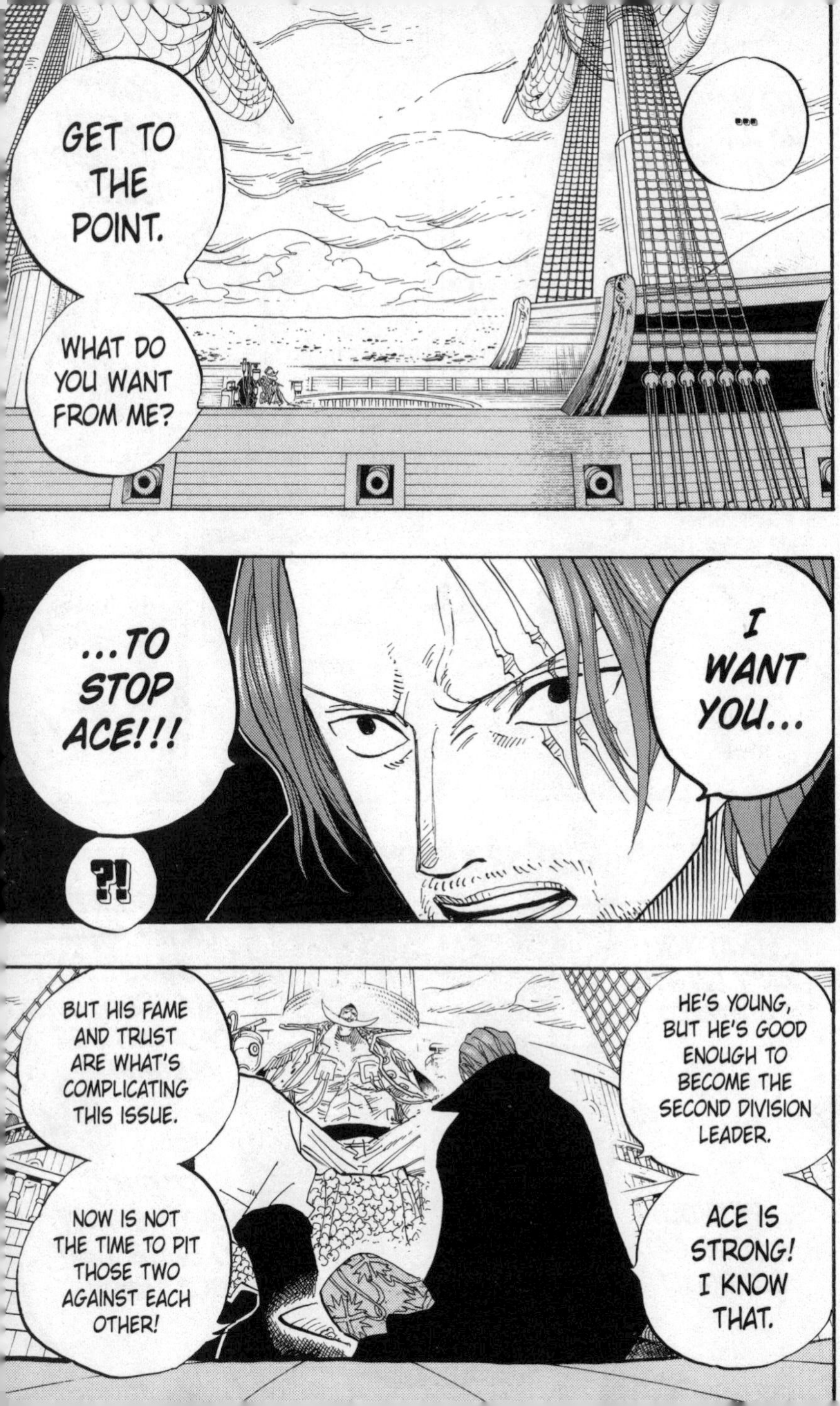
...
GET TO THE POINT.
WHAT DO YOU WANT FROM ME?
I WANT YOU...
...TO STOP ACE!!!
?!
HE'S YOUNG, BUT HE'S GOOD ENOUGH TO BECOME THE SECOND DIVISION LEADER.
ACE IS STRONG! I KNOW THAT.
BUT HIS FAME AND TRUST ARE WHAT'S COMPLICATING THIS ISSUE.
NOW IS NOT THE TIME TO PIT THOSE TWO AGAINST EACH OTHER!

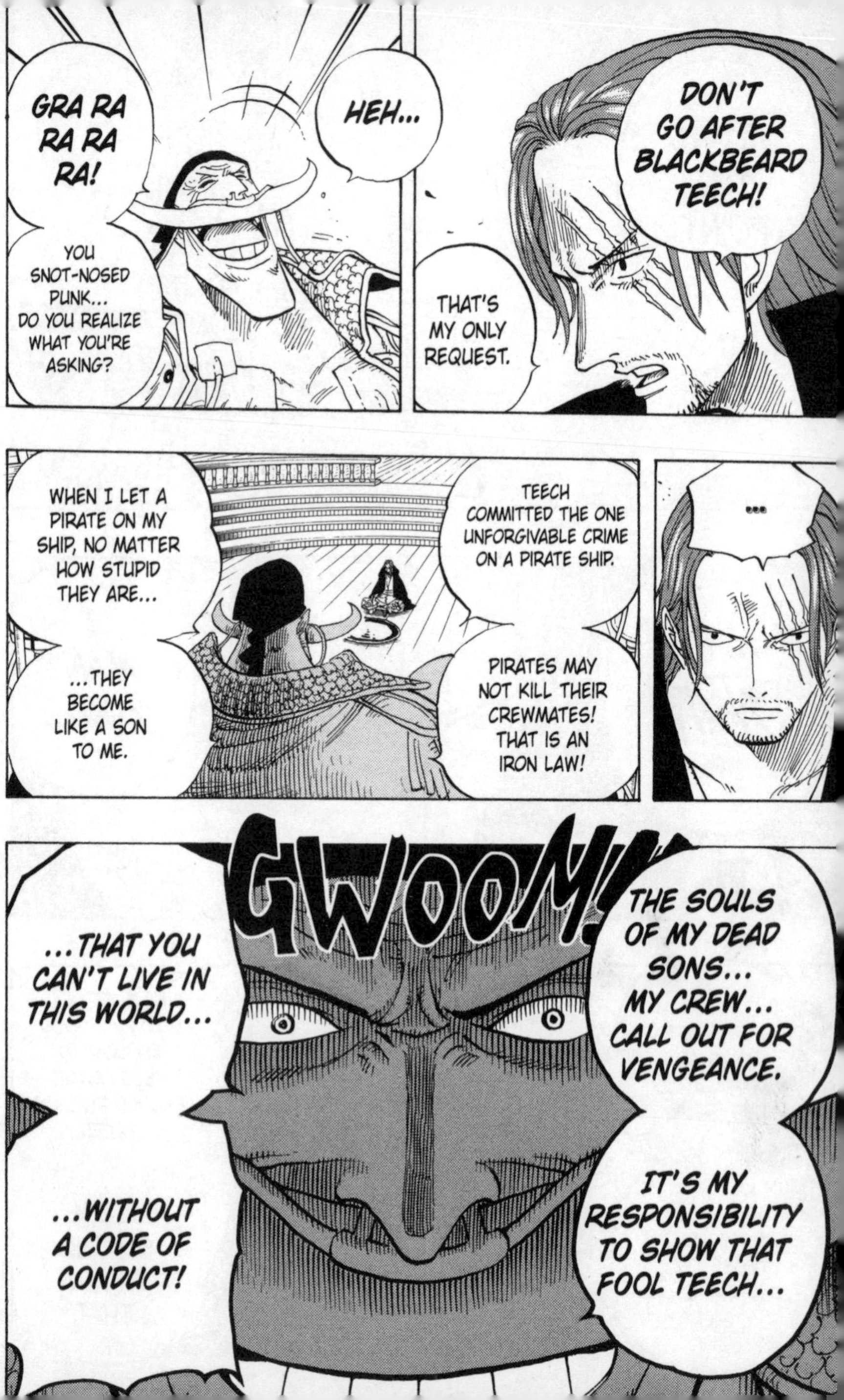

DON'T GO AFTER BLACKBEARD TEECH!
THAT'S MY ONLY REQUEST.
HEH...
GRA RA RA RA RA!
YOU SNOT-NOSED PUNK... DO YOU REALIZE WHAT YOU'RE ASKING?
...
TEECH COMMITTED THE ONE UNFORGIVABLE CRIME ON A PIRATE SHIP.
PIRATES MAY NOT KILL THEIR CREWMATES! THAT IS AN IRON LAW!
WHEN I LET A PIRATE ON MY SHIP, NO MATTER HOW STUPID THEY ARE...
...THEY BECOME LIKE A SON TO ME.
GWOOM!!
THE SOULS OF MY DEAD SONS... MY CREW... CALL OUT FOR VENGEANCE.
IT'S MY RESPONSIBILITY TO SHOW THAT FOOL TEECH...
...THAT YOU CAN'T LIVE IN THIS WORLD...
...WITHOUT A CODE OF CONDUCT!

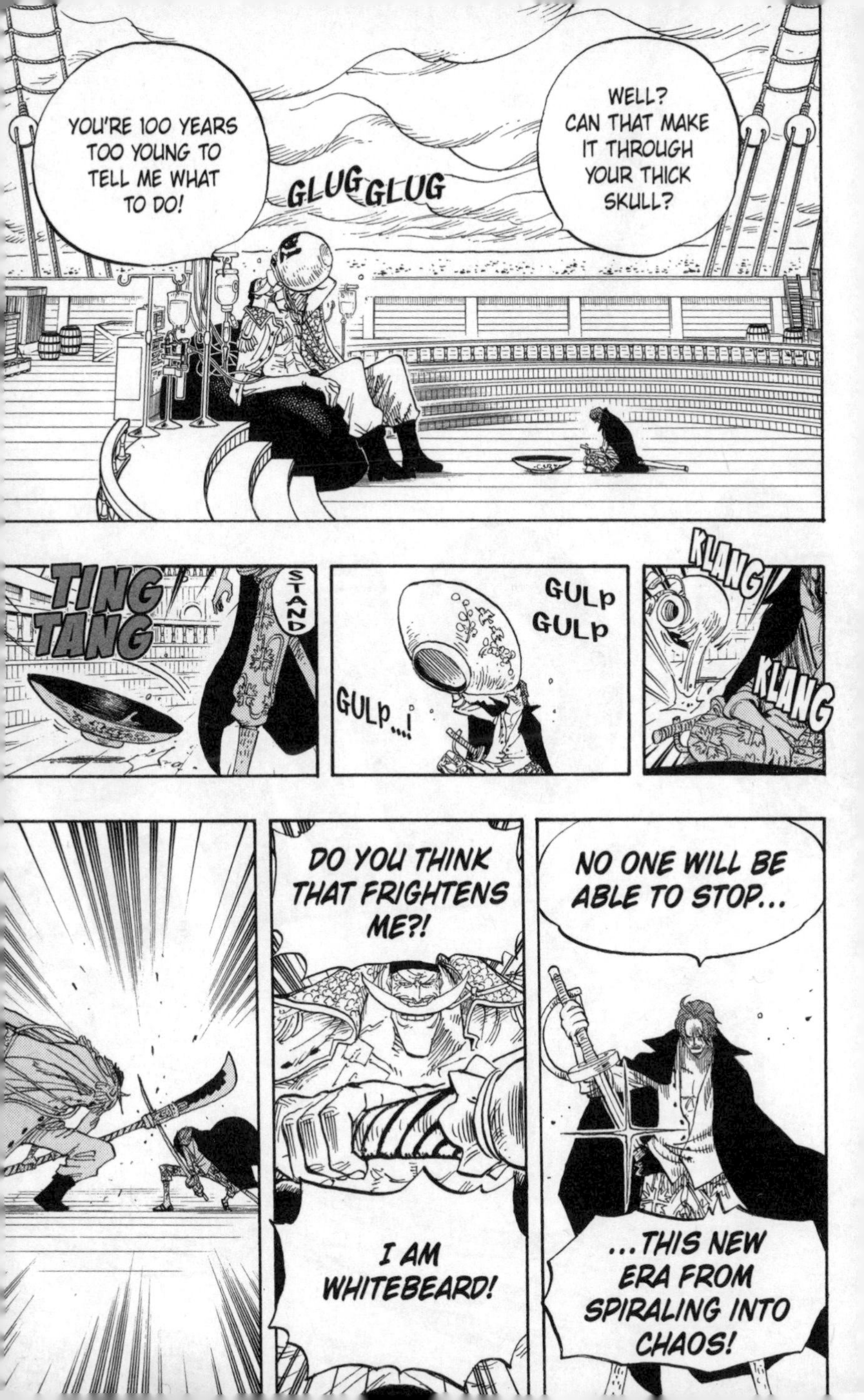
WELL? CAN THAT MAKE IT THROUGH YOUR THICK SKULL?
GLUG GLUG
YOU'RE 100 YEARS TOO YOUNG TO TELL ME WHAT TO DO!
KLANG
KLANG
GULp GULp
GULp...!
STAND
TING TANG
NO ONE WILL BE ABLE TO STOP...
...THIS NEW ERA FROM SPIRALING INTO CHAOS!
DO YOU THINK THAT FRIGHTENS ME?!
I AM WHITEBEARD!

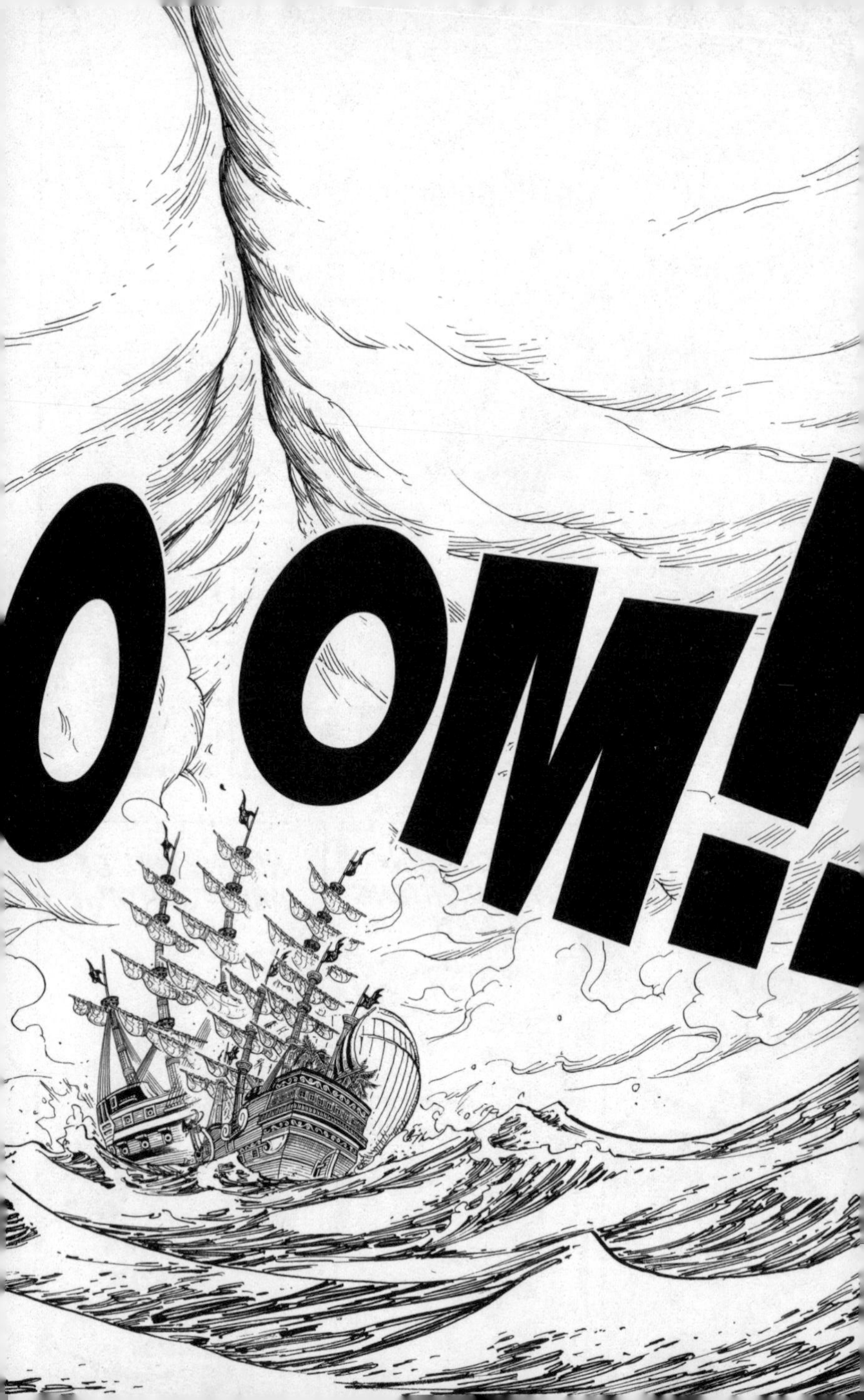
OOM!!

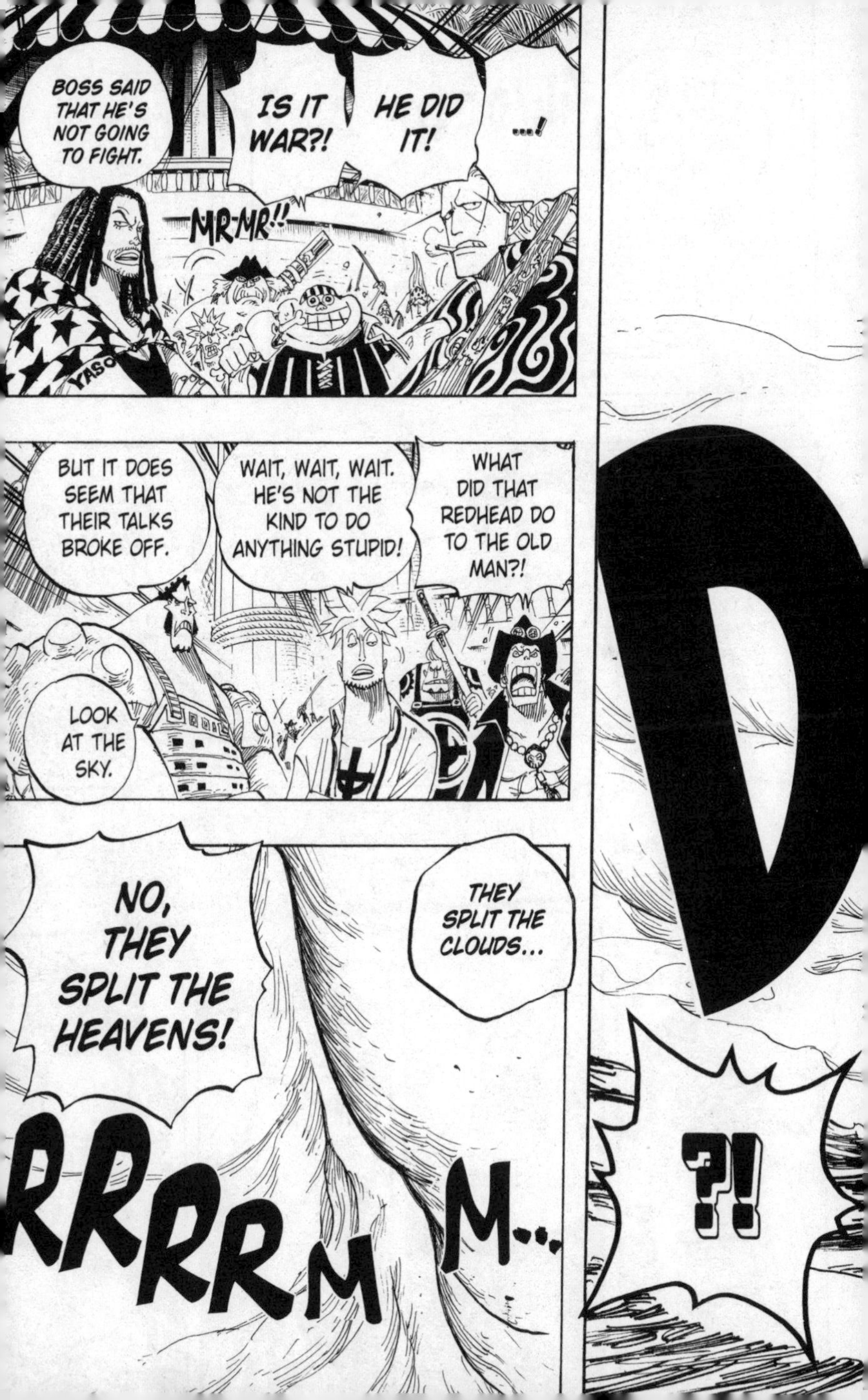
D
?!
...!
HE DID IT!
IS IT WAR?!
BOSS SAID THAT HE'S NOT GOING TO FIGHT.
MR MR!!
YASO
WHAT DID THAT REDHEAD DO TO THE OLD MAN?!
WAIT, WAIT, WAIT. HE'S NOT THE KIND TO DO ANYTHING STUPID!
BUT IT DOES SEEM THAT THEIR TALKS BROKE OFF.
LOOK AT THE SKY.
THEY SPLIT THE CLOUDS...
NO, THEY SPLIT THE HEAVENS!
RRRRRM M M...

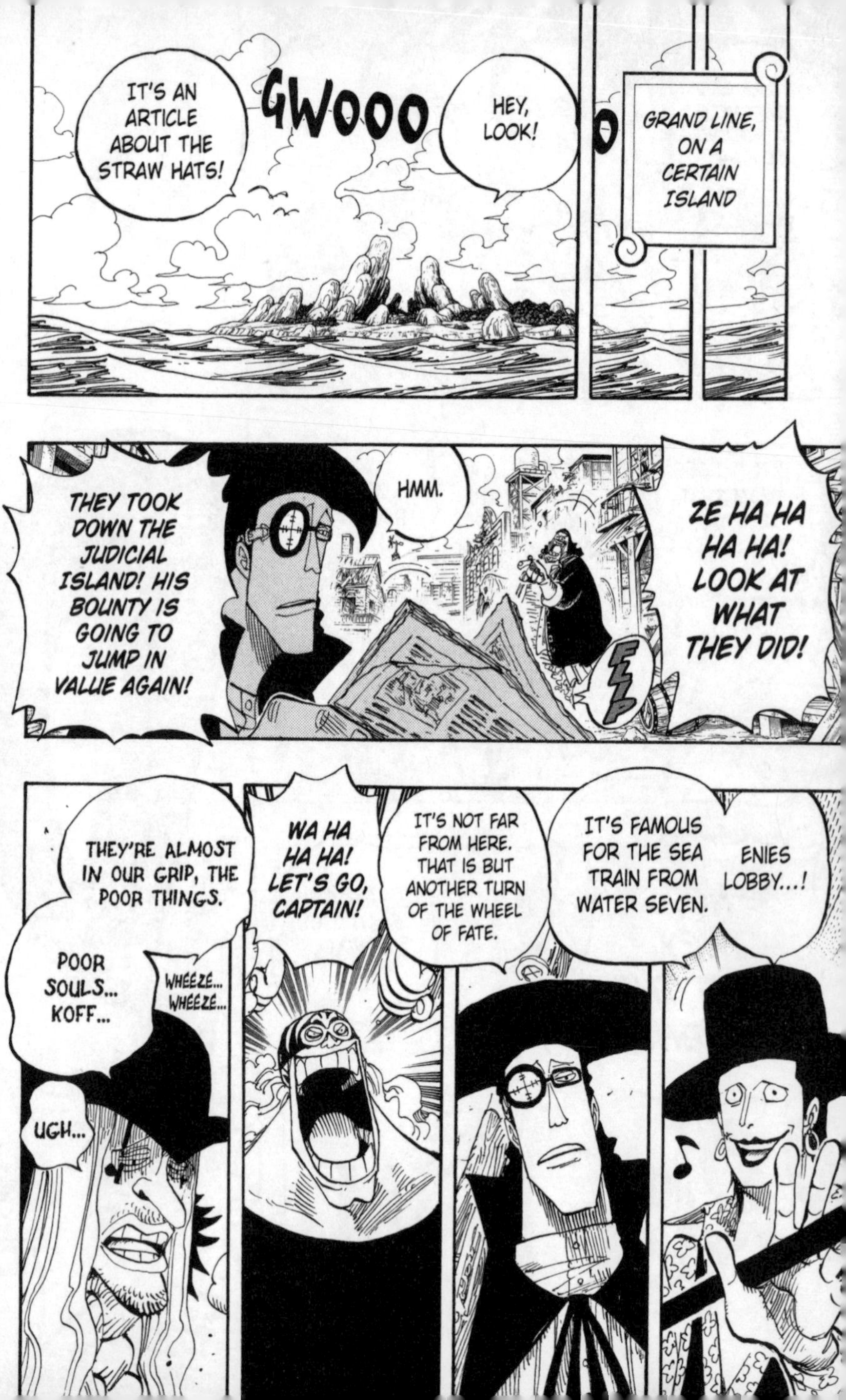
GRAND LINE, ON A CERTAIN ISLAND
GWOOOO
HEY, LOOK!
IT'S AN ARTICLE ABOUT THE STRAW HATS!
ZE HA HA HA HA! LOOK AT WHAT THEY DID!
FLIP
HMM.
THEY TOOK DOWN THE JUDICIAL ISLAND! HIS BOUNTY IS GOING TO JUMP IN VALUE AGAIN!
ENIES LOBBY...!
IT'S FAMOUS FOR THE SEA TRAIN FROM WATER SEVEN.
IT'S NOT FAR FROM HERE. THAT IS BUT ANOTHER TURN OF THE WHEEL OF FATE.
WA HA HA HA! LET'S GO, CAPTAIN!
THEY'RE ALMOST IN OUR GRIP, THE POOR THINGS.
WHEEZE... WHEEZE...
POOR SOULS... KOFF...
UGH...

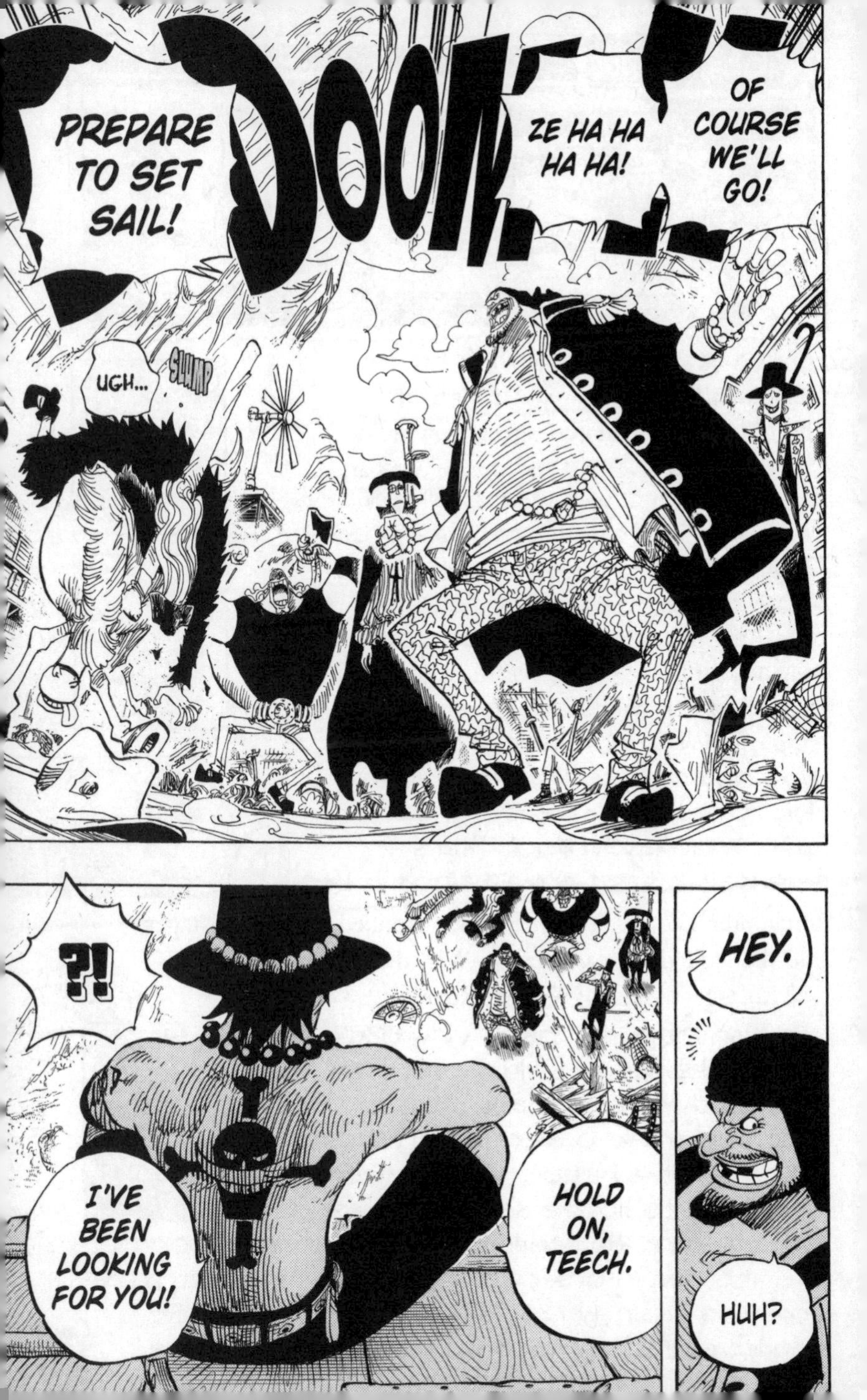
OF COURSE WE'LL GO!
ZE HA HA HA HA!
DOOM
PREPARE TO SET SAIL!
SLUMP
UGH...
HEY.
HUH?
?!
HOLD ON, TEECH.
I'VE BEEN LOOKING FOR YOU!

Q: Kokoro is a mermaid, so why is her grand-daughter, Chimney, a regular human? Don't the mermaid genes pass down?

--Petit Panda

A: When Kokoro was young, a very long time ago, she came with Tom from Fish-Man Island. She married a man from Water Seven and had a son that was half mermaid. That son married a human girl, and they had Chimney. Chimney is a quarter mermaid, so she is very good at swimming. In volume 42, chapter 403, you can see that even a small child like her can save the drowning Luffy from a whirlpool. That's because she has mermaid blood in her.

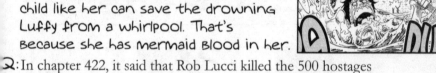

Q: In chapter 422, it said that Rob Lucci killed the 500 hostages and then killed the captain too. Why did he have to kill the 500 hostages?

--Wyper!! Rocks

A: Yeah, isn't that horrible? Why didn't he just kill the bad guys? In short, Lucci believes that being weak is a "sin." In his mind, soldiers who were easily caught and caused the nation to be in jeopardy were likely to do the same thing again in the future. He decided that they weren't worthy of living, and in order to prevent this incident from happening again, he took their lives. He's a cold-blooded guy! Luffy, good job in beating him!

Chapter 435:
YOU HAVE MY SYMPATHIES

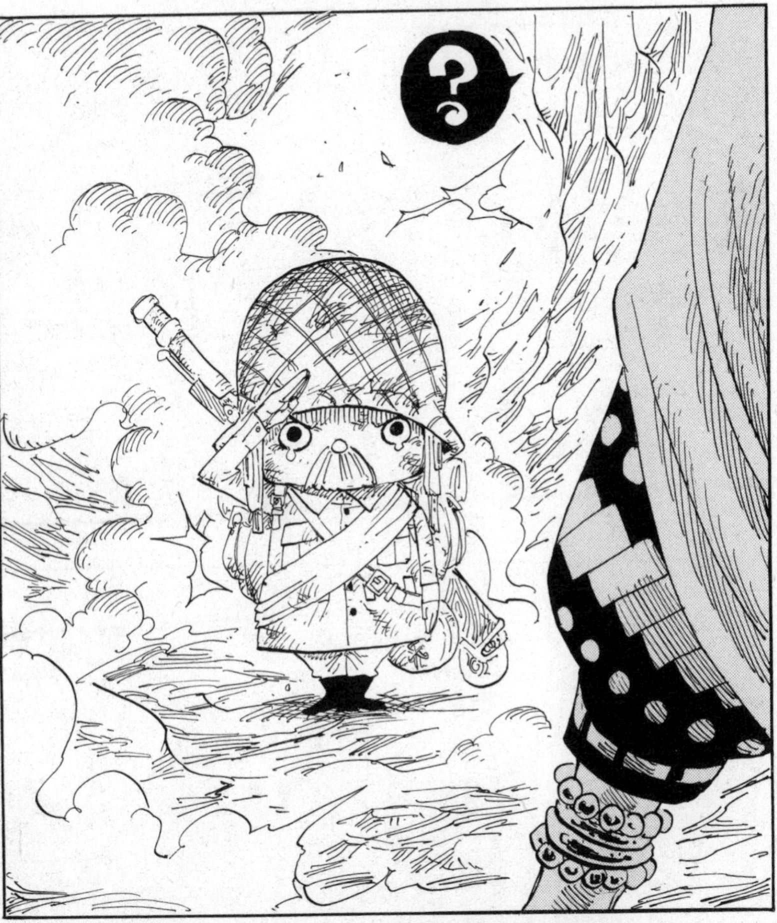
?

ENERU'S GREAT SPACE MISSION, VOL. 6:
"I'M SORRY, BUT I'M STILL ALIVE!"

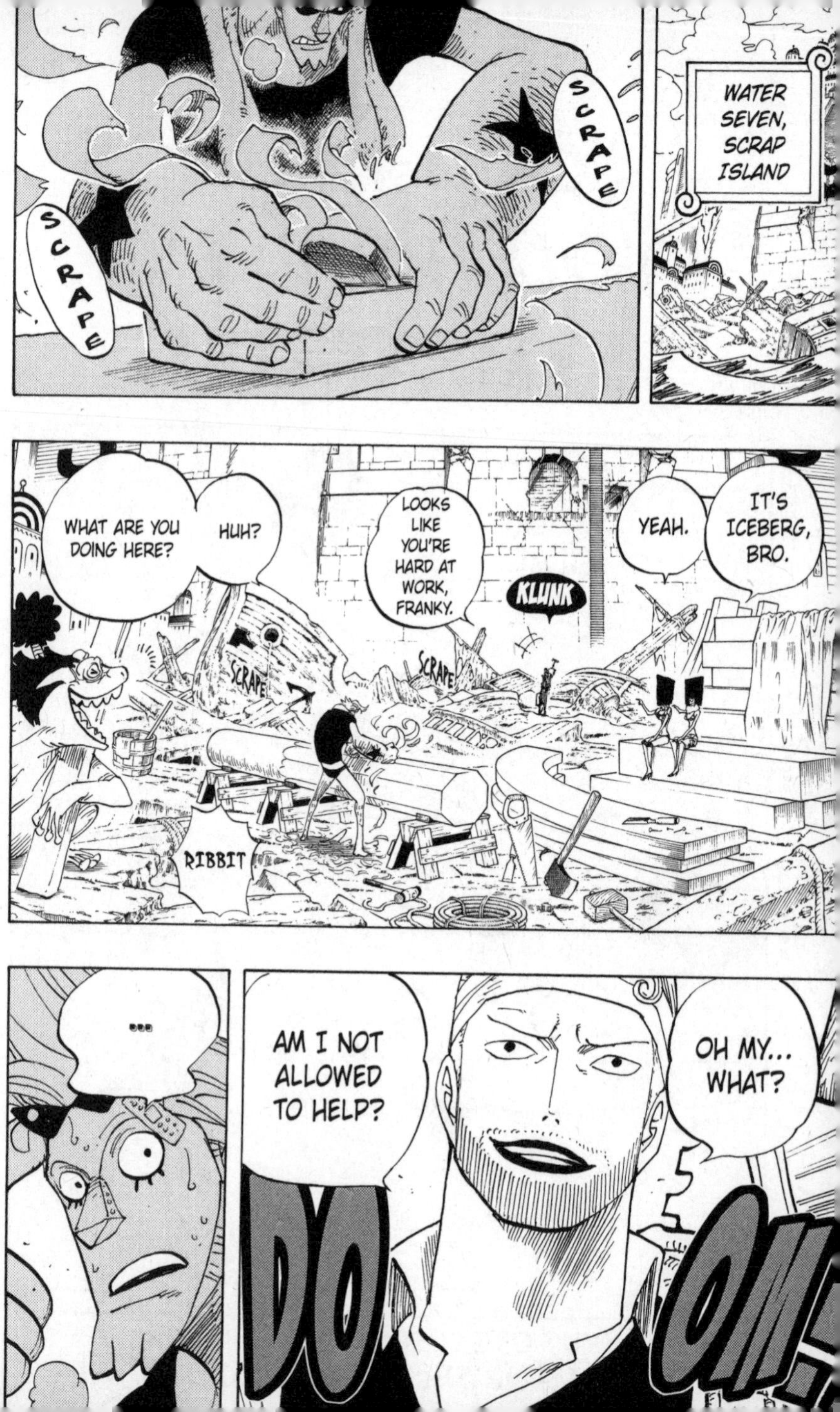
WATER SEVEN, SCRAP ISLAND
SCRAPE
SCRAPE
IT'S ICEBERG, BRO.
YEAH.
KLUNK
LOOKS LIKE YOU'RE HARD AT WORK, FRANKY.
HUH?
WHAT ARE YOU DOING HERE?
SCRAPE
SCRAPE
RIBBIT
OH MY... WHAT?
AM I NOT ALLOWED TO HELP?
DO
...

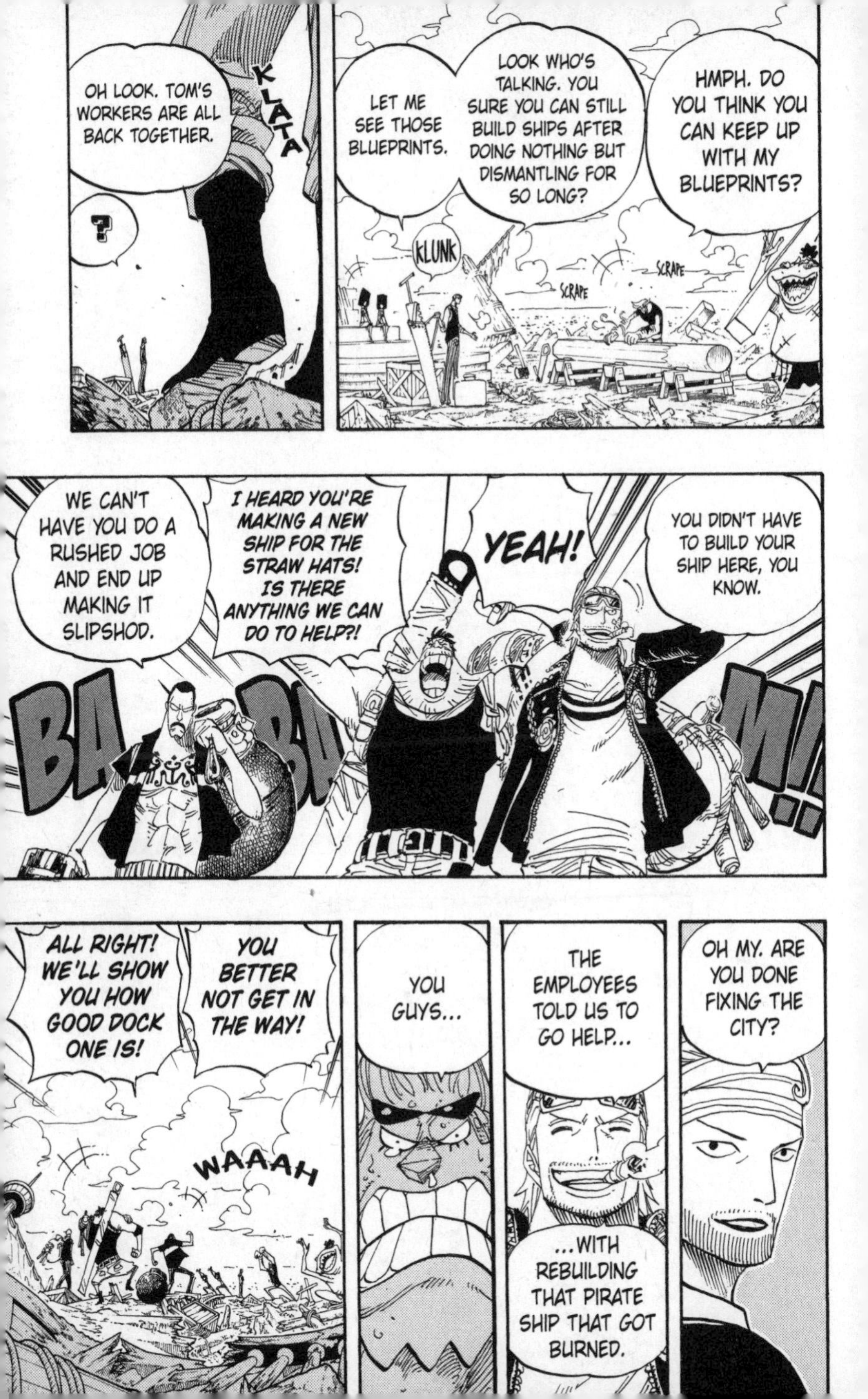
HMPH. DO YOU THINK YOU CAN KEEP UP WITH MY BLUEPRINTS?
LOOK WHO'S TALKING. YOU SURE YOU CAN STILL BUILD SHIPS AFTER DOING NOTHING BUT DISMANTLING FOR SO LONG?
LET ME SEE THOSE BLUEPRINTS.
KLUNK
SCRAPE
SCRAPE
OH LOOK. TOM'S WORKERS ARE ALL BACK TOGETHER.
KLATA
?
YOU DIDN'T HAVE TO BUILD YOUR SHIP HERE, YOU KNOW.
YEAH!
I HEARD YOU'RE MAKING A NEW SHIP FOR THE STRAW HATS! IS THERE ANYTHING WE CAN DO TO HELP?!
WE CAN'T HAVE YOU DO A RUSHED JOB AND END UP MAKING IT SLIPSHOD.
BA
BA
M!!
OH MY. ARE YOU DONE FIXING THE CITY?
THE EMPLOYEES TOLD US TO GO HELP...
...WITH REBUILDING THAT PIRATE SHIP THAT GOT BURNED.
YOU GUYS...
YOU BETTER NOT GET IN THE WAY!
ALL RIGHT! WE'LL SHOW YOU HOW GOOD DOCK ONE IS!
WAAAH

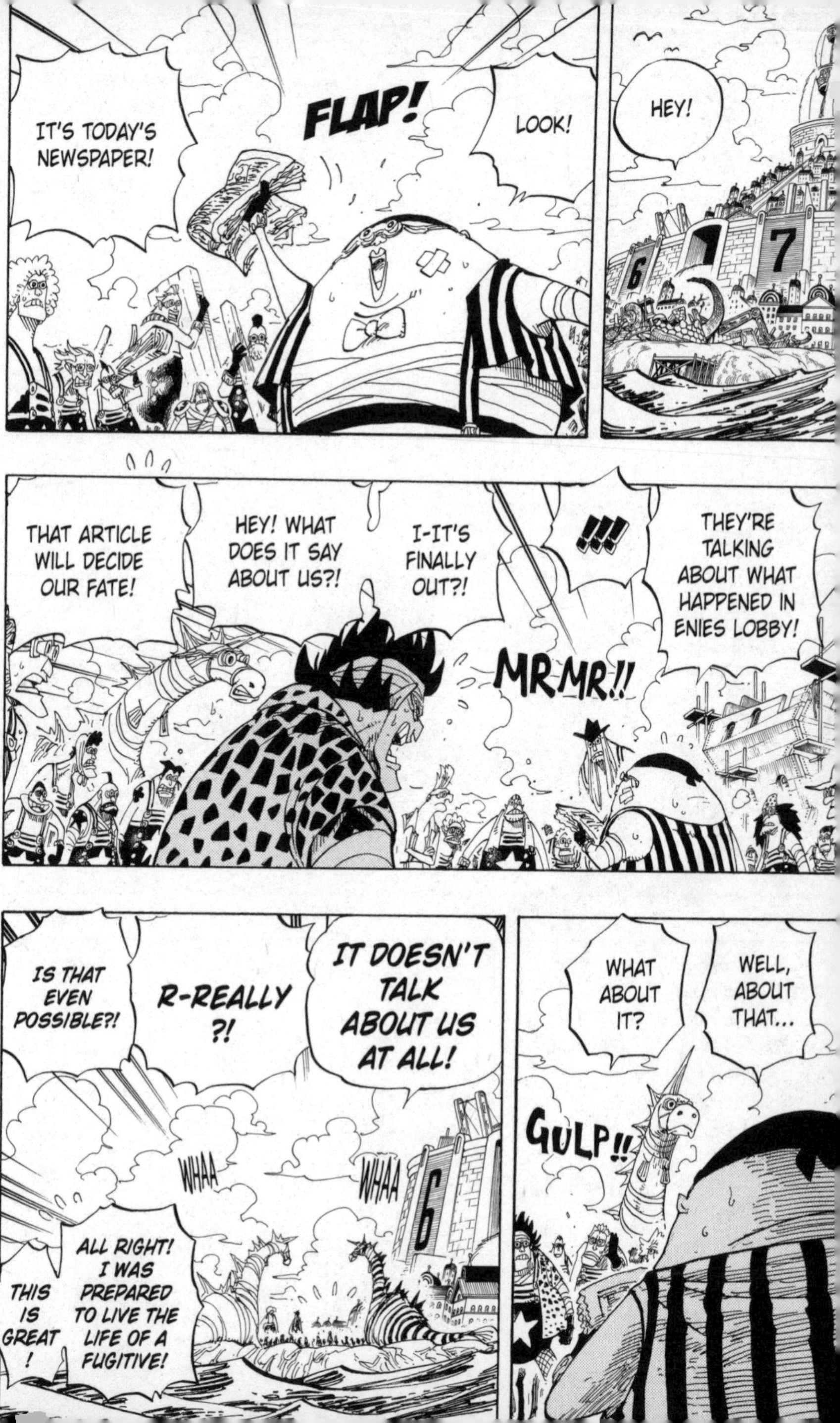
HEY!
LOOK!
FLAP!
IT'S TODAY'S NEWSPAPER!
THEY'RE TALKING ABOUT WHAT HAPPENED IN ENIES LOBBY!
!!!
I-IT'S FINALLY OUT?!
HEY! WHAT DOES IT SAY ABOUT US?!
THAT ARTICLE WILL DECIDE OUR FATE!
MR MR!!
WELL, ABOUT THAT...
WHAT ABOUT IT?
GULP!!
IT DOESN'T TALK ABOUT US AT ALL!
R-REALLY ?!
IS THAT EVEN POSSIBLE?!
WHAA
WHAA
ALL RIGHT! I WAS PREPARED TO LIVE THE LIFE OF A FUGITIVE!
THIS IS GREAT!

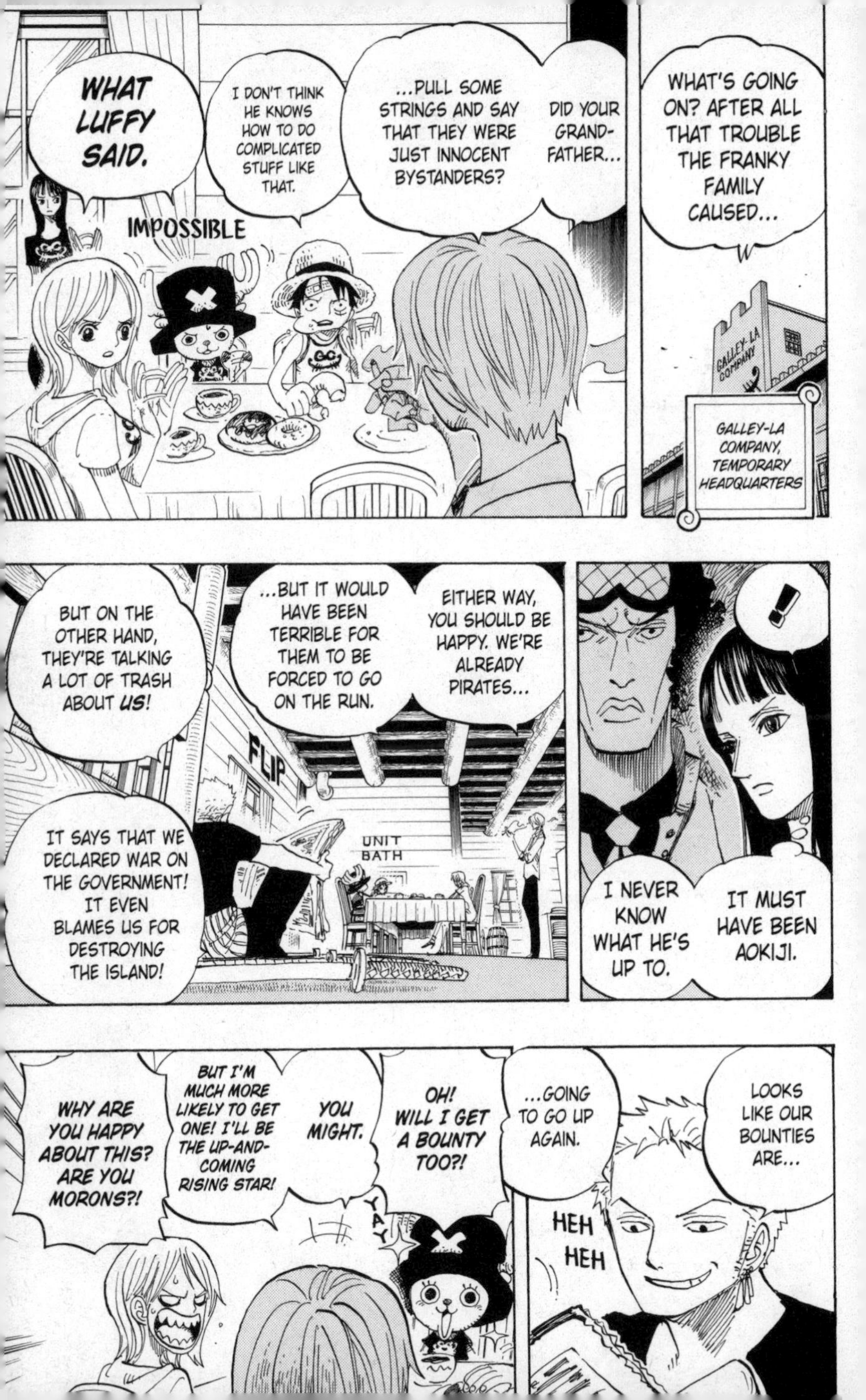
WHAT'S GOING ON? AFTER ALL THAT TROUBLE THE FRANKY FAMILY CAUSED...
GALLEY-LA COMPANY
GALLEY-LA COMPANY, TEMPORARY HEADQUARTERS
DID YOUR GRANDFATHER...
...PULL SOME STRINGS AND SAY THAT THEY WERE JUST INNOCENT BYSTANDERS?
I DON'T THINK HE KNOWS HOW TO DO COMPLICATED STUFF LIKE THAT.
WHAT LUFFY SAID.
IMPOSSIBLE
!
IT MUST HAVE BEEN AOKIJI.
I NEVER KNOW WHAT HE'S UP TO.
EITHER WAY, YOU SHOULD BE HAPPY. WE'RE ALREADY PIRATES...
...BUT IT WOULD HAVE BEEN TERRIBLE FOR THEM TO BE FORCED TO GO ON THE RUN.
BUT ON THE OTHER HAND, THEY'RE TALKING A LOT OF TRASH ABOUT US!
FLIP
UNIT BATH
IT SAYS THAT WE DECLARED WAR ON THE GOVERNMENT! IT EVEN BLAMES US FOR DESTROYING THE ISLAND!
LOOKS LIKE OUR BOUNTIES ARE...
...GOING TO GO UP AGAIN.
HEH HEH
OH! WILL I GET A BOUNTY TOO?!
YAY
YOU MIGHT.
BUT I'M MUCH MORE LIKELY TO GET ONE! I'LL BE THE UP-AND-COMING RISING STAR!
WHY ARE YOU HAPPY ABOUT THIS? ARE YOU MORONS?!

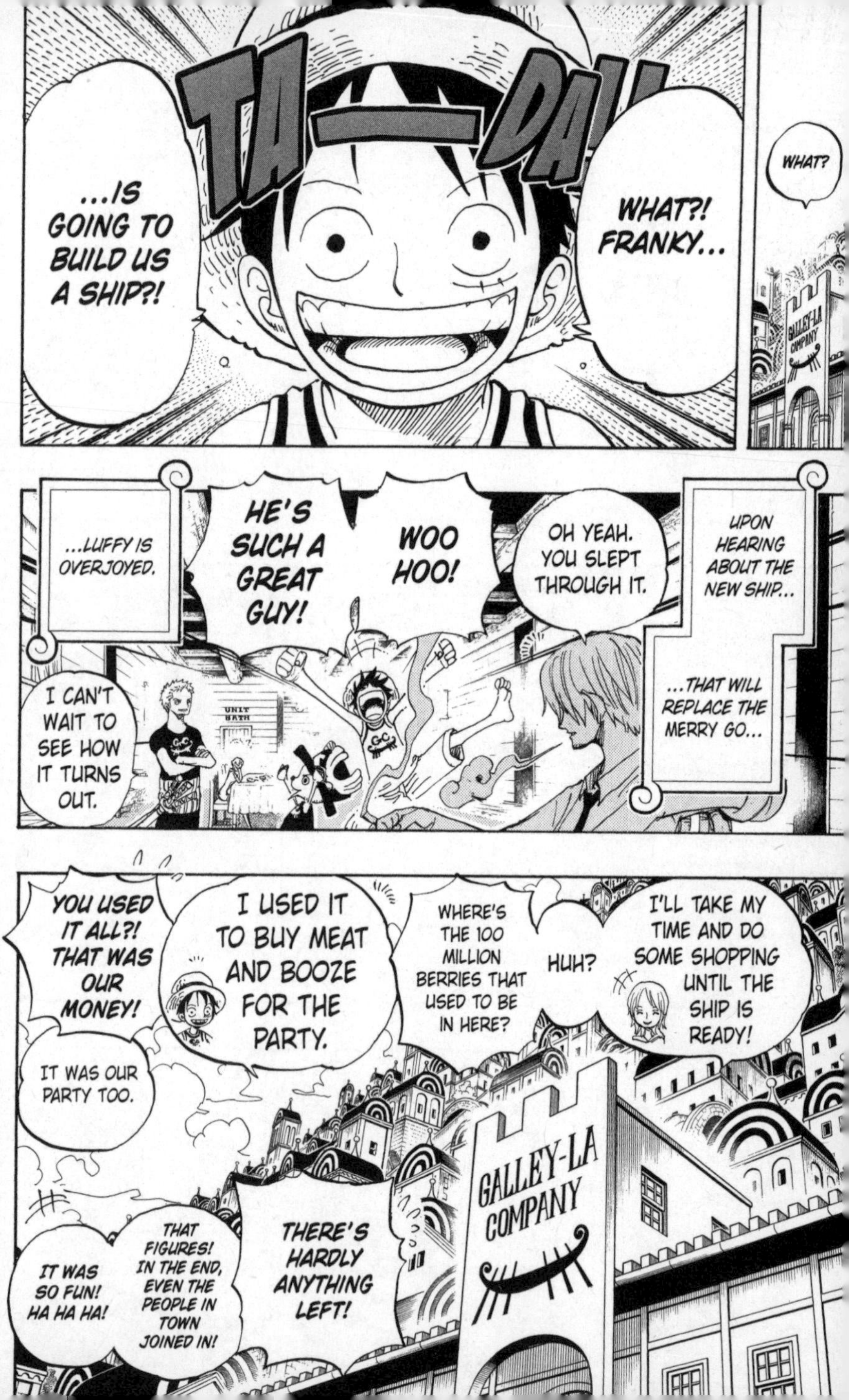
WHAT?
WHAT?! FRANKY...
TA—DA!!
...IS GOING TO BUILD US A SHIP?!
UPON HEARING ABOUT THE NEW SHIP...
...THAT WILL REPLACE THE MERRY GO...
OH YEAH. YOU SLEPT THROUGH IT.
WOO HOO!
HE'S SUCH A GREAT GUY!
...LUFFY IS OVERJOYED.
UNIT BATH
I CAN'T WAIT TO SEE HOW IT TURNS OUT.
I'LL TAKE MY TIME AND DO SOME SHOPPING UNTIL THE SHIP IS READY!
HUH?
WHERE'S THE 100 MILLION BERRIES THAT USED TO BE IN HERE?
I USED IT TO BUY MEAT AND BOOZE FOR THE PARTY.
YOU USED IT ALL?! THAT WAS OUR MONEY!
IT WAS OUR PARTY TOO.
GALLEY-LA COMPANY
THERE'S HARDLY ANYTHING LEFT!
THAT FIGURES! IN THE END, EVEN THE PEOPLE IN TOWN JOINED IN!
IT WAS SO FUN! HA HA HA!

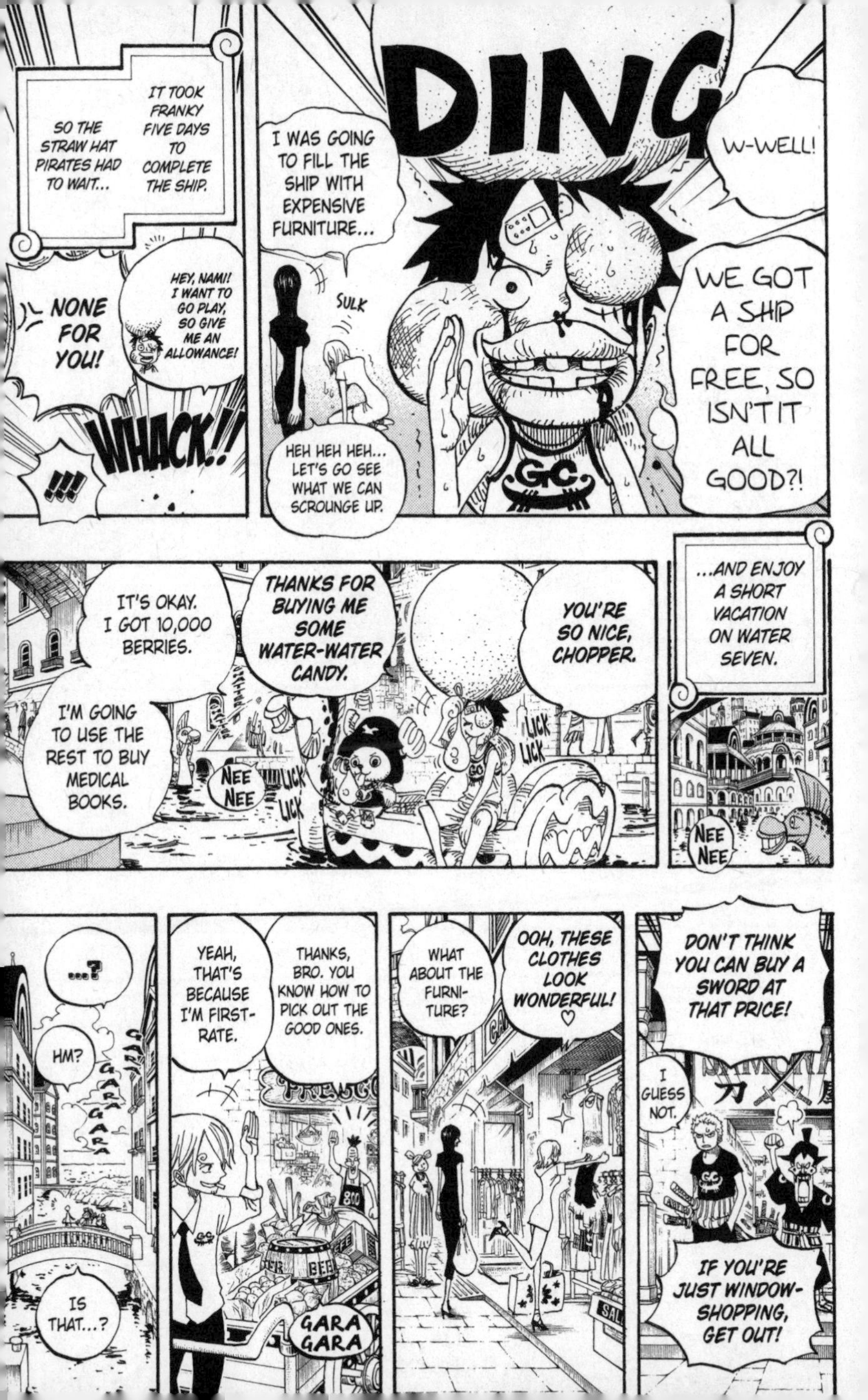
DING
W-WELL!
WE GOT A SHIP FOR FREE, SO ISN'T IT ALL GOOD?!
I WAS GOING TO FILL THE SHIP WITH EXPENSIVE FURNITURE...
SULK
HEH HEH HEH... LET'S GO SEE WHAT WE CAN SCROUNGE UP.
IT TOOK FRANKY FIVE DAYS TO COMPLETE THE SHIP.
SO THE STRAW HAT PIRATES HAD TO WAIT...
HEY, NAMI! I WANT TO GO PLAY, SO GIVE ME AN ALLOWANCE!
NONE FOR YOU!
WHACK!!
!!!
...AND ENJOY A SHORT VACATION ON WATER SEVEN.
NEE NEE
YOU'RE SO NICE, CHOPPER.
THANKS FOR BUYING ME SOME WATER-WATER CANDY.
LICK LICK
IT'S OKAY. I GOT 10,000 BERRIES.
I'M GOING TO USE THE REST TO BUY MEDICAL BOOKS.
NEE NEE
LICK LICK
DON'T THINK YOU CAN BUY A SWORD AT THAT PRICE!
I GUESS NOT.
IF YOU'RE JUST WINDOW-SHOPPING, GET OUT!
OOH, THESE CLOTHES LOOK WONDERFUL! ♡
WHAT ABOUT THE FURNITURE?
THANKS, BRO. YOU KNOW HOW TO PICK OUT THE GOOD ONES.
YEAH, THAT'S BECAUSE I'M FIRST-RATE.
GARA GARA
...?
HM?
GARA GARA GARA GARA
IS THAT...?

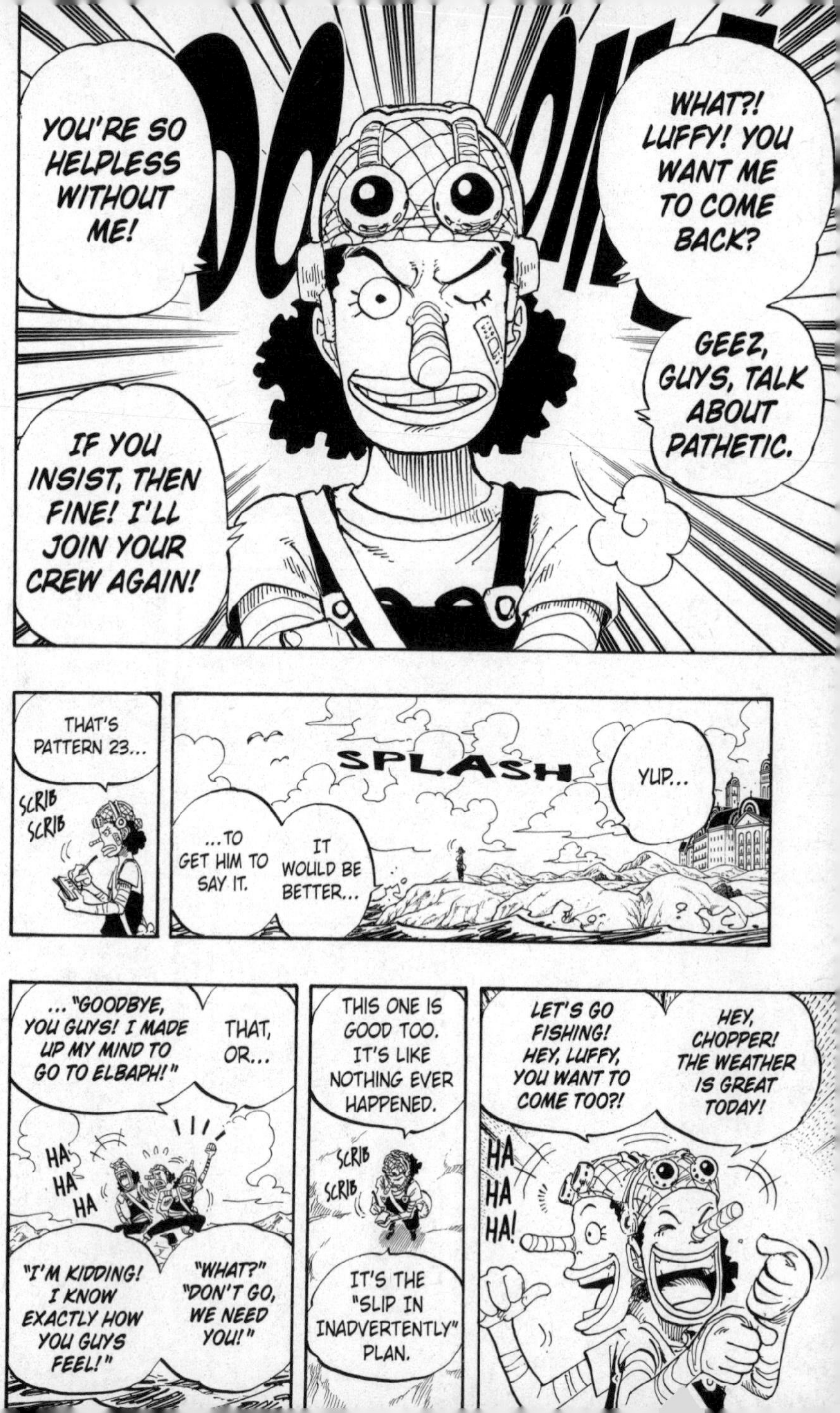
WHAT?! LUFFY! YOU WANT ME TO COME BACK?
YOU'RE SO HELPLESS WITHOUT ME!
GEEZ, GUYS, TALK ABOUT PATHETIC.
IF YOU INSIST, THEN FINE! I'LL JOIN YOUR CREW AGAIN!
YUP...
SPLASH
IT WOULD BE BETTER...
...TO GET HIM TO SAY IT.
THAT'S PATTERN 23...
SCRIB SCRIB
HEY, CHOPPER! THE WEATHER IS GREAT TODAY!
LET'S GO FISHING! HEY, LUFFY, YOU WANT TO COME TOO?!
HA HA HA!
THIS ONE IS GOOD TOO. IT'S LIKE NOTHING EVER HAPPENED.
SCRIB SCRIB
IT'S THE "SLIP IN INADVERTENTLY" PLAN.
THAT, OR...
..."GOODBYE, YOU GUYS! I MADE UP MY MIND TO GO TO ELBAPH!"
HA HA HA
"WHAT?" "DON'T GO, WE NEED YOU!"
"I'M KIDDING! I KNOW EXACTLY HOW YOU GUYS FEEL!"

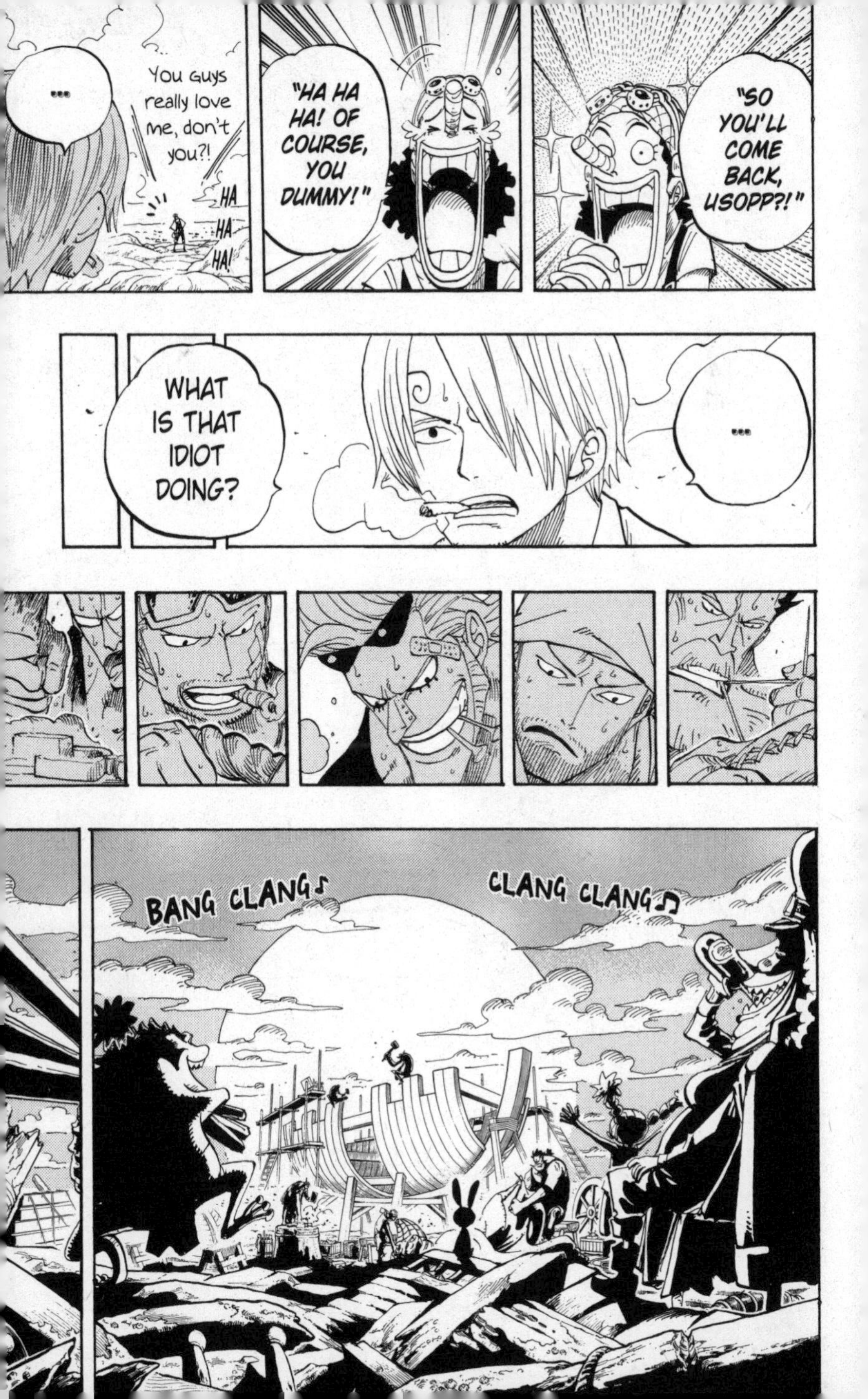
"SO YOU'LL COME BACK, USOPP?!"
"HA HA HA! OF COURSE, YOU DUMMY!"
You guys really love me, don't you?!
HA HA HA!
...
...
WHAT IS THAT IDIOT DOING?
CLANG CLANG♫
BANG CLANG♪

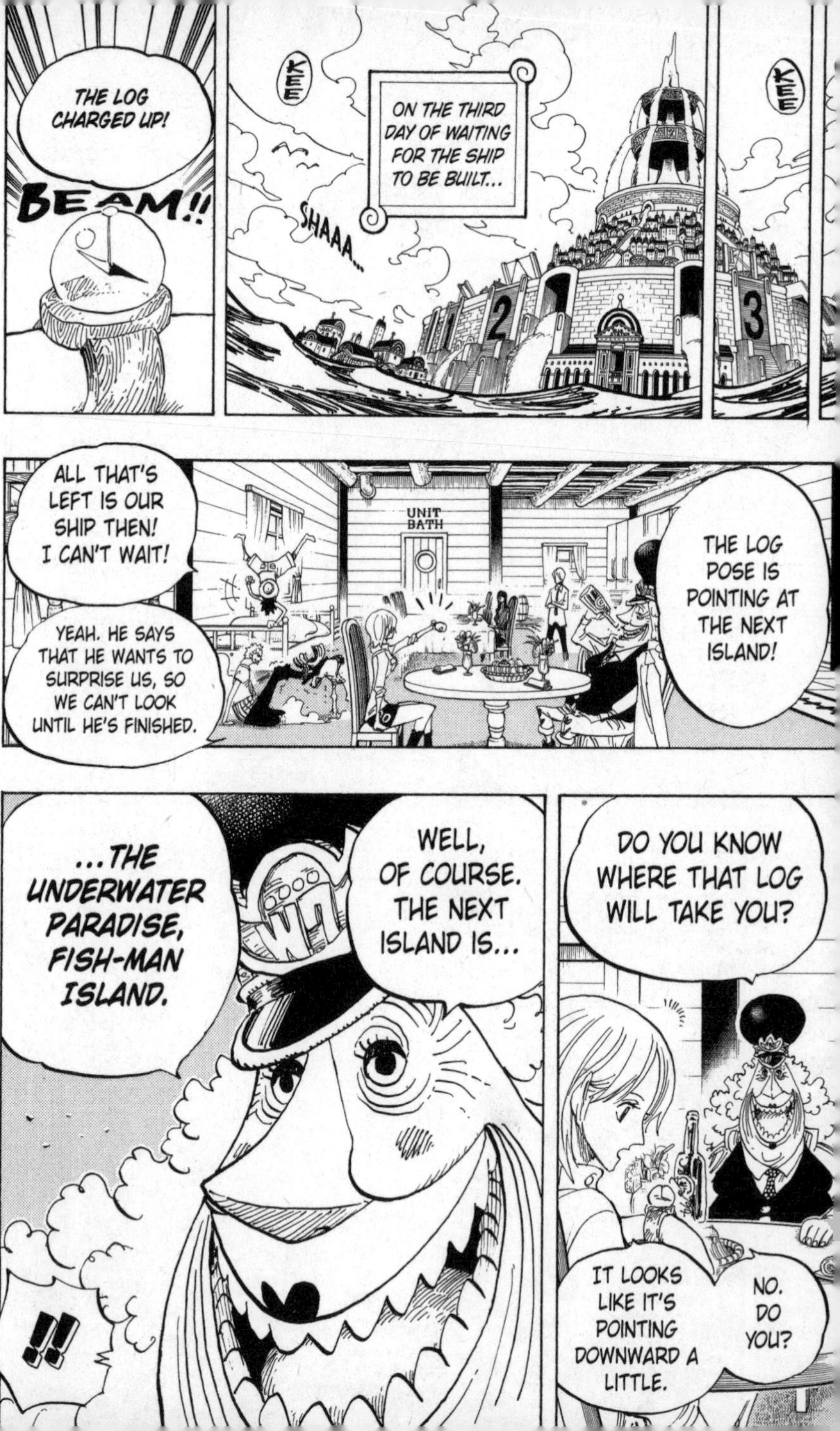
KEE
KEE
ON THE THIRD DAY OF WAITING FOR THE SHIP TO BE BUILT...
SHAAA...
THE LOG CHARGED UP!
BEAM!!
THE LOG POSE IS POINTING AT THE NEXT ISLAND!
UNIT BATH
ALL THAT'S LEFT IS OUR SHIP THEN! I CAN'T WAIT!
YEAH. HE SAYS THAT HE WANTS TO SURPRISE US, SO WE CAN'T LOOK UNTIL HE'S FINISHED.
DO YOU KNOW WHERE THAT LOG WILL TAKE YOU?
NO. DO YOU?
IT LOOKS LIKE IT'S POINTING DOWNWARD A LITTLE.
WELL, OF COURSE. THE NEXT ISLAND IS...
...THE UNDERWATER PARADISE, FISH-MAN ISLAND.
!!

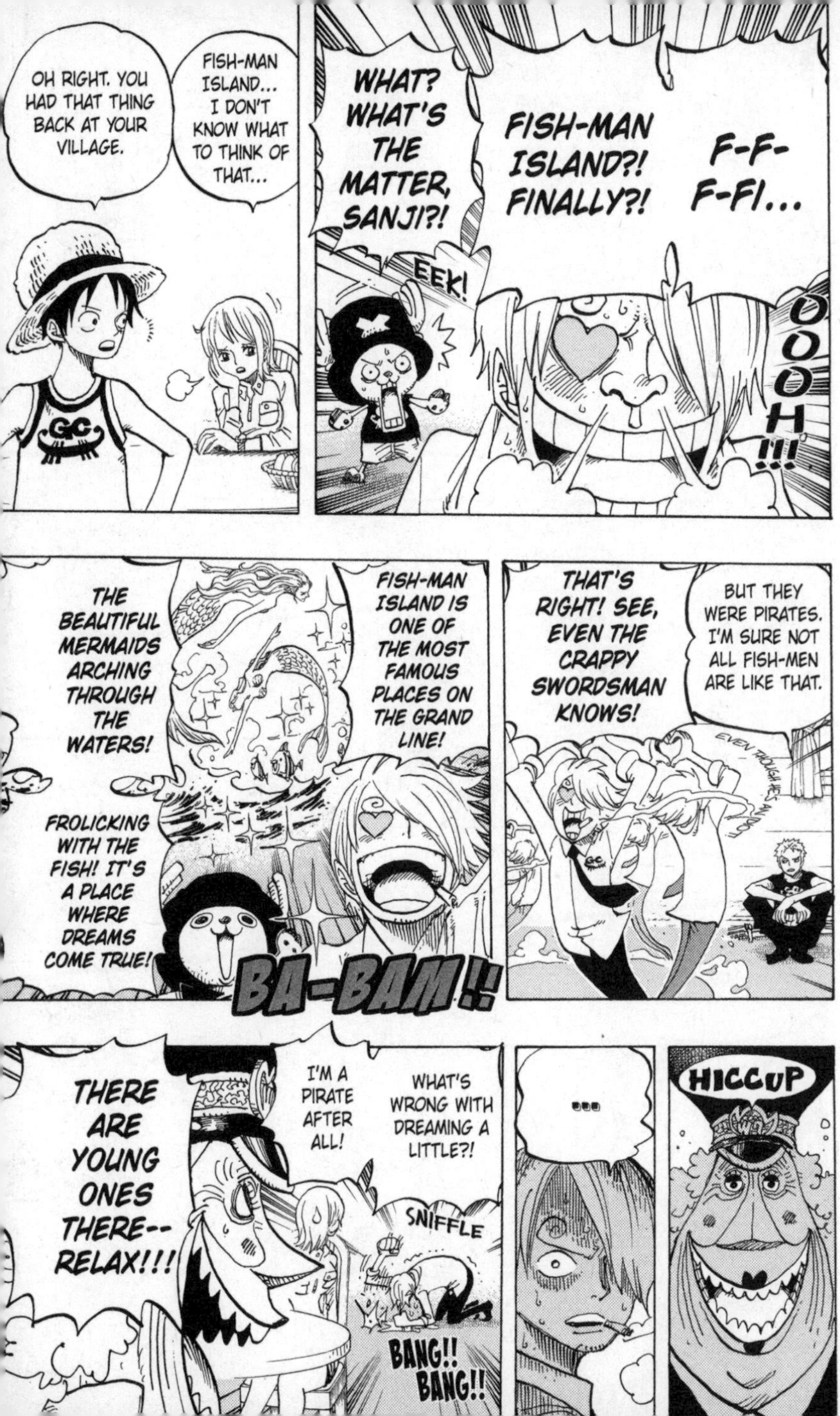
F-F-F-FI...
FISH-MAN ISLAND?! FINALLY?!
OOOOH!!!
WHAT? WHAT'S THE MATTER, SANJI?!
EEK!
FISH-MAN ISLAND... I DON'T KNOW WHAT TO THINK OF THAT...
OH RIGHT. YOU HAD THAT THING BACK AT YOUR VILLAGE.
BUT THEY WERE PIRATES. I'M SURE NOT ALL FISH-MEN ARE LIKE THAT.
THAT'S RIGHT! SEE, EVEN THE CRAPPY SWORDSMAN KNOWS!
EVEN THOUGH HE'S AN IDIOT!
FISH-MAN ISLAND IS ONE OF THE MOST FAMOUS PLACES ON THE GRAND LINE!
THE BEAUTIFUL MERMAIDS ARCHING THROUGH THE WATERS!
FROLICKING WITH THE FISH! IT'S A PLACE WHERE DREAMS COME TRUE!
BA-BAM!!
HICCUP
...
WHAT'S WRONG WITH DREAMING A LITTLE?!
I'M A PIRATE AFTER ALL!
SNIFFLE
BANG!! BANG!!
THERE ARE YOUNG ONES THERE-- RELAX!!!

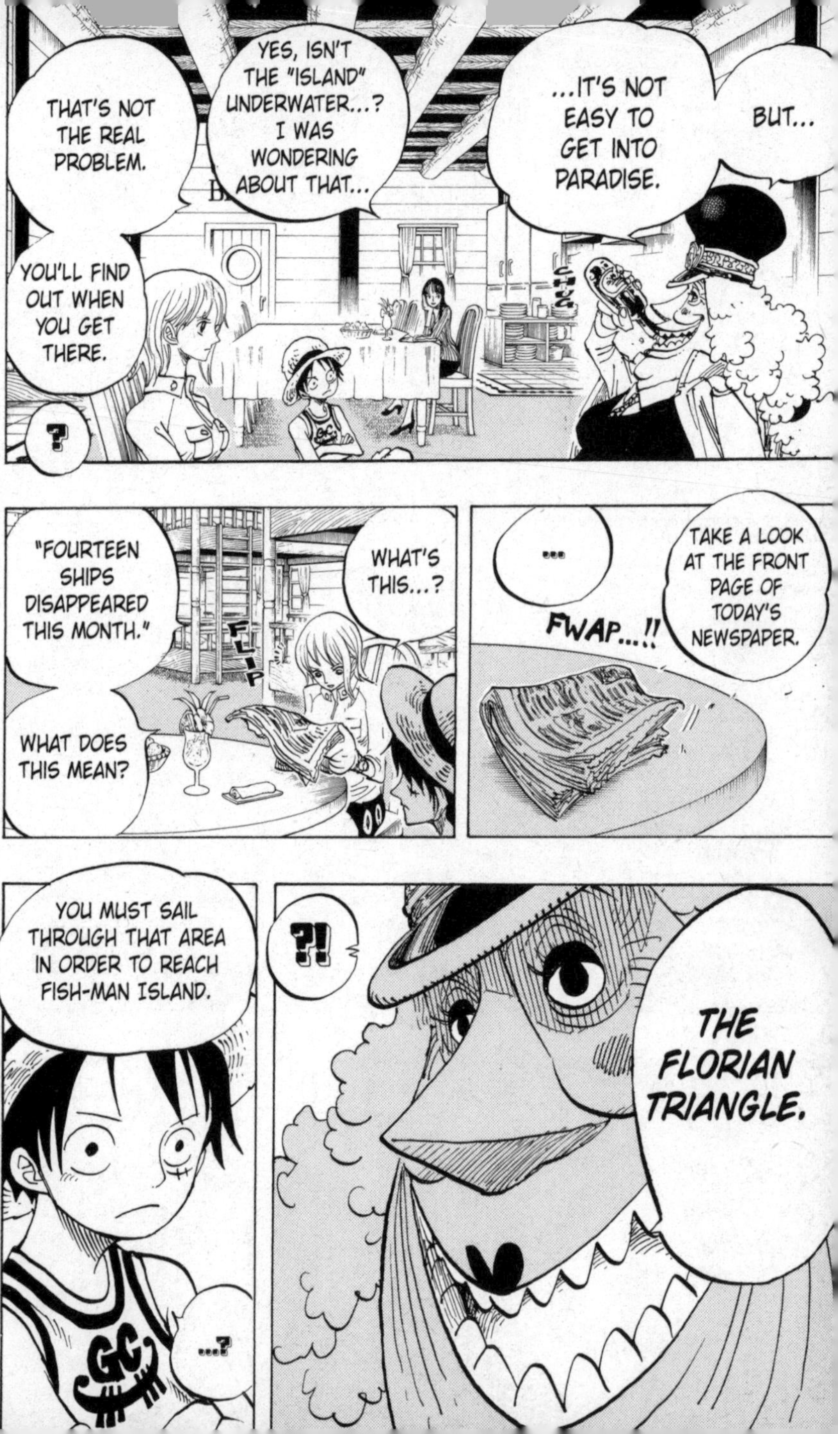
BUT...
...IT'S NOT EASY TO GET INTO PARADISE.
YES, ISN'T THE "ISLAND" UNDERWATER...? I WAS WONDERING ABOUT THAT...
THAT'S NOT THE REAL PROBLEM.
CHUG
YOU'LL FIND OUT WHEN YOU GET THERE.
?
TAKE A LOOK AT THE FRONT PAGE OF TODAY'S NEWSPAPER.
...
FWAP...!!
WHAT'S THIS...?
"FOURTEEN SHIPS DISAPPEARED THIS MONTH."
FLIP
WHAT DOES THIS MEAN?
THE FLORIAN TRIANGLE.
?!
YOU MUST SAIL THROUGH THAT AREA IN ORDER TO REACH FISH-MAN ISLAND.
...?

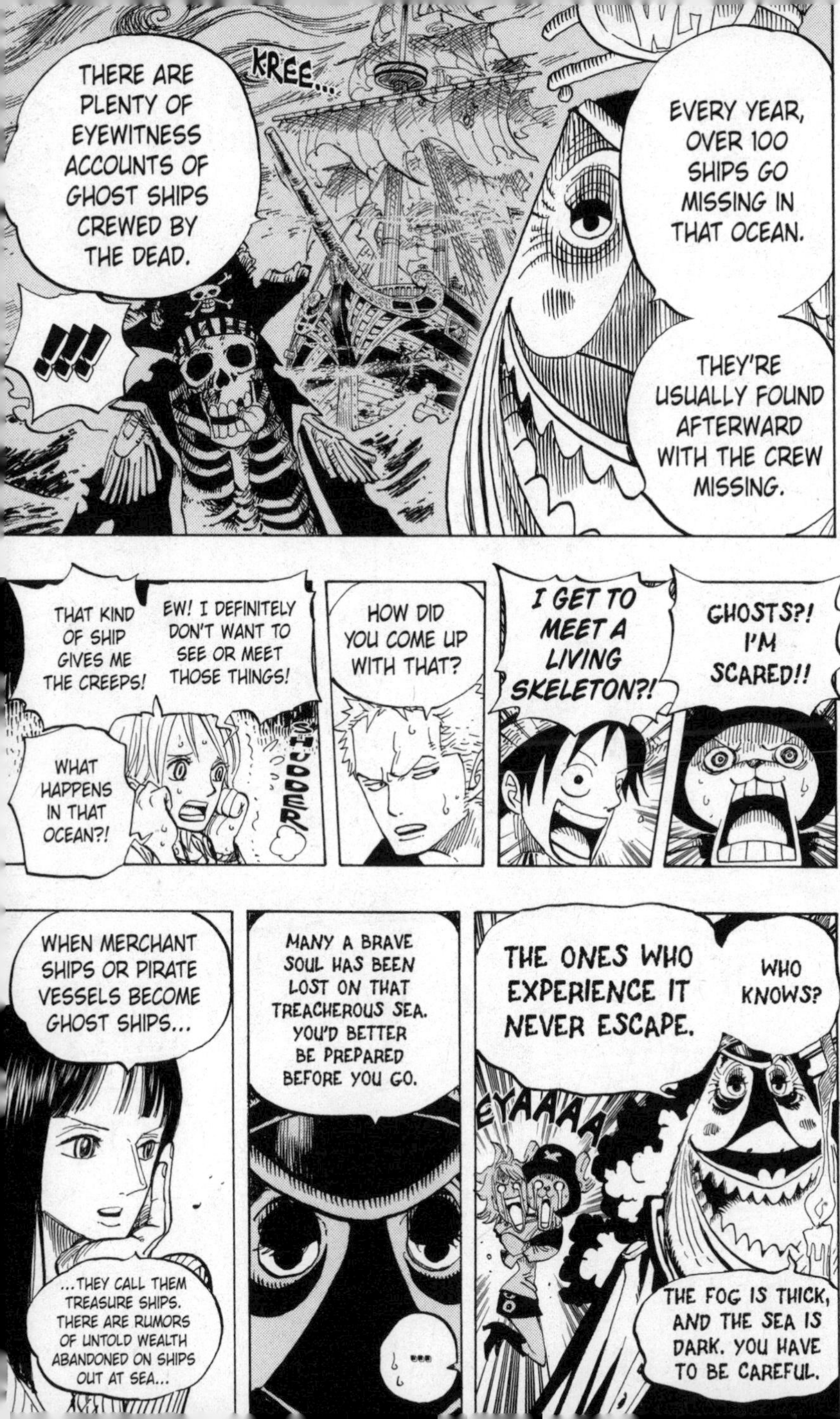
EVERY YEAR, OVER 100 SHIPS GO MISSING IN THAT OCEAN.
THEY'RE USUALLY FOUND AFTERWARD WITH THE CREW MISSING.
KREE...
THERE ARE PLENTY OF EYEWITNESS ACCOUNTS OF GHOST SHIPS CREWED BY THE DEAD.
!!!
GHOSTS?! I'M SCARED!!
I GET TO MEET A LIVING SKELETON?!
HOW DID YOU COME UP WITH THAT?
EW! I DEFINITELY DON'T WANT TO SEE OR MEET THOSE THINGS!
THAT KIND OF SHIP GIVES ME THE CREEPS!
SHUDDER
WHAT HAPPENS IN THAT OCEAN?!
WHO KNOWS?
THE ONES WHO EXPERIENCE IT NEVER ESCAPE.
EYAAAA
THE FOG IS THICK, AND THE SEA IS DARK. YOU HAVE TO BE CAREFUL.
MANY A BRAVE SOUL HAS BEEN LOST ON THAT TREACHEROUS SEA. YOU'D BETTER BE PREPARED BEFORE YOU GO.
...
WHEN MERCHANT SHIPS OR PIRATE VESSELS BECOME GHOST SHIPS...
...THEY CALL THEM TREASURE SHIPS. THERE ARE RUMORS OF UNTOLD WEALTH ABANDONED ON SHIPS OUT AT SEA...

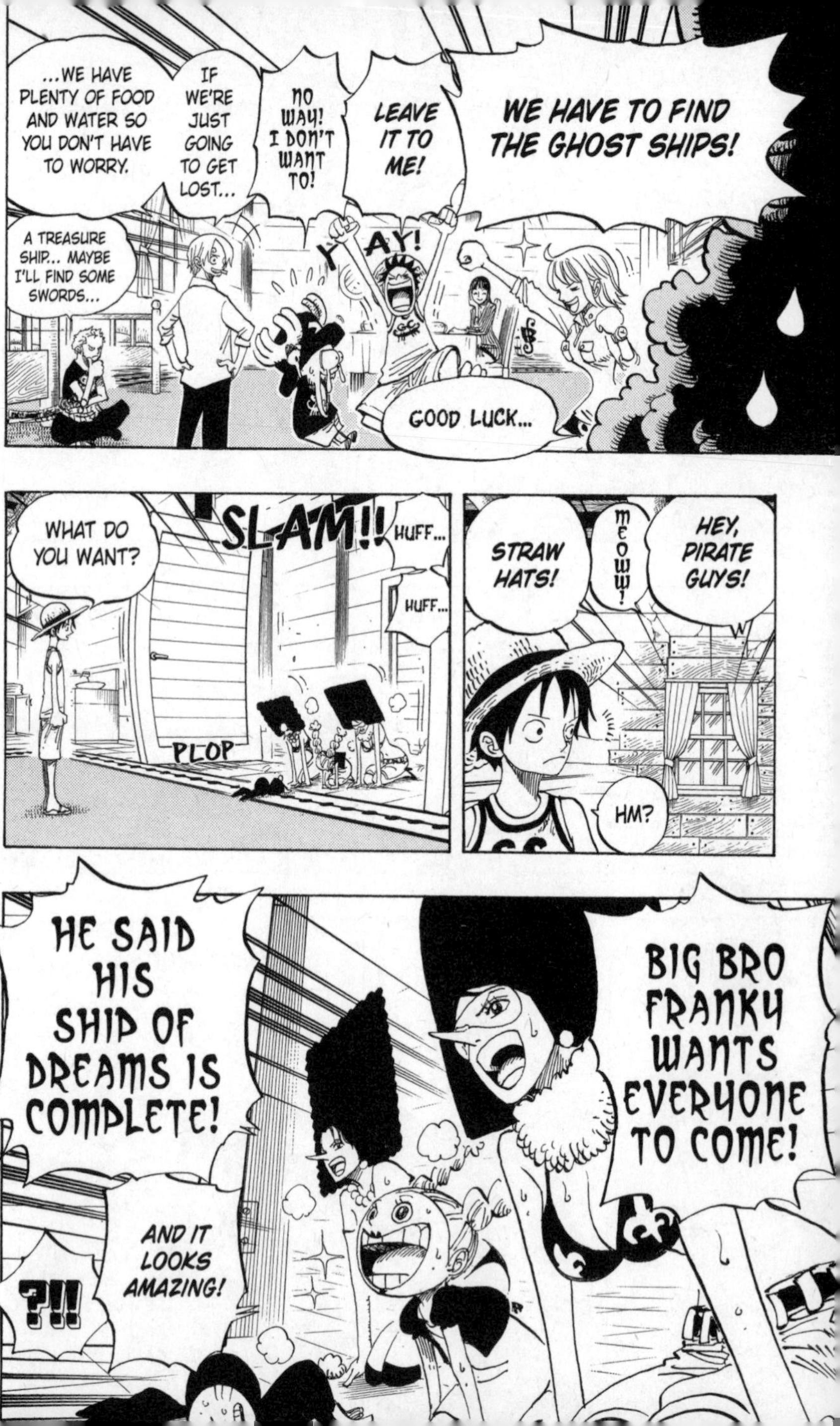
WE HAVE TO FIND THE GHOST SHIPS!
LEAVE IT TO ME!
NO WAY! I DON'T WANT TO!
IF WE'RE JUST GOING TO GET LOST...
...WE HAVE PLENTY OF FOOD AND WATER SO YOU DON'T HAVE TO WORRY.
YAY!
A TREASURE SHIP... MAYBE I'LL FIND SOME SWORDS...
GOOD LUCK...
HEY, PIRATE GUYS!
MEOWW!
STRAW HATS!
HM?
HUFF...
HUFF...
SLAM!!
WHAT DO YOU WANT?
PLOP
BIG BRO FRANKY WANTS EVERYONE TO COME!
HE SAID HIS SHIP OF DREAMS IS COMPLETE!
AND IT LOOKS AMAZING!
?!!

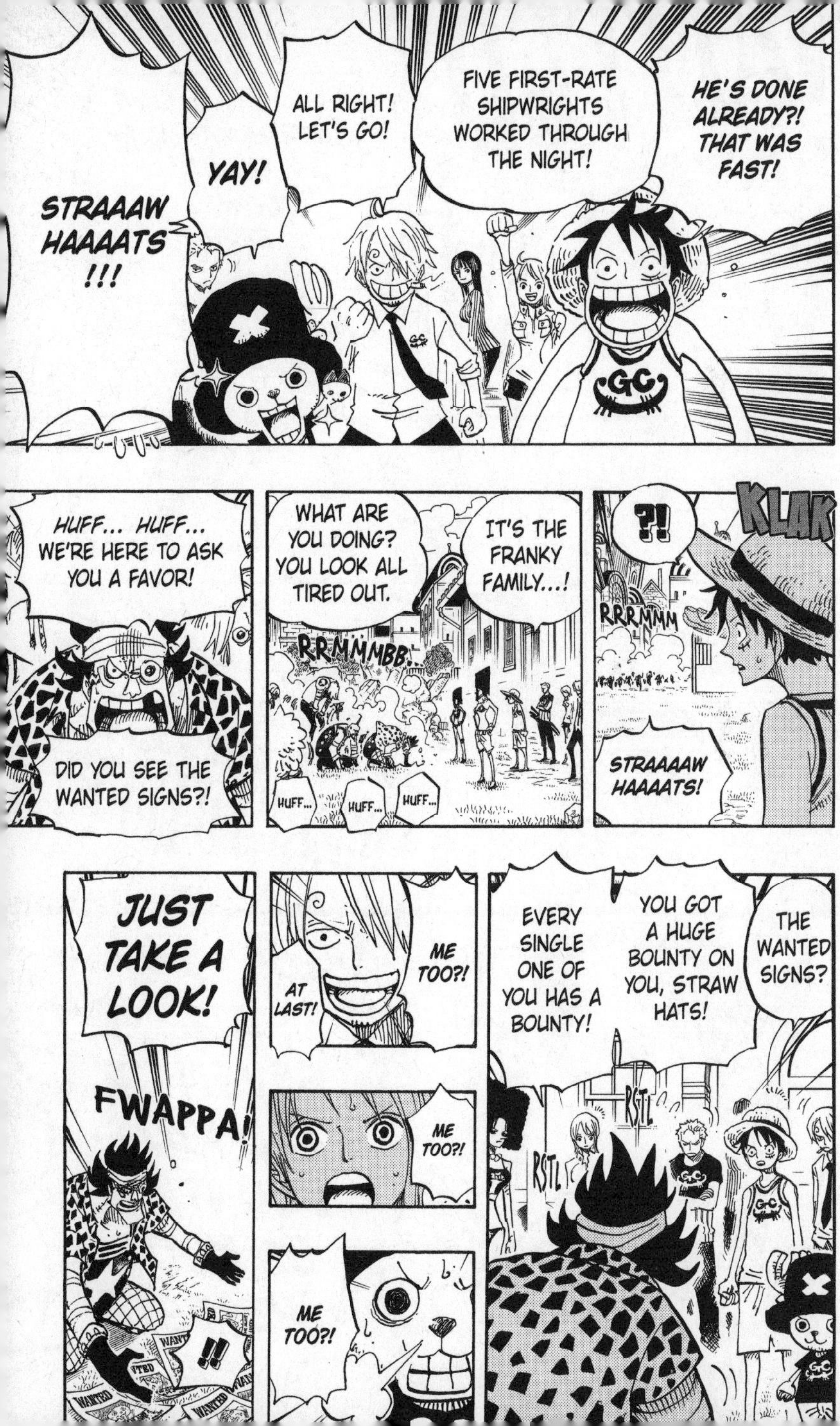
HE'S DONE ALREADY?! THAT WAS FAST!
FIVE FIRST-RATE SHIPWRIGHTS WORKED THROUGH THE NIGHT!
ALL RIGHT! LET'S GO!
YAY!
STRAAAW HAAAATS!!!
KLAK
?!
RRRMMM
STRAAAAW HAAAATS!
IT'S THE FRANKY FAMILY...!
WHAT ARE YOU DOING? YOU LOOK ALL TIRED OUT.
RRMMMBB..
HUFF...
HUFF...
HUFF...
HUFF... HUFF... WE'RE HERE TO ASK YOU A FAVOR!
DID YOU SEE THE WANTED SIGNS?!
THE WANTED SIGNS?
YOU GOT A HUGE BOUNTY ON YOU, STRAW HATS!
EVERY SINGLE ONE OF YOU HAS A BOUNTY!
RSTL
RSTL
ME TOO?!
AT LAST!
ME TOO?!
ME TOO?!
JUST TAKE A LOOK!
FWAPPA
!!

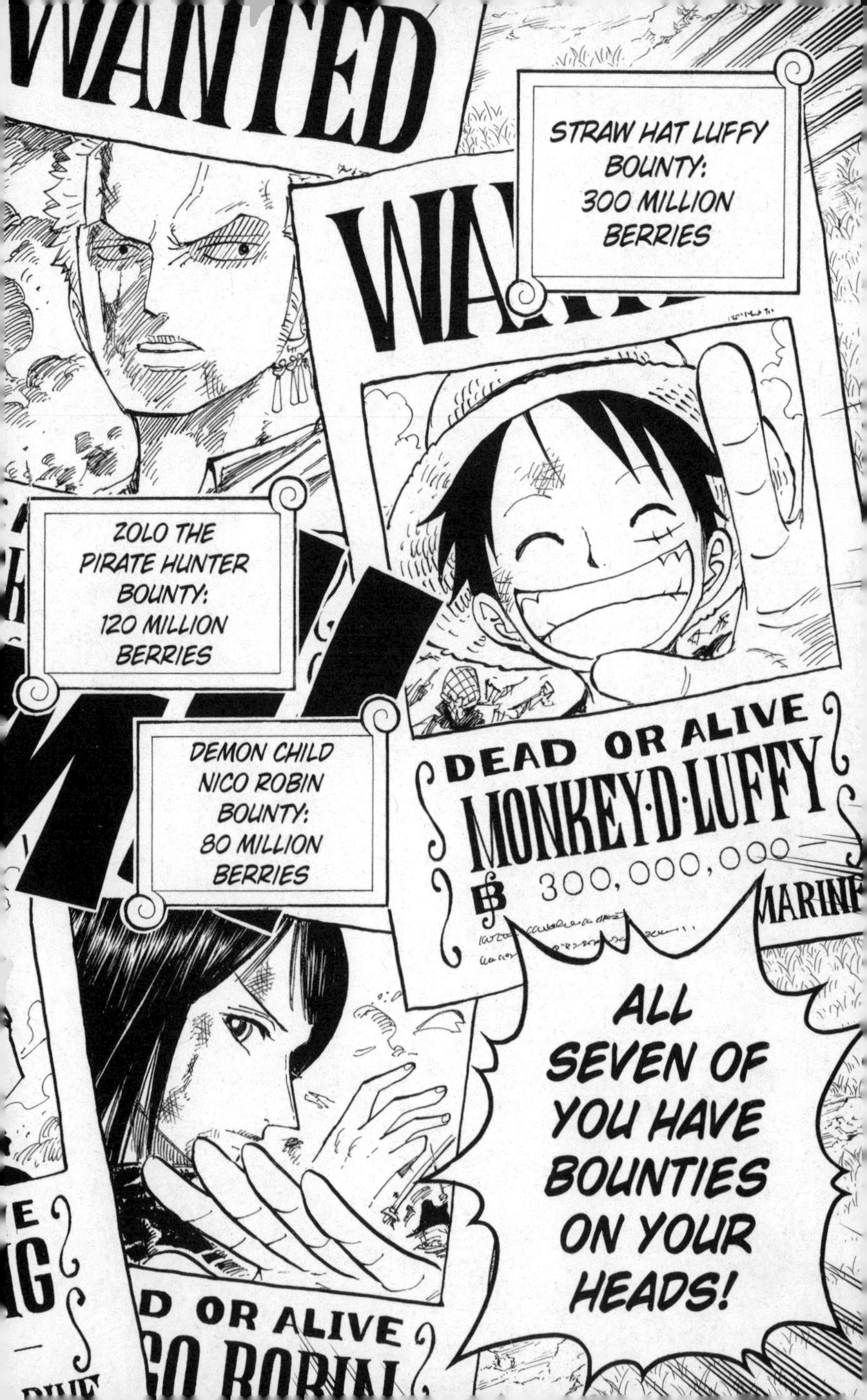
STRAW HAT LUFFY BOUNTY: 300 MILLION BERRIES
ZOLO THE PIRATE HUNTER BOUNTY: 120 MILLION BERRIES
DEMON CHILD NICO ROBIN BOUNTY: 80 MILLION BERRIES
WANTED
DEAD OR ALIVE
MONKEY·D·LUFFY
฿ 300,000,000
DEAD OR ALIVE
ALL SEVEN OF YOU HAVE BOUNTIES ON YOUR HEADS!

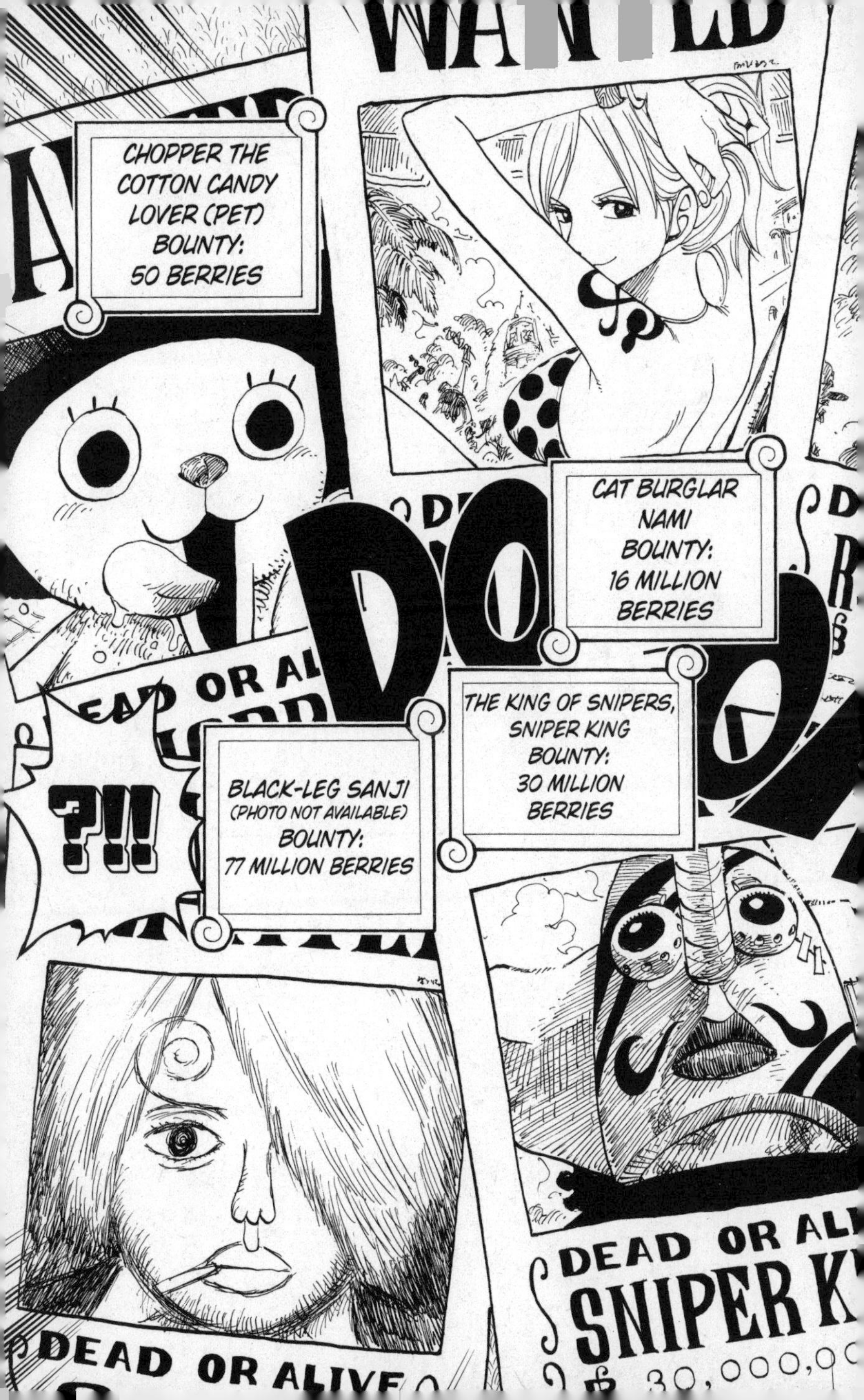
CAT BURGLAR NAMI BOUNTY: 16 MILLION BERRIES
CHOPPER THE COTTON CANDY LOVER (PET) BOUNTY: 50 BERRIES
DO
THE KING OF SNIPERS, SNIPER KING BOUNTY: 30 MILLION BERRIES
BLACK-LEG SANJI (PHOTO NOT AVAILABLE) BOUNTY: 77 MILLION BERRIES
?!!
DEAD OR ALIVE

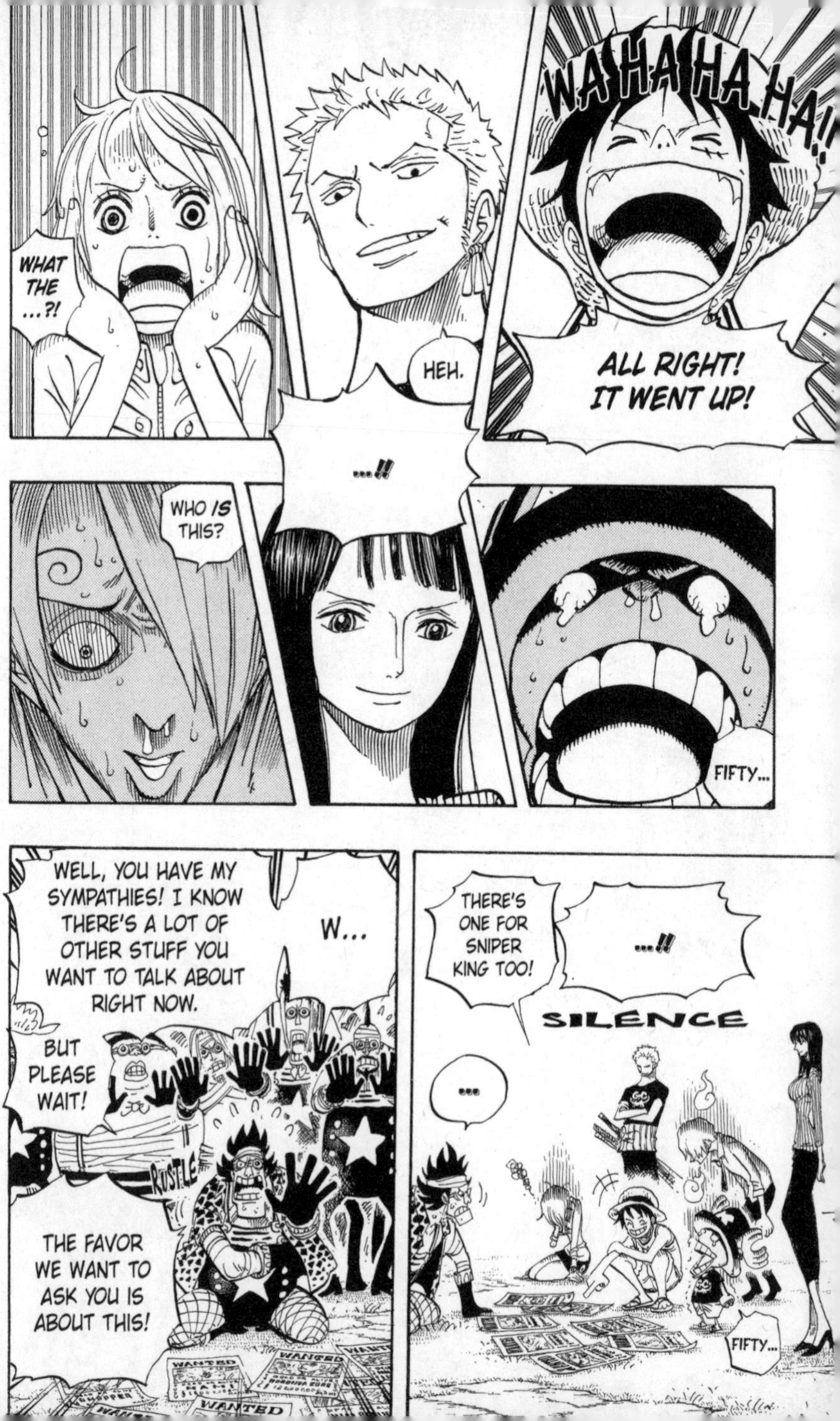
WA HA HA HA!!
ALL RIGHT! IT WENT UP!
HEH.
WHAT THE ...?!
...!!
FIFTY...
WHO IS THIS?
...!!
THERE'S ONE FOR SNIPER KING TOO!
SILENCE
...
FIFTY...
W...
WELL, YOU HAVE MY SYMPATHIES! I KNOW THERE'S A LOT OF OTHER STUFF YOU WANT TO TALK ABOUT RIGHT NOW.
BUT PLEASE WAIT!
RUSTLE
THE FAVOR WE WANT TO ASK YOU IS ABOUT THIS!
WANTED

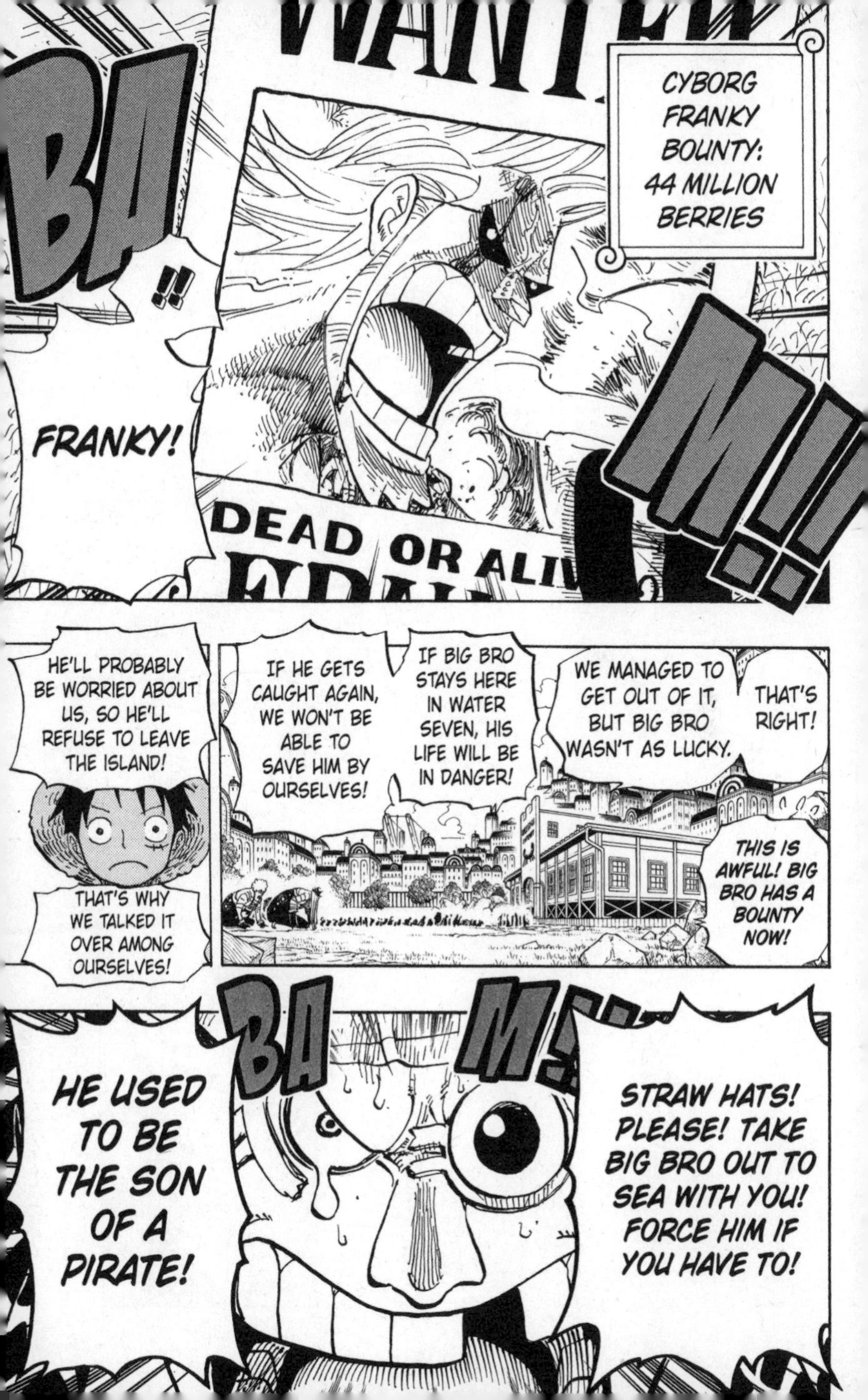
CYBORG FRANKY BOUNTY: 44 MILLION BERRIES
DEAD OR ALIV
M!!
BA!!
FRANKY!
THAT'S RIGHT!
WE MANAGED TO GET OUT OF IT, BUT BIG BRO WASN'T AS LUCKY.
IF BIG BRO STAYS HERE IN WATER SEVEN, HIS LIFE WILL BE IN DANGER!
IF HE GETS CAUGHT AGAIN, WE WON'T BE ABLE TO SAVE HIM BY OURSELVES!
THIS IS AWFUL! BIG BRO HAS A BOUNTY NOW!
HE'LL PROBABLY BE WORRIED ABOUT US, SO HE'LL REFUSE TO LEAVE THE ISLAND!
THAT'S WHY WE TALKED IT OVER AMONG OURSELVES!
BA
STRAW HATS! PLEASE! TAKE BIG BRO OUT TO SEA WITH YOU! FORCE HIM IF YOU HAVE TO!
HE USED TO BE THE SON OF A PIRATE!

Chapter 436:
TRUNKS FROM FRANKY HOUSE

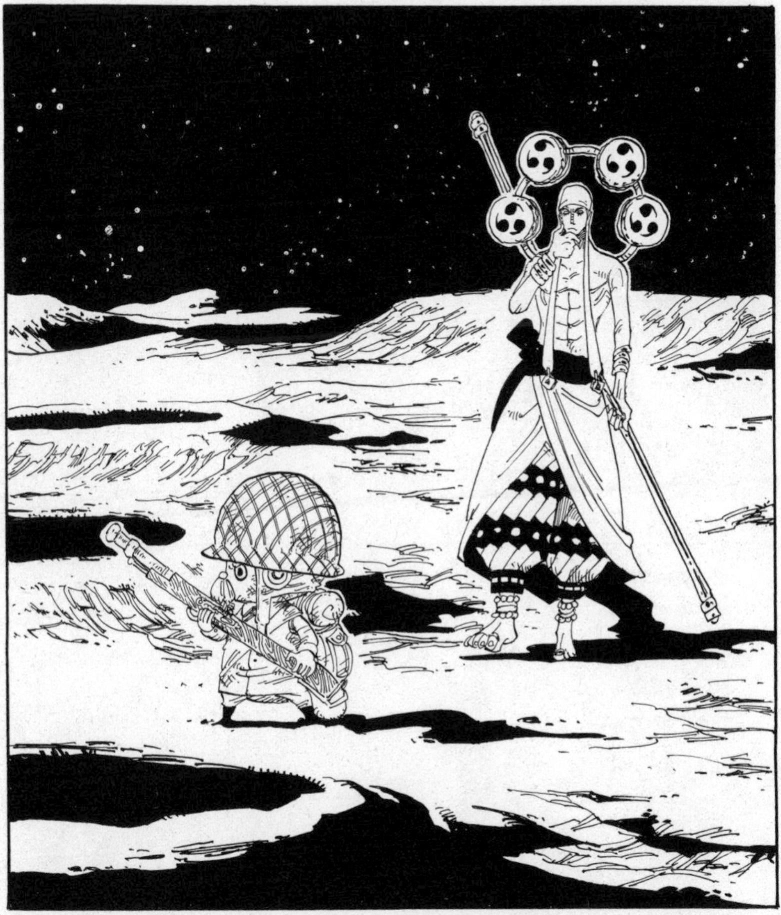

ENERU'S GREAT SPACE MISSION, VOL. 7:
"LIEUTENANT SPACEY REGRETS GOING AWOL"

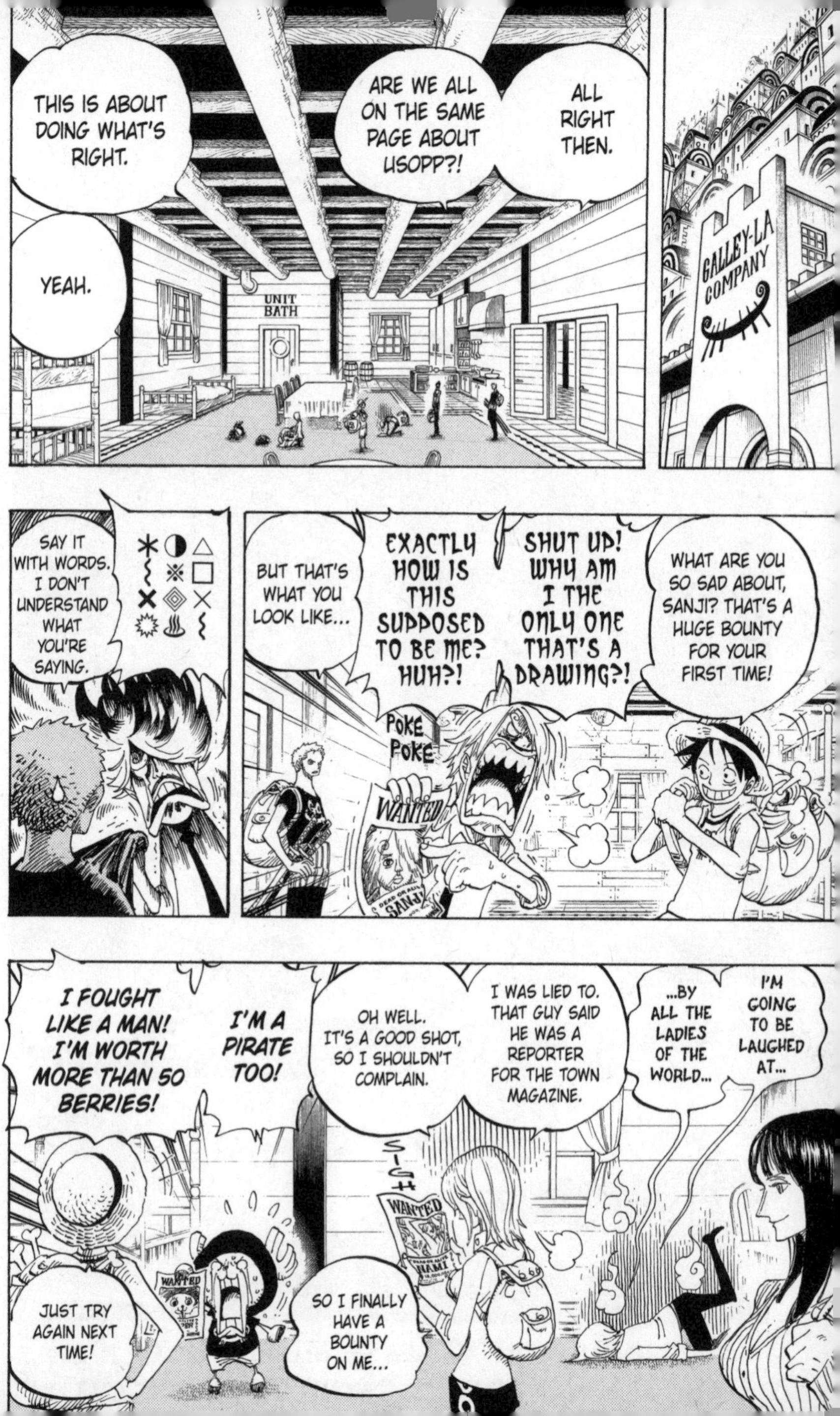
GALLEY-LA COMPANY
ALL RIGHT THEN.
ARE WE ALL ON THE SAME PAGE ABOUT USOPP?!
THIS IS ABOUT DOING WHAT'S RIGHT.
YEAH.
UNIT BATH
WHAT ARE YOU SO SAD ABOUT, SANJI? THAT'S A HUGE BOUNTY FOR YOUR FIRST TIME!
SHUT UP! WHY AM I THE ONLY ONE THAT'S A DRAWING?!
EXACTLY HOW IS THIS SUPPOSED TO BE ME? HUH?!
BUT THAT'S WHAT YOU LOOK LIKE...
POKE POKE
WANTED
SANJI
SAY IT WITH WORDS. I DON'T UNDERSTAND WHAT YOU'RE SAYING.
I'M GOING TO BE LAUGHED AT...
...BY ALL THE LADIES OF THE WORLD...
I WAS LIED TO. THAT GUY SAID HE WAS A REPORTER FOR THE TOWN MAGAZINE.
OH WELL. IT'S A GOOD SHOT, SO I SHOULDN'T COMPLAIN.
SIGH
WANTED
NAMI
SO I FINALLY HAVE A BOUNTY ON ME...
I'M A PIRATE TOO!
I FOUGHT LIKE A MAN! I'M WORTH MORE THAN 50 BERRIES!
WANTED
JUST TRY AGAIN NEXT TIME!

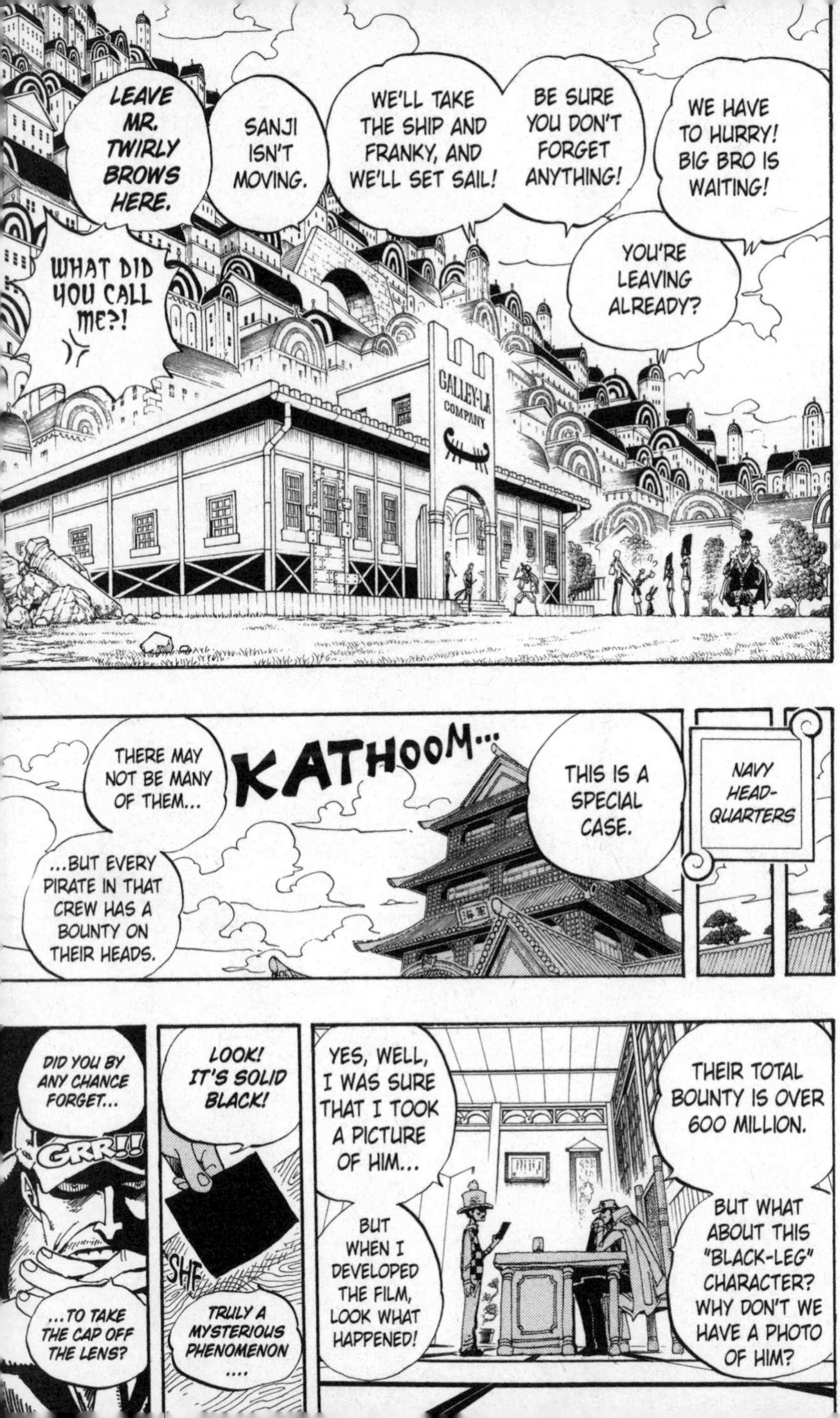
WE HAVE TO HURRY! BIG BRO IS WAITING!
YOU'RE LEAVING ALREADY?
BE SURE YOU DON'T FORGET ANYTHING!
WE'LL TAKE THE SHIP AND FRANKY, AND WE'LL SET SAIL!
SANJI ISN'T MOVING.
LEAVE MR. TWIRLY BROWS HERE.
WHAT DID YOU CALL ME?!
GALLEY-LA COMPANY
NAVY HEADQUARTERS
THIS IS A SPECIAL CASE.
KATHOOM...
THERE MAY NOT BE MANY OF THEM...
...BUT EVERY PIRATE IN THAT CREW HAS A BOUNTY ON THEIR HEADS.
THEIR TOTAL BOUNTY IS OVER 600 MILLION.
BUT WHAT ABOUT THIS "BLACK-LEG" CHARACTER? WHY DON'T WE HAVE A PHOTO OF HIM?
YES, WELL, I WAS SURE THAT I TOOK A PICTURE OF HIM...
BUT WHEN I DEVELOPED THE FILM, LOOK WHAT HAPPENED!
LOOK! IT'S SOLID BLACK!
SHF
TRULY A MYSTERIOUS PHENOMENON ....
DID YOU BY ANY CHANCE FORGET...
GRR!!
...TO TAKE THE CAP OFF THE LENS?

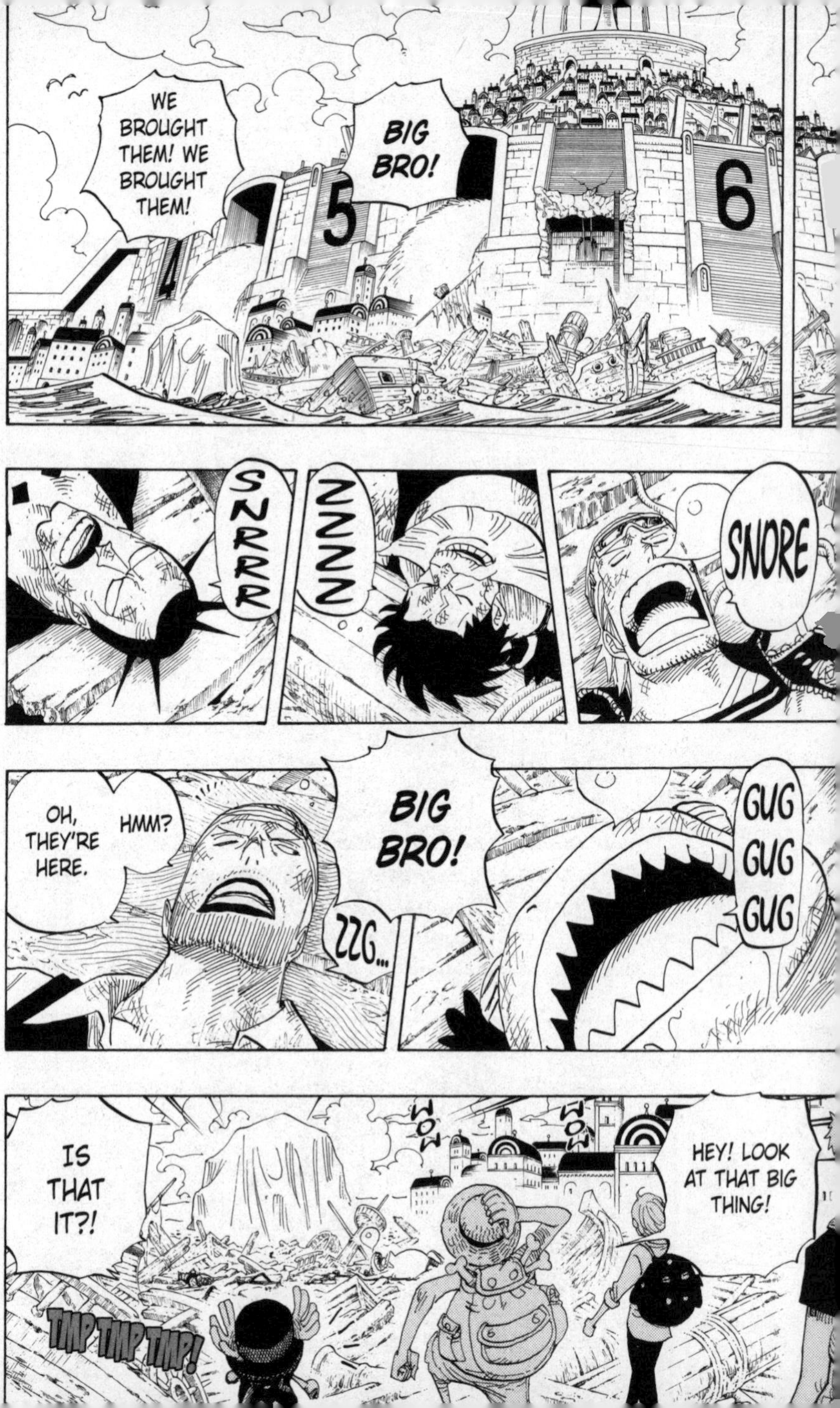
BIG BRO!
WE BROUGHT THEM! WE BROUGHT THEM!
SNORE
ZZZZZ
SNRRR
GUG GUG GUG
BIG BRO!
ZZG...
HMM?
OH, THEY'RE HERE.
HEY! LOOK AT THAT BIG THING!
WOW
WOW
IS THAT IT?!
TMP TMP TMP!

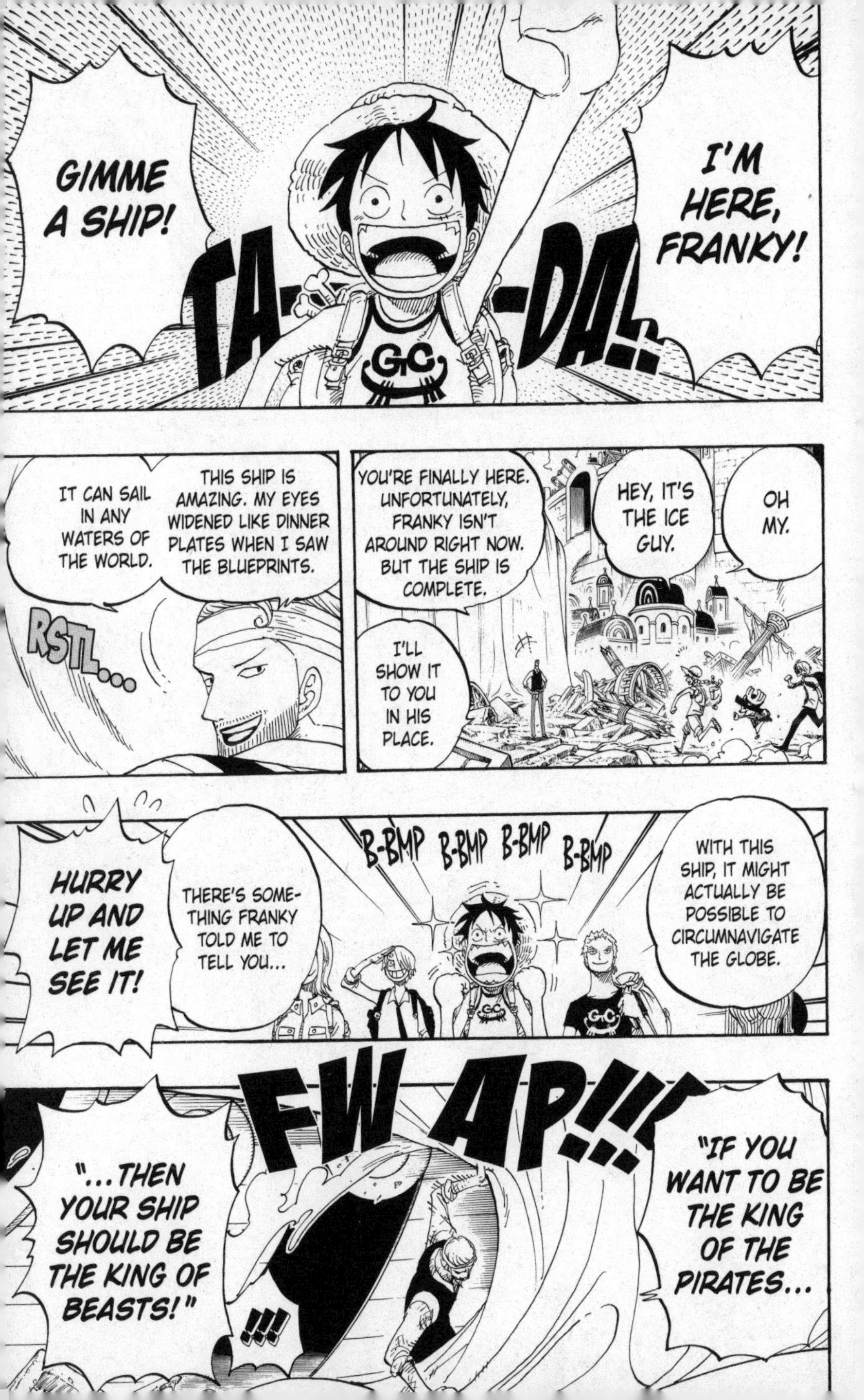
I'M HERE, FRANKY!
TA-DA!!
GIMME A SHIP!
OH MY.
HEY, IT'S THE ICE GUY.
YOU'RE FINALLY HERE. UNFORTUNATELY, FRANKY ISN'T AROUND RIGHT NOW. BUT THE SHIP IS COMPLETE.
I'LL SHOW IT TO YOU IN HIS PLACE.
THIS SHIP IS AMAZING. MY EYES WIDENED LIKE DINNER PLATES WHEN I SAW THE BLUEPRINTS.
IT CAN SAIL IN ANY WATERS OF THE WORLD.
RSTL...
WITH THIS SHIP, IT MIGHT ACTUALLY BE POSSIBLE TO CIRCUMNAVIGATE THE GLOBE.
B-BMP B-BMP B-BMP B-BMP
THERE'S SOME-THING FRANKY TOLD ME TO TELL YOU...
HURRY UP AND LET ME SEE IT!
"IF YOU WANT TO BE THE KING OF THE PIRATES...
FWAP!!!
"...THEN YOUR SHIP SHOULD BE THE KING OF BEASTS!"
!!!

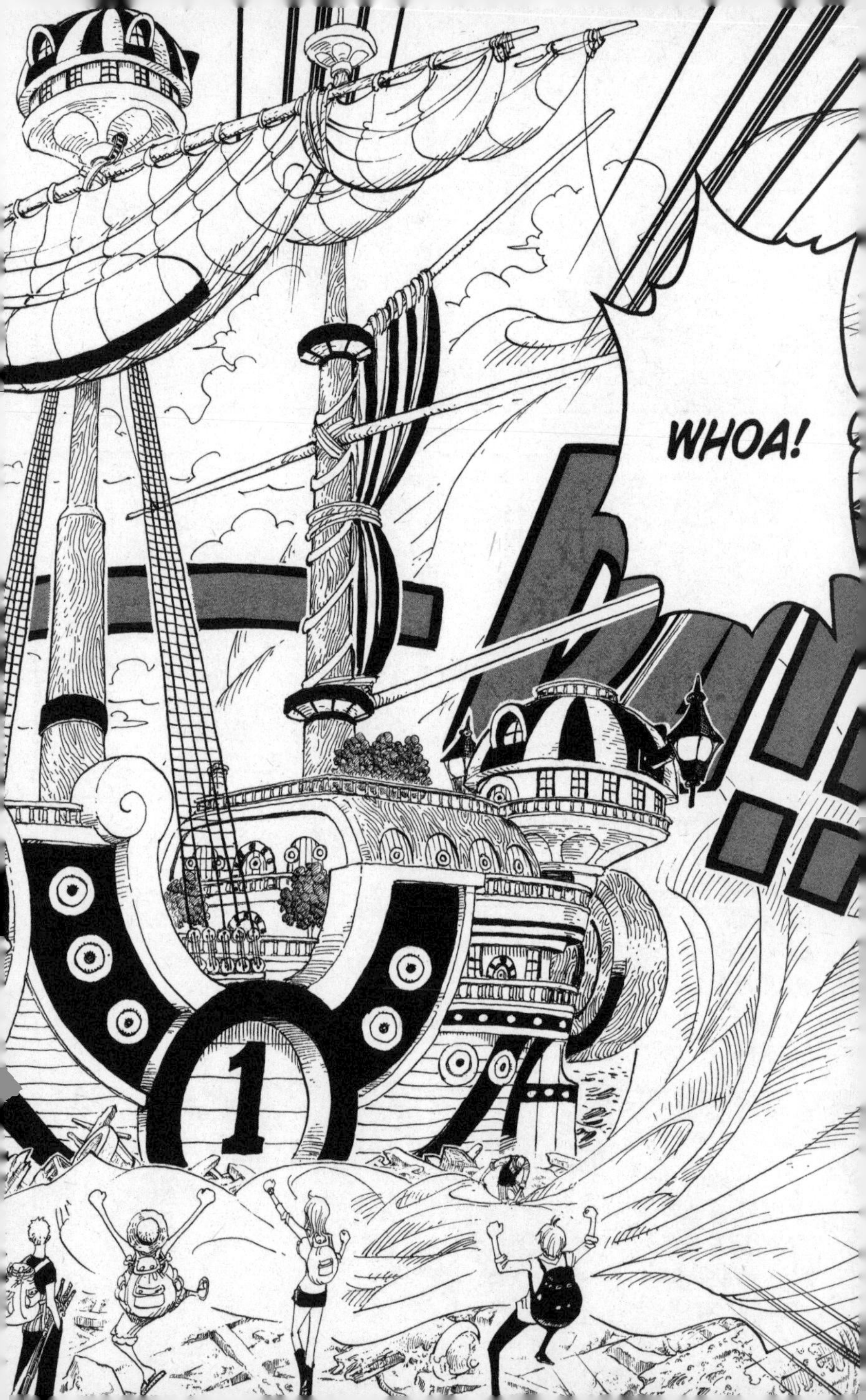
WHOA!

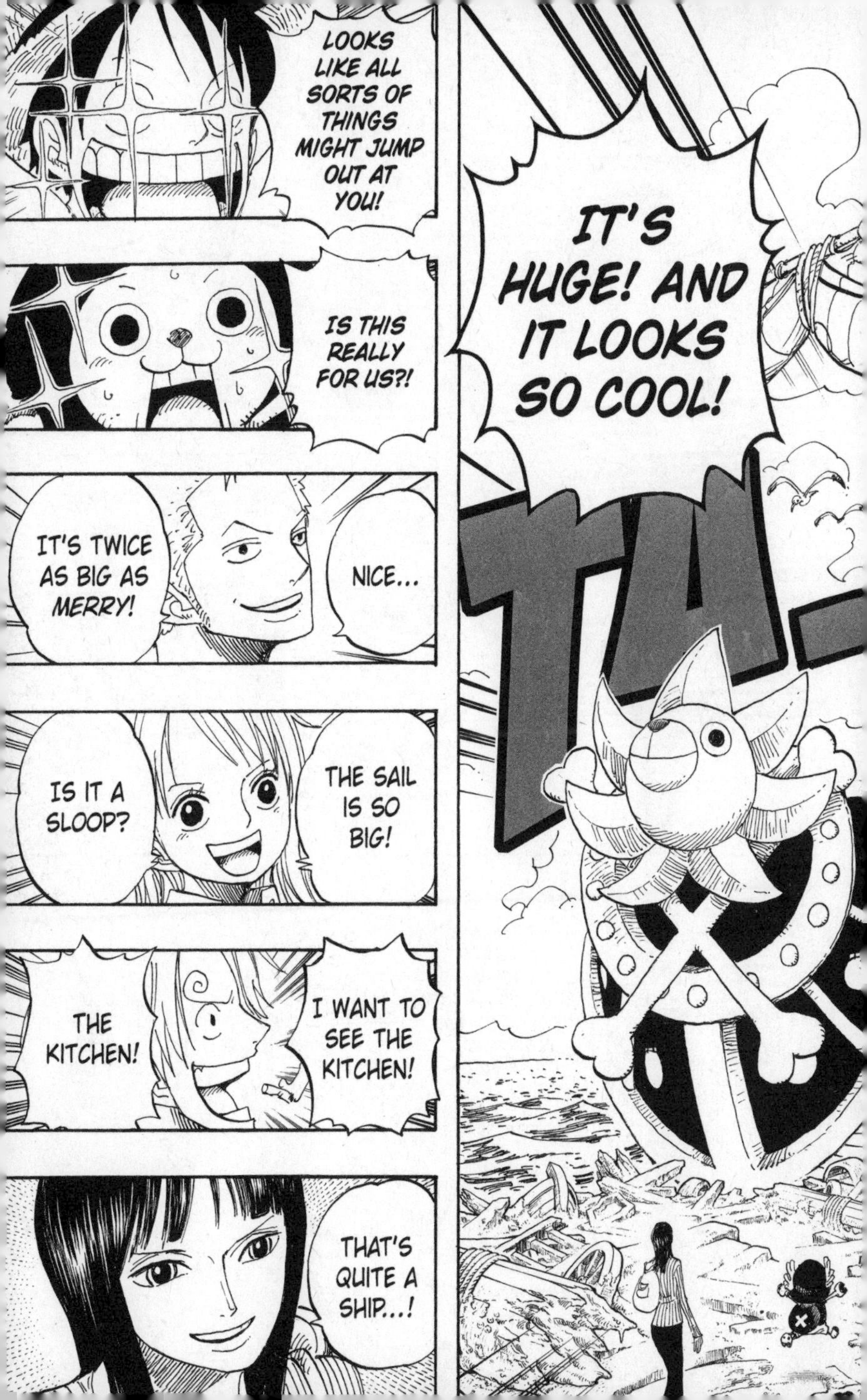
IT'S HUGE! AND IT LOOKS SO COOL!
LOOKS LIKE ALL SORTS OF THINGS MIGHT JUMP OUT AT YOU!
IS THIS REALLY FOR US?!
NICE...
IT'S TWICE AS BIG AS MERRY!
THE SAIL IS SO BIG!
IS IT A SLOOP?
I WANT TO SEE THE KITCHEN!
THE KITCHEN!
THAT'S QUITE A SHIP...!

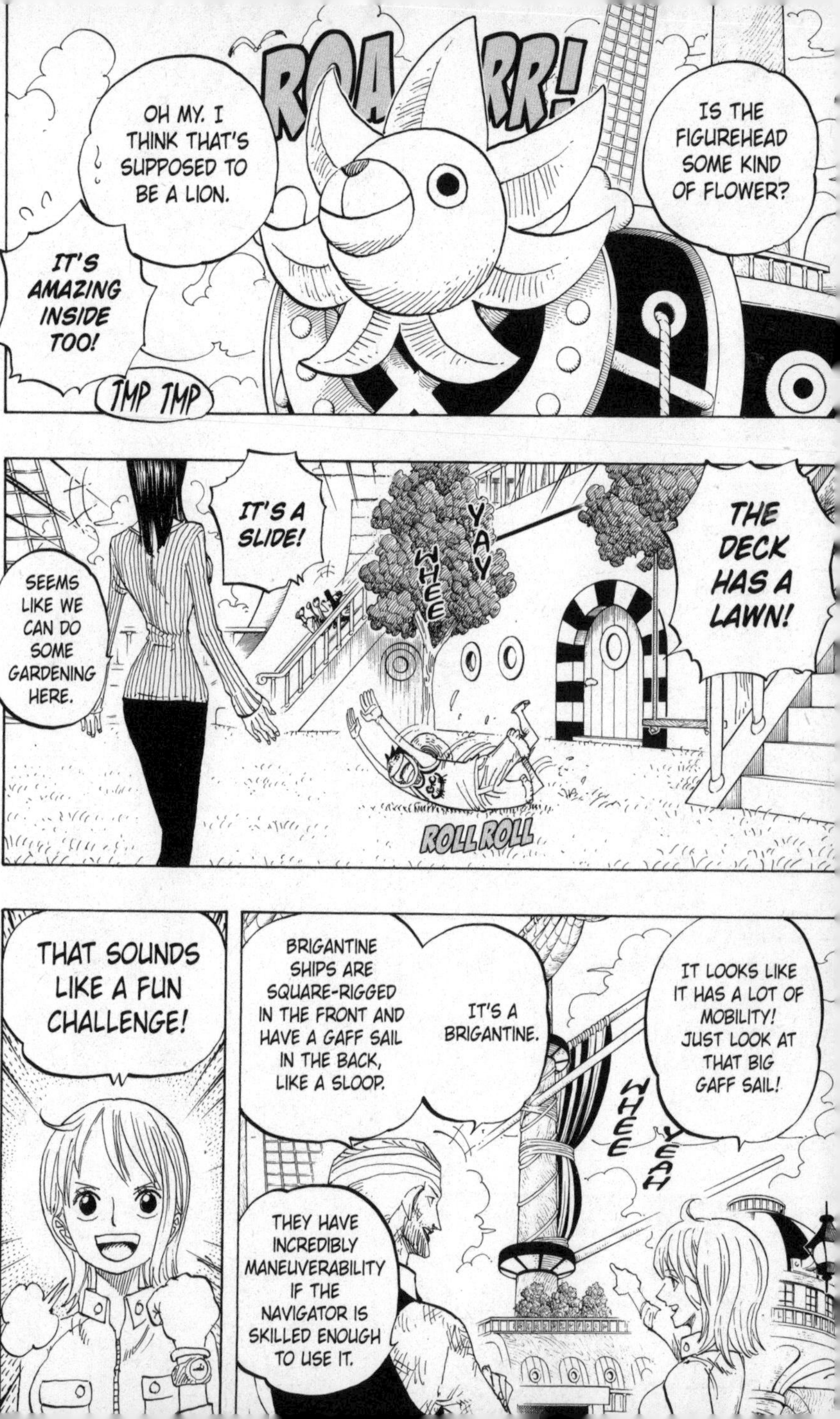
IS THE FIGUREHEAD SOME KIND OF FLOWER?
ROA RR!
OH MY. I THINK THAT'S SUPPOSED TO BE A LION.
IT'S AMAZING INSIDE TOO!
TMP TMP
THE DECK HAS A LAWN!
YAY
WHEE
IT'S A SLIDE!
SEEMS LIKE WE CAN DO SOME GARDENING HERE.
ROLL ROLL
IT LOOKS LIKE IT HAS A LOT OF MOBILITY! JUST LOOK AT THAT BIG GAFF SAIL!
YEAH
WHEE
IT'S A BRIGANTINE.
BRIGANTINE SHIPS ARE SQUARE-RIGGED IN THE FRONT AND HAVE A GAFF SAIL IN THE BACK, LIKE A SLOOP.
THEY HAVE INCREDIBLY MANEUVERABILITY IF THE NAVIGATOR IS SKILLED ENOUGH TO USE IT.
THAT SOUNDS LIKE A FUN CHALLENGE!

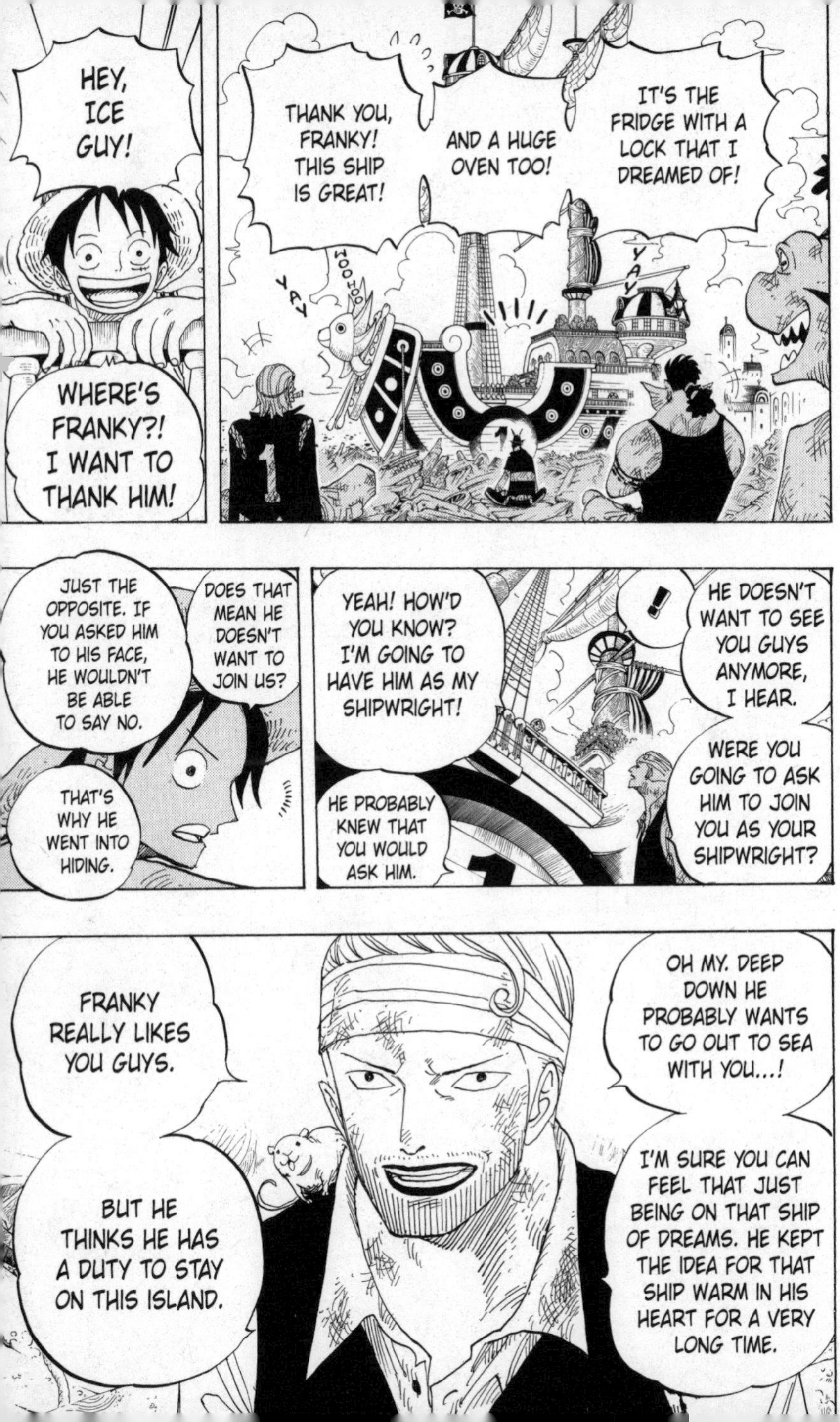
IT'S THE FRIDGE WITH A LOCK THAT I DREAMED OF!
AND A HUGE OVEN TOO!
THANK YOU, FRANKY! THIS SHIP IS GREAT!
YAY
WOOHOO
YAY
HEY, ICE GUY!
WHERE'S FRANKY?! I WANT TO THANK HIM!
HE DOESN'T WANT TO SEE YOU GUYS ANYMORE, I HEAR.
!
WERE YOU GOING TO ASK HIM TO JOIN YOU AS YOUR SHIPWRIGHT?
YEAH! HOW'D YOU KNOW? I'M GOING TO HAVE HIM AS MY SHIPWRIGHT!
HE PROBABLY KNEW THAT YOU WOULD ASK HIM.
DOES THAT MEAN HE DOESN'T WANT TO JOIN US?
JUST THE OPPOSITE. IF YOU ASKED HIM TO HIS FACE, HE WOULDN'T BE ABLE TO SAY NO.
THAT'S WHY HE WENT INTO HIDING.
OH MY. DEEP DOWN HE PROBABLY WANTS TO GO OUT TO SEA WITH YOU...!
I'M SURE YOU CAN FEEL THAT JUST BEING ON THAT SHIP OF DREAMS. HE KEPT THE IDEA FOR THAT SHIP WARM IN HIS HEART FOR A VERY LONG TIME.
FRANKY REALLY LIKES YOU GUYS.
BUT HE THINKS HE HAS A DUTY TO STAY ON THIS ISLAND.

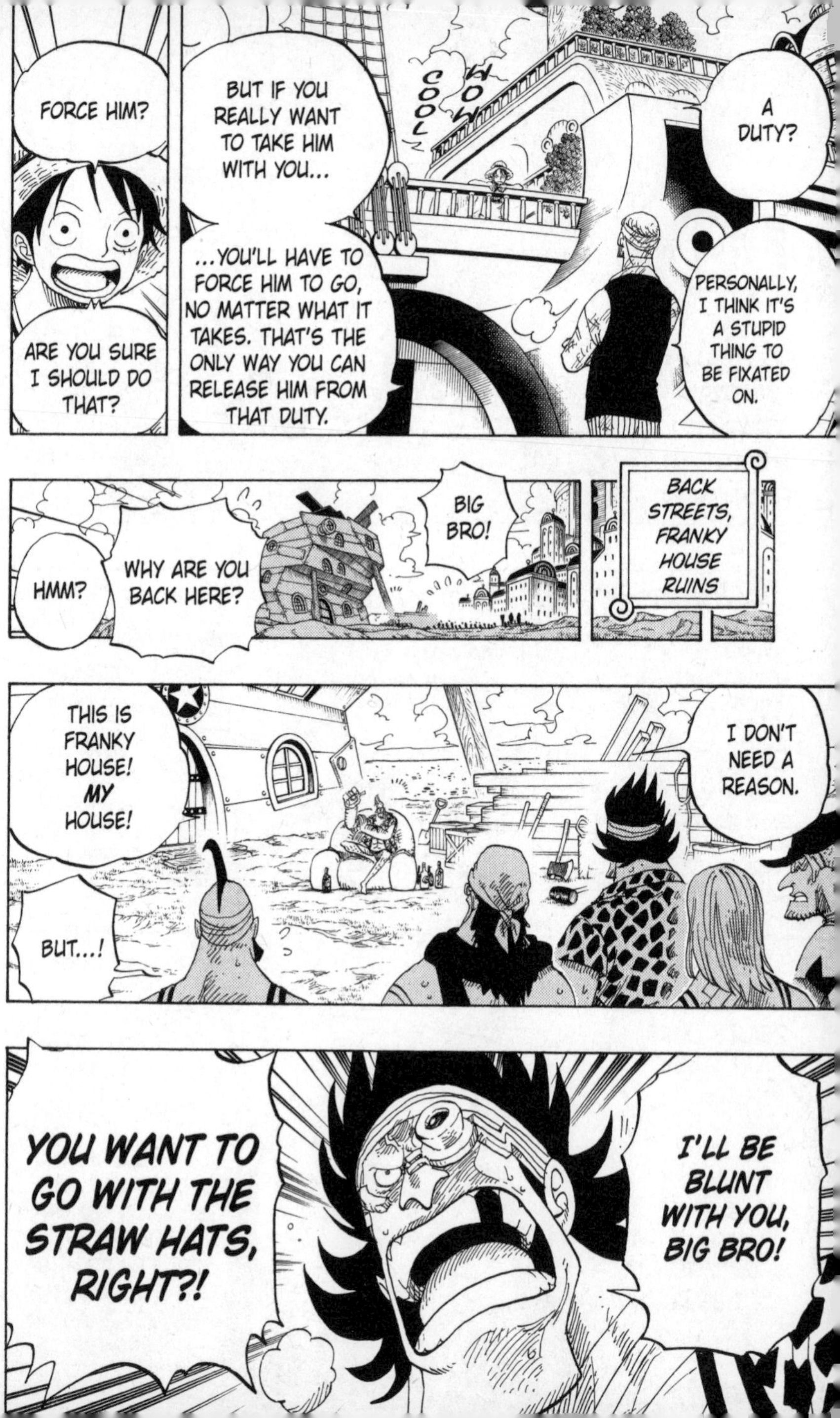
A DUTY?
PERSONALLY, I THINK IT'S A STUPID THING TO BE FIXATED ON.
WOW
COOL
BUT IF YOU REALLY WANT TO TAKE HIM WITH YOU...
...YOU'LL HAVE TO FORCE HIM TO GO, NO MATTER WHAT IT TAKES. THAT'S THE ONLY WAY YOU CAN RELEASE HIM FROM THAT DUTY.
FORCE HIM?
ARE YOU SURE I SHOULD DO THAT?
BACK STREETS, FRANKY HOUSE RUINS
BIG BRO!
WHY ARE YOU BACK HERE?
HMM?
I DON'T NEED A REASON.
THIS IS FRANKY HOUSE! MY HOUSE!
BUT...!
I'LL BE BLUNT WITH YOU, BIG BRO!
YOU WANT TO GO WITH THE STRAW HATS, RIGHT?!

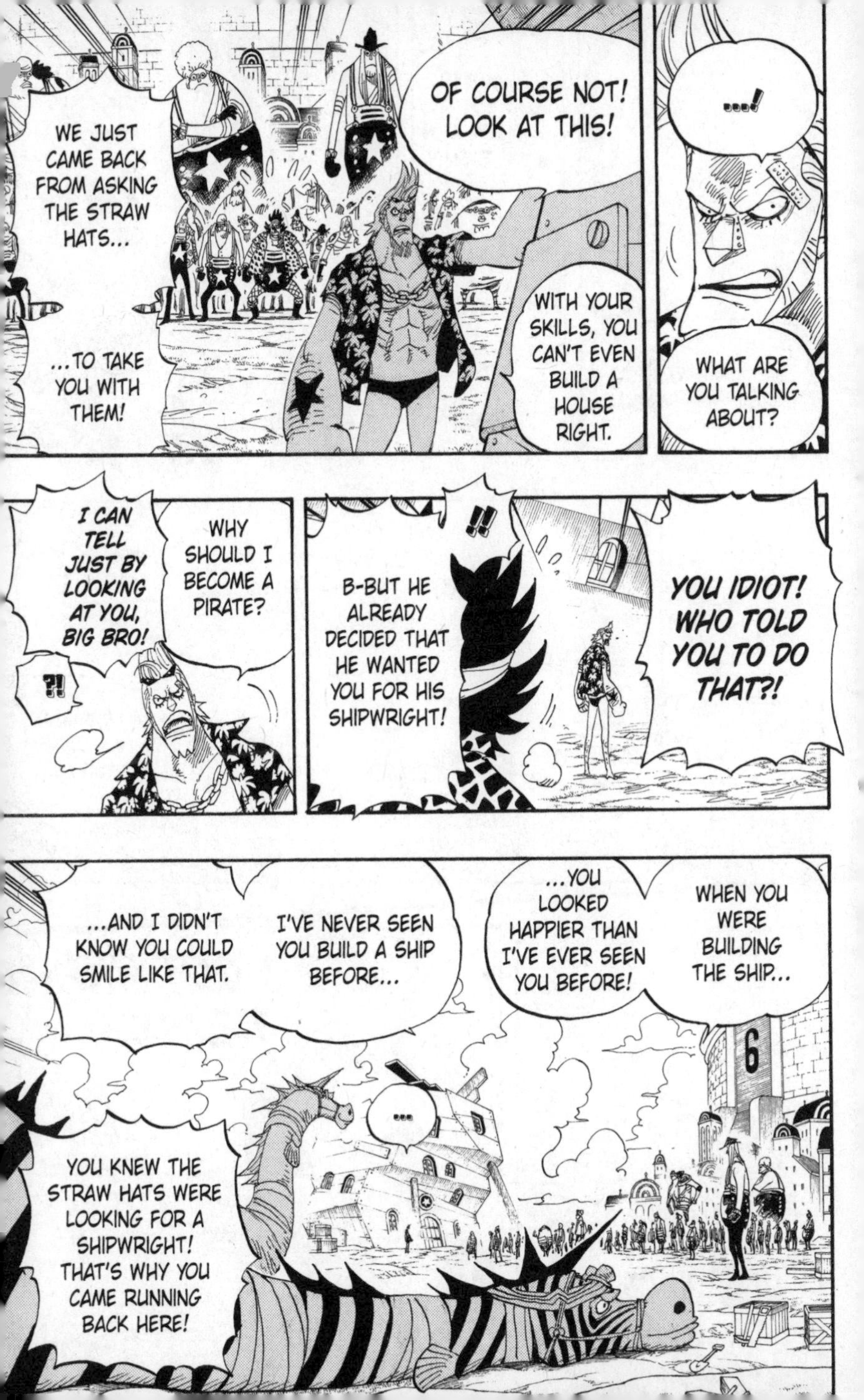
...!
WHAT ARE YOU TALKING ABOUT?
OF COURSE NOT! LOOK AT THIS!
WITH YOUR SKILLS, YOU CAN'T EVEN BUILD A HOUSE RIGHT.
WE JUST CAME BACK FROM ASKING THE STRAW HATS...
...TO TAKE YOU WITH THEM!
!!
YOU IDIOT! WHO TOLD YOU TO DO THAT?!
B-BUT HE ALREADY DECIDED THAT HE WANTED YOU FOR HIS SHIPWRIGHT!
WHY SHOULD I BECOME A PIRATE?
I CAN TELL JUST BY LOOKING AT YOU, BIG BRO!
?!
WHEN YOU WERE BUILDING THE SHIP...
...YOU LOOKED HAPPIER THAN I'VE EVER SEEN YOU BEFORE!
I'VE NEVER SEEN YOU BUILD A SHIP BEFORE...
...AND I DIDN'T KNOW YOU COULD SMILE LIKE THAT.
6
...
YOU KNEW THE STRAW HATS WERE LOOKING FOR A SHIPWRIGHT! THAT'S WHY YOU CAME RUNNING BACK HERE!

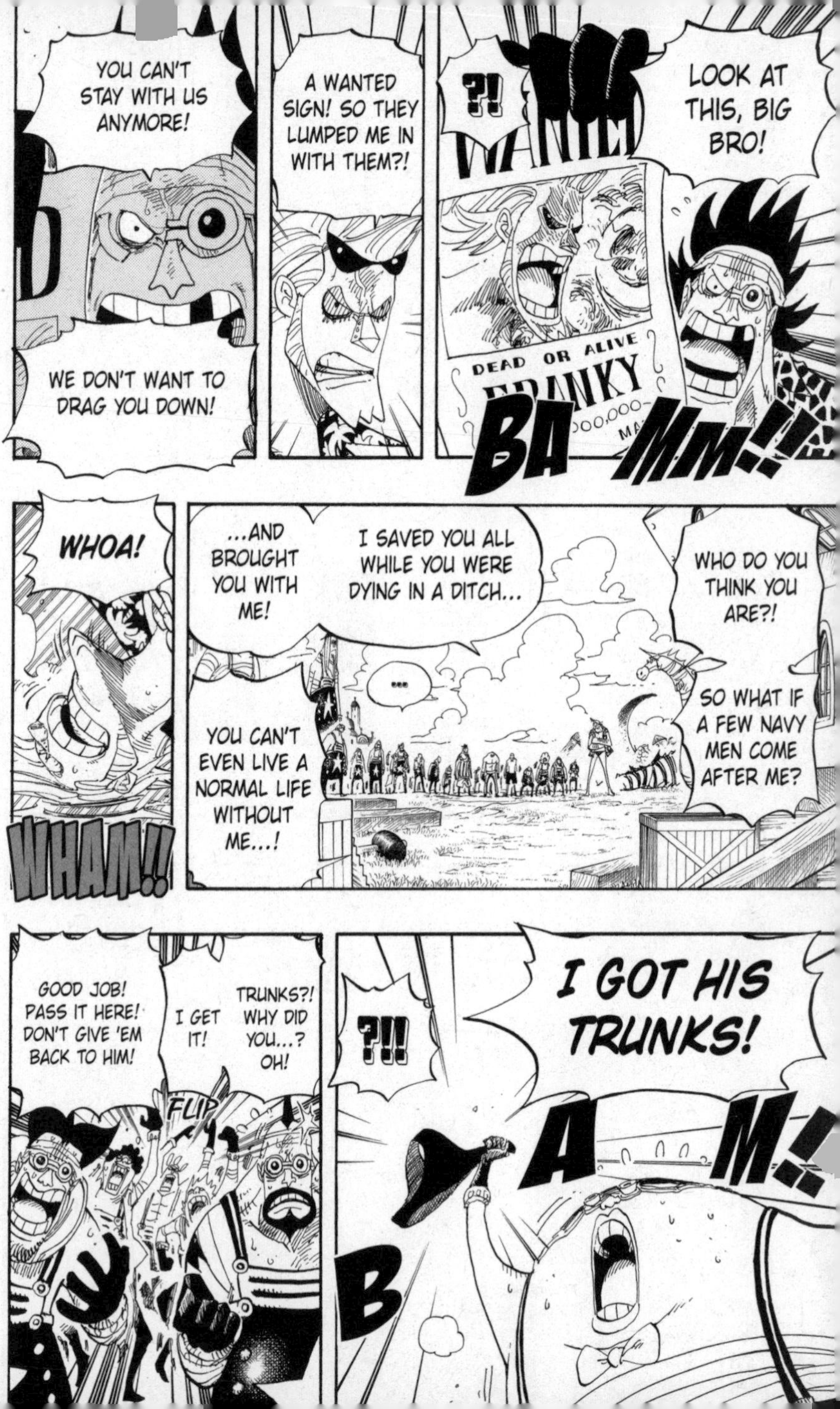
LOOK AT THIS, BIG BRO!
?!
DEAD OR ALIVE
BAMM!!
A WANTED SIGN! SO THEY LUMPED ME IN WITH THEM?!
YOU CAN'T STAY WITH US ANYMORE!
WE DON'T WANT TO DRAG YOU DOWN!
WHO DO YOU THINK YOU ARE?!
SO WHAT IF A FEW NAVY MEN COME AFTER ME?
I SAVED YOU ALL WHILE YOU WERE DYING IN A DITCH...
...AND BROUGHT YOU WITH ME!
...
YOU CAN'T EVEN LIVE A NORMAL LIFE WITHOUT ME...!
WHOA!
WHAM!!
I GOT HIS TRUNKS!
?!!
BAM!!
TRUNKS?! WHY DID YOU...? OH!
I GET IT!
GOOD JOB! PASS IT HERE! DON'T GIVE 'EM BACK TO HIM!
FLIP

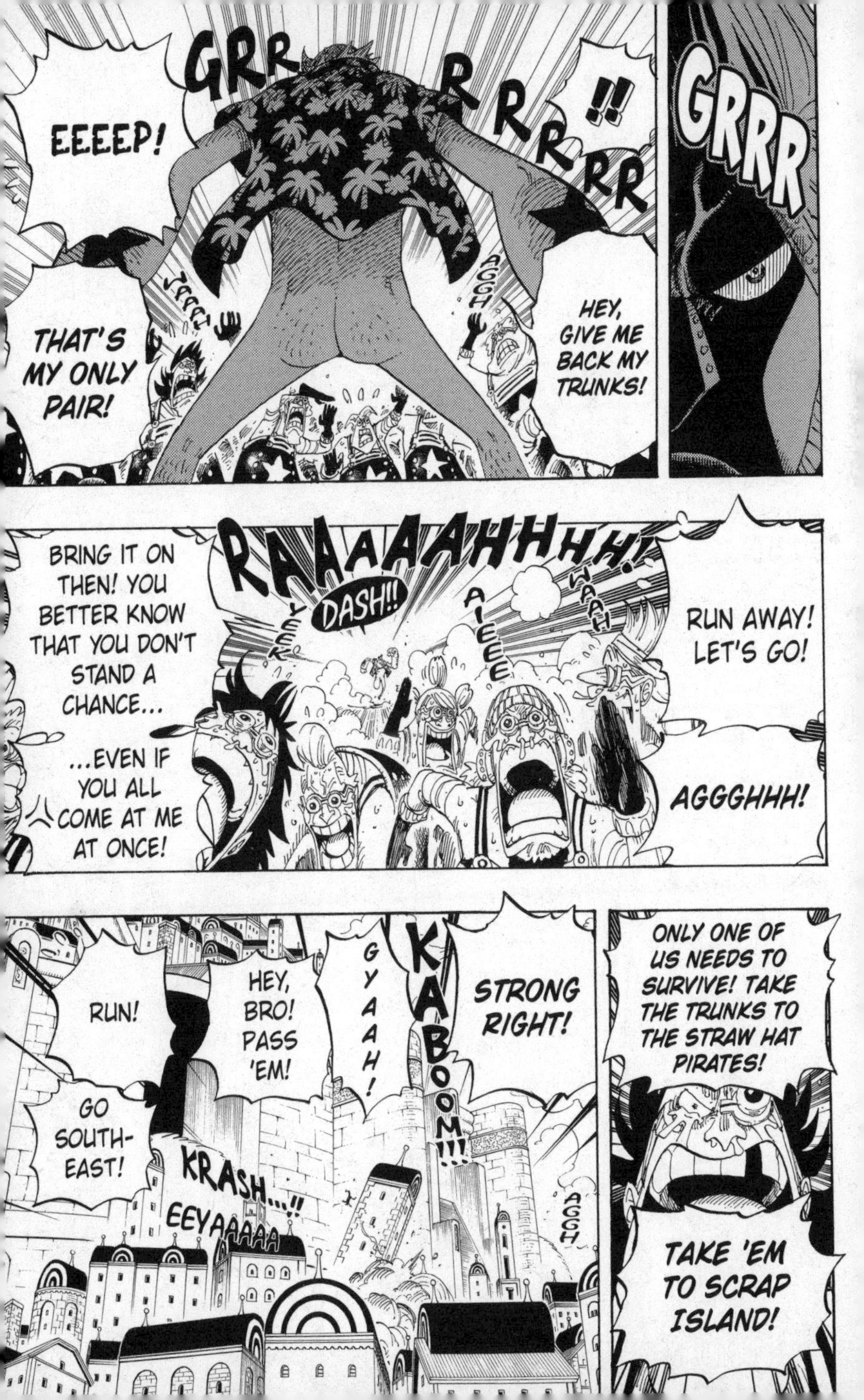
GRRR
GRRRRRRR!!
EEEEP!
HEY, GIVE ME BACK MY TRUNKS!
AGGH
THAT'S MY ONLY PAIR!
RAAAAAHHHH!
RUN AWAY! LET'S GO!
WAAAH
AIEEE
DASH!!
YEEEK
BRING IT ON THEN! YOU BETTER KNOW THAT YOU DON'T STAND A CHANCE...
...EVEN IF YOU ALL COME AT ME AT ONCE!
AGGGHHH!
ONLY ONE OF US NEEDS TO SURVIVE! TAKE THE TRUNKS TO THE STRAW HAT PIRATES!
TAKE 'EM TO SCRAP ISLAND!
STRONG RIGHT!
KABOOM!!!
GYAAAH!
HEY, BRO! PASS 'EM!
RUN!
GO SOUTH-EAST!
AGGH
KRASH...!!
EEYAAAAA

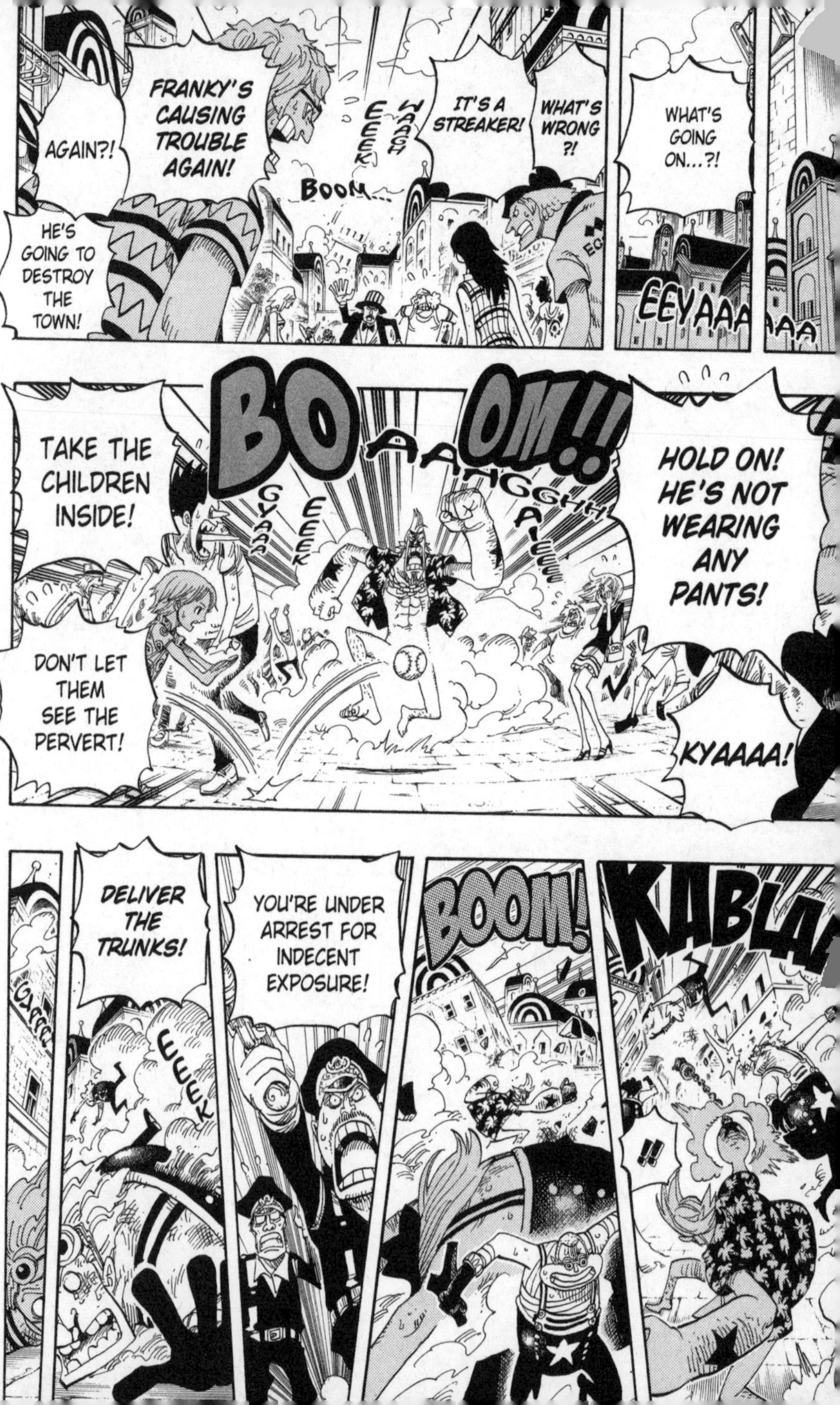
WHAT'S GOING ON...?!
EEYAAAAAA
WHAT'S WRONG?!
IT'S A STREAKER!
WAAGH
EEEK
BOOM...
FRANKY'S CAUSING TROUBLE AGAIN!
AGAIN?!
HE'S GOING TO DESTROY THE TOWN!
HOLD ON! HE'S NOT WEARING ANY PANTS!
BOOM!!
AAAGGHH
AIEEE
EEEK
GYAAA
TAKE THE CHILDREN INSIDE!
KYAAAA!
DON'T LET THEM SEE THE PERVERT!
BOOM!
YOU'RE UNDER ARREST FOR INDECENT EXPOSURE!
DELIVER THE TRUNKS!
EEEEK

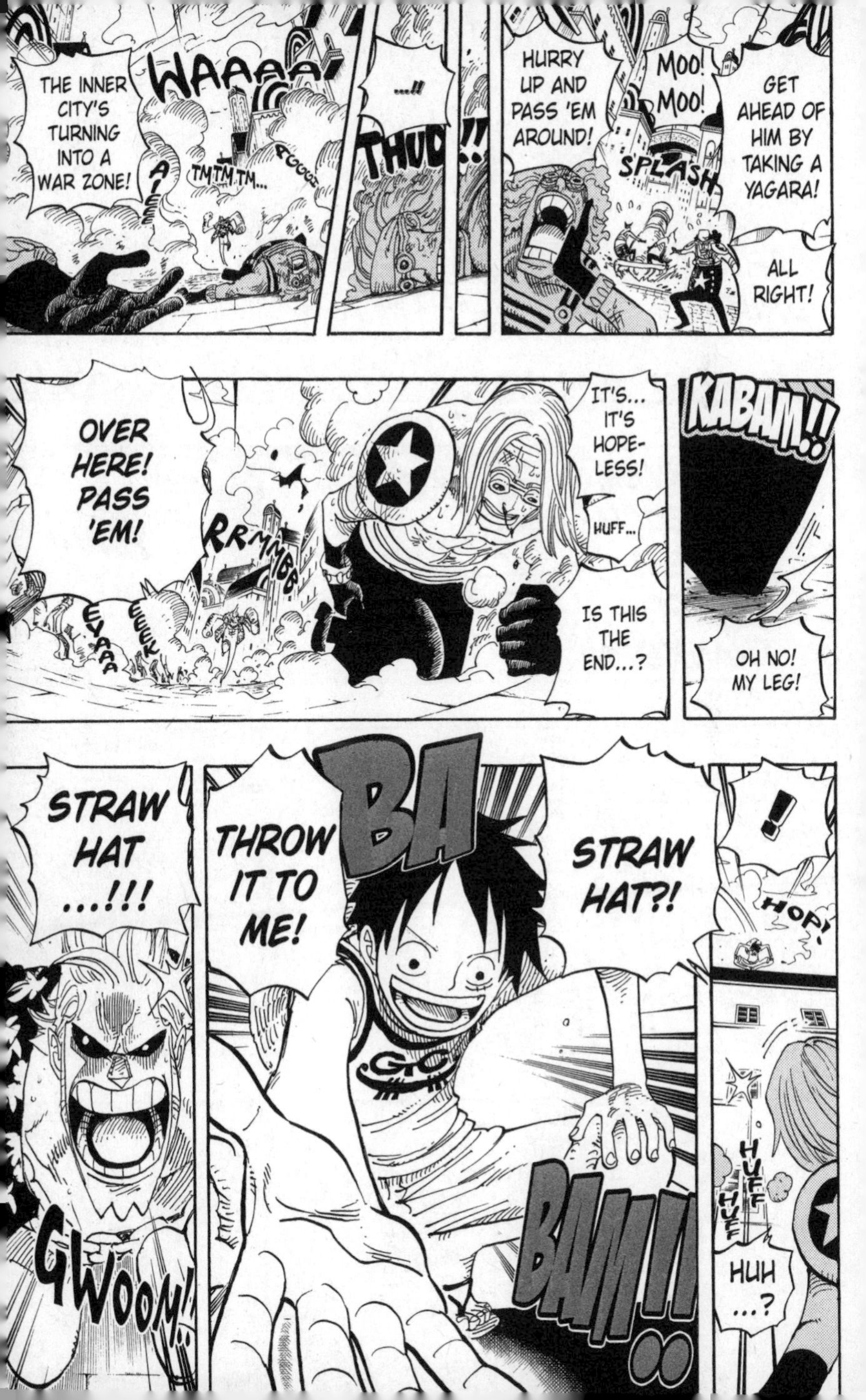
GET AHEAD OF HIM BY TAKING A YAGARA!
MOO! MOO!
HURRY UP AND PASS 'EM AROUND!
SPLASH
ALL RIGHT!
...!!
THUD!!
WAAAA!
THE INNER CITY'S TURNING INTO A WAR ZONE!
TMTMTM...
AIEEE
KABAM!!
OH NO! MY LEG!
IT'S... IT'S HOPE-LESS!
HUFF...
IS THIS THE END...?
RRMMBB
OVER HERE! PASS 'EM!
EEEK
EYAAA
!
HOP!
HUFF HUFF
HUH ...?
STRAW HAT?!
BA
THROW IT TO ME!
BAM!!
STRAW HAT ...!!!
GWOOM!!

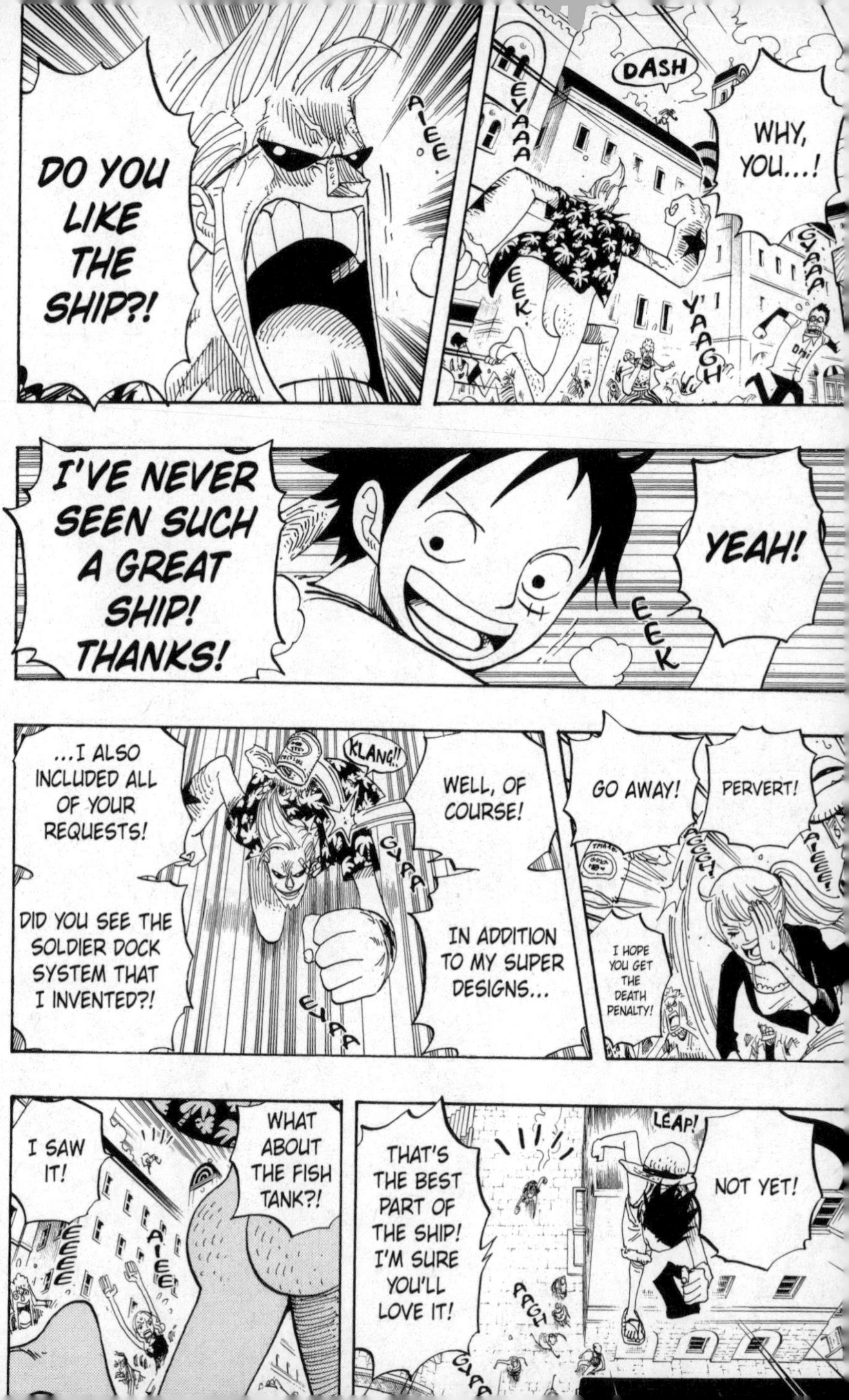
DASH
EYAAA
WHY, YOU...!
EEK
GYAAA
Y'AAGH
DO YOU LIKE THE SHIP?!
AIEE
YEAH!
I'VE NEVER SEEN SUCH A GREAT SHIP! THANKS!
EEK
PERVERT!
GO AWAY!
AIEEE
AGGGH
I HOPE YOU GET THE DEATH PENALTY!
WELL, OF COURSE!
IN ADDITION TO MY SUPER DESIGNS...
KLANG!!
GYAA
...I ALSO INCLUDED ALL OF YOUR REQUESTS!
DID YOU SEE THE SOLDIER DOCK SYSTEM THAT I INVENTED?!
EYAA
LEAP!
NOT YET!
THAT'S THE BEST PART OF THE SHIP! I'M SURE YOU'LL LOVE IT!
AAGH
GYAA
WHAT ABOUT THE FISH TANK?!
I SAW IT!
AIEE
EEEE

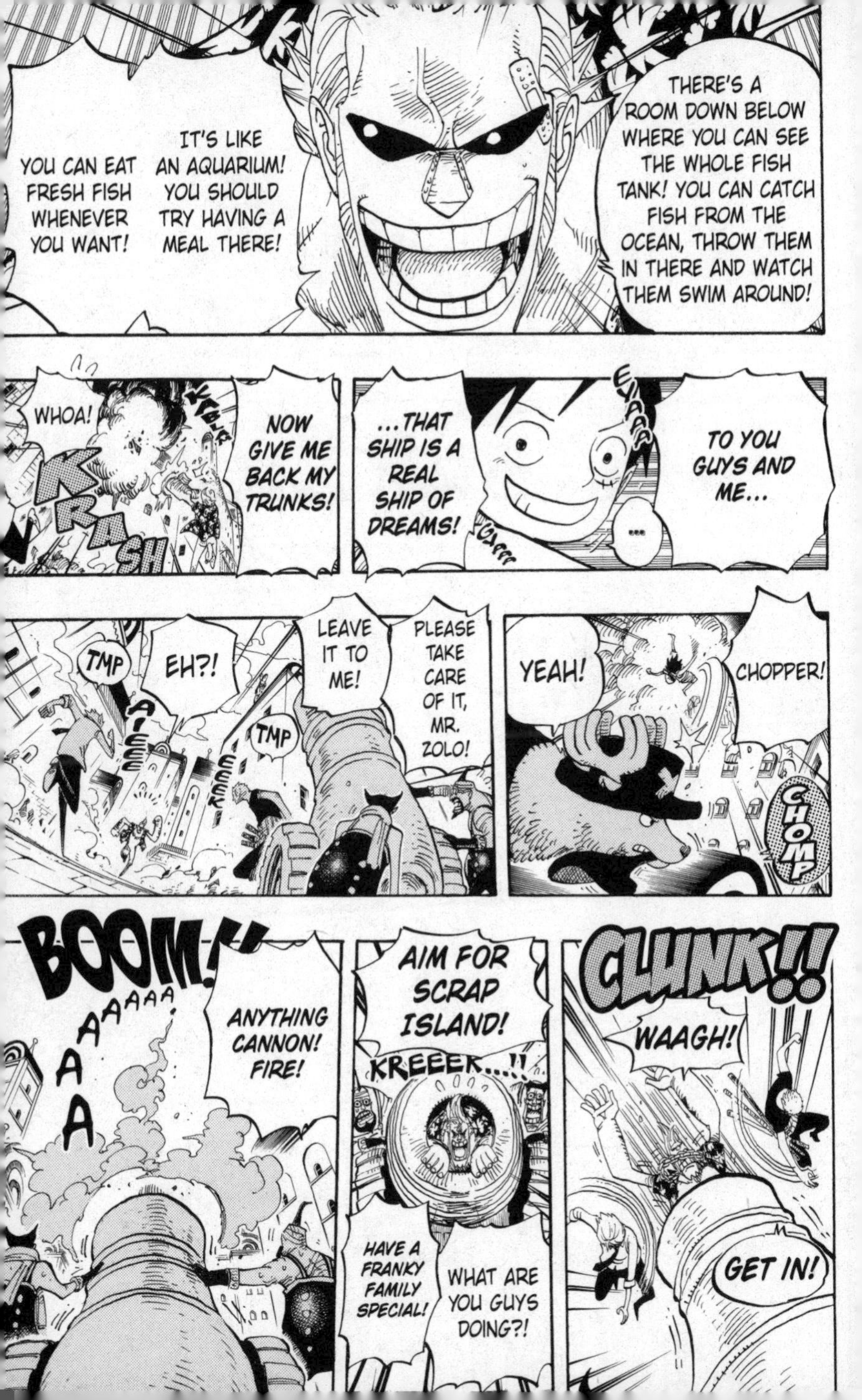
THERE'S A ROOM DOWN BELOW WHERE YOU CAN SEE THE WHOLE FISH TANK! YOU CAN CATCH FISH FROM THE OCEAN, THROW THEM IN THERE AND WATCH THEM SWIM AROUND!
IT'S LIKE AN AQUARIUM! YOU SHOULD TRY HAVING A MEAL THERE!
YOU CAN EAT FRESH FISH WHENEVER YOU WANT!
TO YOU GUYS AND ME...
EYAAA
...
...THAT SHIP IS A REAL SHIP OF DREAMS!
NOW GIVE ME BACK MY TRUNKS!
WHOA!
KRASH
CHOPPER!
YEAH!
CHOMP
PLEASE TAKE CARE OF IT, MR. ZOLO!
LEAVE IT TO ME!
TMP
EEEK
EH?!
TMP
AIEEE
CLUNK!!
WAAGH!
GET IN!
AIM FOR SCRAP ISLAND!
KREEEK...!!
WHAT ARE YOU GUYS DOING?!
HAVE A FRANKY FAMILY SPECIAL!
BOOM!!
ANYTHING CANNON! FIRE!
AAAAAAA

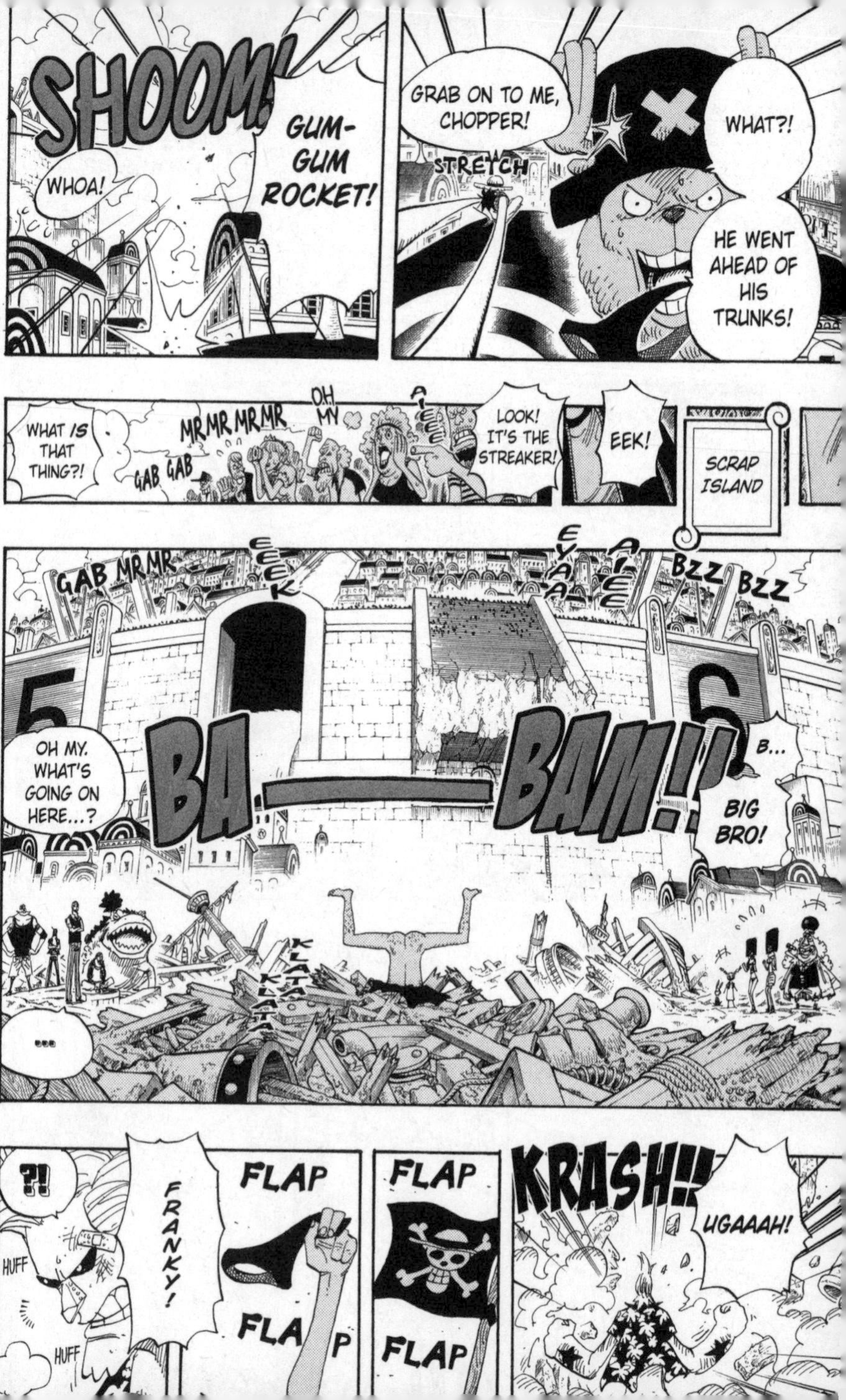
GRAB ON TO ME, CHOPPER!
WHAT?!
STRETCH
HE WENT AHEAD OF HIS TRUNKS!
SHOOM!
GUM-GUM ROCKET!
WHOA!
SCRAP ISLAND
EEK!
LOOK! IT'S THE STREAKER!
AIEEE
OH MY
MRMR MRMR
GAB GAB
WHAT IS THAT THING?!
BZZ BZZ
AIEEE
EYAAA
EEEK
GAB MRMR
B... BIG BRO!
BA—BAM!!
OH MY. WHAT'S GOING ON HERE...?
KLATA KLATA
...
KRASH!!
UGAAAH!
FLAP FLAP
FLAP FLAP
FRANKY!
?!
HUFF
HUFF

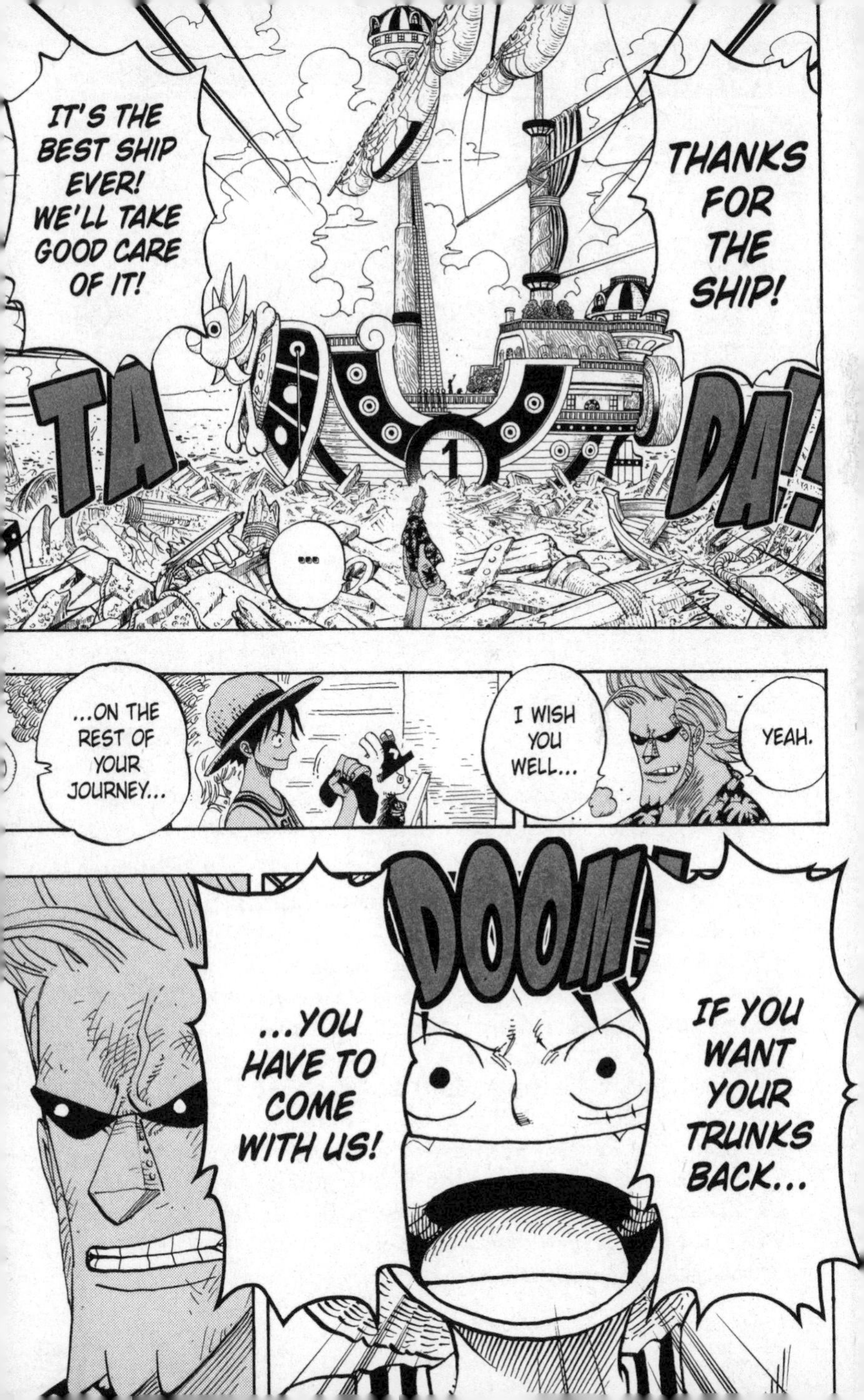
THANKS FOR THE SHIP!
IT'S THE BEST SHIP EVER! WE'LL TAKE GOOD CARE OF IT!
TA
DA!!
...
YEAH.
I WISH YOU WELL...
...ON THE REST OF YOUR JOURNEY...
DOOM
IF YOU WANT YOUR TRUNKS BACK...
...YOU HAVE TO COME WITH US!

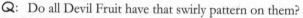

Q: Please tell me this guy's name. Between me and my spouse, we just call him "Round Dude."

--Patty

A: Hmm. Tama... Tamagon.
(Decided just now) *Tamago means egg –Ed

Q: Do all Devil Fruit have that swirly pattern on them?

A: Yes, they do. That's one of their features, it seems. There are times that I think that Sanji himself is a Devil Fruit.

Q: Oda Sensei, in volume 4's Question Corner, you said that you read every single letter and postcard sent to you. Do you still do that?

--Koji

A: Yes, I still read all of them. But to be honest, there was a time when I couldn't read all of them. Back then, I received like a thousand to two thousand letters at a time. I had the editors pick out a couple hundred for me. But recently, the number of letters being sent to me has calmed down (the number of letters I got from girls decreased significantly after I got married...LOL). I still read 100 percent of the letters now. Thinking back, I'm very grateful for receiving these praising letters every single week for the past ten years. Thank you all. I do feel a lot of support from my readers. I keep the letters in a room at my workplace. My staff are worried that the floor is going to fall out from underneath someday.

Chapter 437:
NAKED MANIA

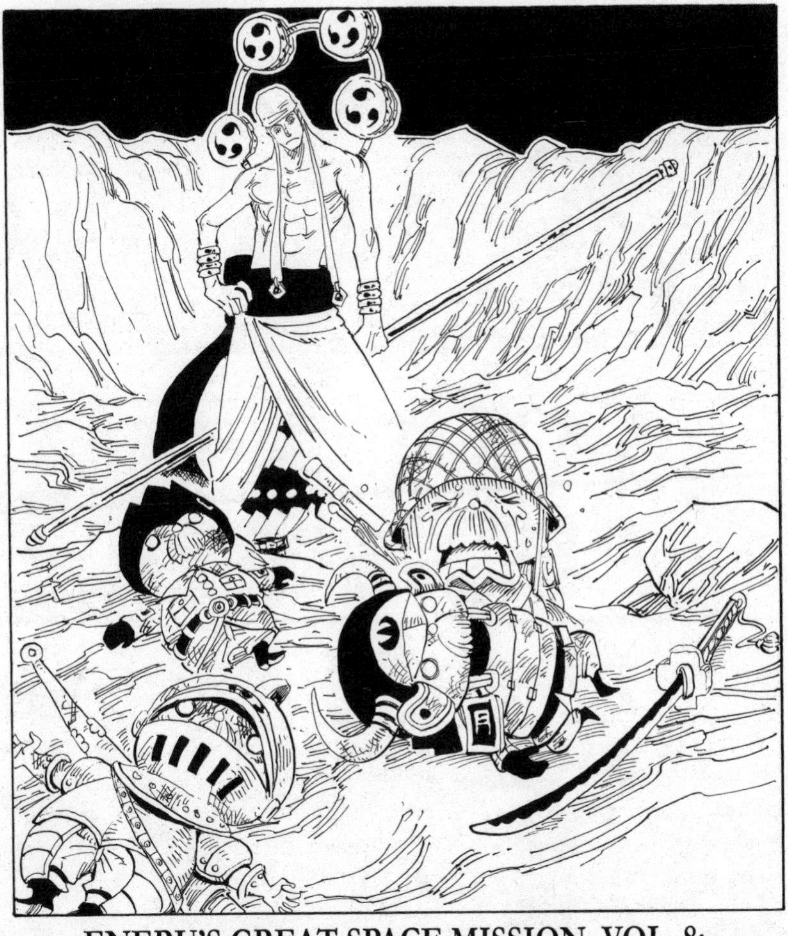

ENERU'S GREAT SPACE MISSION, VOL. 8:
"THE OLD BATTLEFIELD"

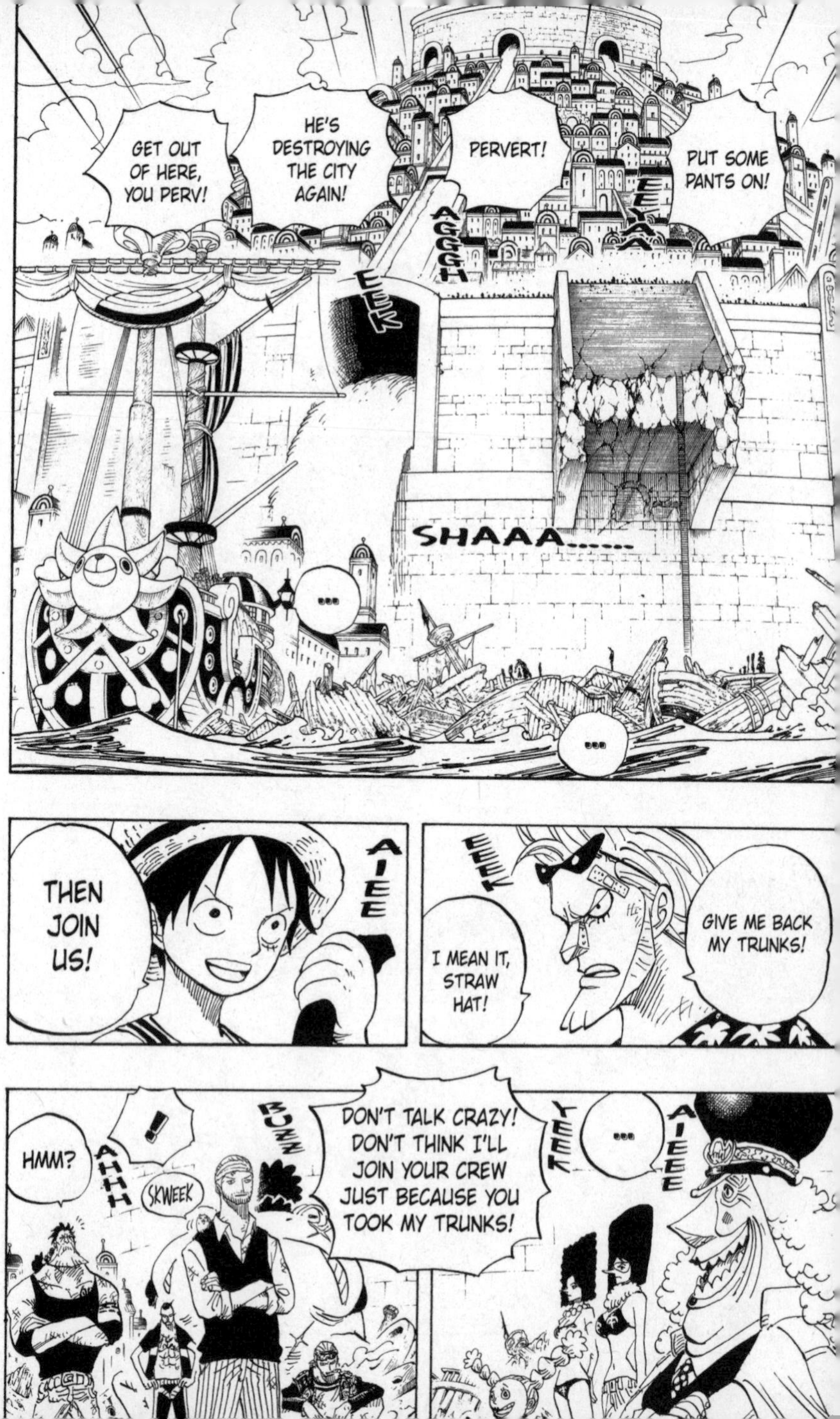
PUT SOME PANTS ON!
EEYAA
PERVERT!
AGGGH
HE'S DESTROYING THE CITY AGAIN!
GET OUT OF HERE, YOU PERV!
EEK
SHAAA......
...
...
GIVE ME BACK MY TRUNKS!
EEEK
I MEAN IT, STRAW HAT!
AIEE
THEN JOIN US!
AIEEE
...
YEEK
DON'T TALK CRAZY! DON'T THINK I'LL JOIN YOUR CREW JUST BECAUSE YOU TOOK MY TRUNKS!
BUZZ
SKWEEK
!
AHHH
HMM?

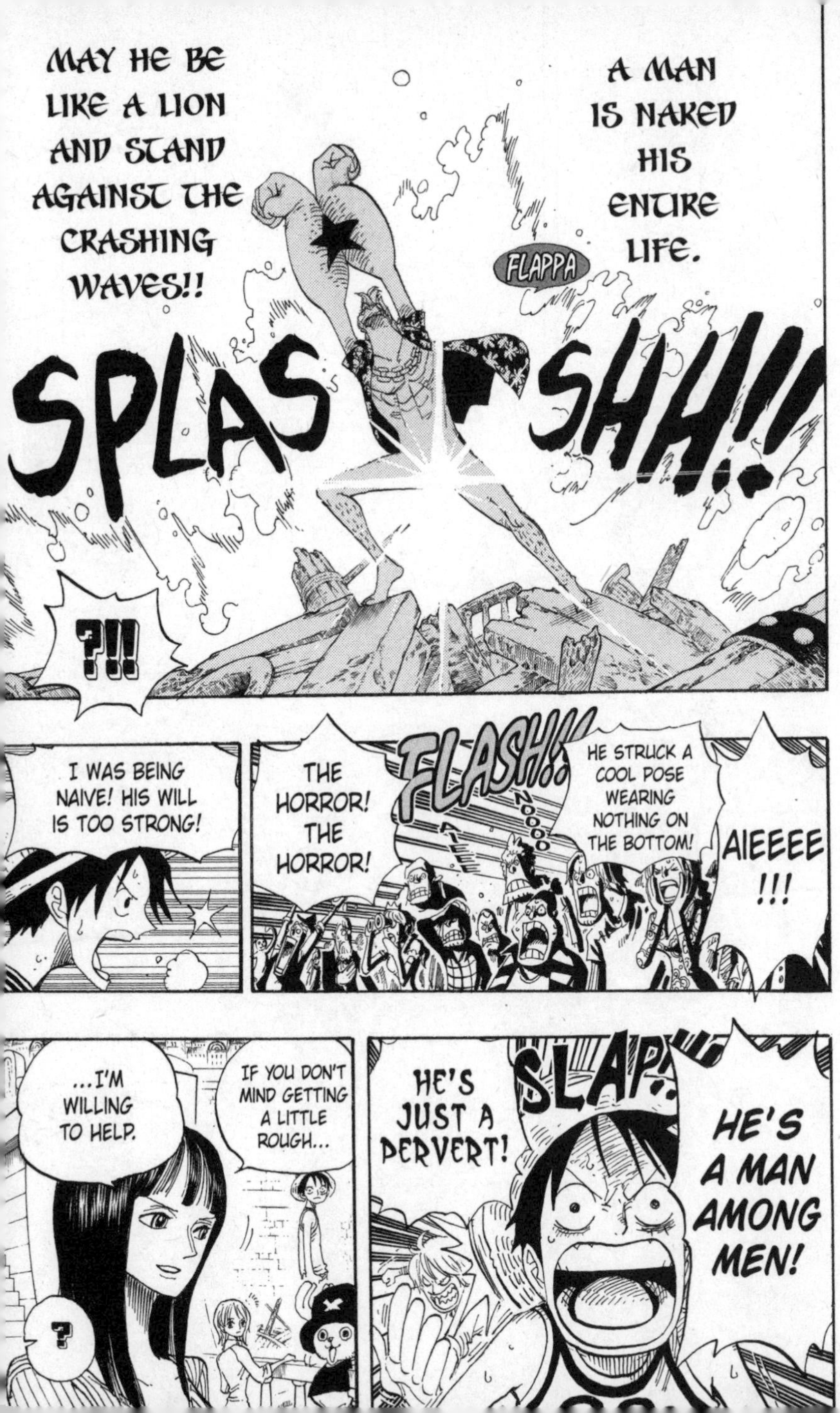
A MAN IS NAKED HIS ENTIRE LIFE.
MAY HE BE LIKE A LION AND STAND AGAINST THE CRASHING WAVES!!
FLAPPA
SPLASSHH!!
?!!
AIEEEE!!!
HE STRUCK A COOL POSE WEARING NOTHING ON THE BOTTOM!
FLASH!!
THE HORROR! THE HORROR!
I WAS BEING NAIVE! HIS WILL IS TOO STRONG!
HE'S A MAN AMONG MEN!
SLAP!!
HE'S JUST A PERVERT!
IF YOU DON'T MIND GETTING A LITTLE ROUGH...
...I'M WILLING TO HELP.
?

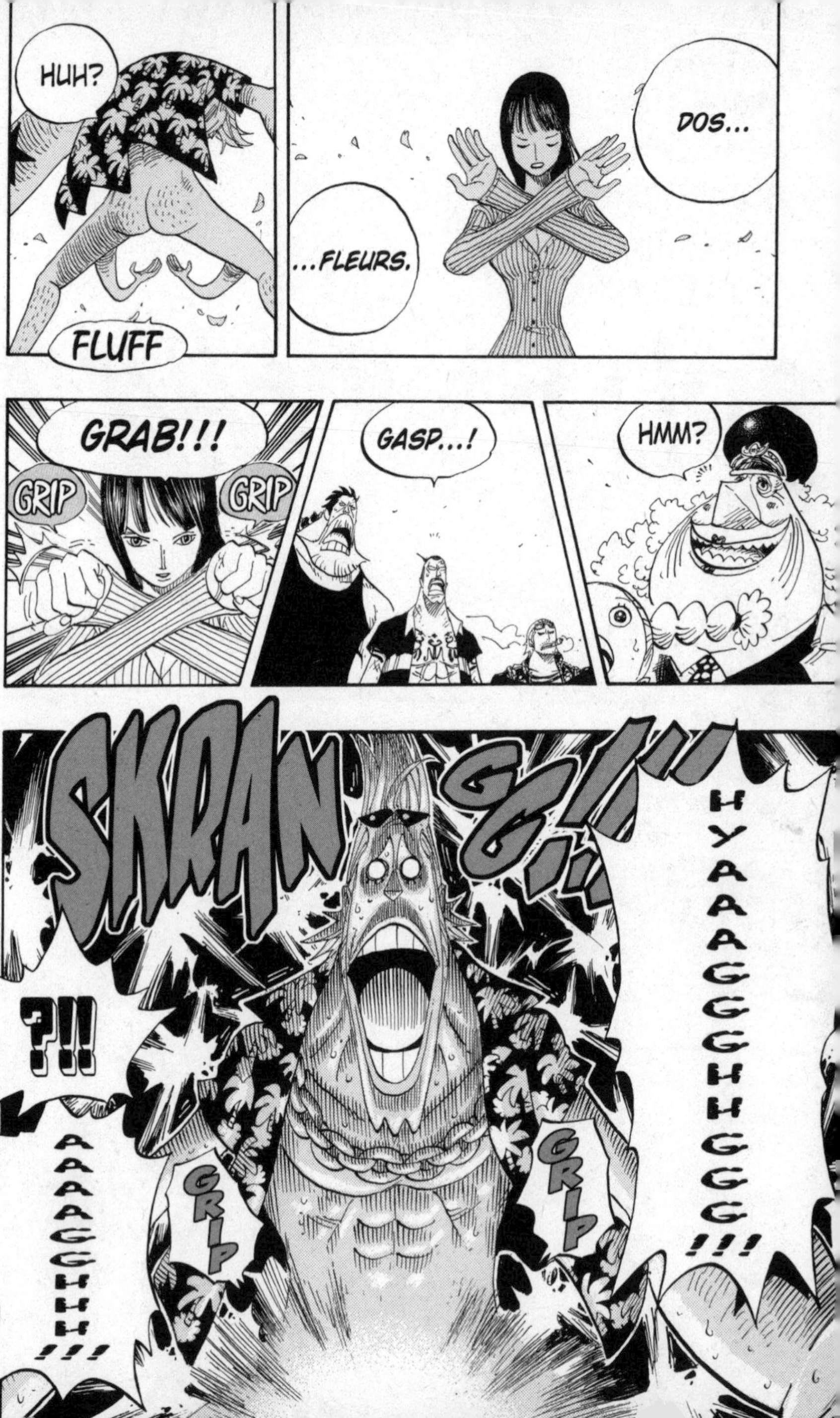
DOS...
...FLEURS.
HUH?
FLUFF
HMM?
GASP...!
GRAB!!!
GRIP
GRIP
SKRANG!!!
HYAAAAGGGHHGGG!!!
?!!
AAAAAGGHHH!!!
GRIP
GRIP

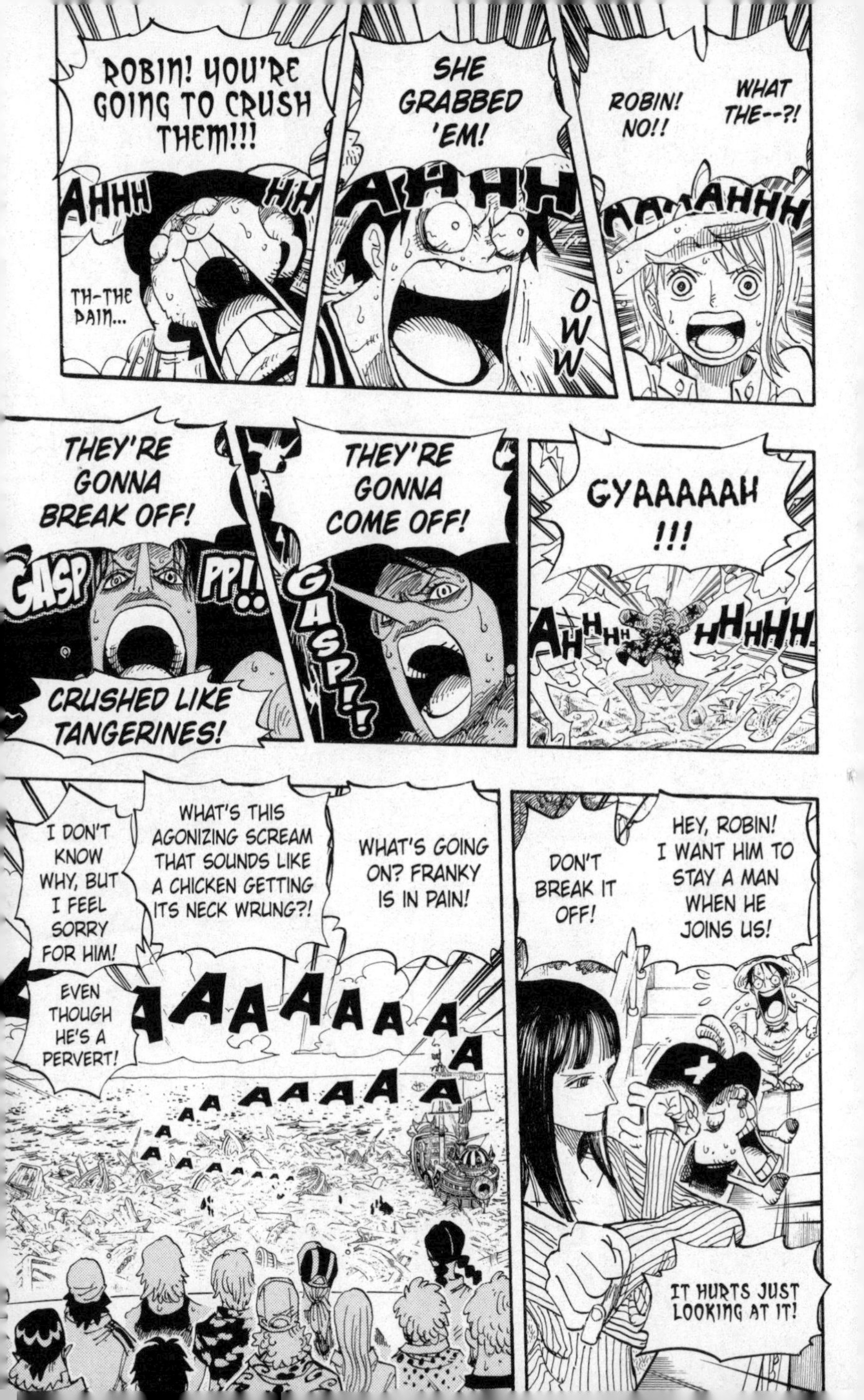
WHAT THE--?!
ROBIN! NO!!
AHHH
SHE GRABBED 'EM!
AHHH
OWW
ROBIN! YOU'RE GOING TO CRUSH THEM!!!
AHHH
TH-THE PAIN...
GYAAAAAH !!!
AHHHHHHHHH
THEY'RE GONNA COME OFF!
GASP!!
THEY'RE GONNA BREAK OFF!
GASP
CRUSHED LIKE TANGERINES!
HEY, ROBIN! I WANT HIM TO STAY A MAN WHEN HE JOINS US!
DON'T BREAK IT OFF!
IT HURTS JUST LOOKING AT IT!
WHAT'S GOING ON? FRANKY IS IN PAIN!
WHAT'S THIS AGONIZING SCREAM THAT SOUNDS LIKE A CHICKEN GETTING ITS NECK WRUNG?!
I DON'T KNOW WHY, BUT I FEEL SORRY FOR HIM!
EVEN THOUGH HE'S A PERVERT!
AAAAAAAAAAAAAAAAAAAA

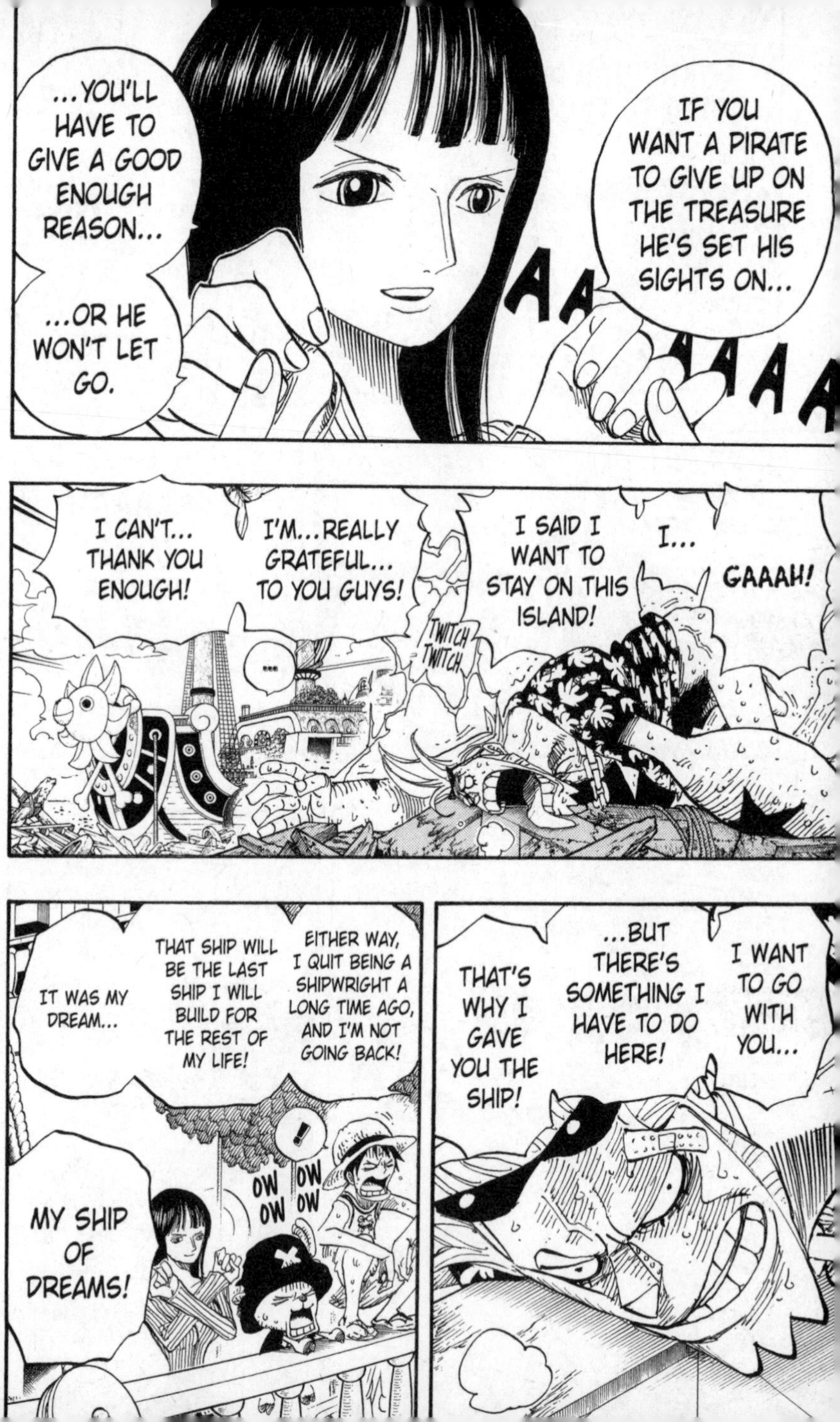
IF YOU WANT A PIRATE TO GIVE UP ON THE TREASURE HE'S SET HIS SIGHTS ON...
...YOU'LL HAVE TO GIVE A GOOD ENOUGH REASON...
...OR HE WON'T LET GO.
AAAAAA
GAAAH!
I...
I SAID I WANT TO STAY ON THIS ISLAND!
TWITCH TWITCH
I'M...REALLY GRATEFUL... TO YOU GUYS!
I CAN'T... THANK YOU ENOUGH!
...
I WANT TO GO WITH YOU...
...BUT THERE'S SOMETHING I HAVE TO DO HERE!
THAT'S WHY I GAVE YOU THE SHIP!
EITHER WAY, I QUIT BEING A SHIPWRIGHT A LONG TIME AGO, AND I'M NOT GOING BACK!
THAT SHIP WILL BE THE LAST SHIP I WILL BUILD FOR THE REST OF MY LIFE!
IT WAS MY DREAM...
!
OW OW
OW OW
MY SHIP OF DREAMS!

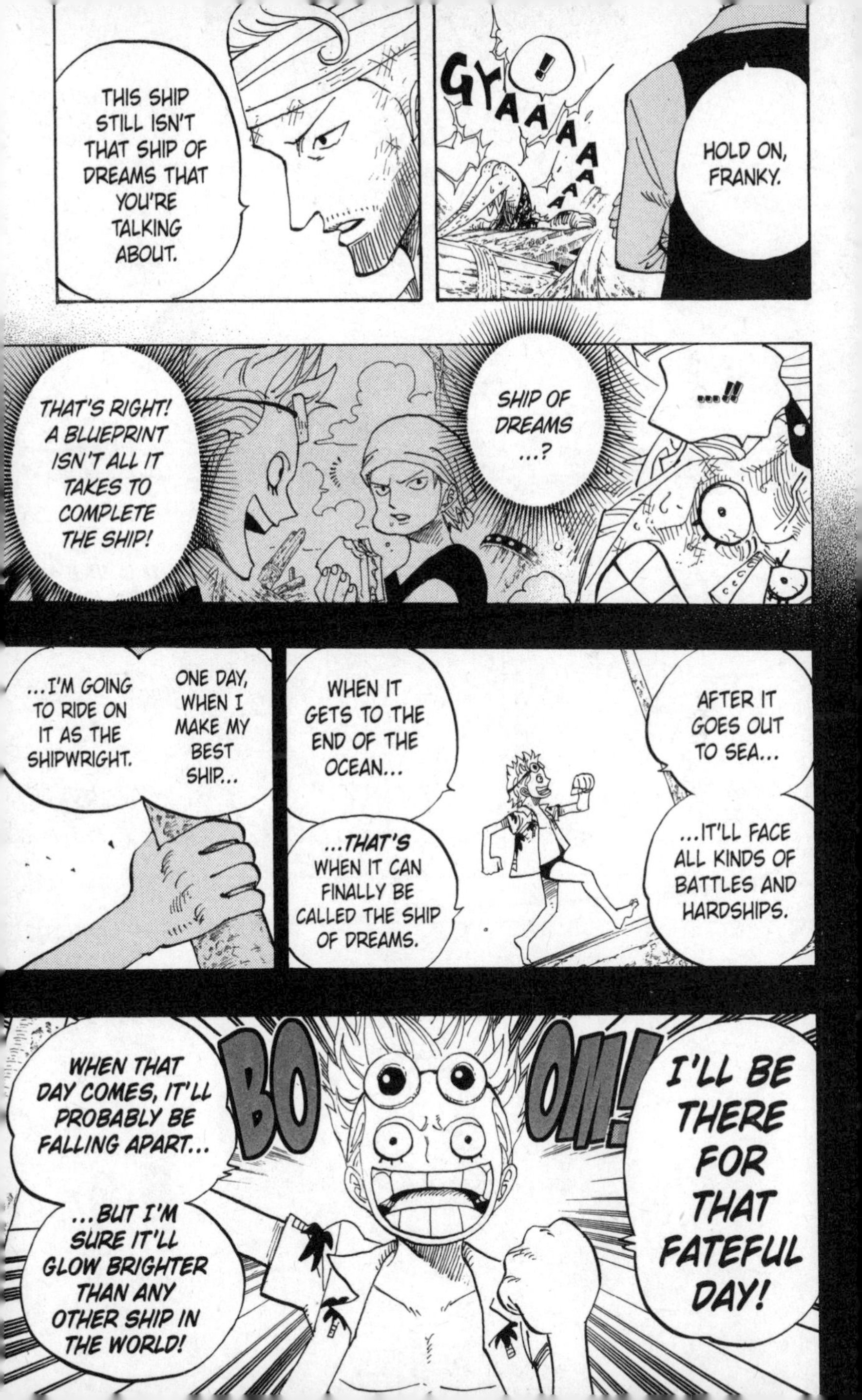
HOLD ON, FRANKY.
GYAAAAAAAA
!
THIS SHIP STILL ISN'T THAT SHIP OF DREAMS THAT YOU'RE TALKING ABOUT.
...!!
SHIP OF DREAMS ...?
THAT'S RIGHT! A BLUEPRINT ISN'T ALL IT TAKES TO COMPLETE THE SHIP!
AFTER IT GOES OUT TO SEA...
...IT'LL FACE ALL KINDS OF BATTLES AND HARDSHIPS.
WHEN IT GETS TO THE END OF THE OCEAN...
...THAT'S WHEN IT CAN FINALLY BE CALLED THE SHIP OF DREAMS.
ONE DAY, WHEN I MAKE MY BEST SHIP...
...I'M GOING TO RIDE ON IT AS THE SHIPWRIGHT.
I'LL BE THERE FOR THAT FATEFUL DAY!
BOOM!
WHEN THAT DAY COMES, IT'LL PROBABLY BE FALLING APART...
...BUT I'M SURE IT'LL GLOW BRIGHTER THAN ANY OTHER SHIP IN THE WORLD!

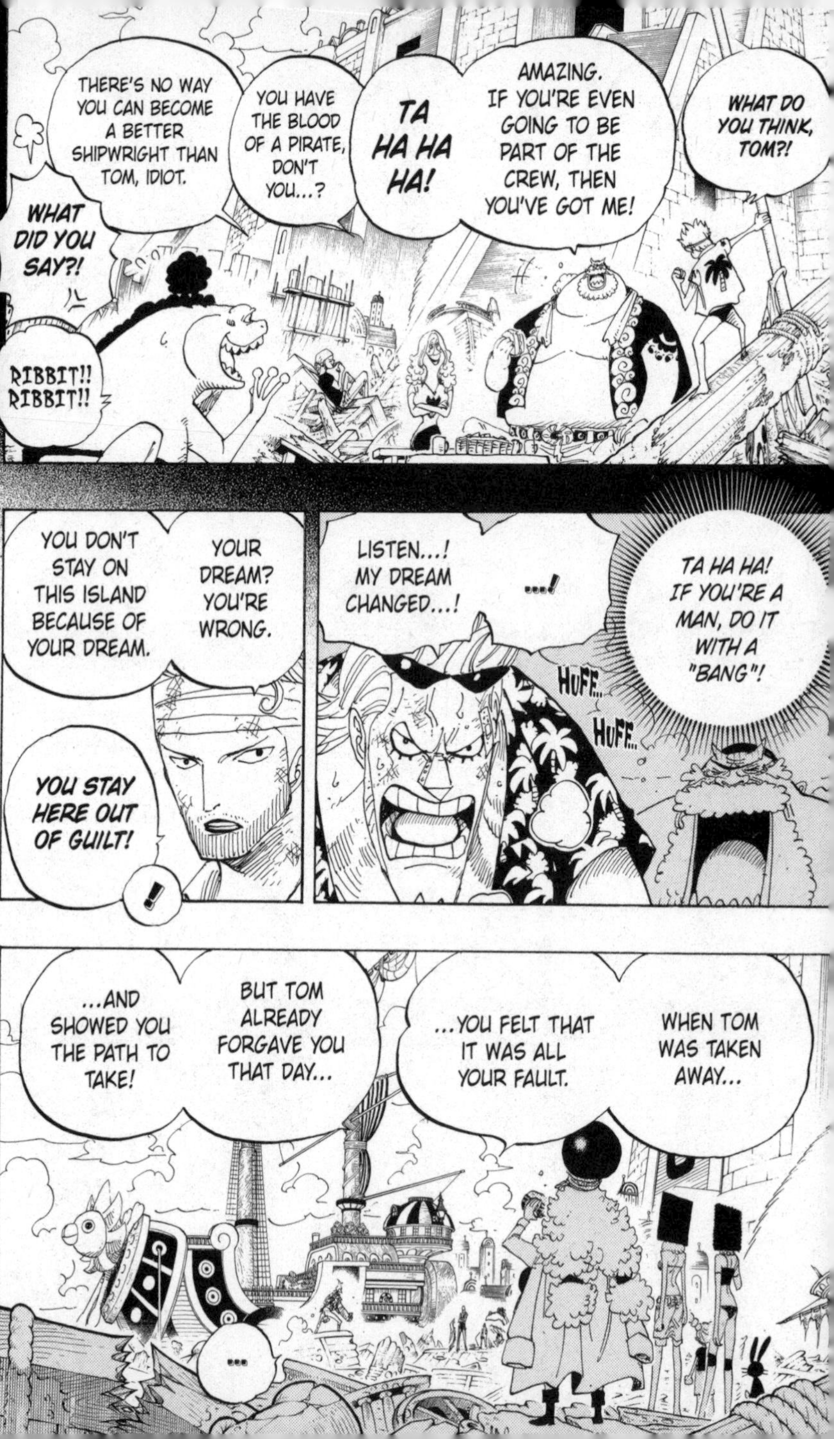
WHAT DO YOU THINK, TOM?!
AMAZING. IF YOU'RE EVEN GOING TO BE PART OF THE CREW, THEN YOU'VE GOT ME!
TA HA HA HA!
YOU HAVE THE BLOOD OF A PIRATE, DON'T YOU...?
THERE'S NO WAY YOU CAN BECOME A BETTER SHIPWRIGHT THAN TOM, IDIOT.
WHAT DID YOU SAY?!
RIBBIT!! RIBBIT!!
TA HA HA! IF YOU'RE A MAN, DO IT WITH A "BANG"!
...!
LISTEN...! MY DREAM CHANGED...!
HUFF...
HUFF...
YOUR DREAM? YOU'RE WRONG.
YOU DON'T STAY ON THIS ISLAND BECAUSE OF YOUR DREAM.
YOU STAY HERE OUT OF GUILT!
!
WHEN TOM WAS TAKEN AWAY...
...YOU FELT THAT IT WAS ALL YOUR FAULT.
BUT TOM ALREADY FORGAVE YOU THAT DAY...
...AND SHOWED YOU THE PATH TO TAKE!
...

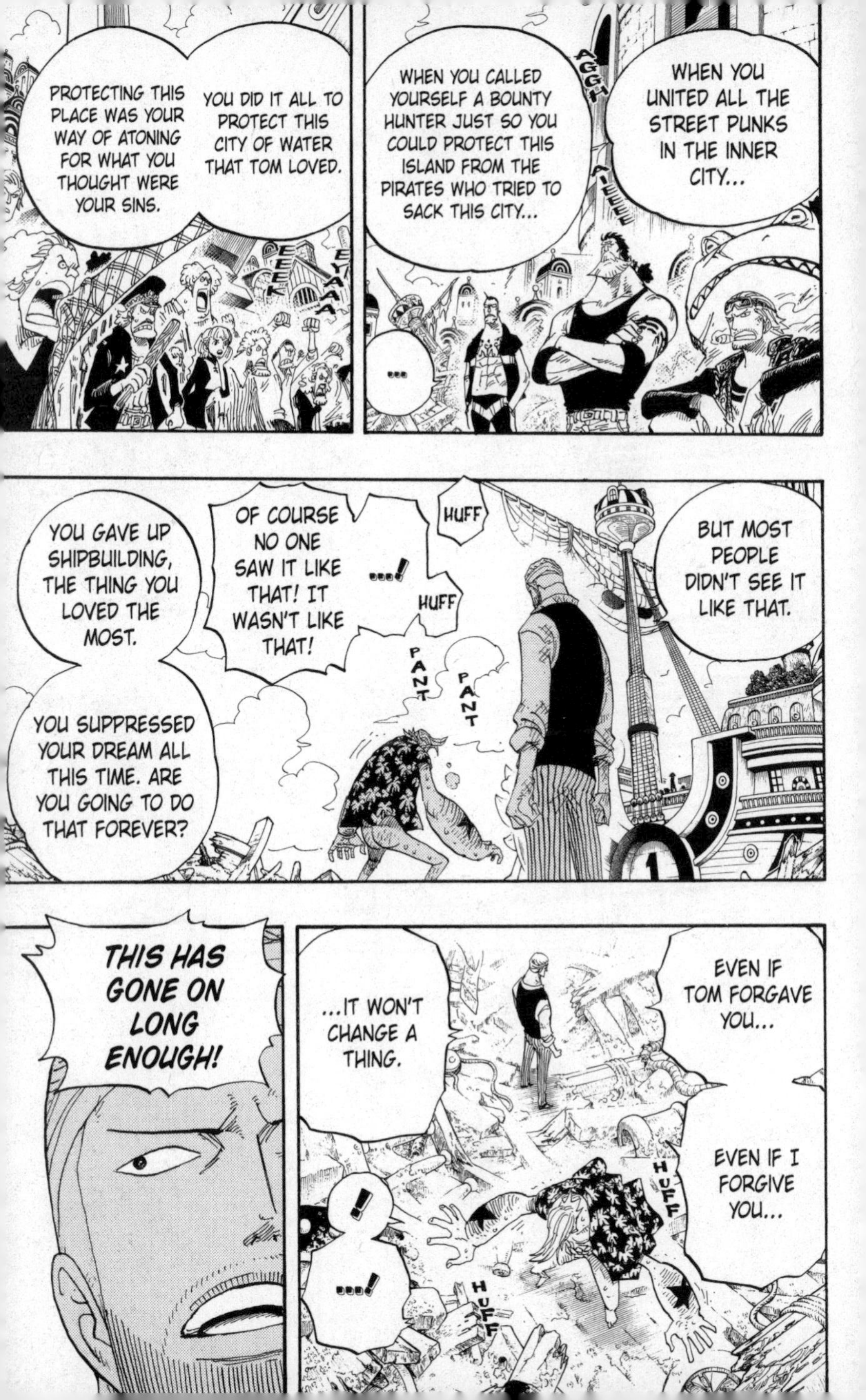
WHEN YOU UNITED ALL THE STREET PUNKS IN THE INNER CITY...
WHEN YOU CALLED YOURSELF A BOUNTY HUNTER JUST SO YOU COULD PROTECT THIS ISLAND FROM THE PIRATES WHO TRIED TO SACK THIS CITY...
AGGH
AIEEEE
...
YOU DID IT ALL TO PROTECT THIS CITY OF WATER THAT TOM LOVED.
PROTECTING THIS PLACE WAS YOUR WAY OF ATONING FOR WHAT YOU THOUGHT WERE YOUR SINS.
EYAAAA
EEEEK
BUT MOST PEOPLE DIDN'T SEE IT LIKE THAT.
HUFF
HUFF
...!
OF COURSE NO ONE SAW IT LIKE THAT! IT WASN'T LIKE THAT!
YOU GAVE UP SHIPBUILDING, THE THING YOU LOVED THE MOST.
YOU SUPPRESSED YOUR DREAM ALL THIS TIME. ARE YOU GOING TO DO THAT FOREVER?
PANT
PANT
EVEN IF TOM FORGAVE YOU...
EVEN IF I FORGIVE YOU...
...IT WON'T CHANGE A THING.
HUFF
!
...!
HUFF
THIS HAS GONE ON LONG ENOUGH!

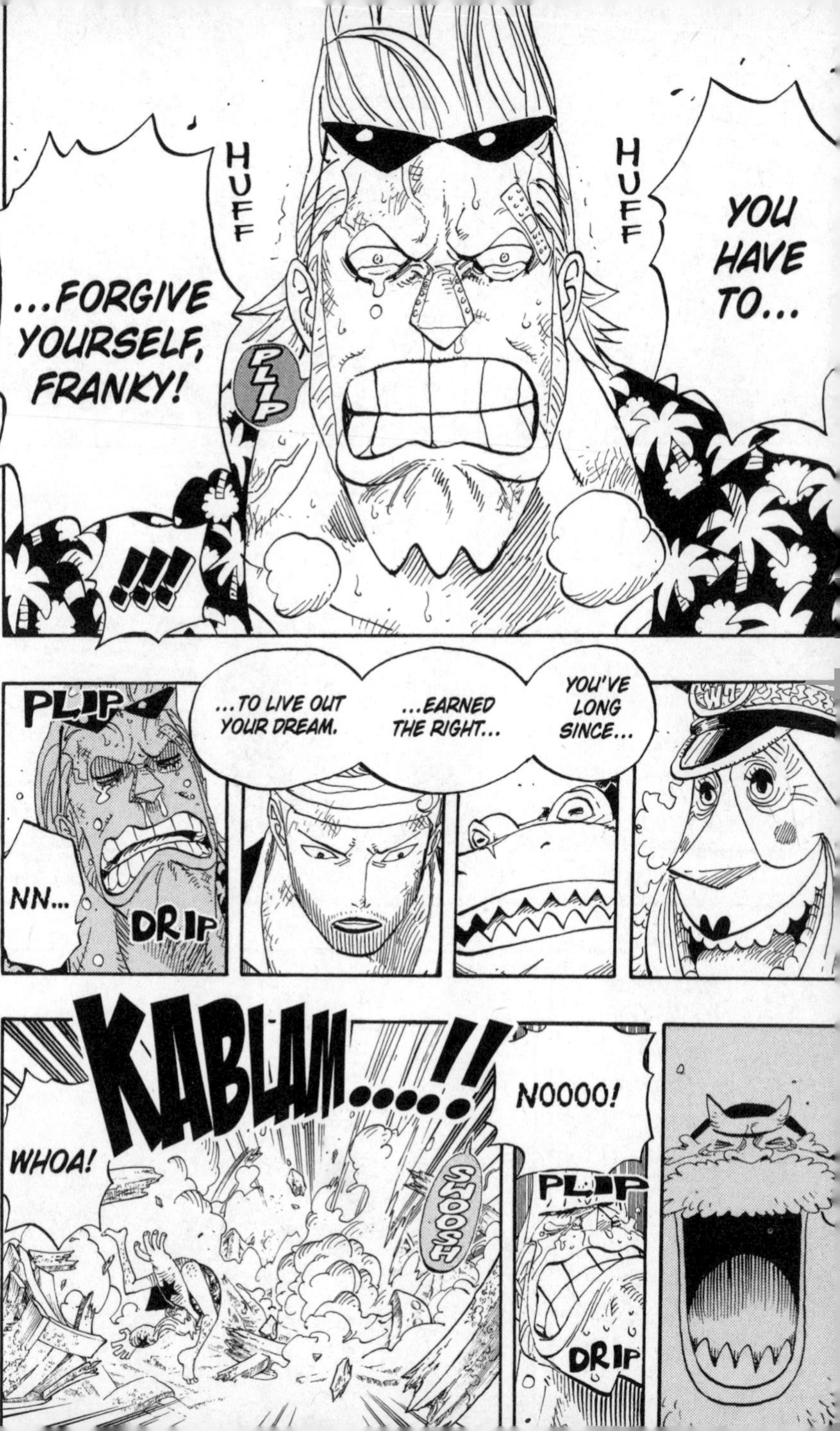
YOU HAVE TO...
HUFF
HUFF
PLIP
...FORGIVE YOURSELF, FRANKY!
!!!
YOU'VE LONG SINCE...
...EARNED THE RIGHT...
...TO LIVE OUT YOUR DREAM.
PLIP
NN...
DRIP
NOOOO!
PLIP
DRIP
KABLAM.....!!
SWOOSH
WHOA!

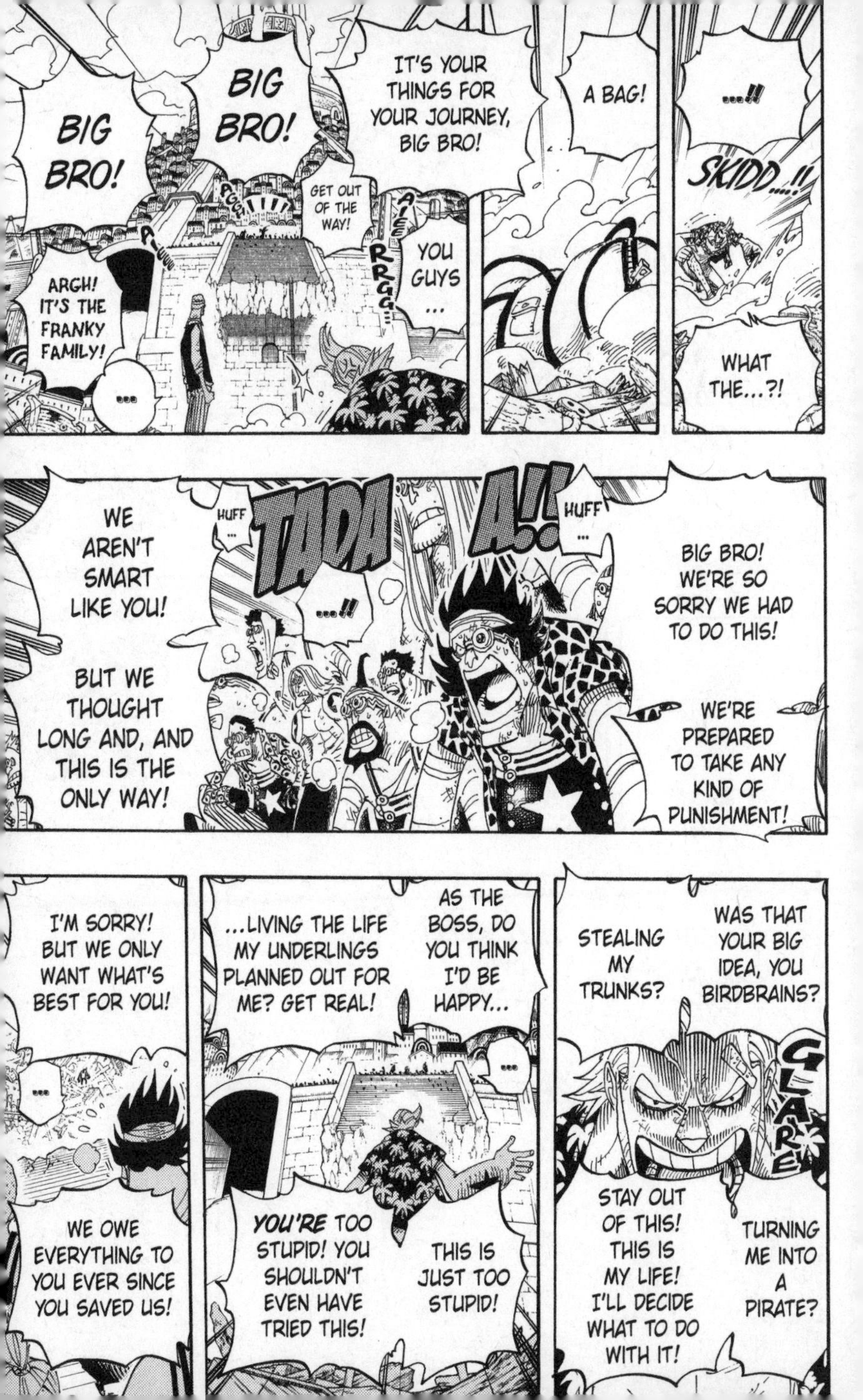
...!!
SKIDD...!!
WHAT THE...?!
A BAG!
IT'S YOUR THINGS FOR YOUR JOURNEY, BIG BRO!
BIG BRO!
BIG BRO!
GET OUT OF THE WAY!
AIEE
RRRGG...
YOU GUYS ...
AGGH
A-UUU
ARGH! IT'S THE FRANKY FAMILY!
...
BIG BRO! WE'RE SO SORRY WE HAD TO DO THIS!
HUFF ...
TADAA!!
HUFF ...
...!!
WE AREN'T SMART LIKE YOU!
WE'RE PREPARED TO TAKE ANY KIND OF PUNISHMENT!
BUT WE THOUGHT LONG AND, AND THIS IS THE ONLY WAY!
WAS THAT YOUR BIG IDEA, YOU BIRDBRAINS?
STEALING MY TRUNKS?
GLARE
TURNING ME INTO A PIRATE?
STAY OUT OF THIS! THIS IS MY LIFE! I'LL DECIDE WHAT TO DO WITH IT!
AS THE BOSS, DO YOU THINK I'D BE HAPPY...
...LIVING THE LIFE MY UNDERLINGS PLANNED OUT FOR ME? GET REAL!
...
THIS IS JUST TOO STUPID!
YOU'RE TOO STUPID! YOU SHOULDN'T EVEN HAVE TRIED THIS!
I'M SORRY! BUT WE ONLY WANT WHAT'S BEST FOR YOU!
...
WE OWE EVERYTHING TO YOU EVER SINCE YOU SAVED US!

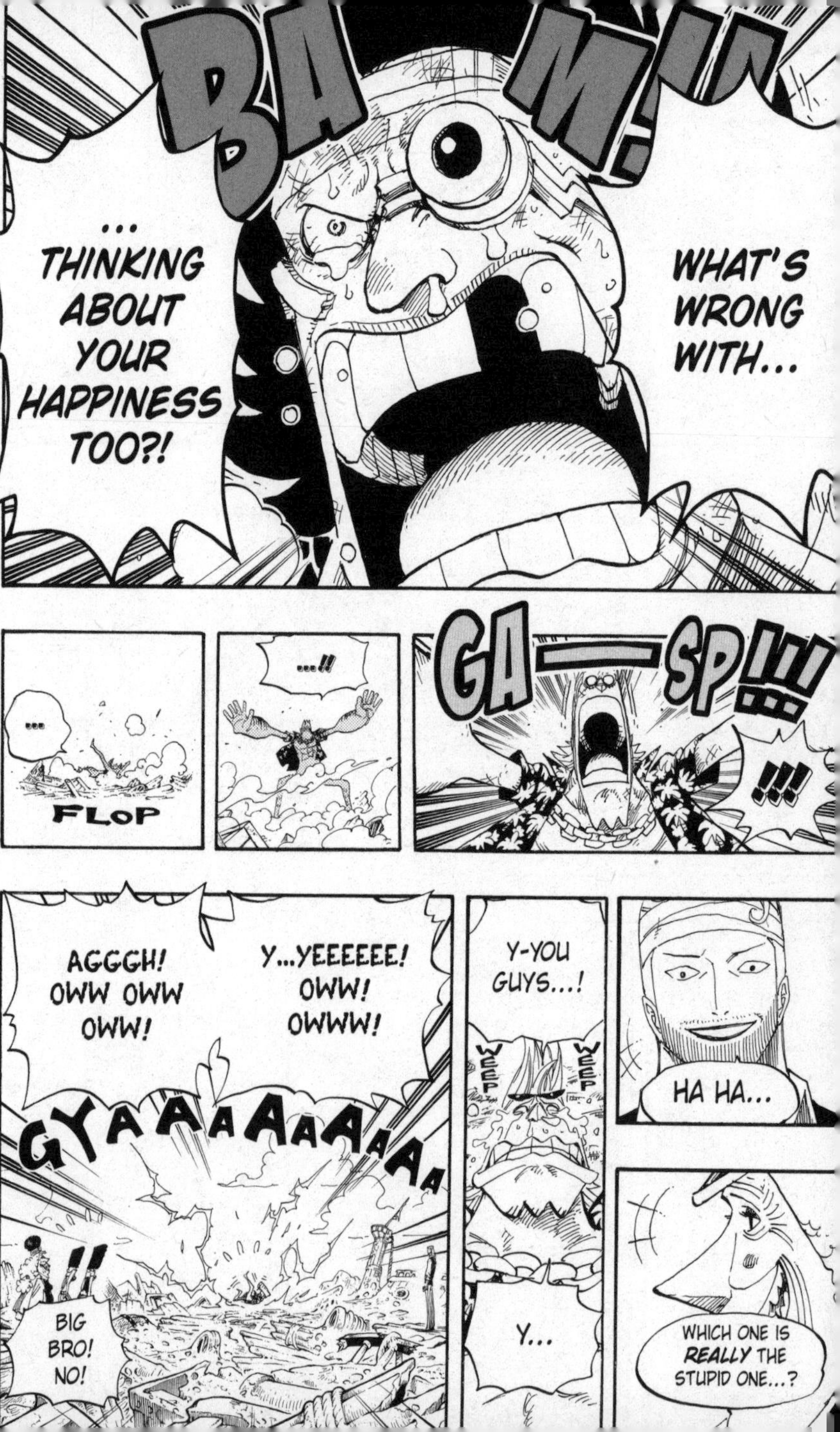
BAM!!
WHAT'S WRONG WITH...
... THINKING ABOUT YOUR HAPPINESS TOO?!
GA—SP!!!
!!!
...!!
...
FLOP
HA HA...
WHICH ONE IS *REALLY* THE STUPID ONE...?
Y-YOU GUYS...!
WEEP
WEEP
Y...
Y...YEEEEEE! OWW! OWWW!
AGGGH! OWW OWW OWW!
GYAAAAAAAAAA
BIG BRO! NO!

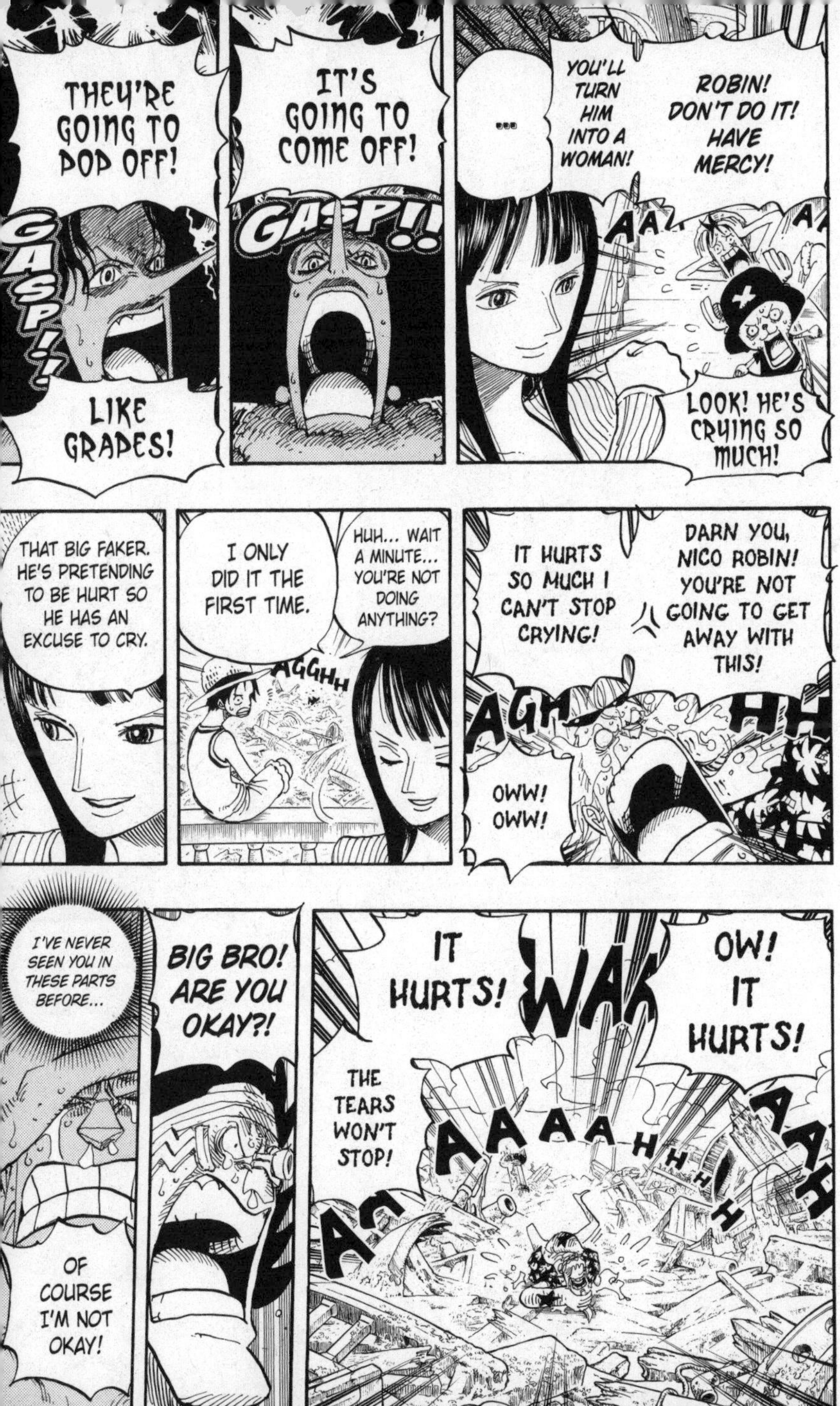

ROBIN! DON'T DO IT! HAVE MERCY!
YOU'LL TURN HIM INTO A WOMAN!
...
LOOK! HE'S CRYING SO MUCH!
IT'S GOING TO COME OFF!
GASP!!
THEY'RE GOING TO POP OFF!
GASP!!
LIKE GRAPES!
DARN YOU, NICO ROBIN! YOU'RE NOT GOING TO GET AWAY WITH THIS!
IT HURTS SO MUCH I CAN'T STOP CRYING!
OWW! OWW!
HUH... WAIT A MINUTE... YOU'RE NOT DOING ANYTHING?
I ONLY DID IT THE FIRST TIME.
AGGHH
THAT BIG FAKER. HE'S PRETENDING TO BE HURT SO HE HAS AN EXCUSE TO CRY.
OW! IT HURTS!
WAK
IT HURTS!
THE TEARS WON'T STOP!
AAAAHHHHH
BIG BRO! ARE YOU OKAY?!
I'VE NEVER SEEN YOU IN THESE PARTS BEFORE...
OF COURSE I'M NOT OKAY!

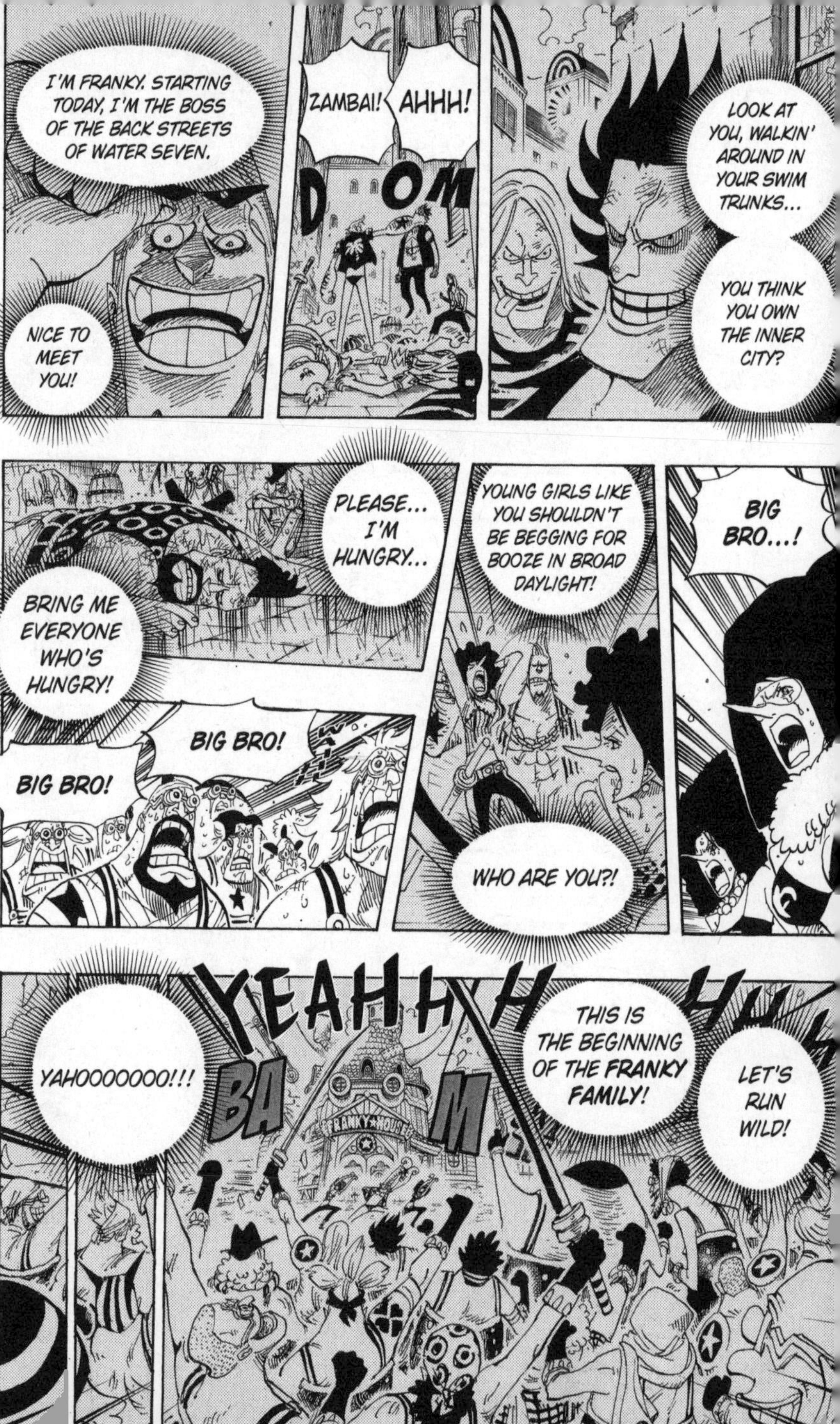
LOOK AT YOU, WALKIN' AROUND IN YOUR SWIM TRUNKS...
YOU THINK YOU OWN THE INNER CITY?
AHHH!
ZAMBAI!
DOM
I'M FRANKY. STARTING TODAY, I'M THE BOSS OF THE BACK STREETS OF WATER SEVEN.
NICE TO MEET YOU!
BIG BRO...!
YOUNG GIRLS LIKE YOU SHOULDN'T BE BEGGING FOR BOOZE IN BROAD DAYLIGHT!
WHO ARE YOU?!
PLEASE... I'M HUNGRY...
BRING ME EVERYONE WHO'S HUNGRY!
BIG BRO!
BIG BRO!
LET'S RUN WILD!
THIS IS THE BEGINNING OF THE FRANKY FAMILY!
YEAHHH
YAHOOOOOOO!!!
BAM
FRANKY HOUSE

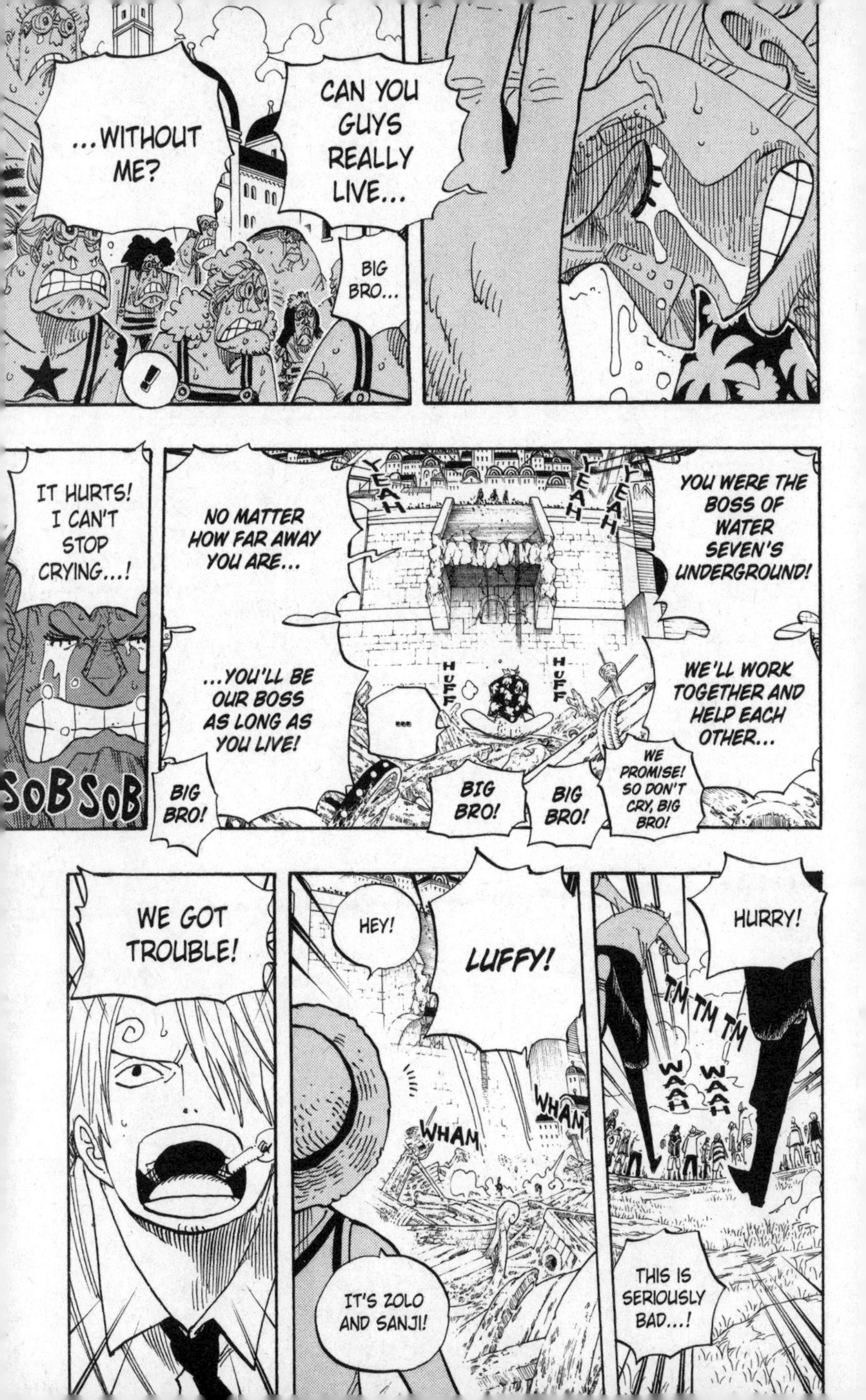
CAN YOU GUYS REALLY LIVE...
...WITHOUT ME?
!
BIG BRO...
YEAH
YEAH
YEAH
YOU WERE THE BOSS OF WATER SEVEN'S UNDERGROUND!
WE'LL WORK TOGETHER AND HELP EACH OTHER...
WE PROMISE! SO DON'T CRY, BIG BRO!
BIG BRO!
BIG BRO!
HUFF
HUFF
...
NO MATTER HOW FAR AWAY YOU ARE...
...YOU'LL BE OUR BOSS AS LONG AS YOU LIVE!
BIG BRO!
IT HURTS! I CAN'T STOP CRYING...!
SOB SOB
HURRY!
TM TM TM
WAAAH
WAAAH
THIS IS SERIOUSLY BAD...!
LUFFY!
HEY!
WHAM
WHAM
IT'S ZOLO AND SANJI!
WE GOT TROUBLE!

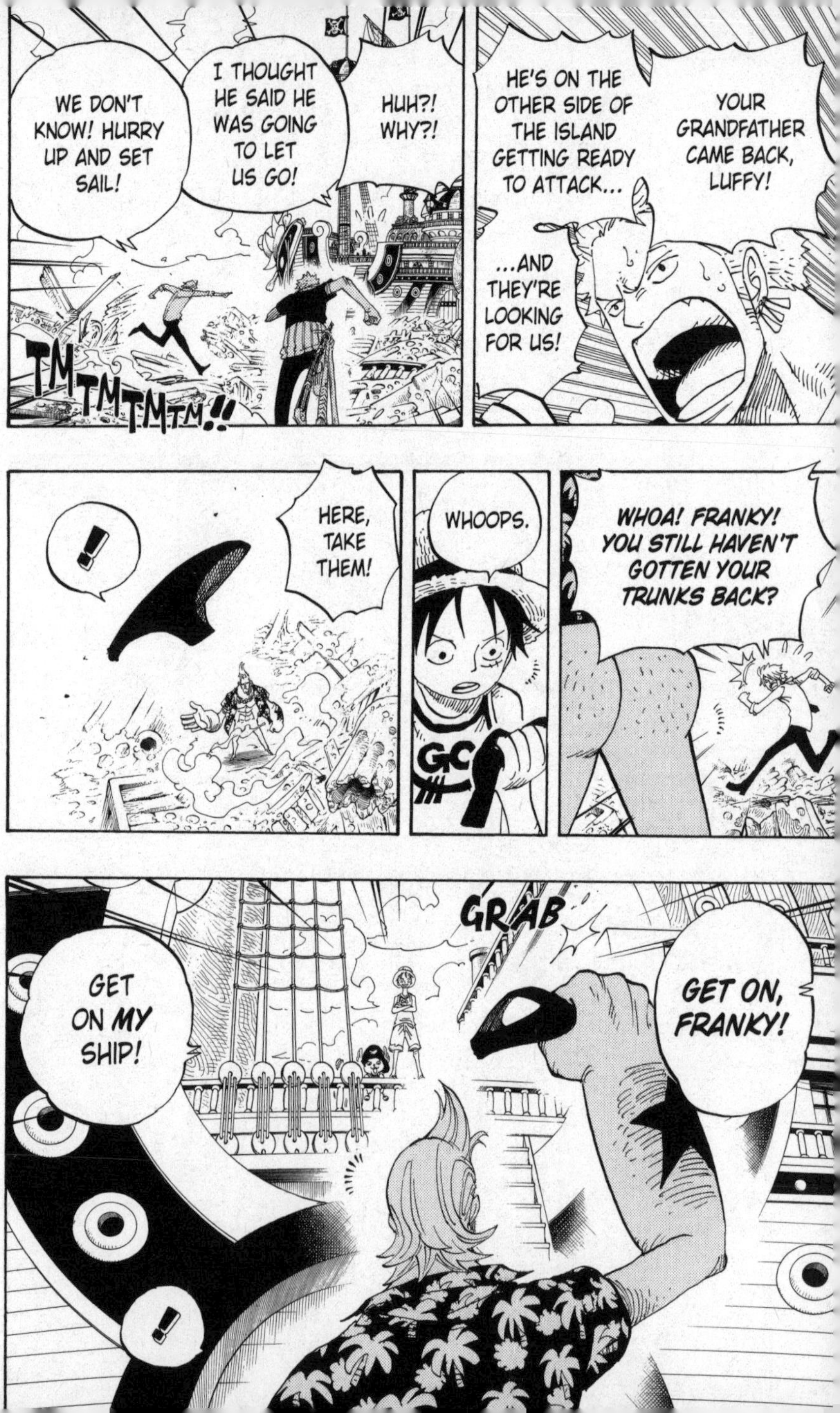
YOUR GRANDFATHER CAME BACK, LUFFY!
HE'S ON THE OTHER SIDE OF THE ISLAND GETTING READY TO ATTACK...
...AND THEY'RE LOOKING FOR US!
HUH?! WHY?!
I THOUGHT HE SAID HE WAS GOING TO LET US GO!
WE DON'T KNOW! HURRY UP AND SET SAIL!
TMTMTMTM!!
WHOA! FRANKY! YOU STILL HAVEN'T GOTTEN YOUR TRUNKS BACK?
WHOOPS.
HERE, TAKE THEM!
!
GRAB
GET ON, FRANKY!
GET ON MY SHIP!
!

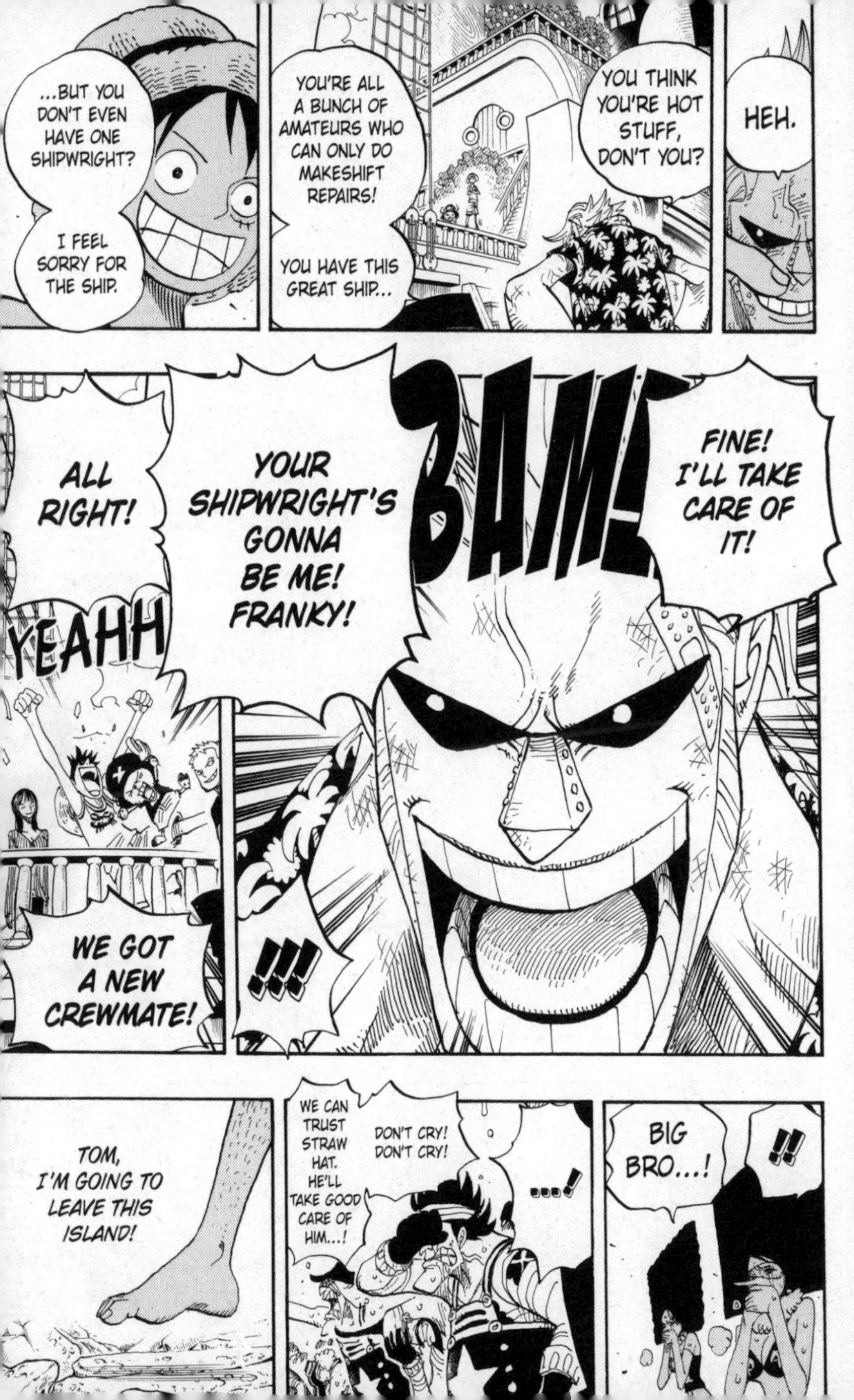
HEH.
YOU THINK YOU'RE HOT STUFF, DON'T YOU?
YOU'RE ALL A BUNCH OF AMATEURS WHO CAN ONLY DO MAKESHIFT REPAIRS!
YOU HAVE THIS GREAT SHIP...
...BUT YOU DON'T EVEN HAVE ONE SHIPWRIGHT?
I FEEL SORRY FOR THE SHIP.
FINE! I'LL TAKE CARE OF IT!
BAM!
YOUR SHIPWRIGHT'S GONNA BE ME! FRANKY!
!!!
ALL RIGHT!
YEAHH
WE GOT A NEW CREWMATE!
!!
BIG BRO...!
...!
DON'T CRY! DON'T CRY!
WE CAN TRUST STRAW HAT. HE'LL TAKE GOOD CARE OF HIM...!
TOM, I'M GOING TO LEAVE THIS ISLAND!

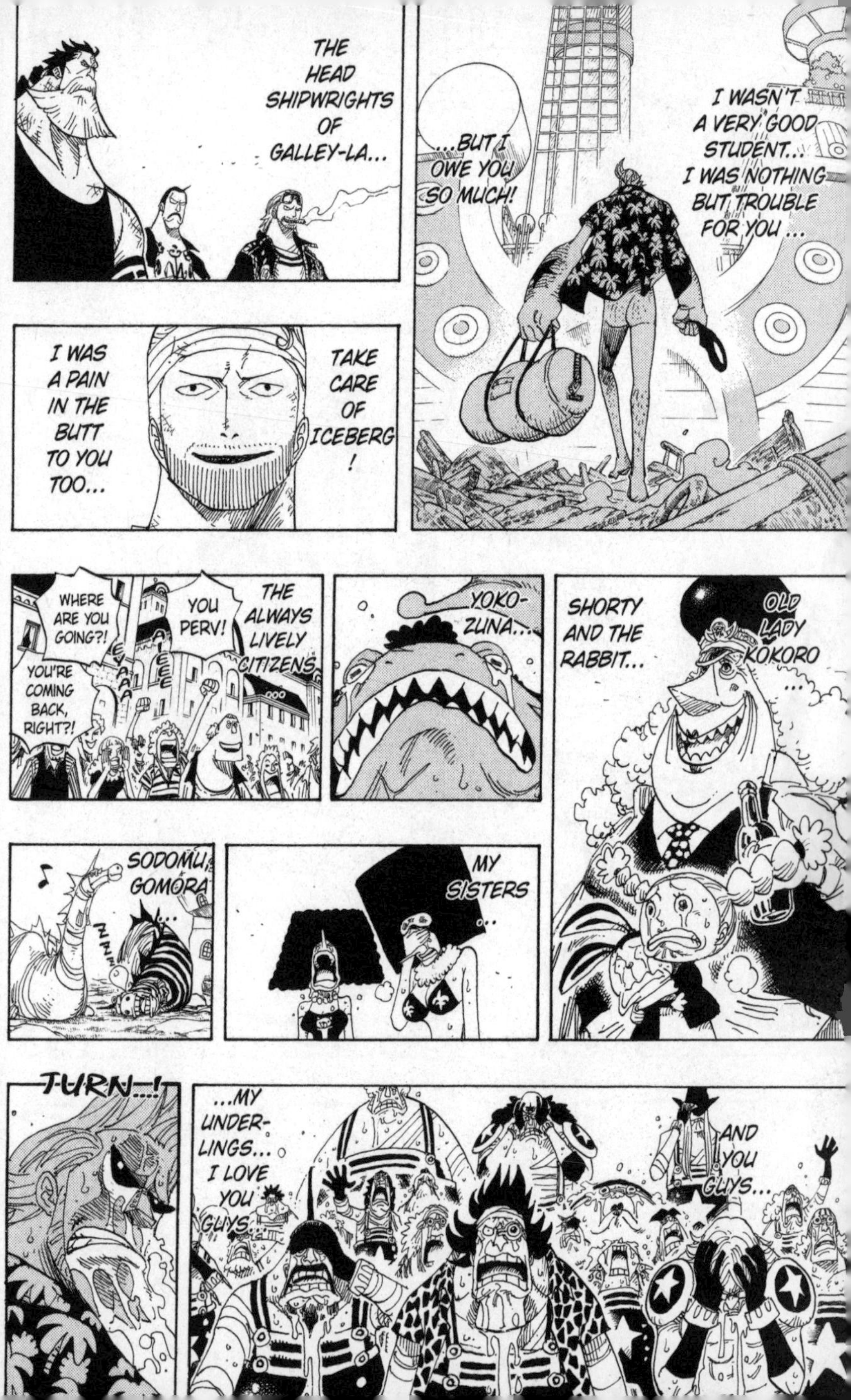
I WASN'T A VERY GOOD STUDENT... I WAS NOTHING BUT TROUBLE FOR YOU ...
...BUT I OWE YOU SO MUCH!
THE HEAD SHIPWRIGHTS OF GALLEY-LA...
TAKE CARE OF ICEBERG!
I WAS A PAIN IN THE BUTT TO YOU TOO...
OLD LADY KOKORO...
SHORTY AND THE RABBIT...
YOKO-ZUNA...
THE ALWAYS LIVELY CITIZENS
YOU PERV!
WHERE ARE YOU GOING?!
AIEEE
EYAAA
YOU'RE COMING BACK, RIGHT?!
MY SISTERS...
SODOMU, GOMORA...
...MY UNDER-LINGS... I LOVE YOU GUYS...
AND YOU GUYS...
TURN...!

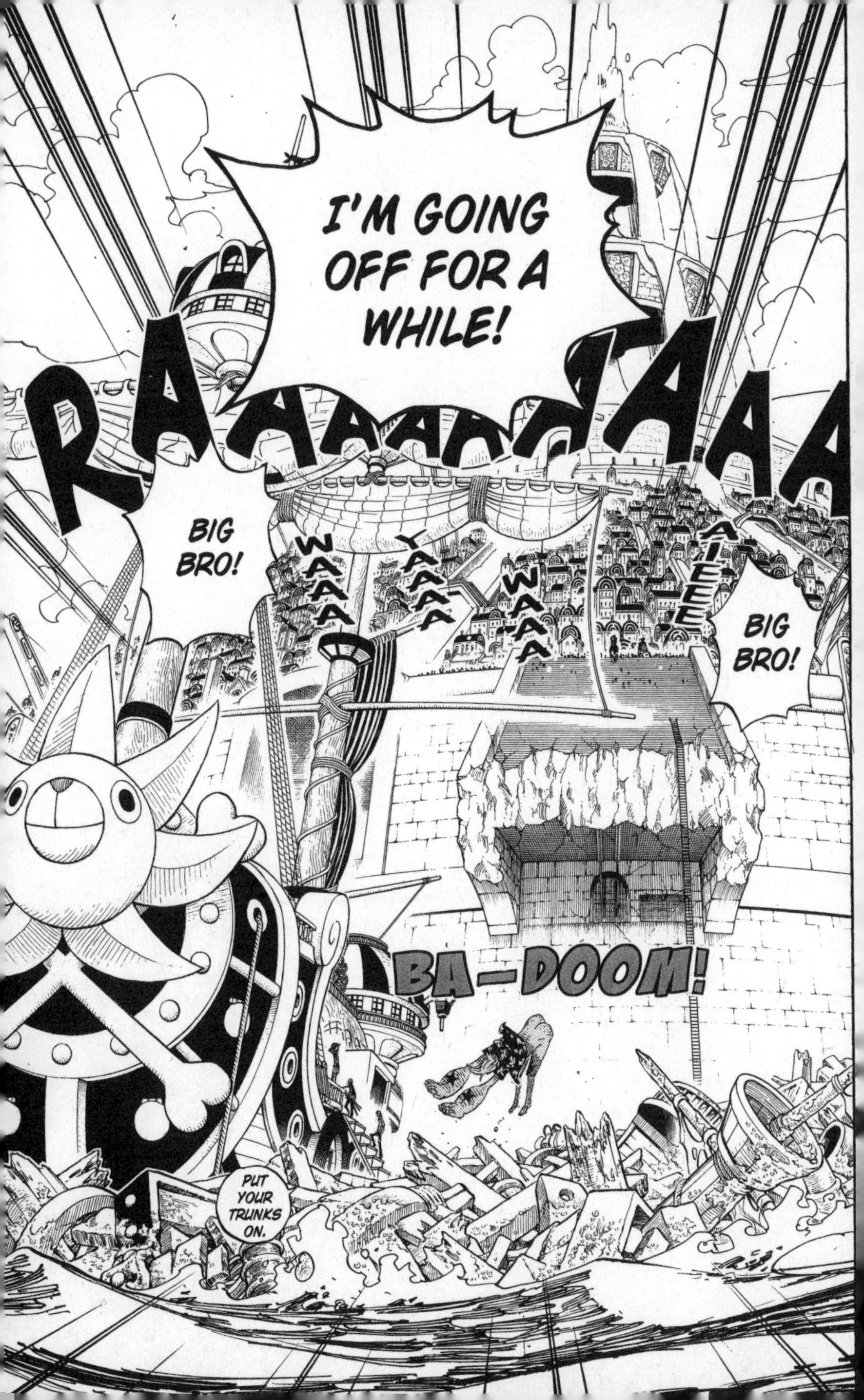

I'M GOING OFF FOR A WHILE!
RAAAAAAAA
BIG BRO!
AIEEEE
WAAAA
YAAAA
WAAAA
BIG BRO!
BA-DOOM!
PUT YOUR TRUNKS ON.

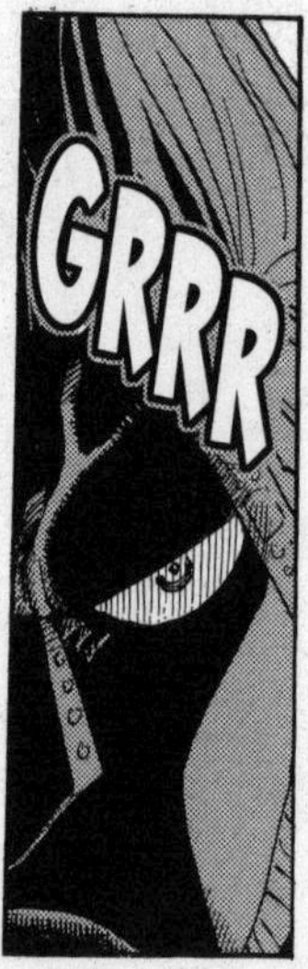
GRRR

Chapter 438:

PRIDE

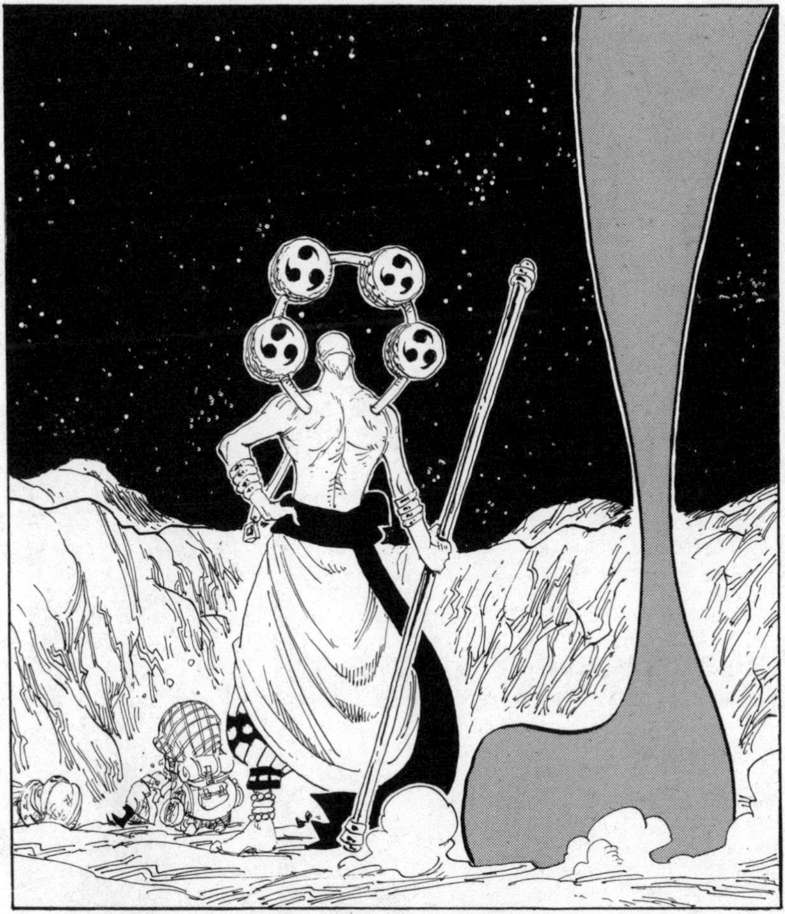

ENERU'S GREAT SPACE MISSION, VOL. 9:
"THE CREEPING SHADOW"

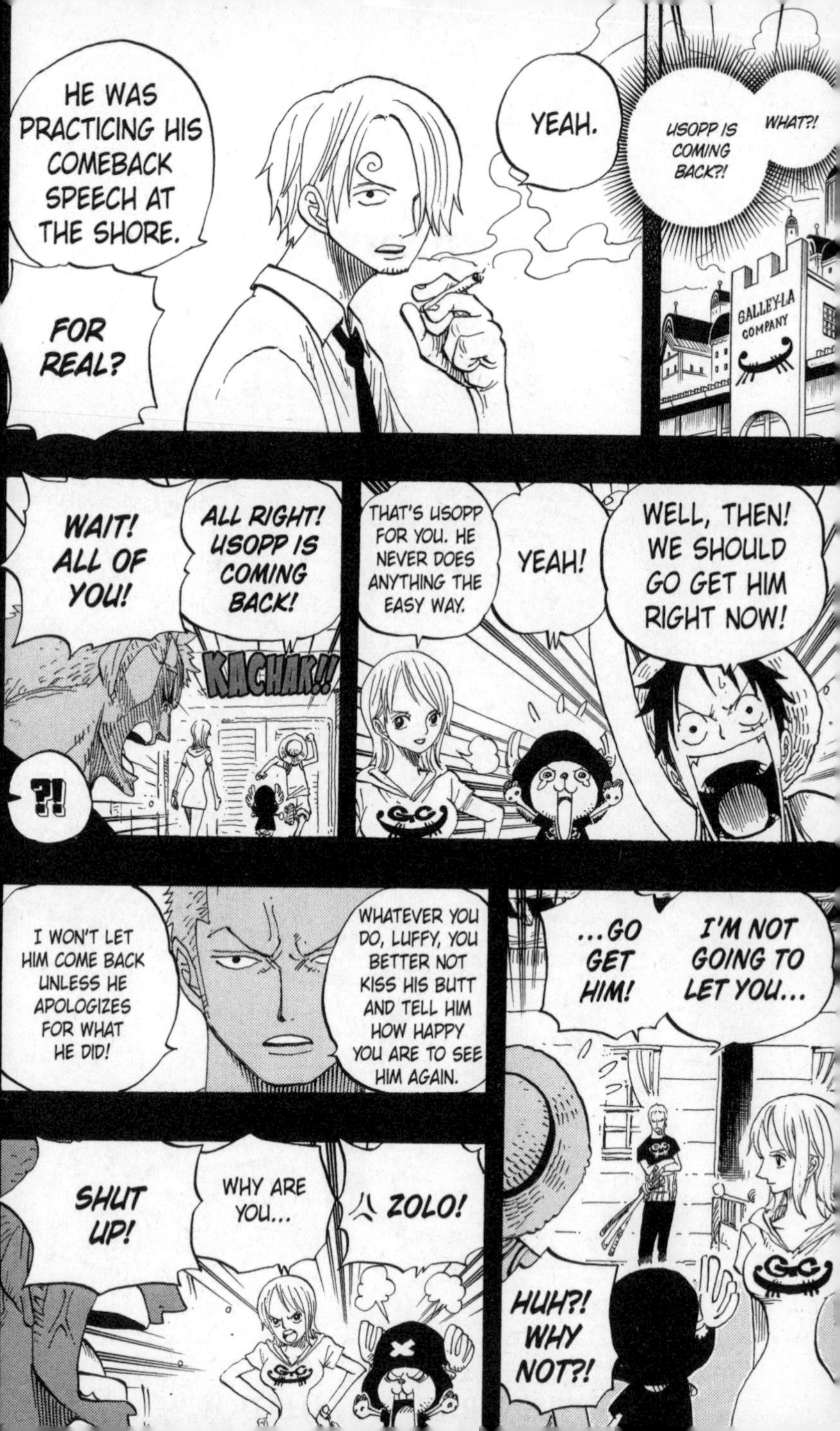
WHAT?!
USOPP IS COMING BACK?!
GALLEY-LA COMPANY
YEAH.
HE WAS PRACTICING HIS COMEBACK SPEECH AT THE SHORE.
FOR REAL?
WELL, THEN! WE SHOULD GO GET HIM RIGHT NOW!
YEAH!
THAT'S USOPP FOR YOU. HE NEVER DOES ANYTHING THE EASY WAY.
ALL RIGHT! USOPP IS COMING BACK!
KACHAK!!
WAIT! ALL OF YOU!
?!
I'M NOT GOING TO LET YOU...
...GO GET HIM!
HUH?! WHY NOT?!
WHATEVER YOU DO, LUFFY, YOU BETTER NOT KISS HIS BUTT AND TELL HIM HOW HAPPY YOU ARE TO SEE HIM AGAIN.
I WON'T LET HIM COME BACK UNLESS HE APOLOGIZES FOR WHAT HE DID!
ZOLO!
WHY ARE YOU...
SHUT UP!

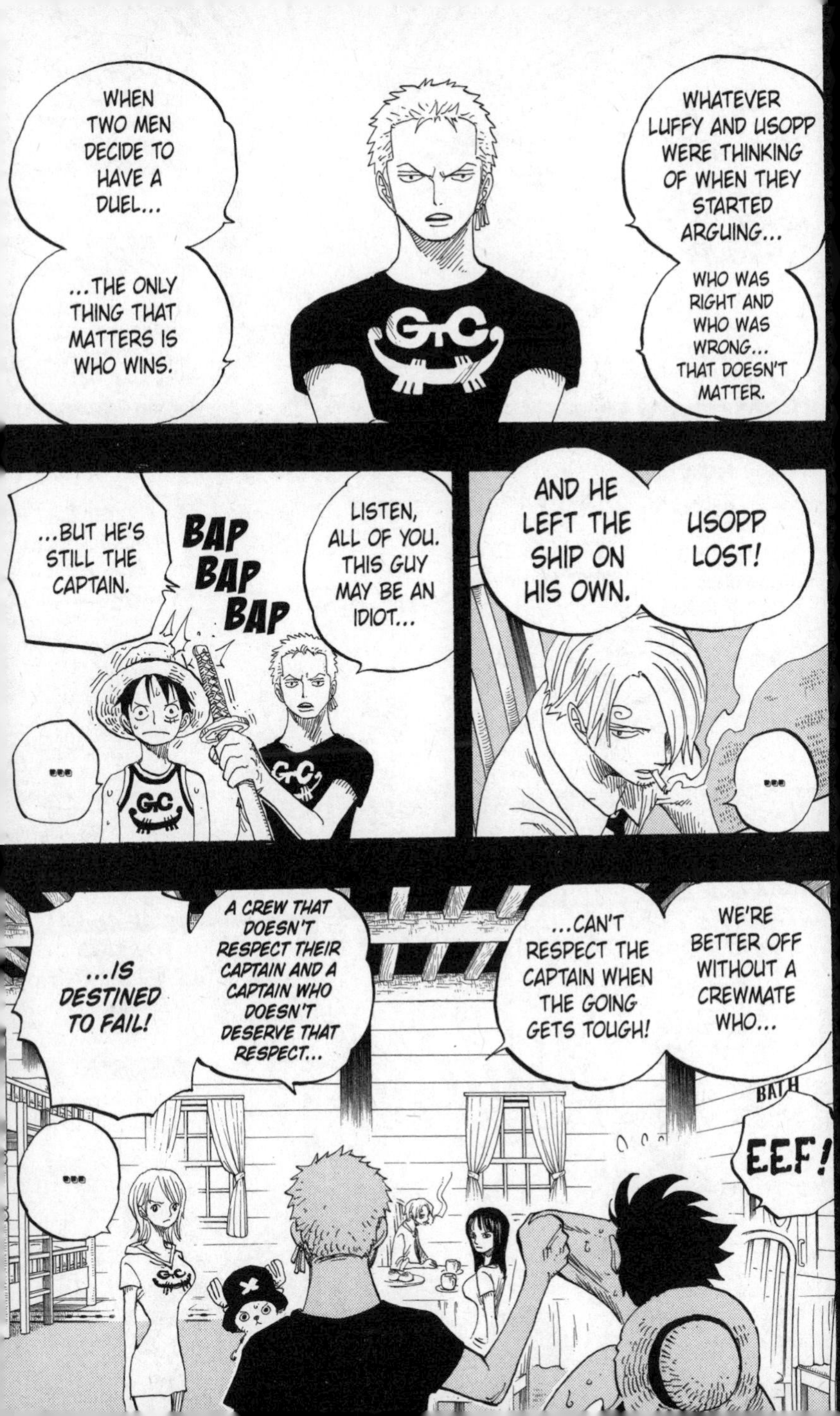
WHATEVER LUFFY AND USOPP WERE THINKING OF WHEN THEY STARTED ARGUING...
WHO WAS RIGHT AND WHO WAS WRONG... THAT DOESN'T MATTER.
WHEN TWO MEN DECIDE TO HAVE A DUEL...
...THE ONLY THING THAT MATTERS IS WHO WINS.
USOPP LOST!
AND HE LEFT THE SHIP ON HIS OWN.
...
LISTEN, ALL OF YOU. THIS GUY MAY BE AN IDIOT...
BAP BAP BAP
...BUT HE'S STILL THE CAPTAIN.
...
WE'RE BETTER OFF WITHOUT A CREWMATE WHO...
...CAN'T RESPECT THE CAPTAIN WHEN THE GOING GETS TOUGH!
A CREW THAT DOESN'T RESPECT THEIR CAPTAIN AND A CAPTAIN WHO DOESN'T DESERVE THAT RESPECT...
...IS DESTINED TO FAIL!
BATH
EEF!
...

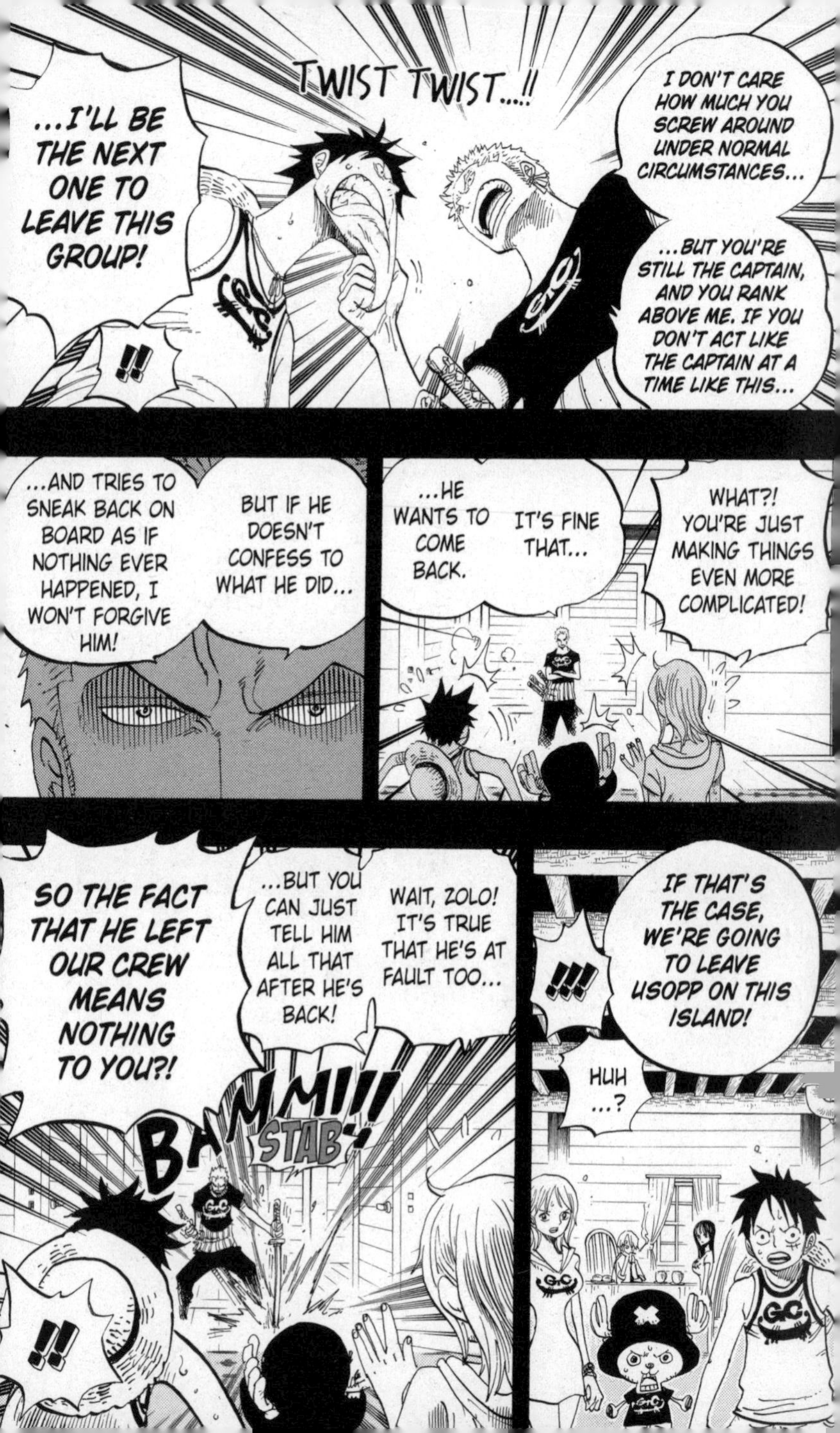
TWIST TWIST...!!
I DON'T CARE HOW MUCH YOU SCREW AROUND UNDER NORMAL CIRCUMSTANCES...
...BUT YOU'RE STILL THE CAPTAIN, AND YOU RANK ABOVE ME. IF YOU DON'T ACT LIKE THE CAPTAIN AT A TIME LIKE THIS...
...I'LL BE THE NEXT ONE TO LEAVE THIS GROUP!
!!
WHAT?! YOU'RE JUST MAKING THINGS EVEN MORE COMPLICATED!
IT'S FINE THAT...
...HE WANTS TO COME BACK.
BUT IF HE DOESN'T CONFESS TO WHAT HE DID...
...AND TRIES TO SNEAK BACK ON BOARD AS IF NOTHING EVER HAPPENED, I WON'T FORGIVE HIM!
IF THAT'S THE CASE, WE'RE GOING TO LEAVE USOPP ON THIS ISLAND!
!!!
HUH ...?
WAIT, ZOLO! IT'S TRUE THAT HE'S AT FAULT TOO...
...BUT YOU CAN JUST TELL HIM ALL THAT AFTER HE'S BACK!
SO THE FACT THAT HE LEFT OUR CREW MEANS NOTHING TO YOU?!
BAMM!!!
STAB
!!

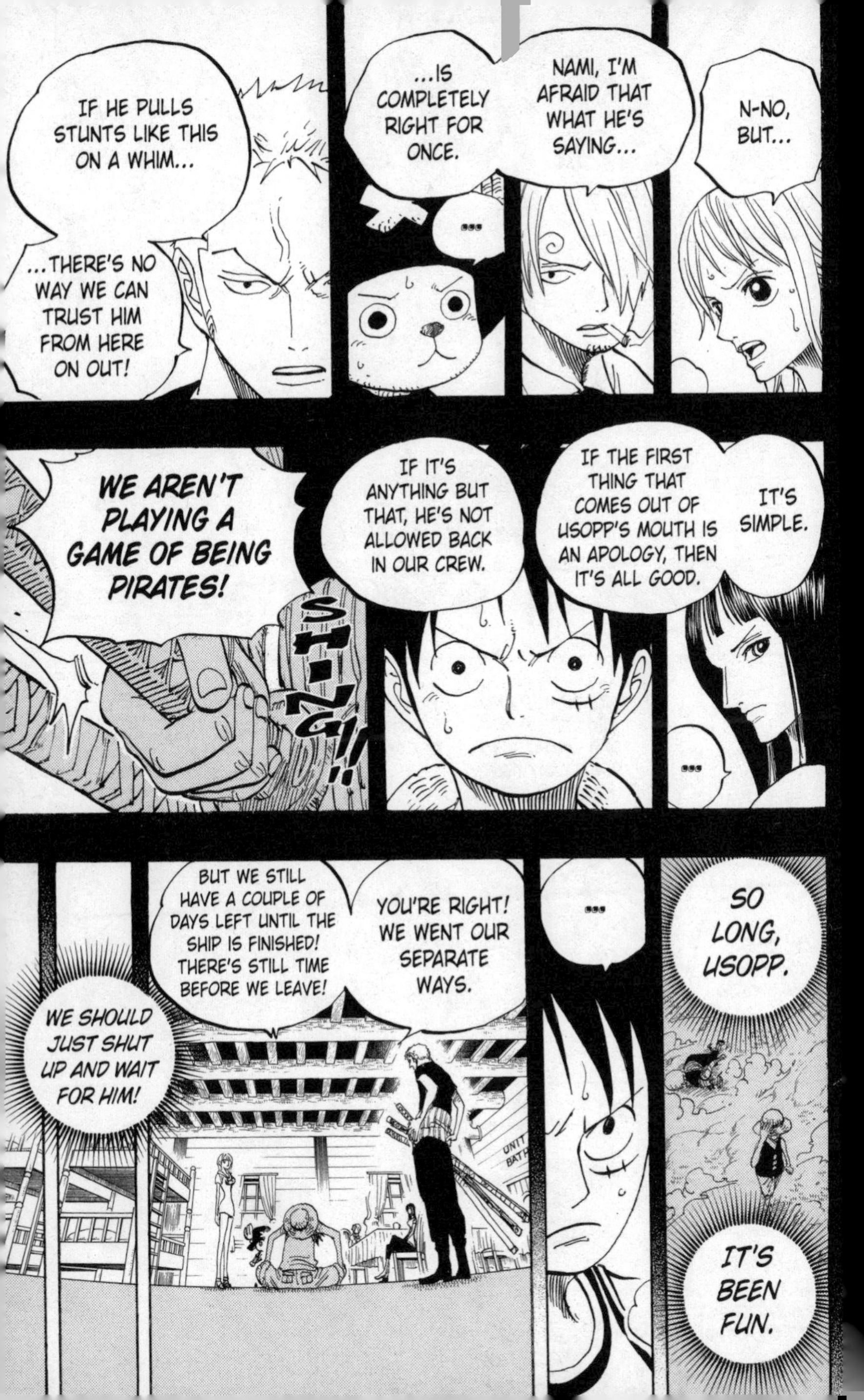
N-NO, BUT...
NAMI, I'M AFRAID THAT WHAT HE'S SAYING...
...IS COMPLETELY RIGHT FOR ONCE.
...
IF HE PULLS STUNTS LIKE THIS ON A WHIM...
...THERE'S NO WAY WE CAN TRUST HIM FROM HERE ON OUT!
IT'S SIMPLE.
IF THE FIRST THING THAT COMES OUT OF USOPP'S MOUTH IS AN APOLOGY, THEN IT'S ALL GOOD.
...
IF IT'S ANYTHING BUT THAT, HE'S NOT ALLOWED BACK IN OUR CREW.
WE AREN'T PLAYING A GAME OF BEING PIRATES!
SHING!!
SO LONG, USOPP.
IT'S BEEN FUN.
...
YOU'RE RIGHT! WE WENT OUR SEPARATE WAYS.
BUT WE STILL HAVE A COUPLE OF DAYS LEFT UNTIL THE SHIP IS FINISHED! THERE'S STILL TIME BEFORE WE LEAVE!
UNIT BATH
WE SHOULD JUST SHUT UP AND WAIT FOR HIM!

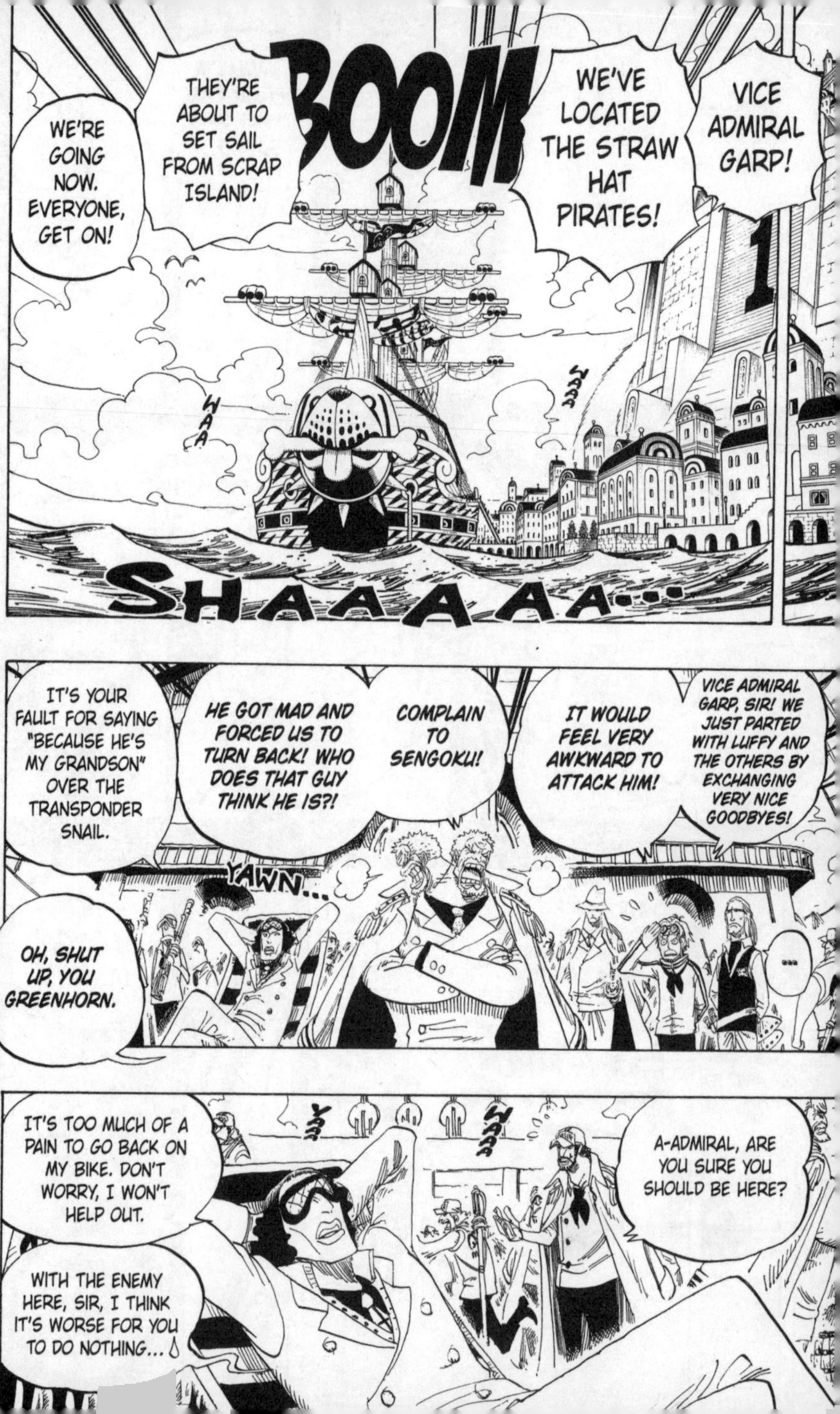
VICE ADMIRAL GARP!
WE'VE LOCATED THE STRAW HAT PIRATES!
BOOM
THEY'RE ABOUT TO SET SAIL FROM SCRAP ISLAND!
WE'RE GOING NOW. EVERYONE, GET ON!
WAAA
WAAA
SHAAAAA...
VICE ADMIRAL GARP, SIR! WE JUST PARTED WITH LUFFY AND THE OTHERS BY EXCHANGING VERY NICE GOODBYES!
IT WOULD FEEL VERY AWKWARD TO ATTACK HIM!
COMPLAIN TO SENGOKU!
HE GOT MAD AND FORCED US TO TURN BACK! WHO DOES THAT GUY THINK HE IS?!
IT'S YOUR FAULT FOR SAYING "BECAUSE HE'S MY GRANDSON" OVER THE TRANSPONDER SNAIL.
...
YAWN...
OH, SHUT UP, YOU GREENHORN.
A-ADMIRAL, ARE YOU SURE YOU SHOULD BE HERE?
WAAA
WAAA
IT'S TOO MUCH OF A PAIN TO GO BACK ON MY BIKE. DON'T WORRY, I WON'T HELP OUT.
WITH THE ENEMY HERE, SIR, I THINK IT'S WORSE FOR YOU TO DO NOTHING...

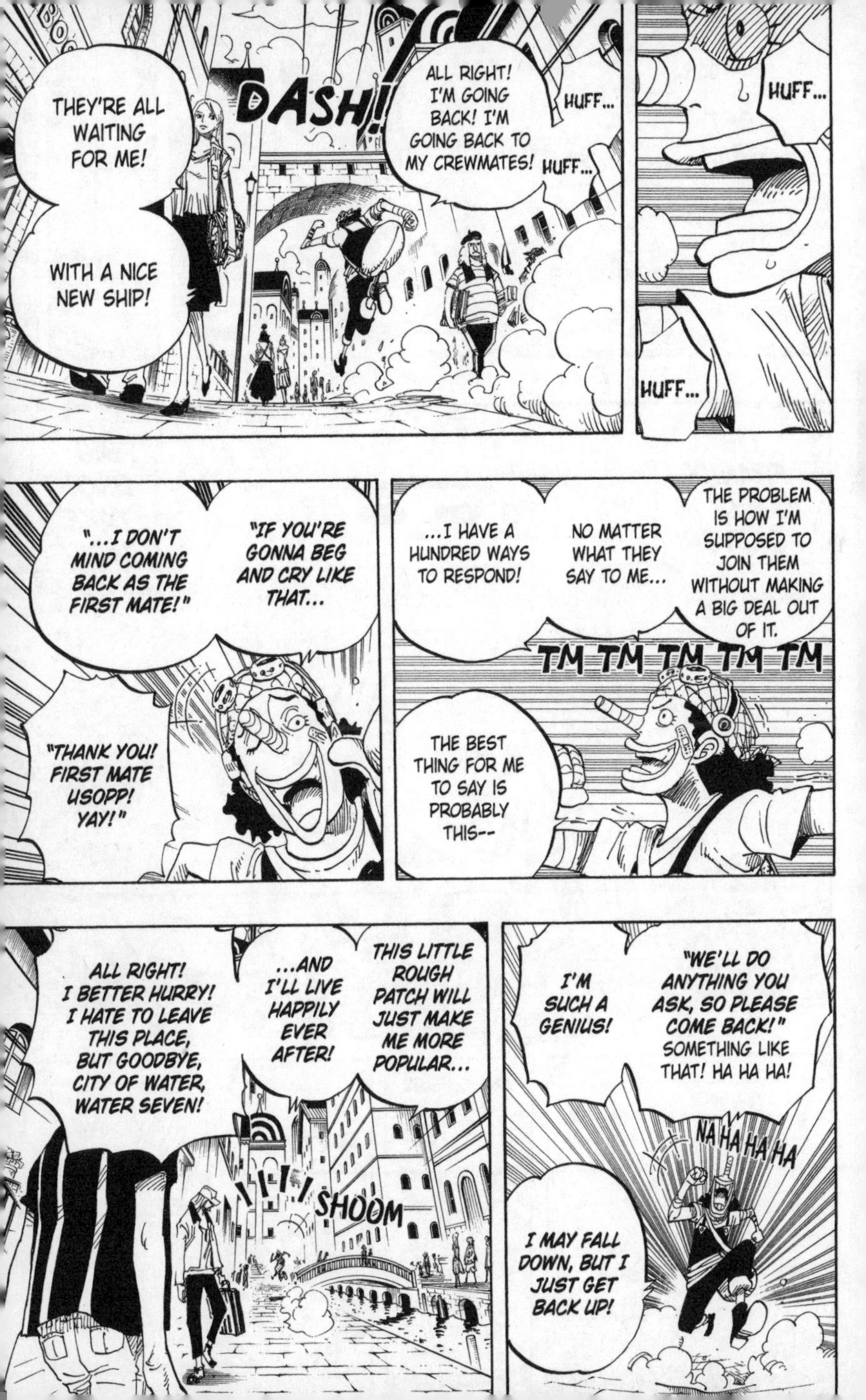
HUFF...
HUFF...
HUFF...
HUFF...
ALL RIGHT! I'M GOING BACK! I'M GOING BACK TO MY CREWMATES!
DASH!!
THEY'RE ALL WAITING FOR ME!
WITH A NICE NEW SHIP!
THE PROBLEM IS HOW I'M SUPPOSED TO JOIN THEM WITHOUT MAKING A BIG DEAL OUT OF IT.
NO MATTER WHAT THEY SAY TO ME...
...I HAVE A HUNDRED WAYS TO RESPOND!
TM TM TM TM TM
THE BEST THING FOR ME TO SAY IS PROBABLY THIS--
"IF YOU'RE GONNA BEG AND CRY LIKE THAT...
"...I DON'T MIND COMING BACK AS THE FIRST MATE!"
"THANK YOU! FIRST MATE USOPP! YAY!"
"WE'LL DO ANYTHING YOU ASK, SO PLEASE COME BACK!" SOMETHING LIKE THAT! HA HA HA!
I'M SUCH A GENIUS!
NA HA HA HA
I MAY FALL DOWN, BUT I JUST GET BACK UP!
THIS LITTLE ROUGH PATCH WILL JUST MAKE ME MORE POPULAR...
...AND I'LL LIVE HAPPILY EVER AFTER!
ALL RIGHT! I BETTER HURRY! I HATE TO LEAVE THIS PLACE, BUT GOODBYE, CITY OF WATER, WATER SEVEN!
SHOOM

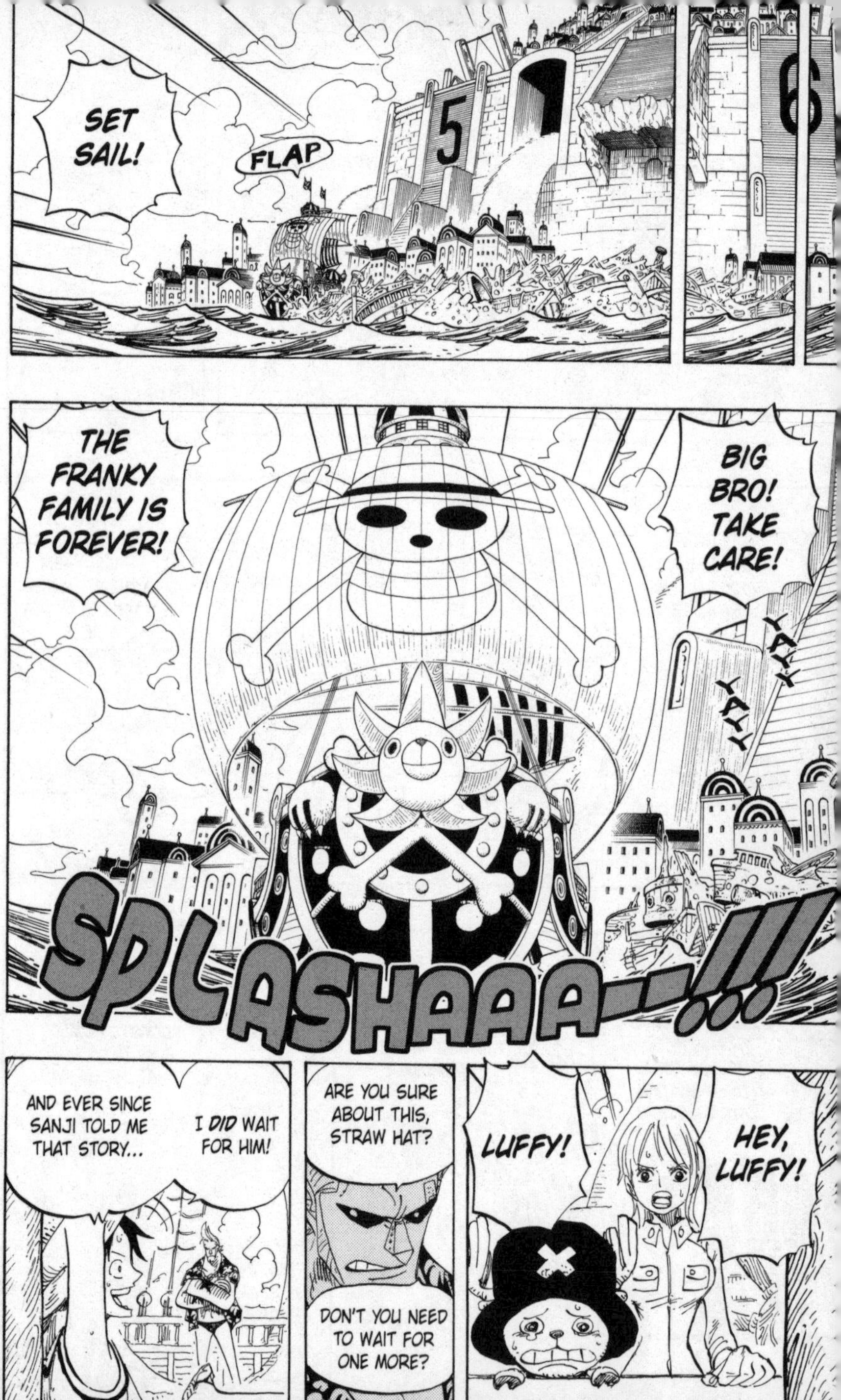
SET SAIL!
FLAP
BIG BRO! TAKE CARE!
YAYY
YAYY
THE FRANKY FAMILY IS FOREVER!
SPLASHAAA--!!!
HEY, LUFFY!
LUFFY!
ARE YOU SURE ABOUT THIS, STRAW HAT?
DON'T YOU NEED TO WAIT FOR ONE MORE?
I *DID* WAIT FOR HIM!
AND EVER SINCE SANJI TOLD ME THAT STORY...

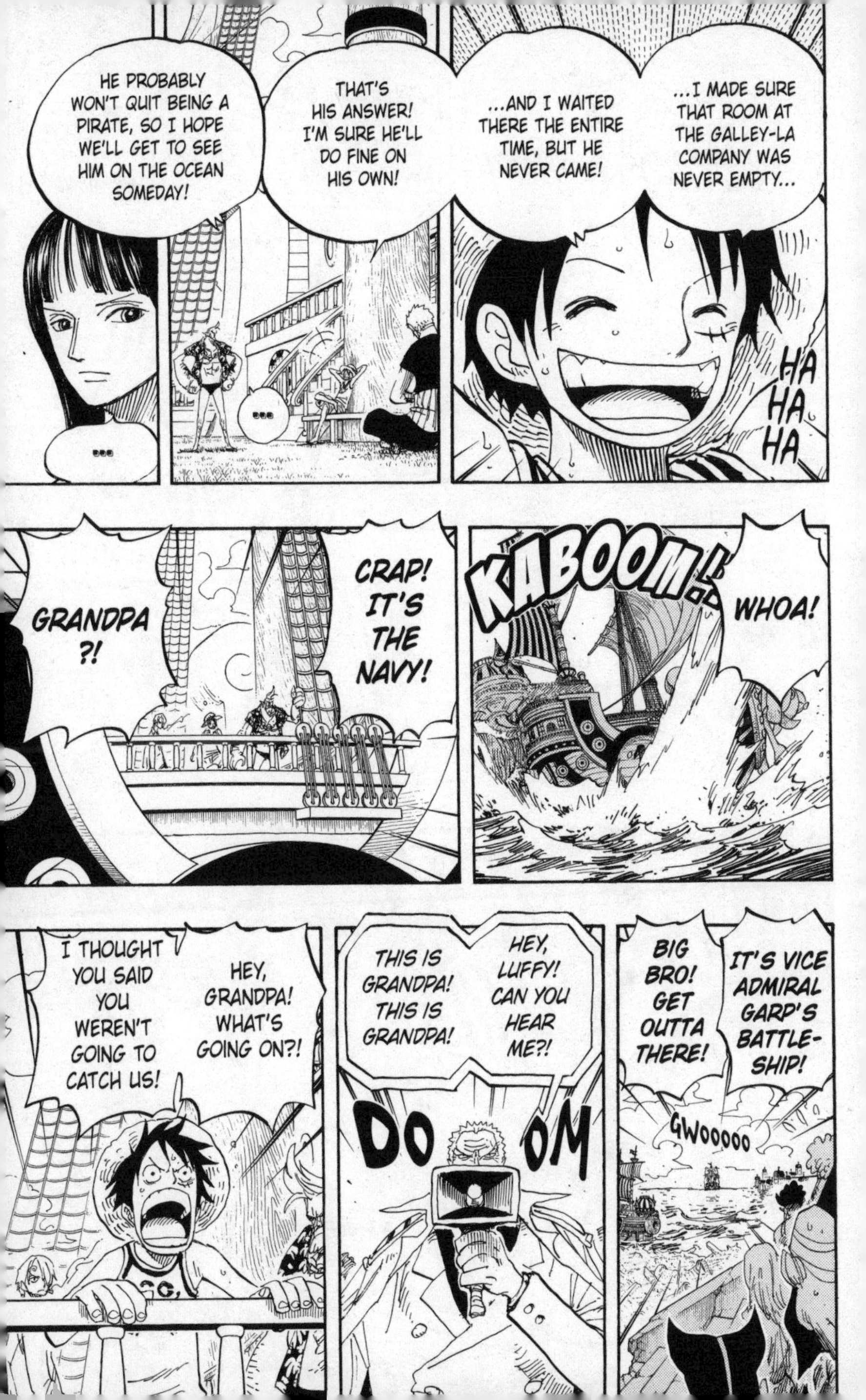
...I MADE SURE THAT ROOM AT THE GALLEY-LA COMPANY WAS NEVER EMPTY...
...AND I WAITED THERE THE ENTIRE TIME, BUT HE NEVER CAME!
HA HA HA
THAT'S HIS ANSWER! I'M SURE HE'LL DO FINE ON HIS OWN!
...
HE PROBABLY WON'T QUIT BEING A PIRATE, SO I HOPE WE'LL GET TO SEE HIM ON THE OCEAN SOMEDAY!
...
WHOA!
KABOOM!!
CRAP! IT'S THE NAVY!
GRANDPA ?!
IT'S VICE ADMIRAL GARP'S BATTLE-SHIP!
BIG BRO! GET OUTTA THERE!
GWOOOOO
HEY, LUFFY! CAN YOU HEAR ME?!
THIS IS GRANDPA! THIS IS GRANDPA!
DO OM
HEY, GRANDPA! WHAT'S GOING ON?!
I THOUGHT YOU SAID YOU WEREN'T GOING TO CATCH US!

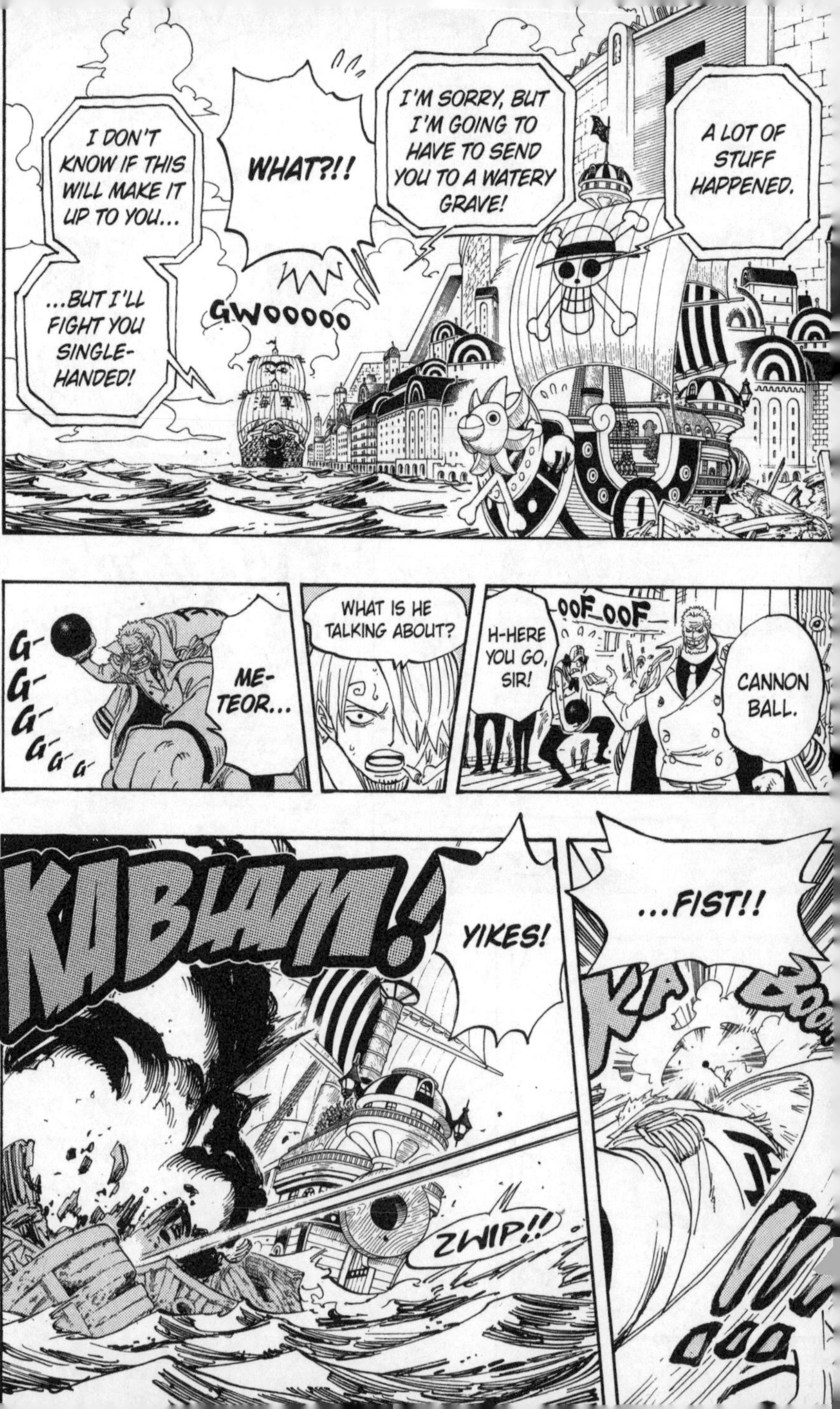
A LOT OF STUFF HAPPENED.
I'M SORRY, BUT I'M GOING TO HAVE TO SEND YOU TO A WATERY GRAVE!
WHAT?!!
I DON'T KNOW IF THIS WILL MAKE IT UP TO YOU...
...BUT I'LL FIGHT YOU SINGLE-HANDED!
GWOOOOO
OOF OOF
CANNON BALL.
H-HERE YOU GO, SIR!
WHAT IS HE TALKING ABOUT?
ME-TEOR...
G-G-G-G-G-G-G
...FIST!!
YIKES!
KABLAM!
ZWIP!!

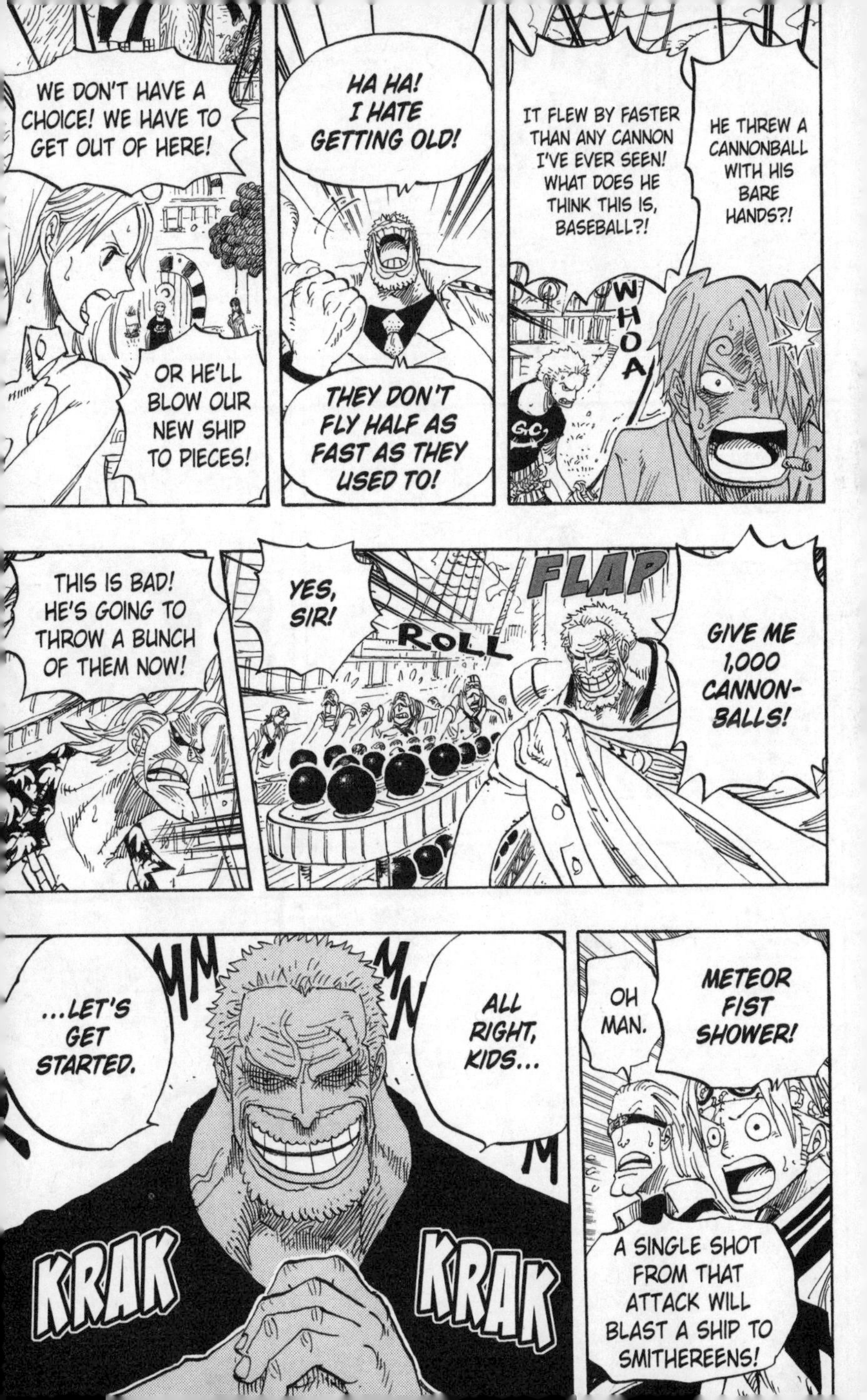
HE THREW A CANNONBALL WITH HIS BARE HANDS?!
IT FLEW BY FASTER THAN ANY CANNON I'VE EVER SEEN! WHAT DOES HE THINK THIS IS, BASEBALL?!
WHOA
HA HA! I HATE GETTING OLD!
THEY DON'T FLY HALF AS FAST AS THEY USED TO!
WE DON'T HAVE A CHOICE! WE HAVE TO GET OUT OF HERE!
OR HE'LL BLOW OUR NEW SHIP TO PIECES!
GIVE ME 1,000 CANNON-BALLS!
FLAP
YES, SIR!
ROLL
THIS IS BAD! HE'S GOING TO THROW A BUNCH OF THEM NOW!
METEOR FIST SHOWER!
OH MAN.
A SINGLE SHOT FROM THAT ATTACK WILL BLAST A SHIP TO SMITHEREENS!
ALL RIGHT, KIDS...
MMM
...LET'S GET STARTED.
KRAK
KRAK

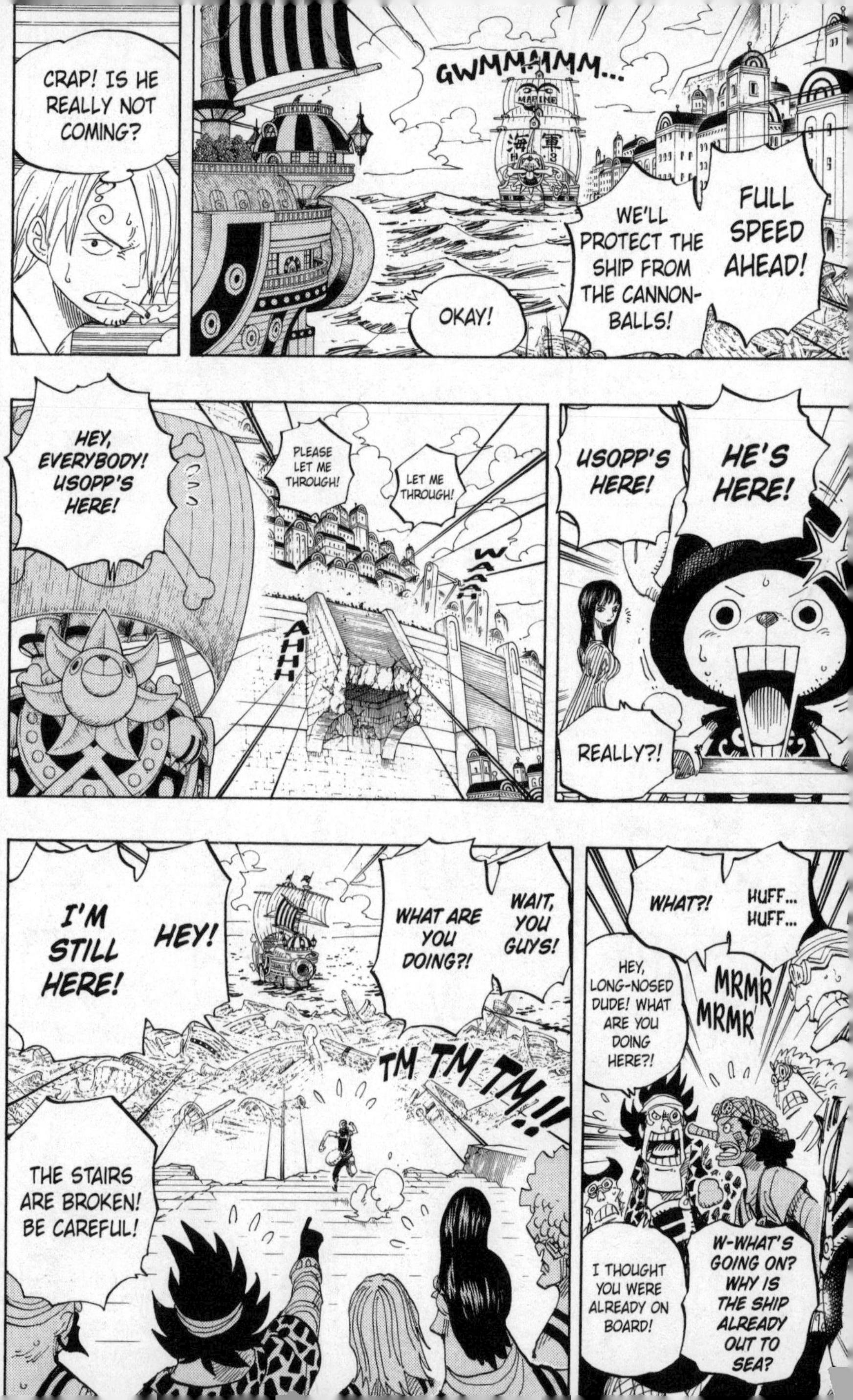
GWMMMMMM...
FULL SPEED AHEAD!
WE'LL PROTECT THE SHIP FROM THE CANNON-BALLS!
OKAY!
CRAP! IS HE REALLY NOT COMING?
HE'S HERE!
USOPP'S HERE!
REALLY?!
LET ME THROUGH!
PLEASE LET ME THROUGH!
HEY, EVERYBODY! USOPP'S HERE!
WAAA
AHHH
HUFF... HUFF...
WHAT?!
MRMR MRMR
HEY, LONG-NOSED DUDE! WHAT ARE YOU DOING HERE?!
W-WHAT'S GOING ON? WHY IS THE SHIP ALREADY OUT TO SEA?
I THOUGHT YOU WERE ALREADY ON BOARD!
WAIT, YOU GUYS!
WHAT ARE YOU DOING?!
HEY!
I'M STILL HERE!
TM TM TM!!
THE STAIRS ARE BROKEN! BE CAREFUL!

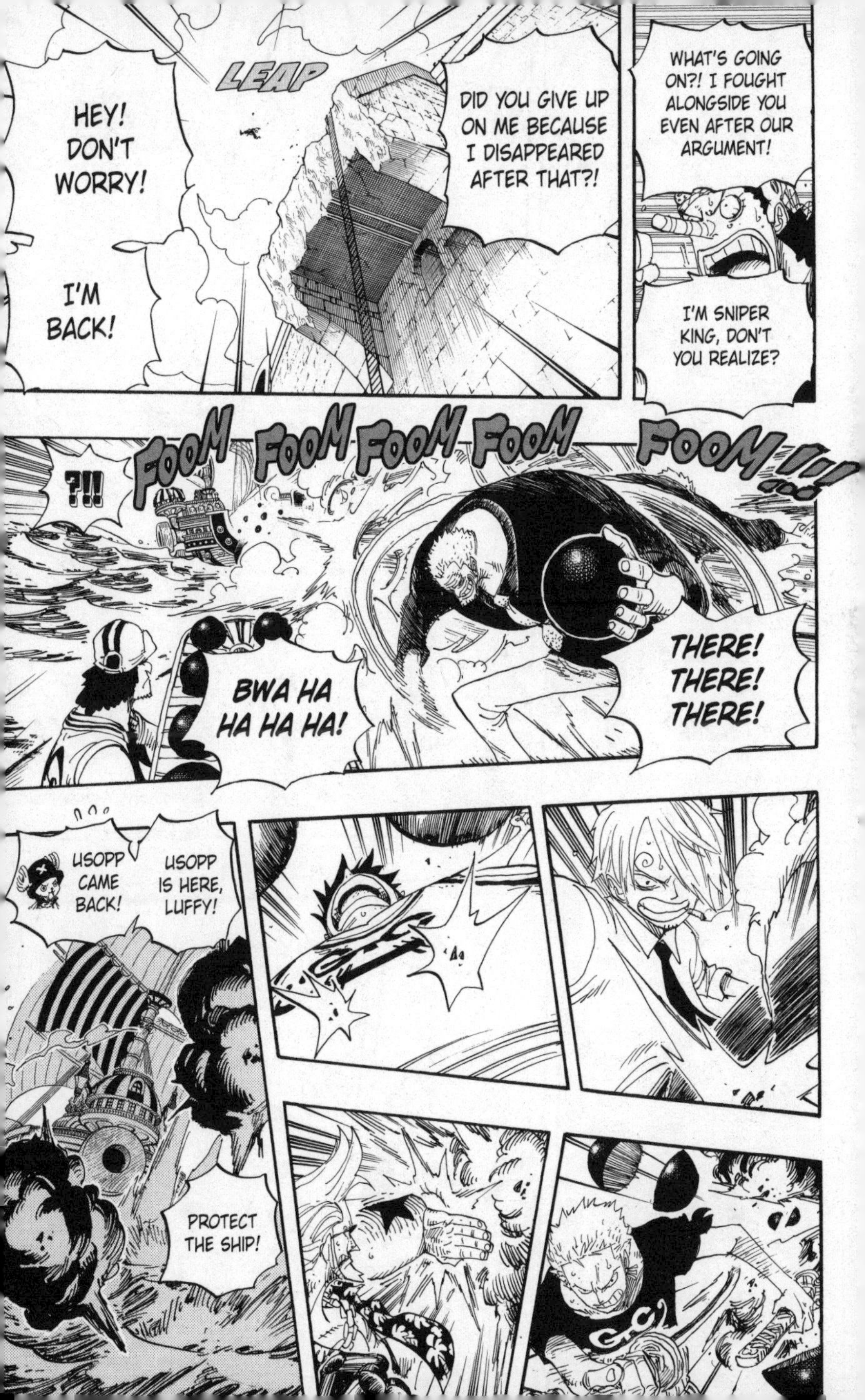
WHAT'S GOING ON?! I FOUGHT ALONGSIDE YOU EVEN AFTER OUR ARGUMENT!
I'M SNIPER KING, DON'T YOU REALIZE?
LEAP
DID YOU GIVE UP ON ME BECAUSE I DISAPPEARED AFTER THAT?!
HEY! DON'T WORRY!
I'M BACK!
FOOM FOOM FOOM FOOM FOOM!!!
THERE! THERE! THERE!
BWA HA HA HA HA!
?!!
USOPP IS HERE, LUFFY!
USOPP CAME BACK!
PROTECT THE SHIP!

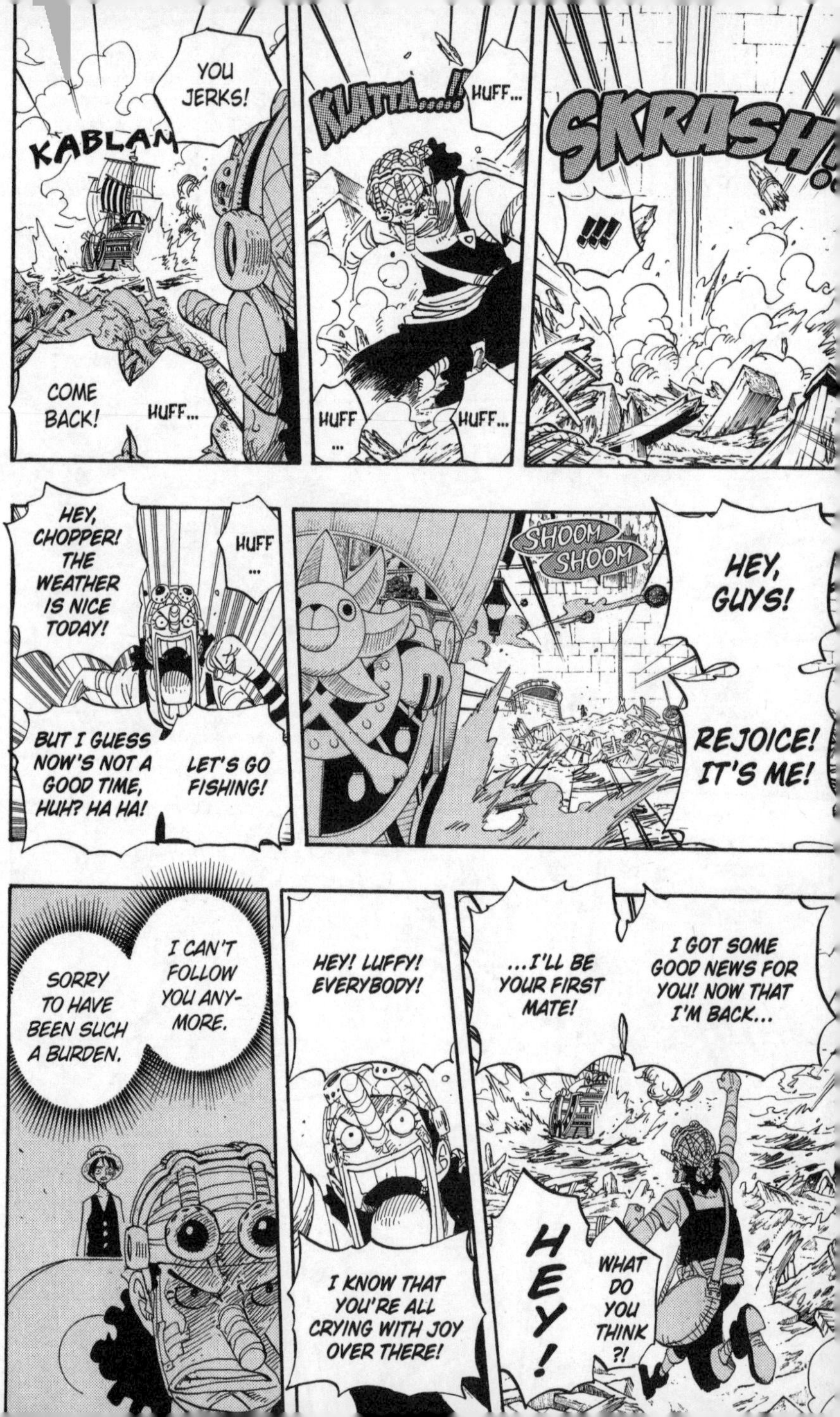
SKRASH!!
!!!
KLATTA...!!
HUFF...
HUFF...
HUFF ...
YOU JERKS!
KABLAM
COME BACK!
HUFF...
HEY, GUYS!
SHOOM SHOOM
REJOICE! IT'S ME!
HUFF ...
HEY, CHOPPER! THE WEATHER IS NICE TODAY!
LET'S GO FISHING!
BUT I GUESS NOW'S NOT A GOOD TIME, HUH? HA HA!
I GOT SOME GOOD NEWS FOR YOU! NOW THAT I'M BACK...
...I'LL BE YOUR FIRST MATE!
WHAT DO YOU THINK?!
HEY!
HEY! LUFFY! EVERYBODY!
I KNOW THAT YOU'RE ALL CRYING WITH JOY OVER THERE!
I CAN'T FOLLOW YOU ANYMORE.
SORRY TO HAVE BEEN SUCH A BURDEN.

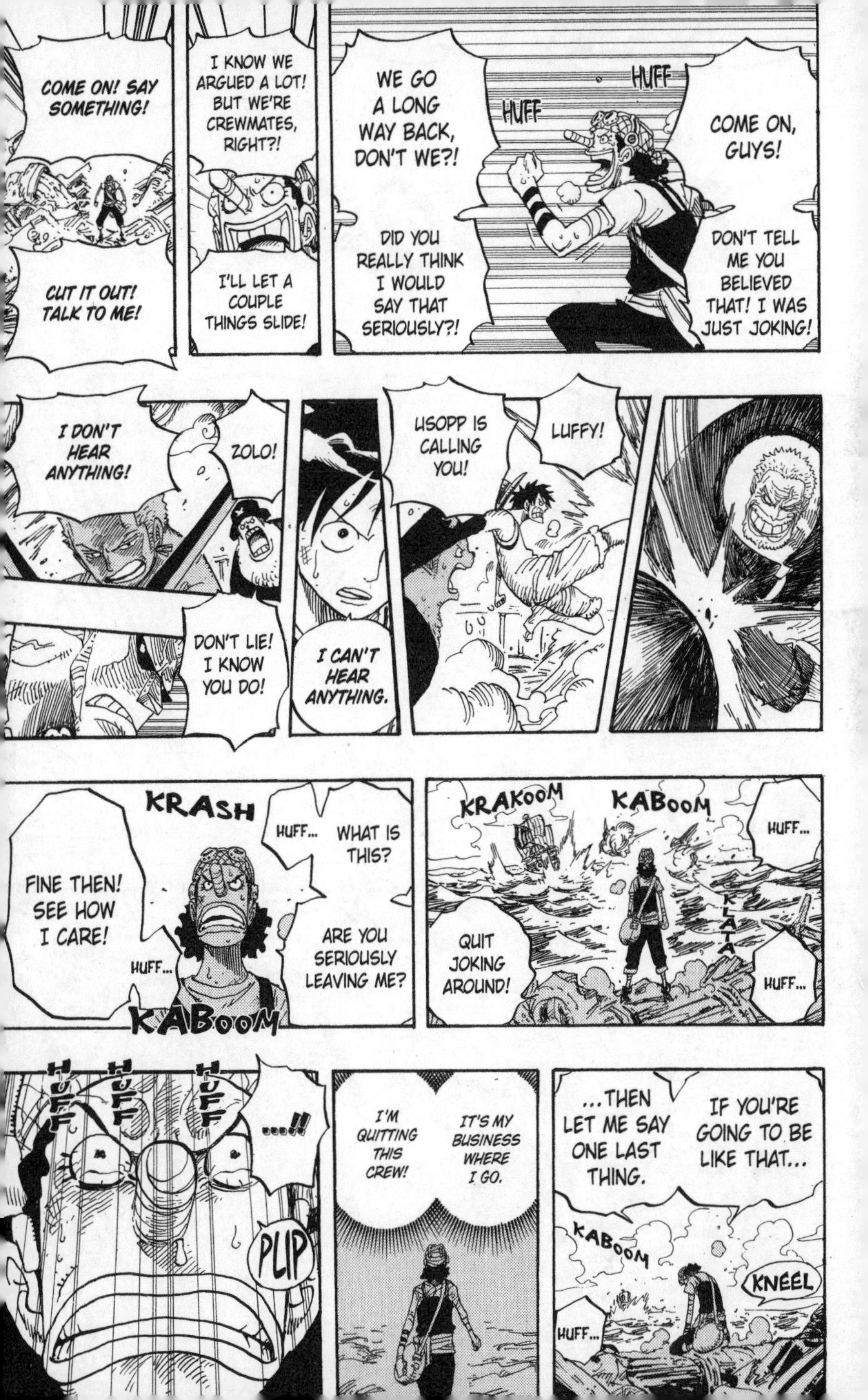
COME ON, GUYS!
HUFF
HUFF
WE GO A LONG WAY BACK, DON'T WE?!
DON'T TELL ME YOU BELIEVED THAT! I WAS JUST JOKING!
DID YOU REALLY THINK I WOULD SAY THAT SERIOUSLY?!
I KNOW WE ARGUED A LOT! BUT WE'RE CREWMATES, RIGHT?!
I'LL LET A COUPLE THINGS SLIDE!
COME ON! SAY SOMETHING!
CUT IT OUT! TALK TO ME!
LUFFY!
USOPP IS CALLING YOU!
I CAN'T HEAR ANYTHING.
ZOLO!
I DON'T HEAR ANYTHING!
DON'T LIE! I KNOW YOU DO!
HUFF...
KABOOM
KRAKOOM
KLATA
QUIT JOKING AROUND!
HUFF...
WHAT IS THIS?
HUFF...
KRASH
ARE YOU SERIOUSLY LEAVING ME?
FINE THEN! SEE HOW I CARE!
HUFF...
KABOOM
IF YOU'RE GOING TO BE LIKE THAT...
...THEN LET ME SAY ONE LAST THING.
KNEEL
KABOOM
HUFF...
IT'S MY BUSINESS WHERE I GO.
I'M QUITTING THIS CREW!
HUFF
HUFF
HUFF
...!!
PLIP

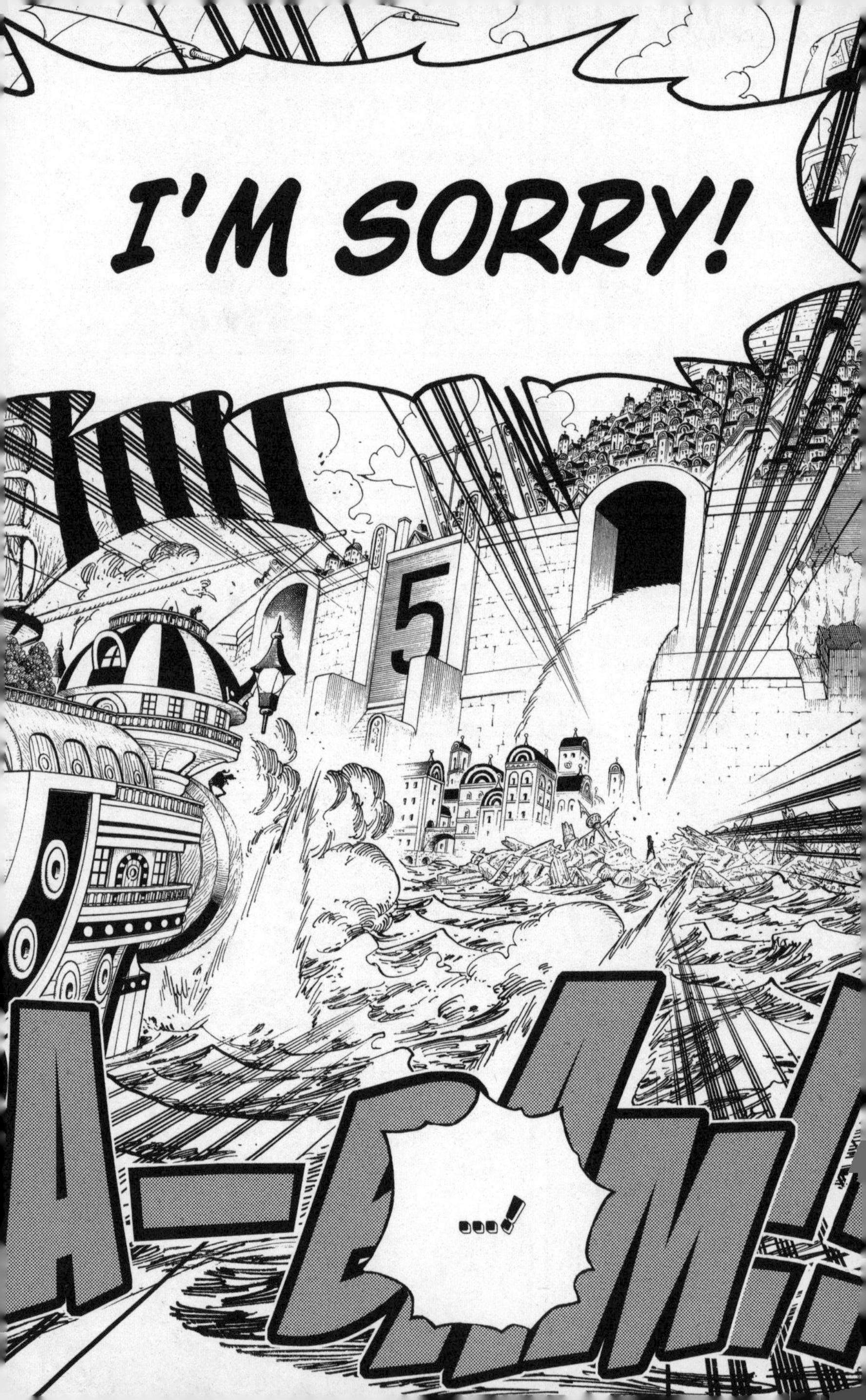
I'M SORRY!
...!

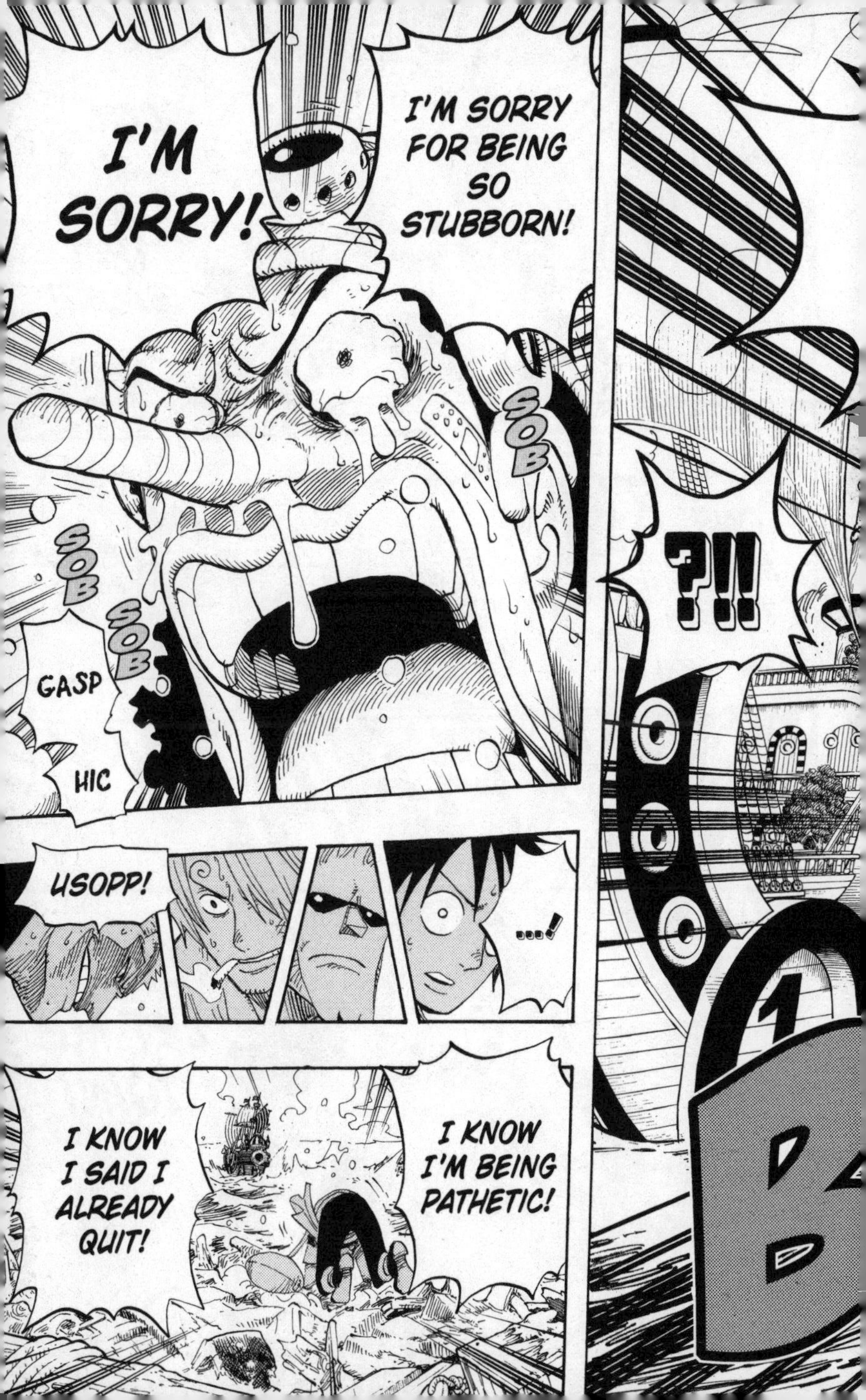
?!!
I'M SORRY FOR BEING SO STUBBORN!
I'M SORRY!
SOB
SOB
SOB
GASP
HIC
...!
USOPP!
I KNOW I'M BEING PATHETIC!
I KNOW I SAID I ALREADY QUIT!

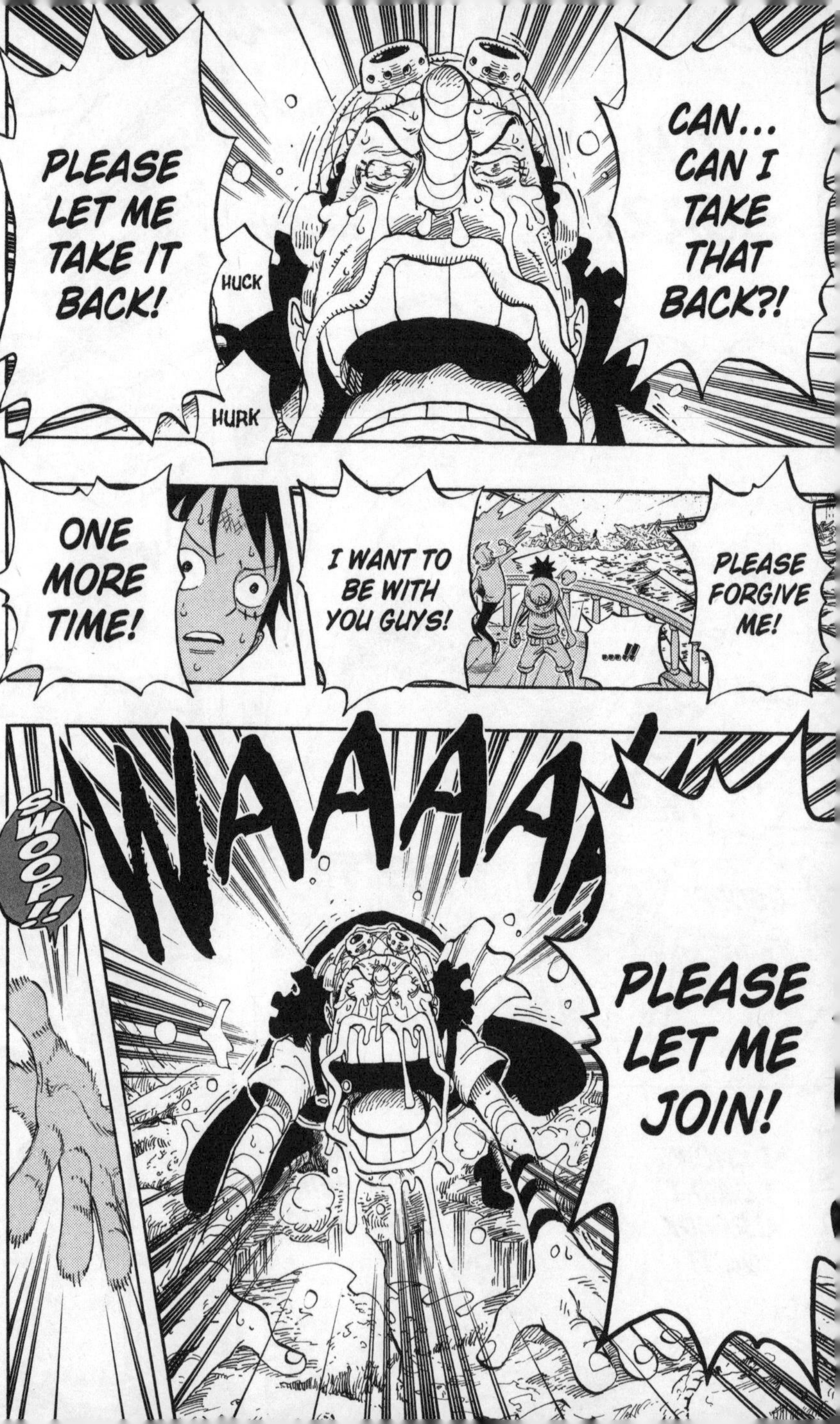
CAN... CAN I TAKE THAT BACK?!
PLEASE LET ME TAKE IT BACK!
HUCK
HURK
PLEASE FORGIVE ME!
...!!
I WANT TO BE WITH YOU GUYS!
ONE MORE TIME!
WAAAA
PLEASE LET ME JOIN!
SWOOP!!

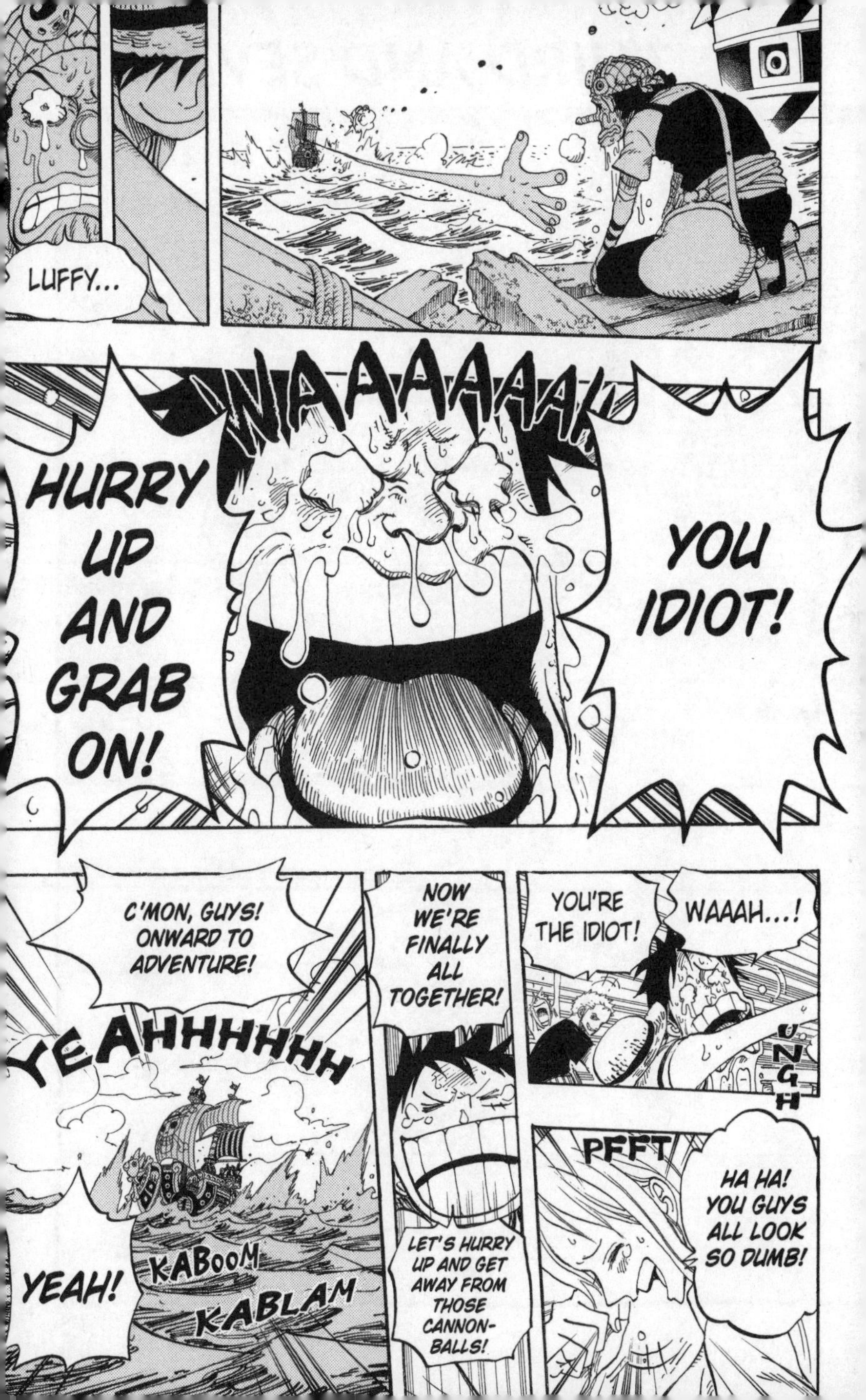
LUFFY...
WAAAAAAH
HURRY UP AND GRAB ON! YOU IDIOT!
WAAAH...!
YOU'RE THE IDIOT!
UNGH
PFFT
HA HA! YOU GUYS ALL LOOK SO DUMB!
NOW WE'RE FINALLY ALL TOGETHER!
LET'S HURRY UP AND GET AWAY FROM THOSE CANNON-BALLS!
C'MON, GUYS! ONWARD TO ADVENTURE!
YEAHHHHHH
KABOOM
KABLAM
YEAH!

THIRD AND SEVENTH

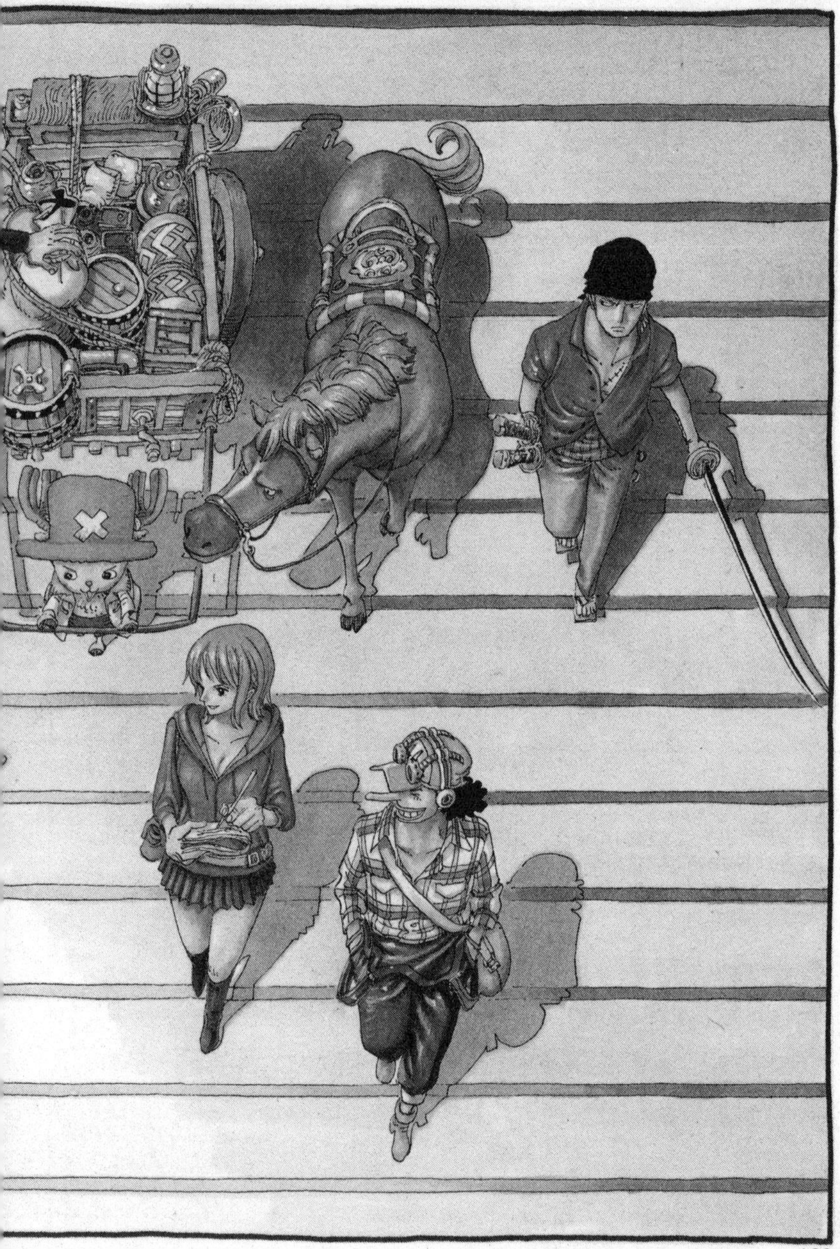

Chapter 439:

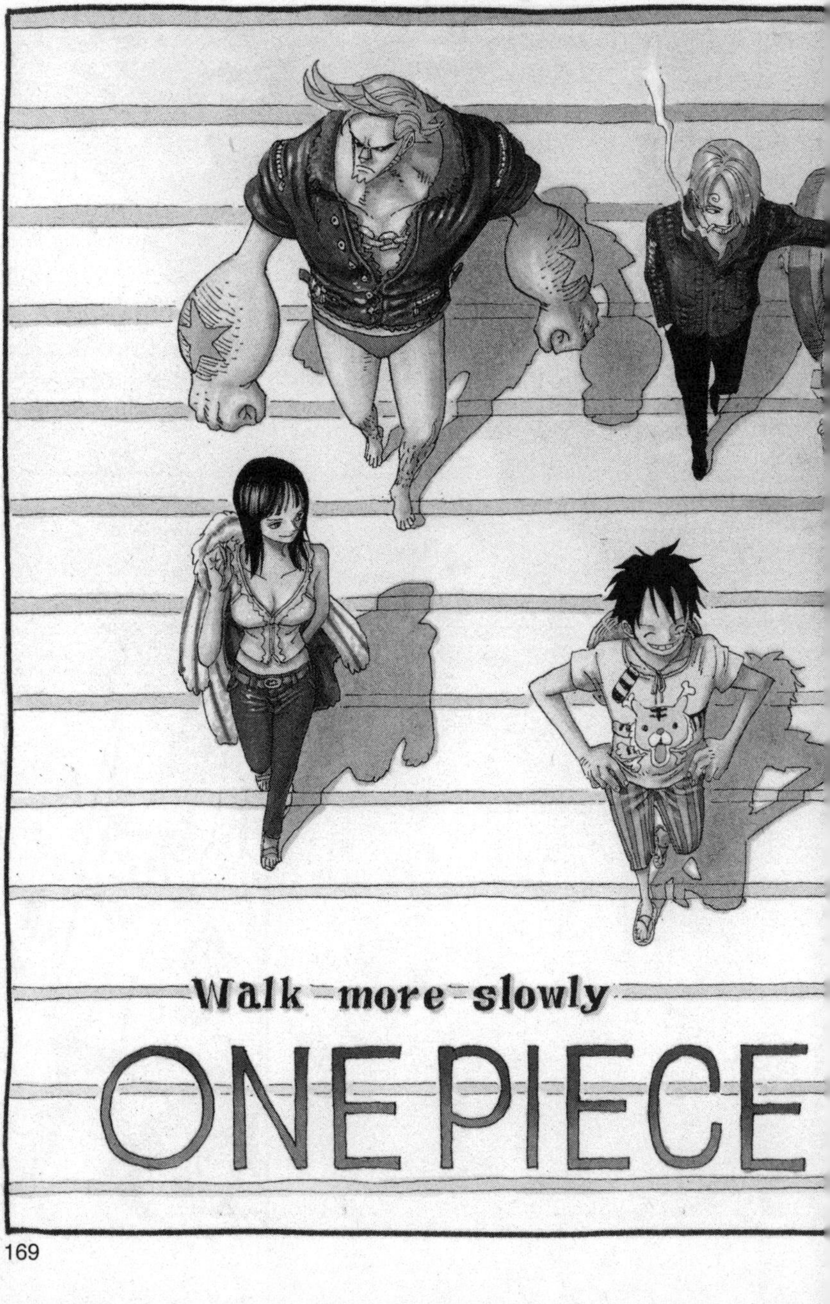
Walk more slowly
ONE PIECE

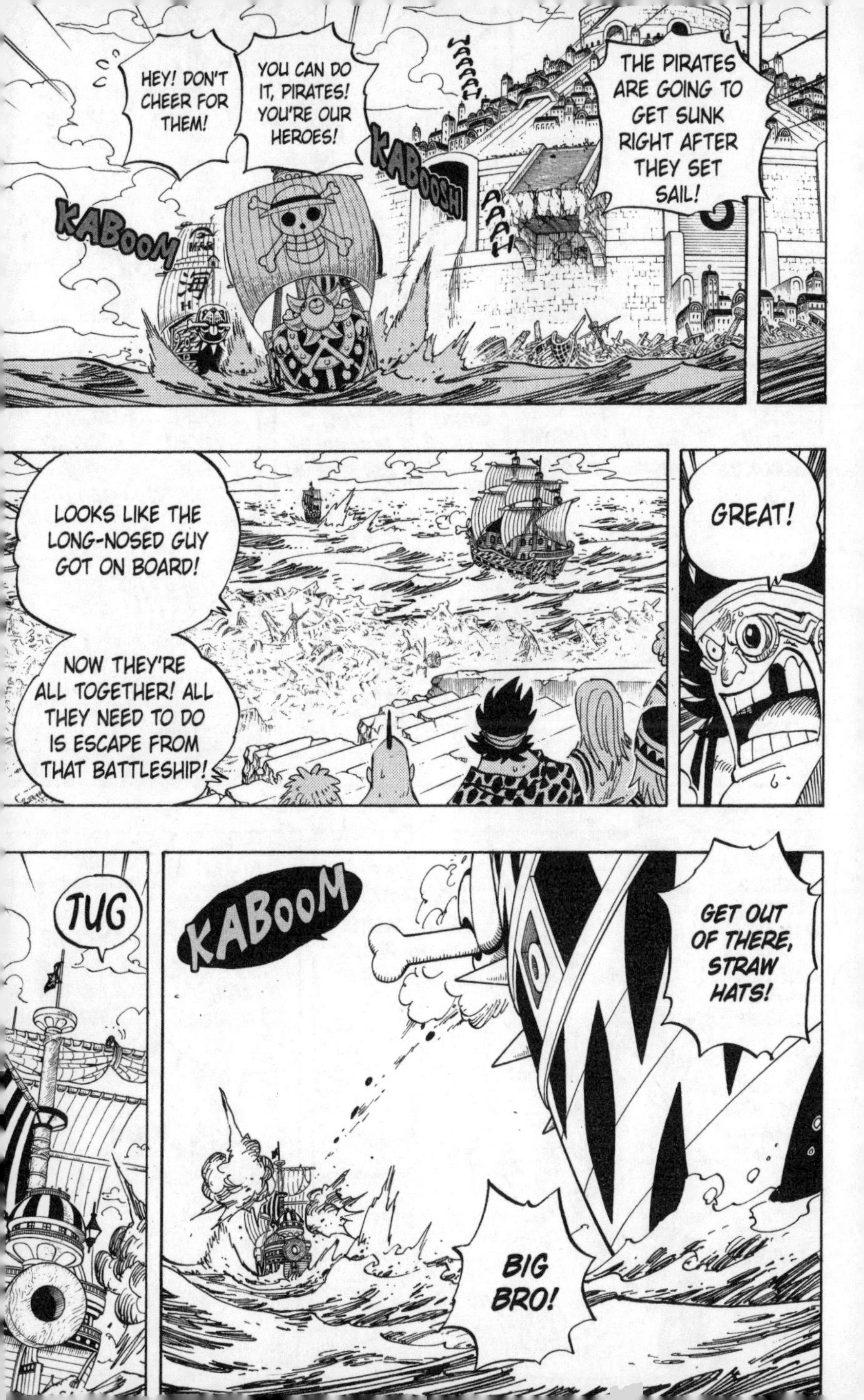
THE PIRATES ARE GOING TO GET SUNK RIGHT AFTER THEY SET SAIL!
WAAAAH
KABOOSH
AAAAH
YOU CAN DO IT, PIRATES! YOU'RE OUR HEROES!
HEY! DON'T CHEER FOR THEM!
KABOOM
GREAT!
LOOKS LIKE THE LONG-NOSED GUY GOT ON BOARD!
NOW THEY'RE ALL TOGETHER! ALL THEY NEED TO DO IS ESCAPE FROM THAT BATTLESHIP!
GET OUT OF THERE, STRAW HATS!
KABOOM
BIG BRO!
TUG

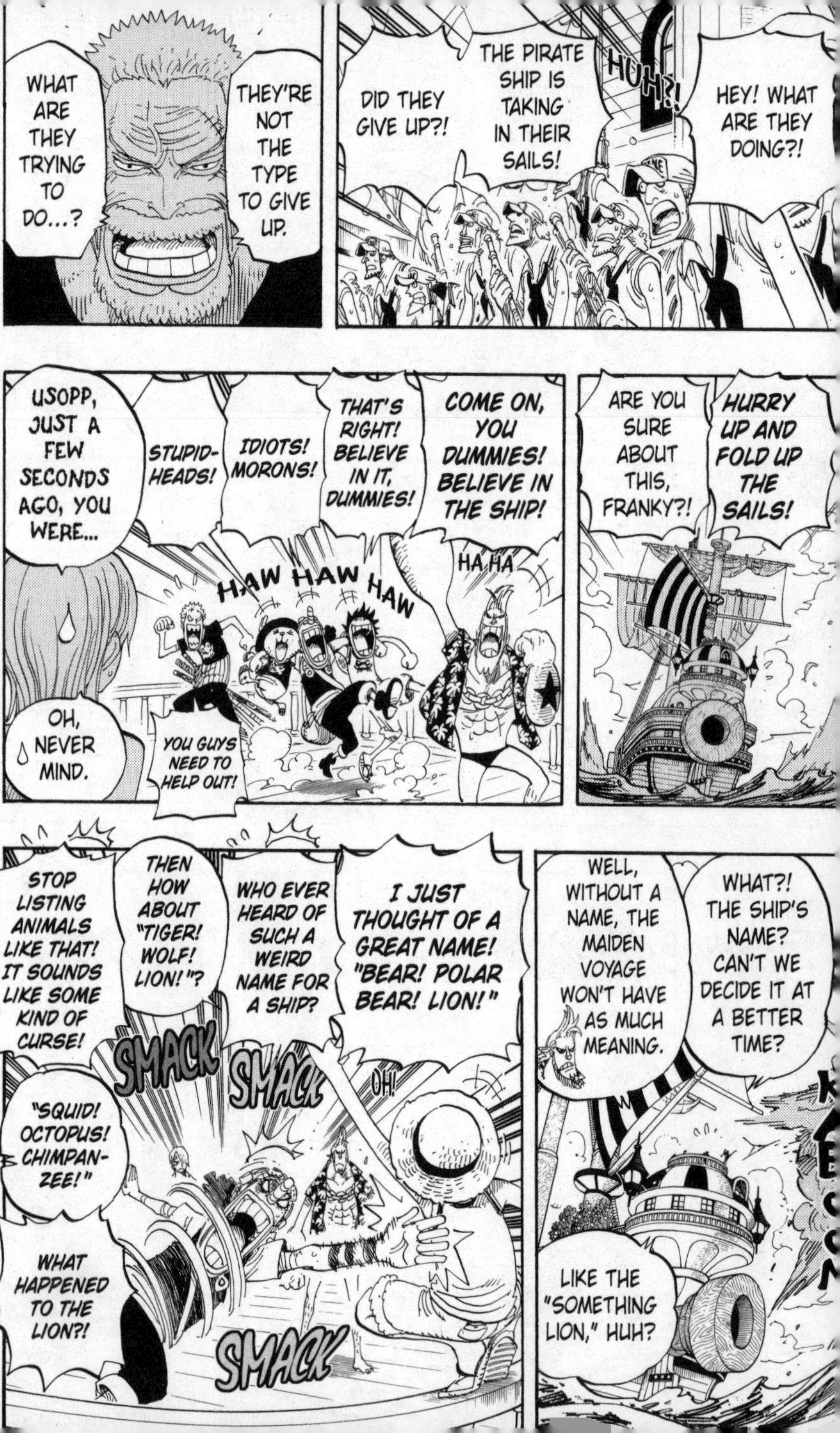
HEY! WHAT ARE THEY DOING?!
HUH?!
THE PIRATE SHIP IS TAKING IN THEIR SAILS!
DID THEY GIVE UP?!
THEY'RE NOT THE TYPE TO GIVE UP.
WHAT ARE THEY TRYING TO DO...?
HURRY UP AND FOLD UP THE SAILS!
ARE YOU SURE ABOUT THIS, FRANKY?!
COME ON, YOU DUMMIES! BELIEVE IN THE SHIP!
THAT'S RIGHT! BELIEVE IN IT, DUMMIES!
IDIOTS! MORONS!
STUPID-HEADS!
USOPP, JUST A FEW SECONDS AGO, YOU WERE...
HA HA
HAW HAW HAW
YOU GUYS NEED TO HELP OUT!
OH, NEVER MIND.
WHAT?! THE SHIP'S NAME? CAN'T WE DECIDE IT AT A BETTER TIME?
WELL, WITHOUT A NAME, THE MAIDEN VOYAGE WON'T HAVE AS MUCH MEANING.
LIKE THE "SOMETHING LION," HUH?
I JUST THOUGHT OF A GREAT NAME! "BEAR! POLAR BEAR! LION!"
WHO EVER HEARD OF SUCH A WEIRD NAME FOR A SHIP?
THEN HOW ABOUT "TIGER! WOLF! LION!"?
STOP LISTING ANIMALS LIKE THAT! IT SOUNDS LIKE SOME KIND OF CURSE!
OH!
SMACK
SMACK
"SQUID! OCTOPUS! CHIMPANZEE!"
WHAT HAPPENED TO THE LION?!
SMACK

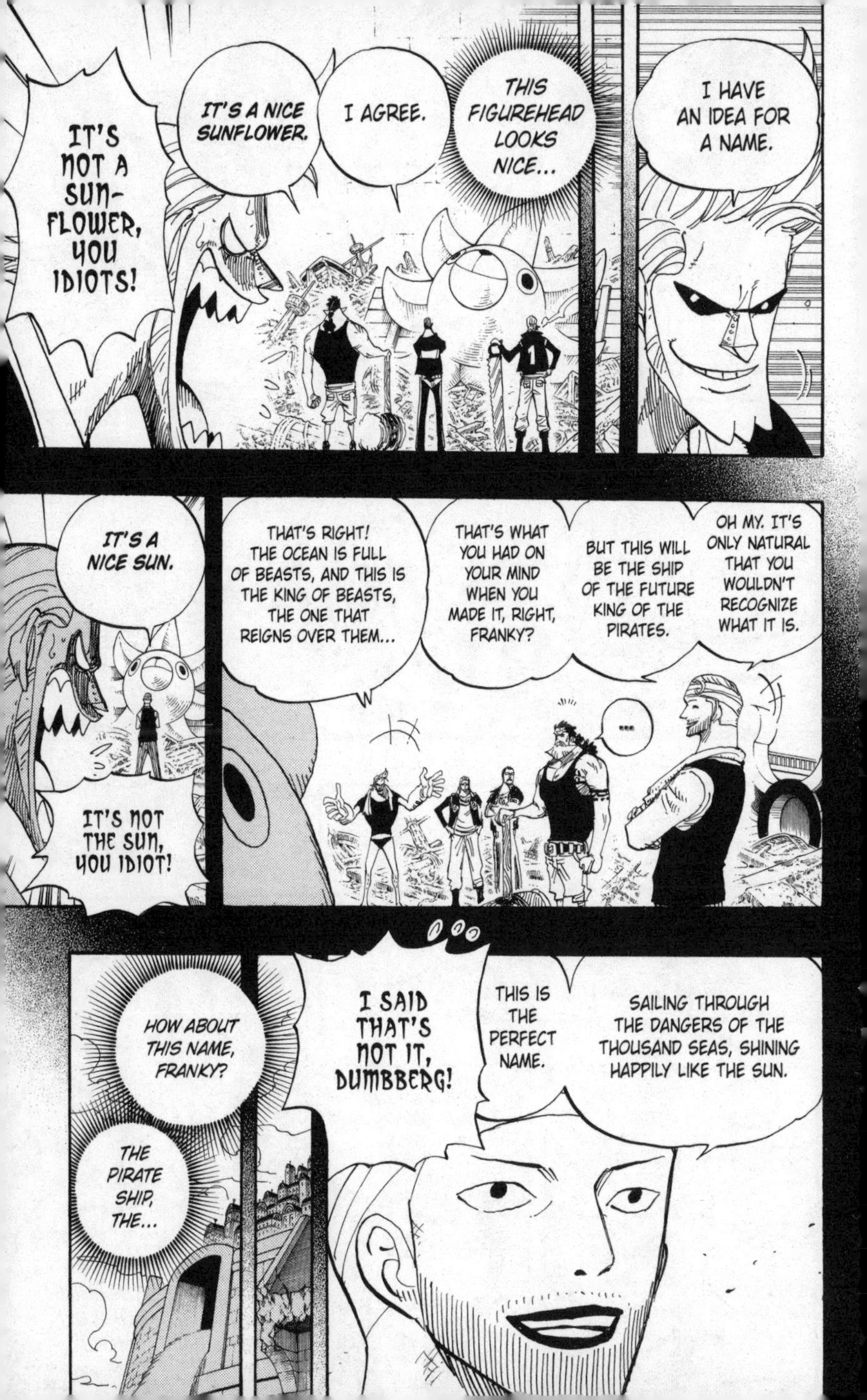
I HAVE AN IDEA FOR A NAME.
THIS FIGUREHEAD LOOKS NICE...
I AGREE.
IT'S A NICE SUNFLOWER.
IT'S NOT A SUNFLOWER, YOU IDIOTS!
OH MY. IT'S ONLY NATURAL THAT YOU WOULDN'T RECOGNIZE WHAT IT IS.
BUT THIS WILL BE THE SHIP OF THE FUTURE KING OF THE PIRATES.
THAT'S WHAT YOU HAD ON YOUR MIND WHEN YOU MADE IT, RIGHT, FRANKY?
THAT'S RIGHT! THE OCEAN IS FULL OF BEASTS, AND THIS IS THE KING OF BEASTS, THE ONE THAT REIGNS OVER THEM...
...
IT'S A NICE SUN.
IT'S NOT THE SUN, YOU IDIOT!
SAILING THROUGH THE DANGERS OF THE THOUSAND SEAS, SHINING HAPPILY LIKE THE SUN.
THIS IS THE PERFECT NAME.
I SAID THAT'S NOT IT, DUMBBERG!
HOW ABOUT THIS NAME, FRANKY?
THE PIRATE SHIP, THE...

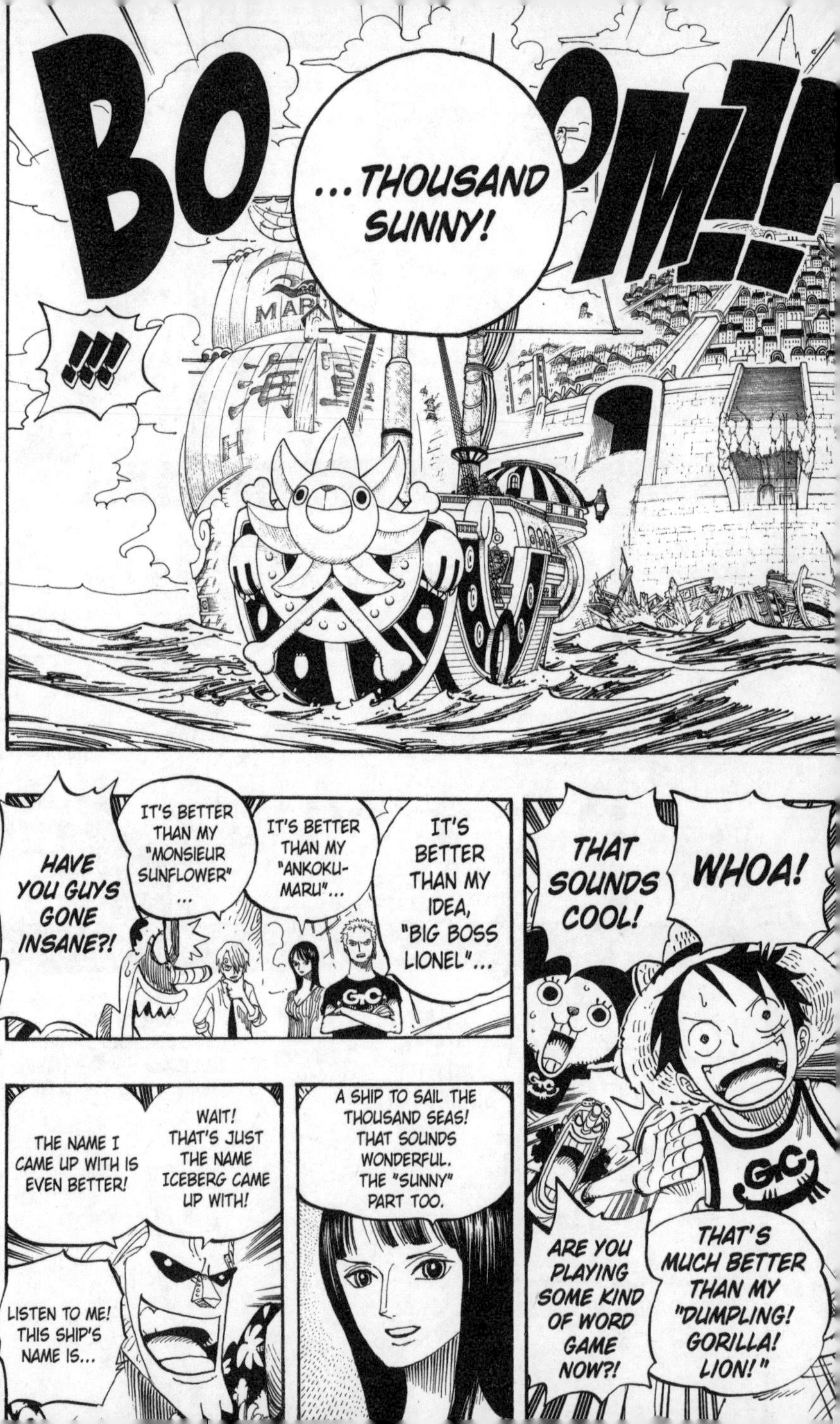
...THOUSAND SUNNY!
BOOM!!
!!!
WHOA!
THAT SOUNDS COOL!
THAT'S MUCH BETTER THAN MY "DUMPLING! GORILLA! LION!"
ARE YOU PLAYING SOME KIND OF WORD GAME NOW?!
IT'S BETTER THAN MY IDEA, "BIG BOSS LIONEL"...
IT'S BETTER THAN MY "ANKOKU-MARU"...
IT'S BETTER THAN MY "MONSIEUR SUNFLOWER"...
HAVE YOU GUYS GONE INSANE?!
A SHIP TO SAIL THE THOUSAND SEAS! THAT SOUNDS WONDERFUL. THE "SUNNY" PART TOO.
WAIT! THAT'S JUST THE NAME ICEBERG CAME UP WITH!
THE NAME I CAME UP WITH IS EVEN BETTER!
LISTEN TO ME! THIS SHIP'S NAME IS...

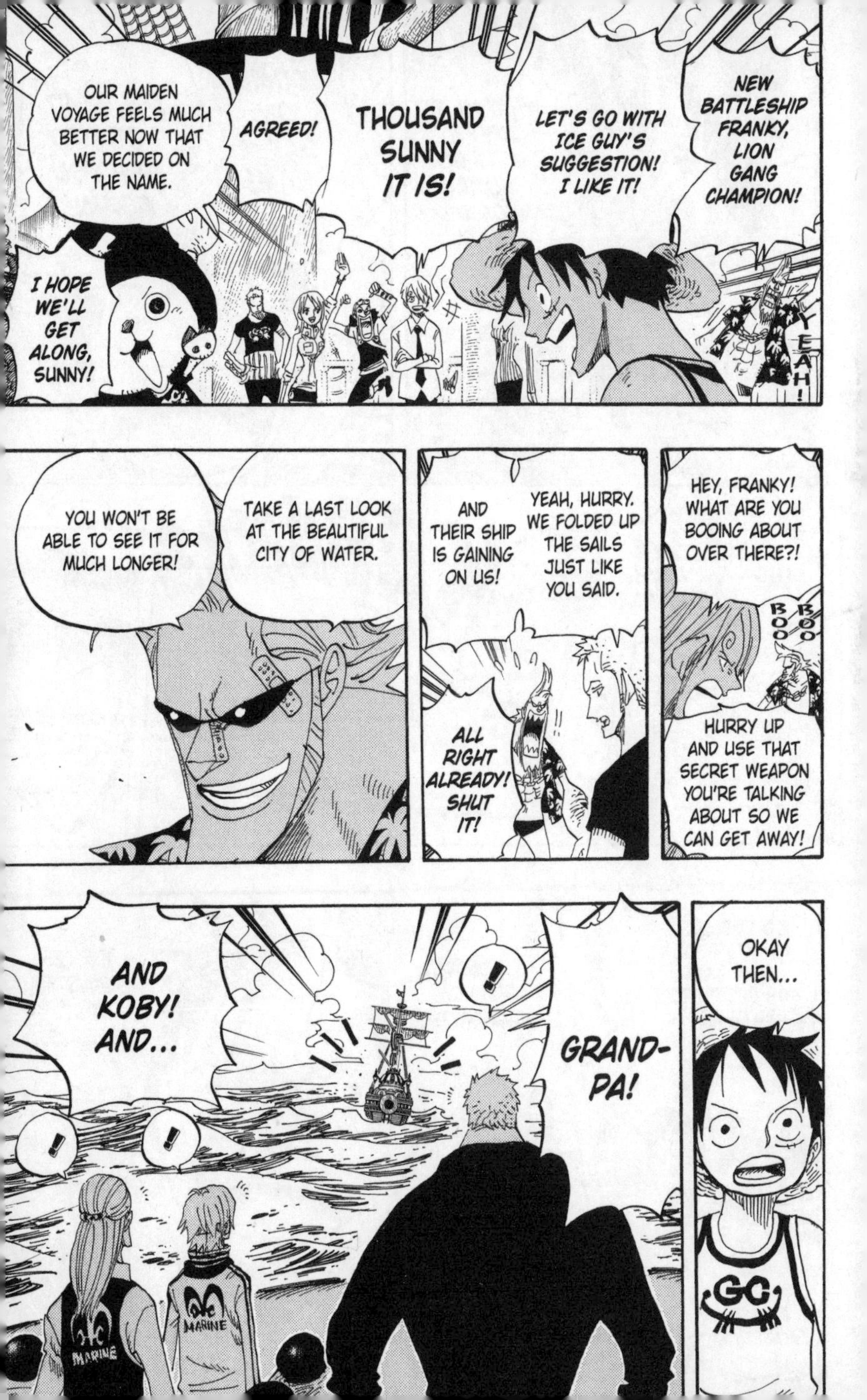
NEW BATTLESHIP FRANKY, LION GANG CHAMPION!
LET'S GO WITH ICE GUY'S SUGGESTION! I LIKE IT!
THOUSAND SUNNY IT IS!
AGREED!
OUR MAIDEN VOYAGE FEELS MUCH BETTER NOW THAT WE DECIDED ON THE NAME.
YEAH!
I HOPE WE'LL GET ALONG, SUNNY!
HEY, FRANKY! WHAT ARE YOU BOOING ABOUT OVER THERE?!
BOO BOO
HURRY UP AND USE THAT SECRET WEAPON YOU'RE TALKING ABOUT SO WE CAN GET AWAY!
YEAH, HURRY. WE FOLDED UP THE SAILS JUST LIKE YOU SAID.
AND THEIR SHIP IS GAINING ON US!
ALL RIGHT ALREADY! SHUT IT!
TAKE A LAST LOOK AT THE BEAUTIFUL CITY OF WATER.
YOU WON'T BE ABLE TO SEE IT FOR MUCH LONGER!
OKAY THEN...
GC
GRAND-PA!
!
AND KOBY! AND...
!
!
MARINE
MARINE

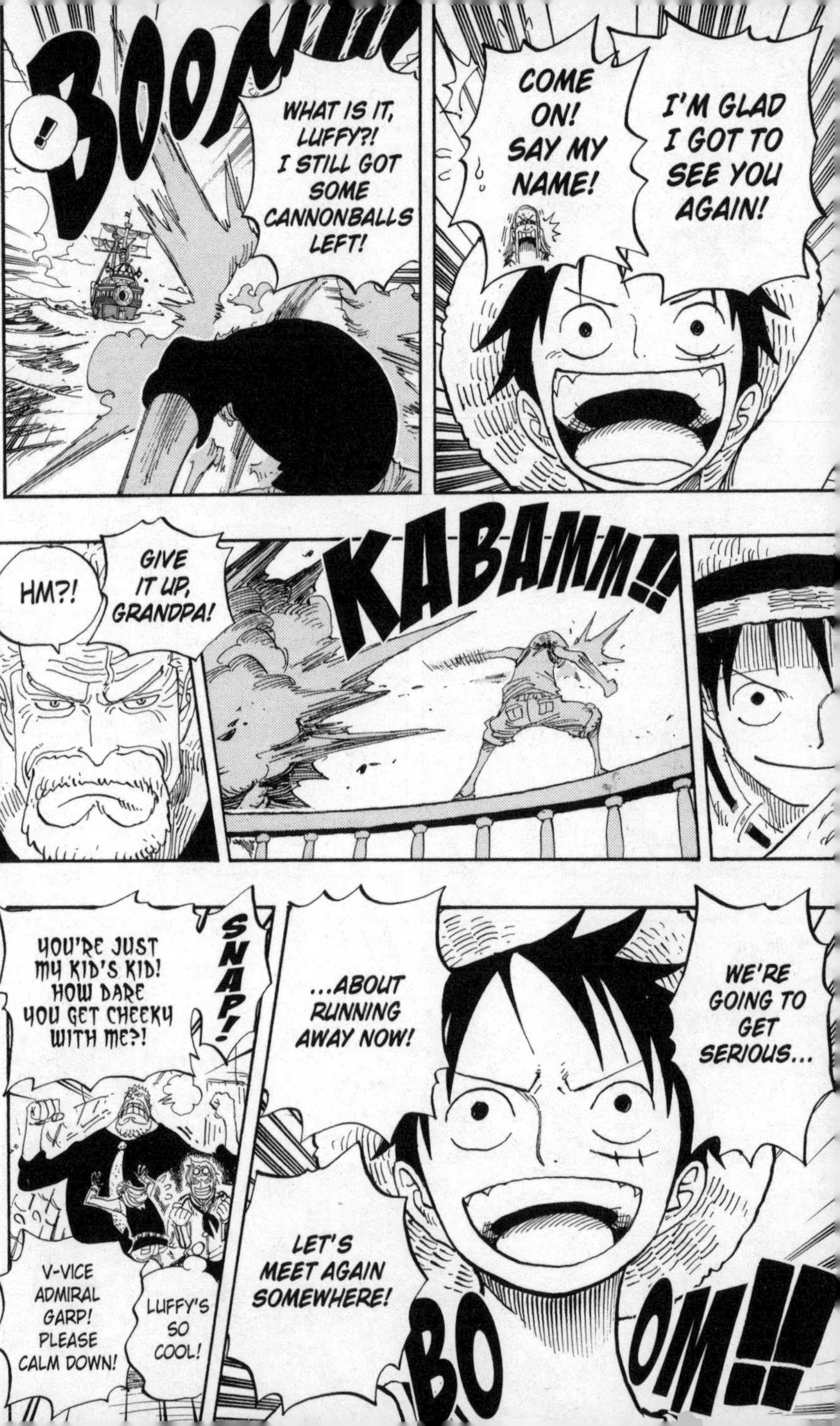
I'M GLAD I GOT TO SEE YOU AGAIN!
COME ON! SAY MY NAME!
BOOM
!
WHAT IS IT, LUFFY?! I STILL GOT SOME CANNONBALLS LEFT!
KABAMM!!
GIVE IT UP, GRANDPA!
HM?!
WE'RE GOING TO GET SERIOUS...
...ABOUT RUNNING AWAY NOW!
LET'S MEET AGAIN SOMEWHERE!
BOOM!!
SNAP!
YOU'RE JUST MY KID'S KID! HOW DARE YOU GET CHEEKY WITH ME?!
LUFFY'S SO COOL!
V-VICE ADMIRAL GARP! PLEASE CALM DOWN!

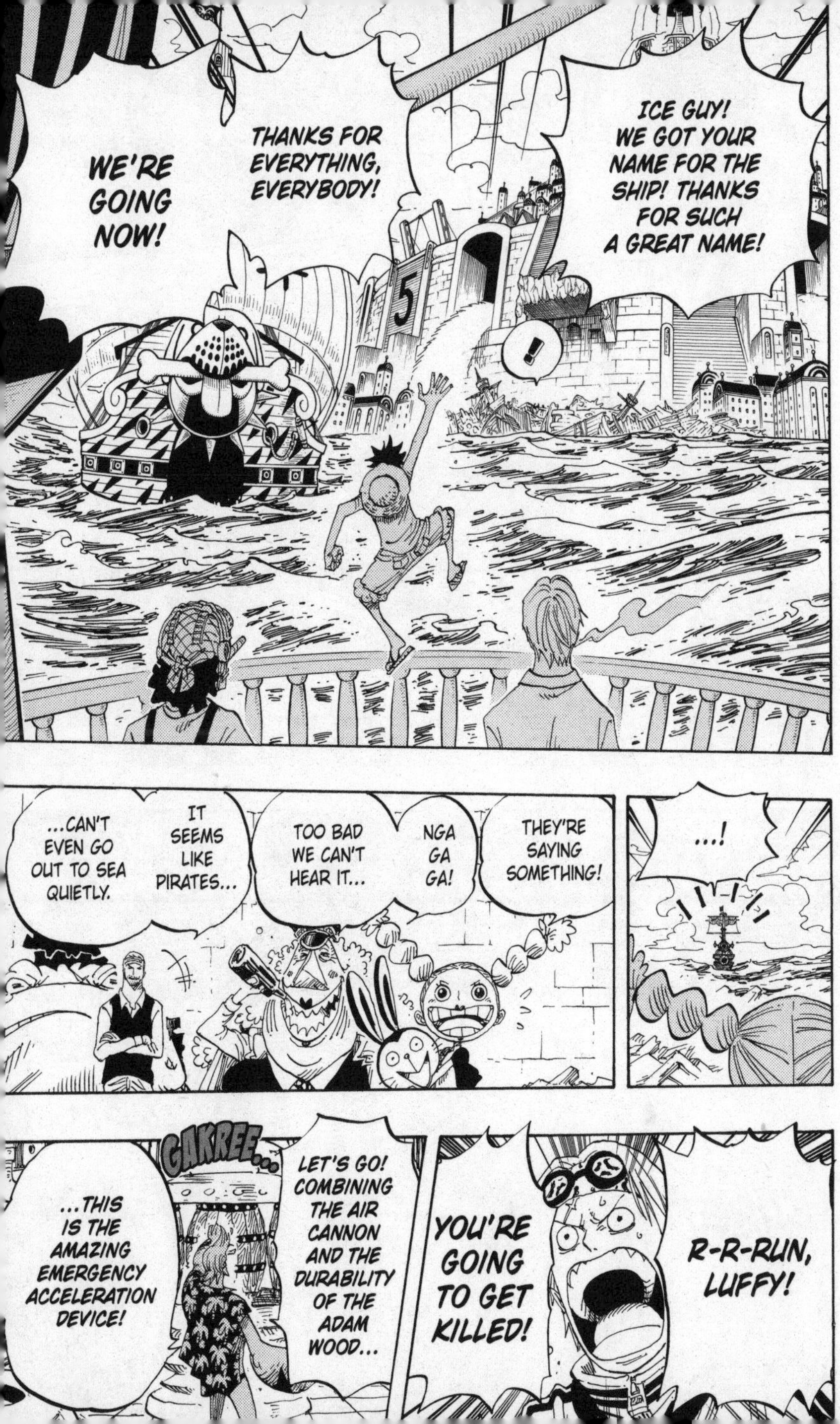
ICE GUY! WE GOT YOUR NAME FOR THE SHIP! THANKS FOR SUCH A GREAT NAME!
THANKS FOR EVERYTHING, EVERYBODY!
WE'RE GOING NOW!
!
...!
THEY'RE SAYING SOMETHING!
NGA GA GA!
TOO BAD WE CAN'T HEAR IT...
IT SEEMS LIKE PIRATES...
...CAN'T EVEN GO OUT TO SEA QUIETLY.
R-R-RUN, LUFFY!
YOU'RE GOING TO GET KILLED!
LET'S GO! COMBINING THE AIR CANNON AND THE DURABILITY OF THE ADAM WOOD...
GAKREE...
...THIS IS THE AMAZING EMERGENCY ACCELERATION DEVICE!

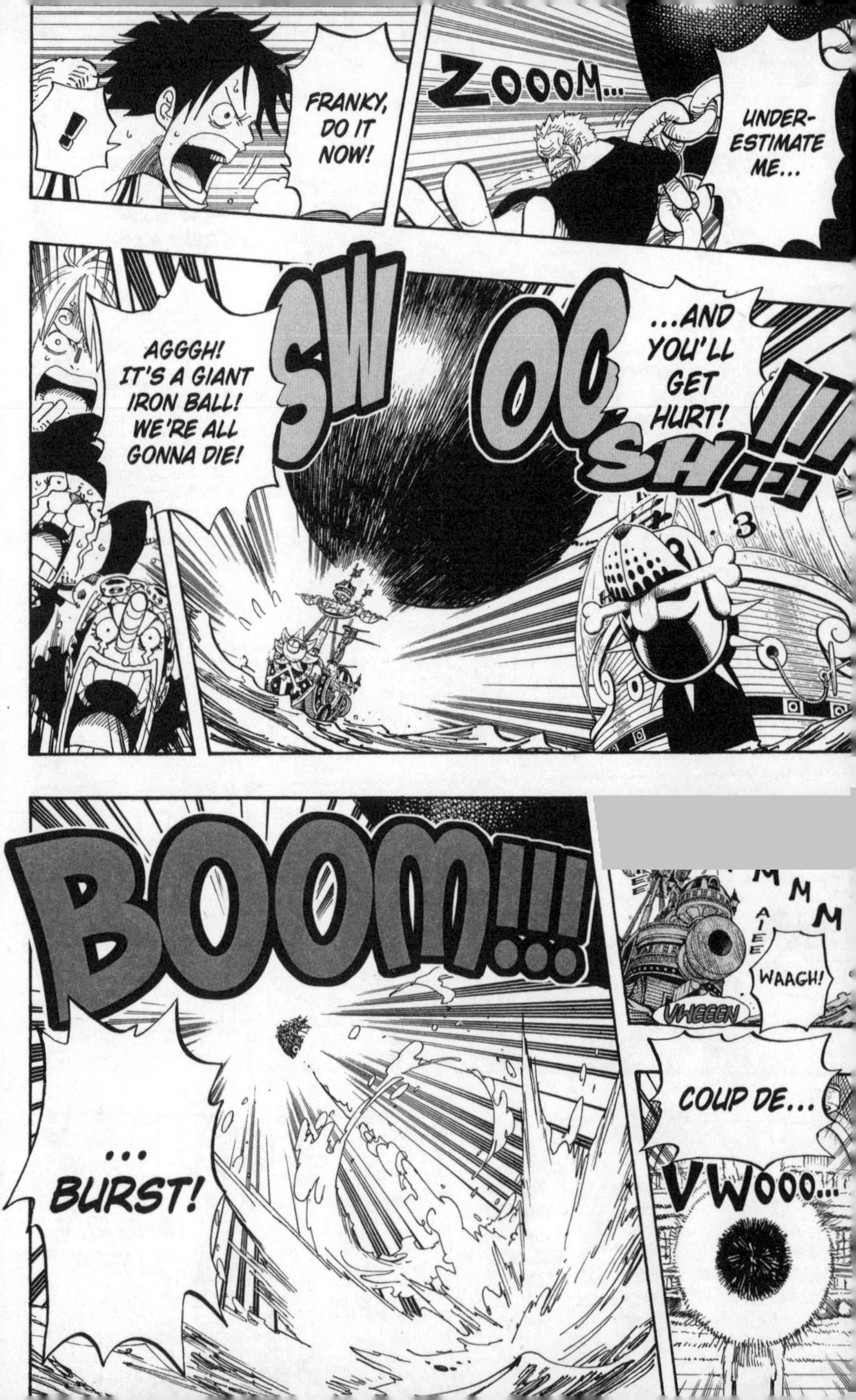
UNDER-ESTIMATE ME...
ZOOOM...
!
FRANKY, DO IT NOW!
...AND YOU'LL GET HURT!
SWOOOSH!!
AGGGH! IT'S A GIANT IRON BALL! WE'RE ALL GONNA DIE!
MMM
AIEE
WAAGH!
VWEEEN
COUP DE...
VWOOO...
BOOM!!!
... BURST!

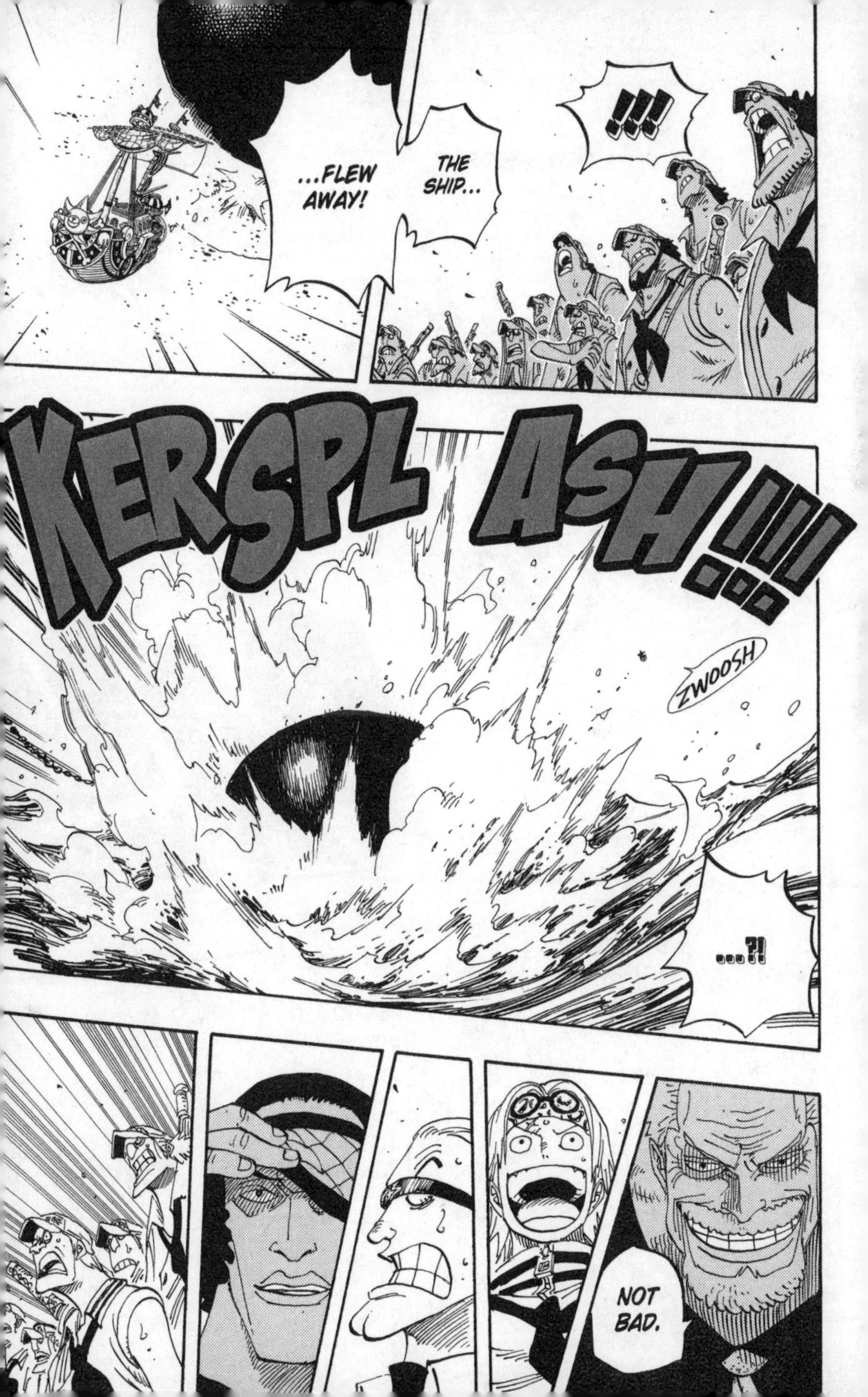
!!!
THE SHIP...
...FLEW AWAY!
KERSPLASH!!!!
ZWOOSH
...?!
NOT BAD.

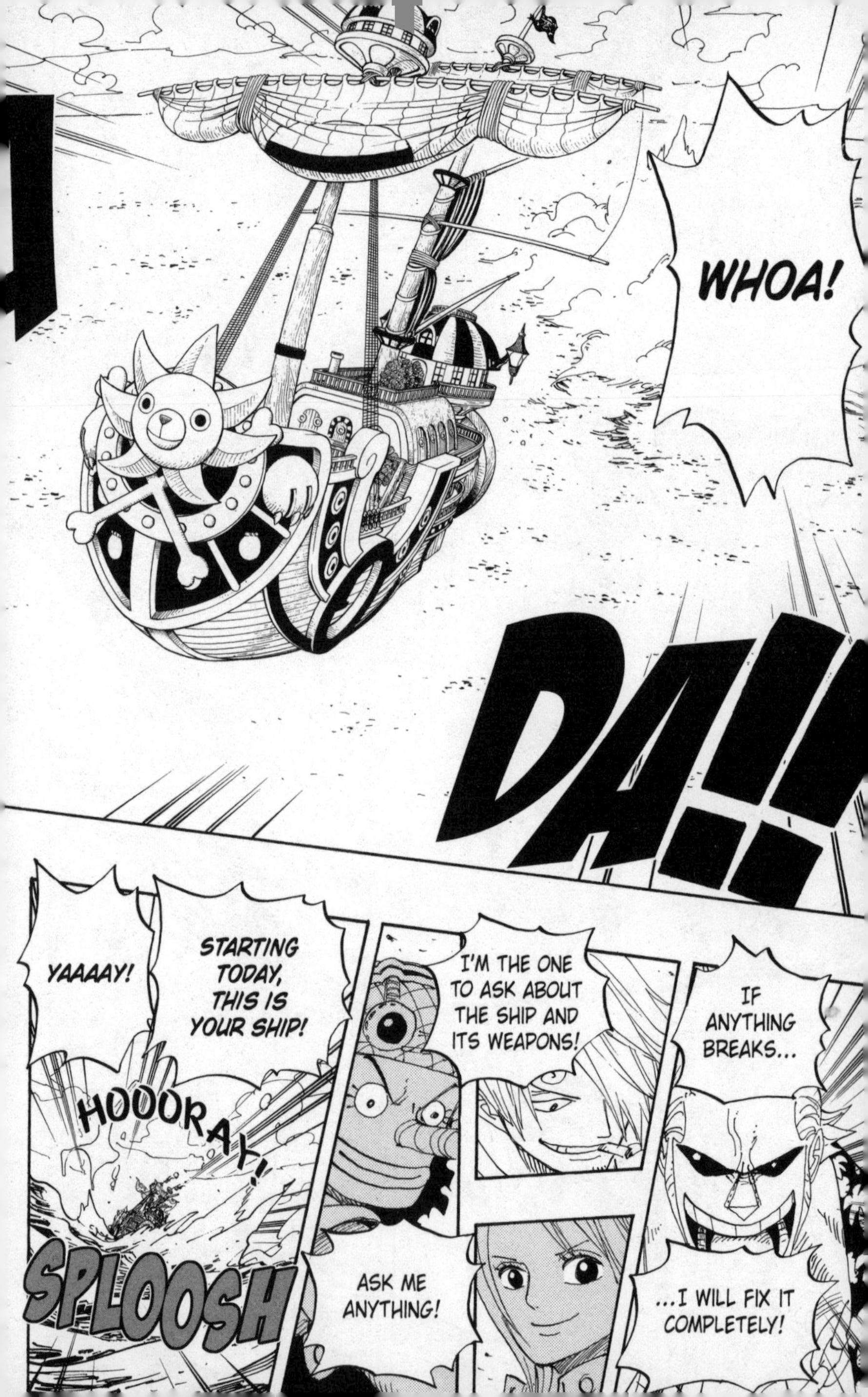
WHOA!
DA!!
IF ANYTHING BREAKS...
...I WILL FIX IT COMPLETELY!
I'M THE ONE TO ASK ABOUT THE SHIP AND ITS WEAPONS!
ASK ME ANYTHING!
STARTING TODAY, THIS IS YOUR SHIP!
YAAAAY!
HOOORAY!
SPLOOSH

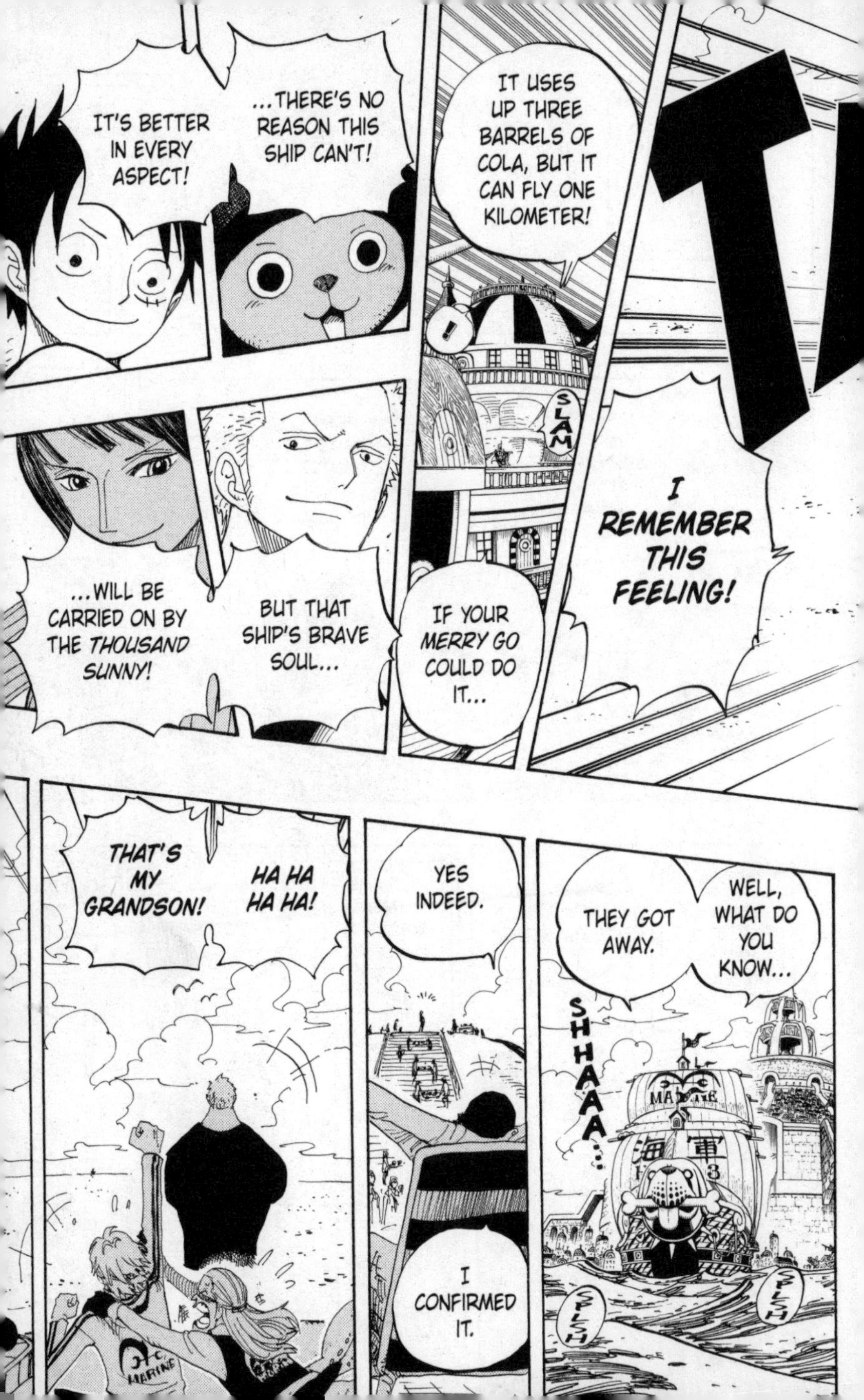
T
I REMEMBER THIS FEELING!
IT USES UP THREE BARRELS OF COLA, BUT IT CAN FLY ONE KILOMETER!
!
SLAM
IF YOUR MERRY GO COULD DO IT...
...THERE'S NO REASON THIS SHIP CAN'T!
IT'S BETTER IN EVERY ASPECT!
BUT THAT SHIP'S BRAVE SOUL...
...WILL BE CARRIED ON BY THE THOUSAND SUNNY!
WELL, WHAT DO YOU KNOW...
THEY GOT AWAY.
SHHAAA...
SPLSH
SPLSH
YES INDEED.
I CONFIRMED IT.
HA HA HA HA!
THAT'S MY GRANDSON!

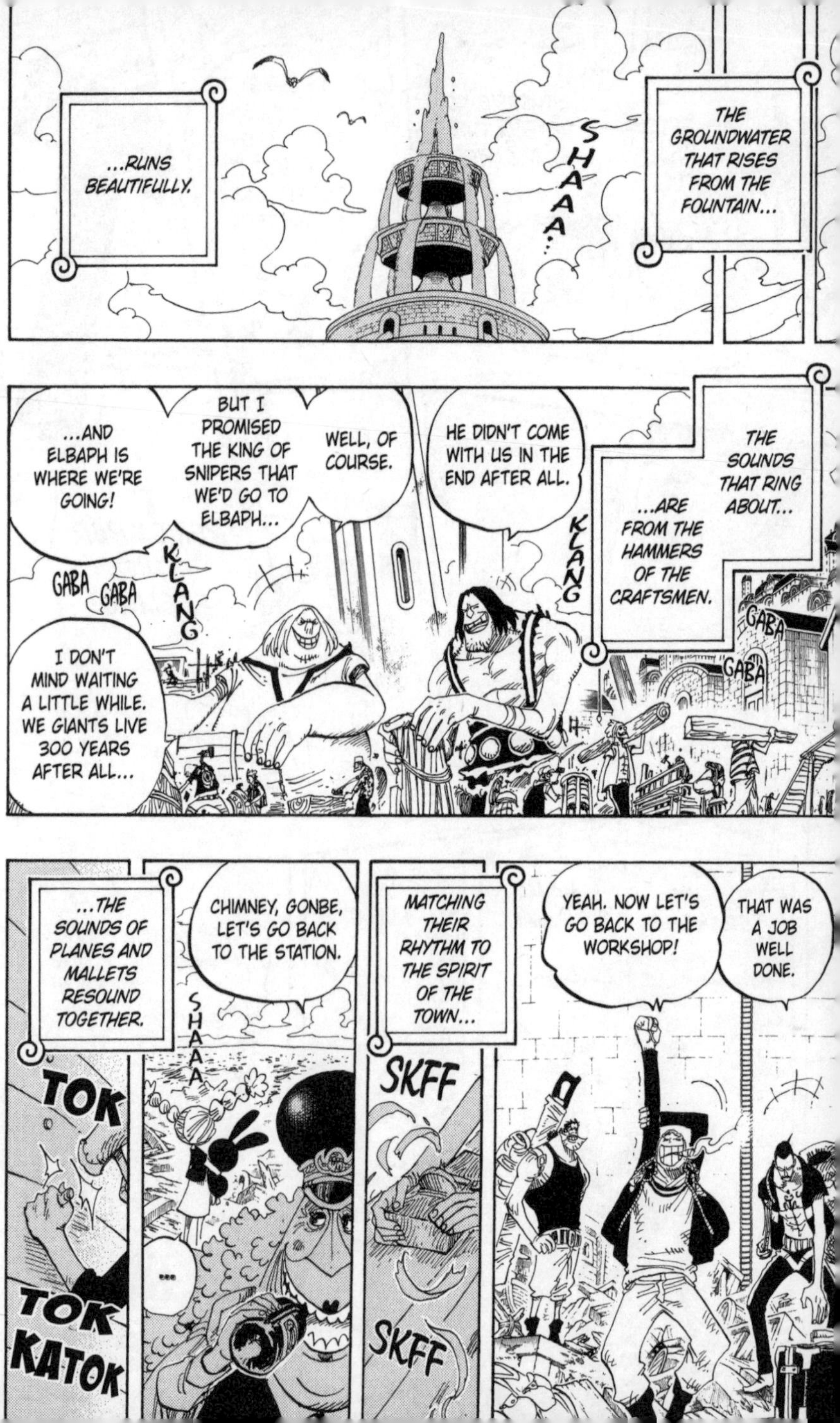
THE GROUNDWATER THAT RISES FROM THE FOUNTAIN...
SHAAAA...
...RUNS BEAUTIFULLY.
THE SOUNDS THAT RING ABOUT...
...ARE FROM THE HAMMERS OF THE CRAFTSMEN.
GABA GABA
HE DIDN'T COME WITH US IN THE END AFTER ALL.
KLANG
WELL, OF COURSE.
BUT I PROMISED THE KING OF SNIPERS THAT WE'D GO TO ELBAPH...
...AND ELBAPH IS WHERE WE'RE GOING!
KLANG
GABA GABA
I DON'T MIND WAITING A LITTLE WHILE. WE GIANTS LIVE 300 YEARS AFTER ALL...
THAT WAS A JOB WELL DONE.
YEAH. NOW LET'S GO BACK TO THE WORKSHOP!
MATCHING THEIR RHYTHM TO THE SPIRIT OF THE TOWN...
SKFF
SKFF
CHIMNEY, GONBE, LET'S GO BACK TO THE STATION.
SHAAA
...
...THE SOUNDS OF PLANES AND MALLETS RESOUND TOGETHER.
TOK
TOK
KATOK

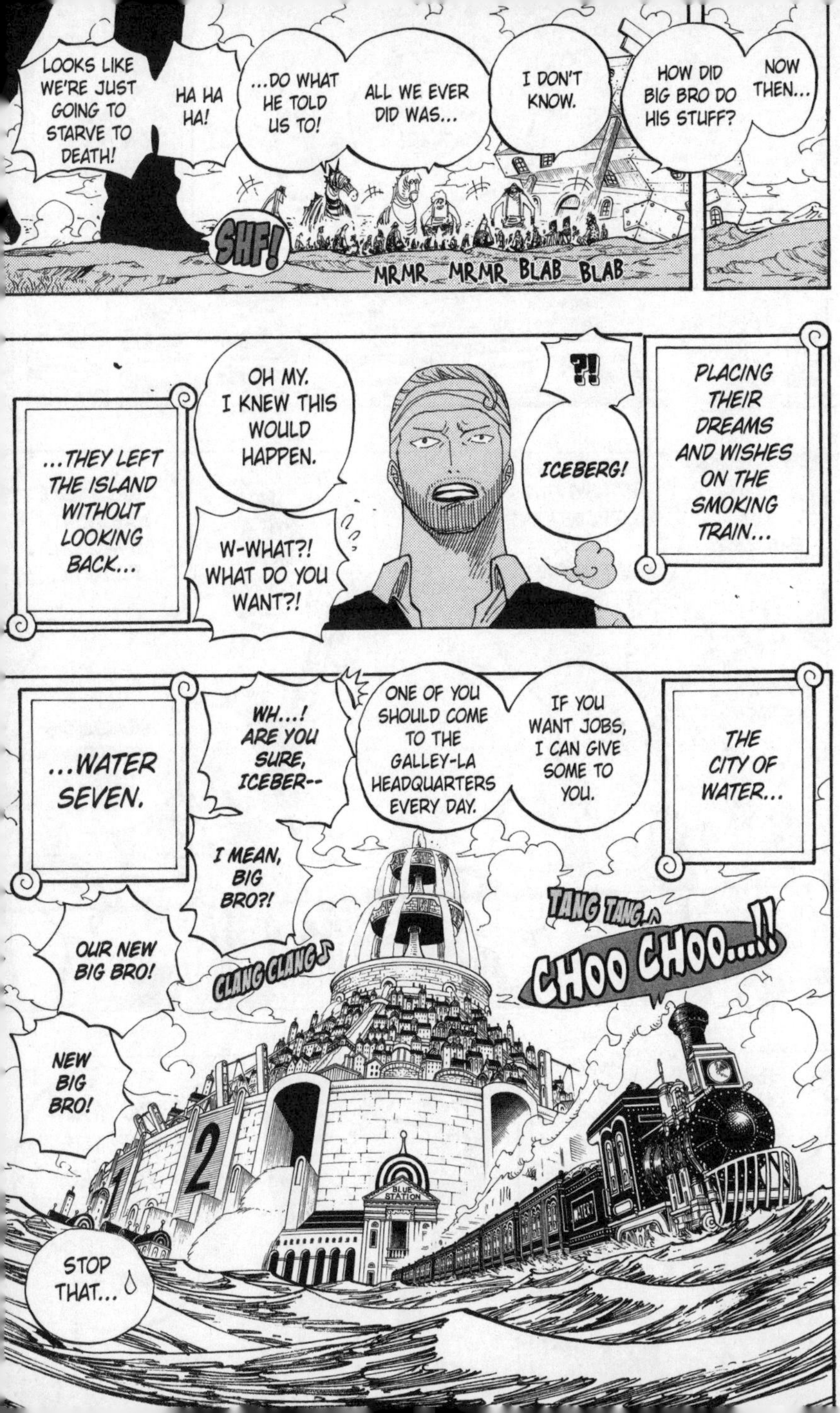
NOW THEN...
HOW DID BIG BRO DO HIS STUFF?
I DON'T KNOW.
ALL WE EVER DID WAS...
...DO WHAT HE TOLD US TO!
HA HA HA!
LOOKS LIKE WE'RE JUST GOING TO STARVE TO DEATH!
SHF!
MRMR MRMR BLAB BLAB
PLACING THEIR DREAMS AND WISHES ON THE SMOKING TRAIN...
?!
ICEBERG!
OH MY. I KNEW THIS WOULD HAPPEN.
W-WHAT?! WHAT DO YOU WANT?!
...THEY LEFT THE ISLAND WITHOUT LOOKING BACK...
THE CITY OF WATER...
IF YOU WANT JOBS, I CAN GIVE SOME TO YOU.
ONE OF YOU SHOULD COME TO THE GALLEY-LA HEADQUARTERS EVERY DAY.
WH...! ARE YOU SURE, ICEBER--
I MEAN, BIG BRO?!
...WATER SEVEN.
TANG TANG♪
CHOO CHOO...!!
CLANG CLANG♪
OUR NEW BIG BRO!
NEW BIG BRO!
BLUE STATION
STOP THAT...

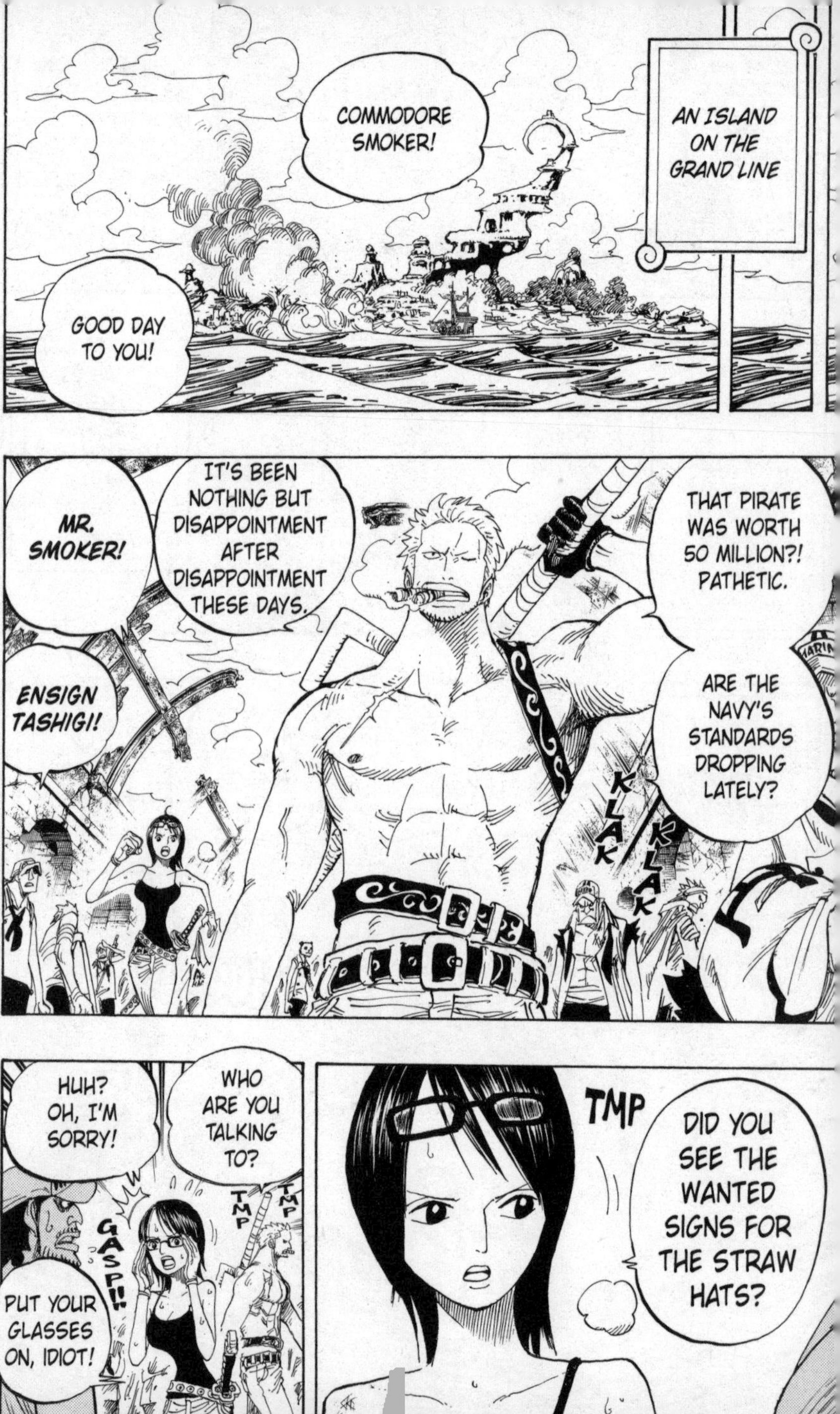

AN ISLAND ON THE GRAND LINE
COMMODORE SMOKER!
GOOD DAY TO YOU!
THAT PIRATE WAS WORTH 50 MILLION?! PATHETIC.
ARE THE NAVY'S STANDARDS DROPPING LATELY?
KLAK
KLAK
IT'S BEEN NOTHING BUT DISAPPOINTMENT AFTER DISAPPOINTMENT THESE DAYS.
MR. SMOKER!
ENSIGN TASHIGI!
TMP
DID YOU SEE THE WANTED SIGNS FOR THE STRAW HATS?
WHO ARE YOU TALKING TO?
TMP
TMP
HUH? OH, I'M SORRY!
GASP!!
PUT YOUR GLASSES ON, IDIOT!

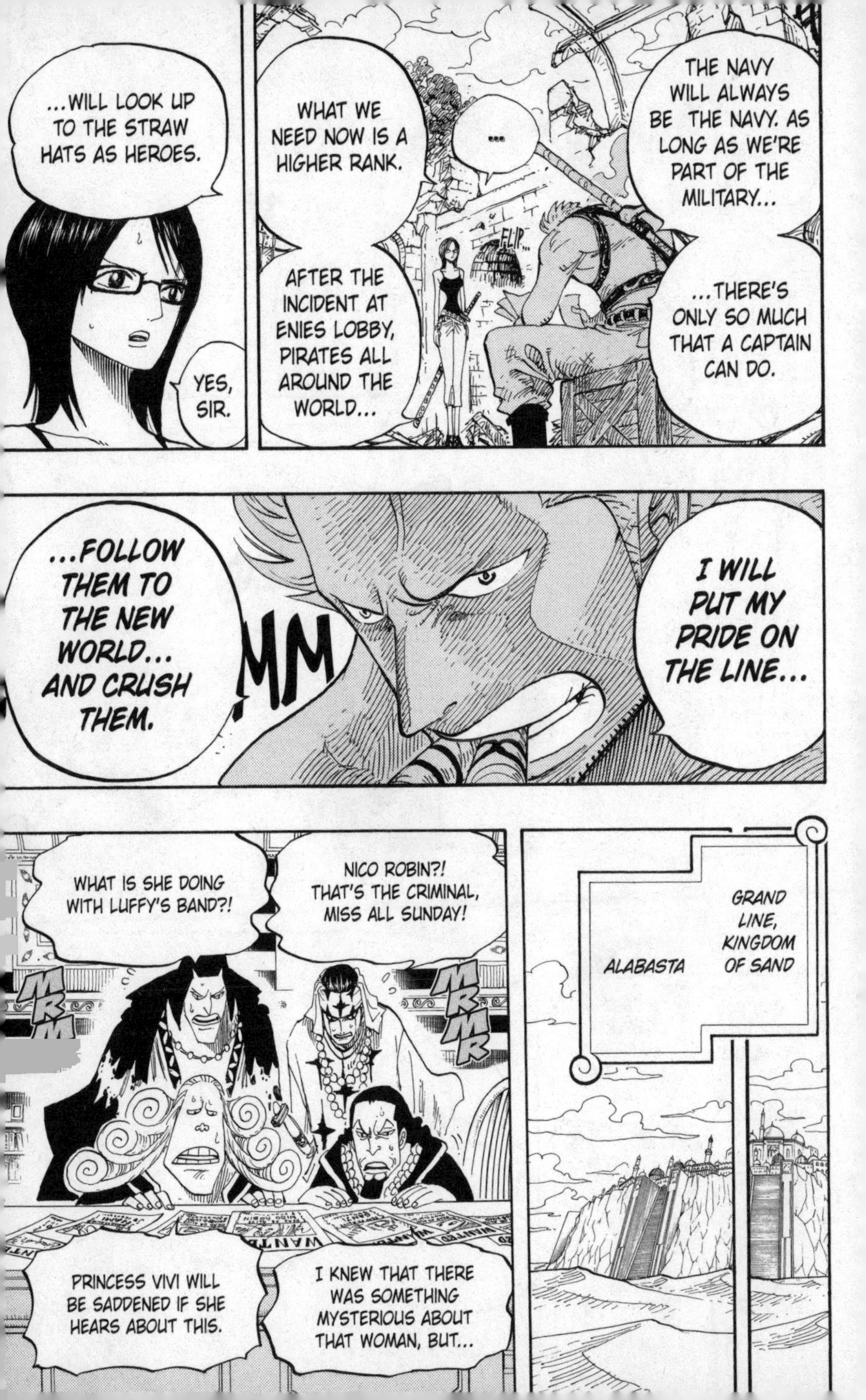
THE NAVY WILL ALWAYS BE THE NAVY. AS LONG AS WE'RE PART OF THE MILITARY...
...THERE'S ONLY SO MUCH THAT A CAPTAIN CAN DO.
FLIP...
...
WHAT WE NEED NOW IS A HIGHER RANK.
AFTER THE INCIDENT AT ENIES LOBBY, PIRATES ALL AROUND THE WORLD...
...WILL LOOK UP TO THE STRAW HATS AS HEROES.
YES, SIR.
I WILL PUT MY PRIDE ON THE LINE...
MM
...FOLLOW THEM TO THE NEW WORLD... AND CRUSH THEM.
GRAND LINE, KINGDOM OF SAND
ALABASTA
NICO ROBIN?! THAT'S THE CRIMINAL, MISS ALL SUNDAY!
MRMR
WHAT IS SHE DOING WITH LUFFY'S BAND?!
MRM
I KNEW THAT THERE WAS SOMETHING MYSTERIOUS ABOUT THAT WOMAN, BUT...
PRINCESS VIVI WILL BE SADDENED IF SHE HEARS ABOUT THIS.

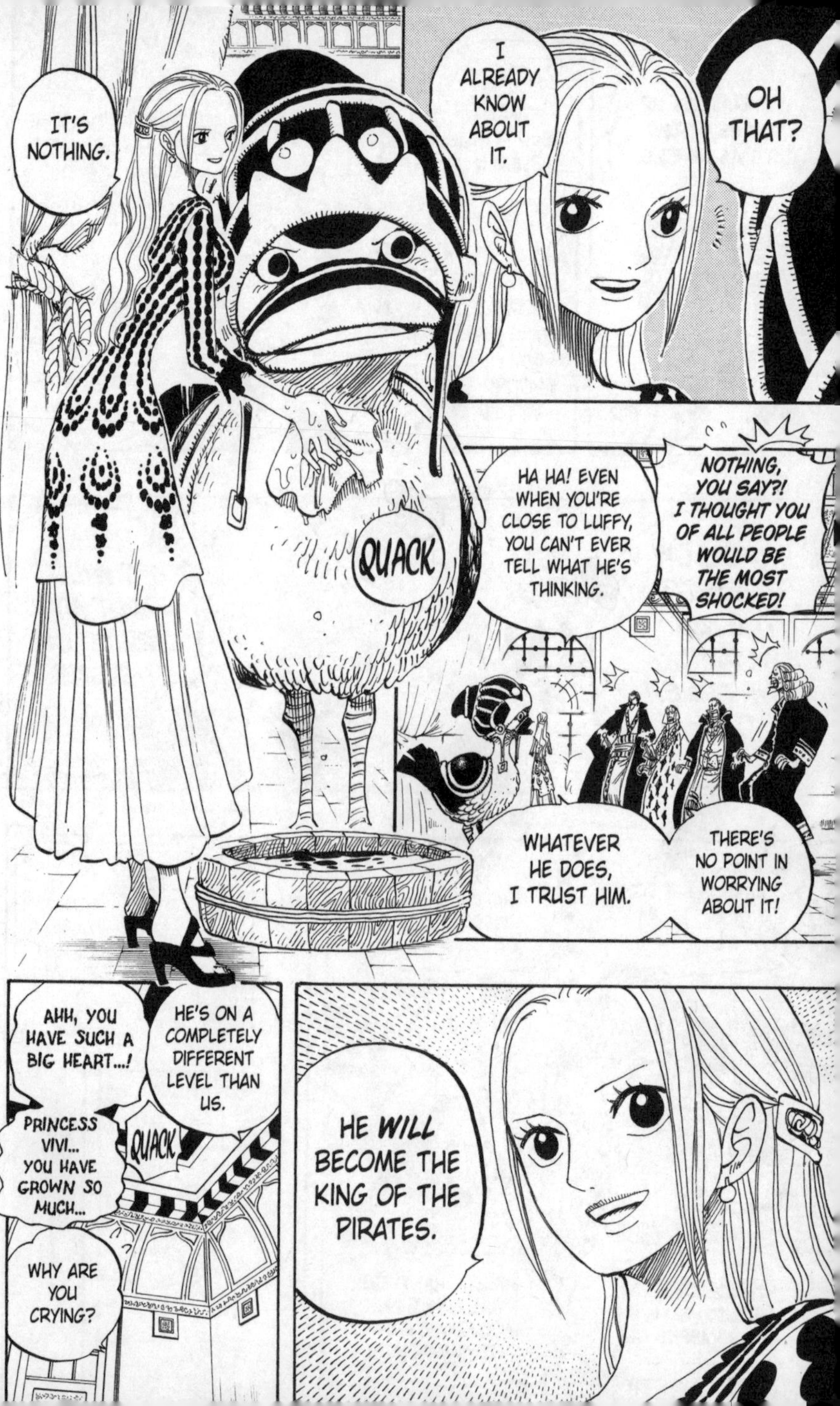
OH THAT?
I ALREADY KNOW ABOUT IT.
NOTHING, YOU SAY?! I THOUGHT YOU OF ALL PEOPLE WOULD BE THE MOST SHOCKED!
HA HA! EVEN WHEN YOU'RE CLOSE TO LUFFY, YOU CAN'T EVER TELL WHAT HE'S THINKING.
THERE'S NO POINT IN WORRYING ABOUT IT!
WHATEVER HE DOES, I TRUST HIM.
IT'S NOTHING.
QUACK
HE *WILL* BECOME THE KING OF THE PIRATES.
HE'S ON A COMPLETELY DIFFERENT LEVEL THAN US.
AHH, YOU HAVE SUCH A BIG HEART...!
QUACK
PRINCESS VIVI... YOU HAVE GROWN SO MUCH...
WHY ARE YOU CRYING?

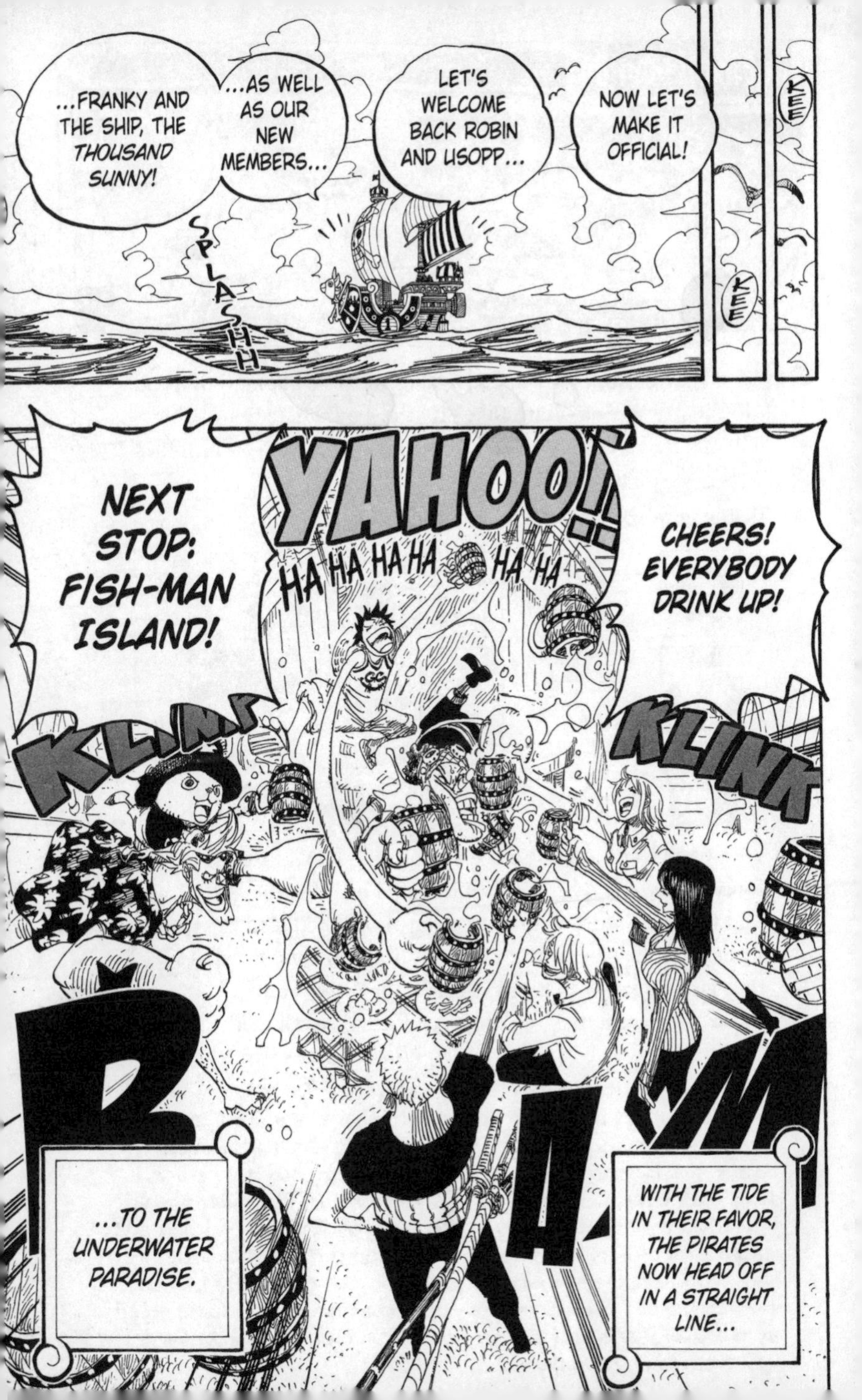
KEE
KEE
NOW LET'S MAKE IT OFFICIAL!
LET'S WELCOME BACK ROBIN AND USOPP...
...AS WELL AS OUR NEW MEMBERS...
...FRANKY AND THE SHIP, THE THOUSAND SUNNY!
SPLASHH
CHEERS! EVERYBODY DRINK UP!
YAHOO!!
HA HA HA HA HA HA
NEXT STOP: FISH-MAN ISLAND!
KLINK
KLINK
BAM
WITH THE TIDE IN THEIR FAVOR, THE PIRATES NOW HEAD OFF IN A STRAIGHT LINE...
...TO THE UNDERWATER PARADISE.

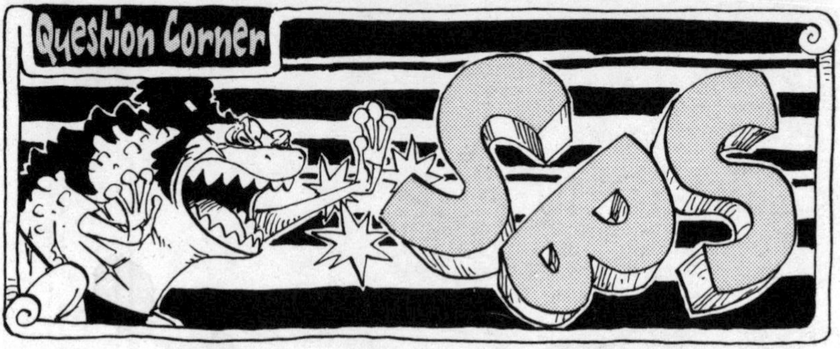
Question Corner
SBS

Q: This may be sudden, but Luffy likes meat. What kind of food do the rest of the pirates like? By the way, what about you? Cha Pa Pa Pa Pa!

--From I Love Cup Noodles!

A: These are their favorite foods!! ↓

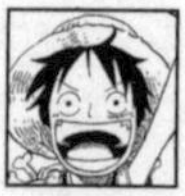

ALL MEAT.

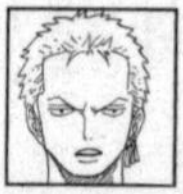

White rice, Neptunian meat, anything that goes well with alcohol.

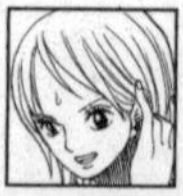

Tangerines, fruits in general.

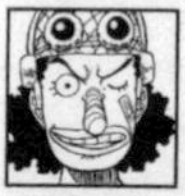

Sauries from the Autumn Islands. He loves fish that are in season.

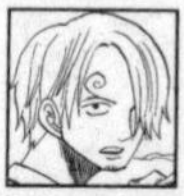

Spicy seafood pasta, anything that goes well with tea.

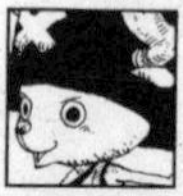

Cotton candy, chocolate, sweets in general.

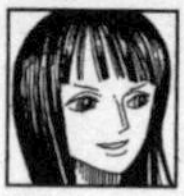

Sandwiches, cake that isn't too sweet, anything that goes well with coffee.

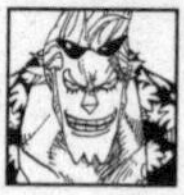

Hamburgers, fries, anything that goes well with cola.

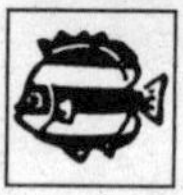

Goes through phases. Likes beef with green peppers right now.

Q: Hey, Oda! I got a question! It's about the Devil Fruit! During the time with Kaku and Kalifa of CP9, they said that they didn't know anything about the Devil Fruit until they ate it. But during Luffy's time, how did they already know that it was called the Gum-Gum Fruit? Please tell me! Tell me now! Pleeeease tell me!

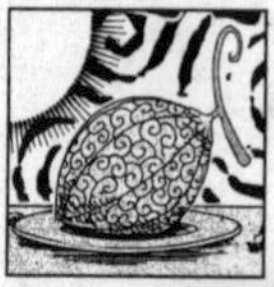

--White Hunter Fan

A: Well, I will go into more detail about the Devil Fruit in the main story at a later time. But there is a sort of identification manual for Devil Fruits. It has information about the name and powers of each fruit, but there are a few that even have pictures to go with it. The Gum-Gum Fruit had a picture in this book, but the fruits for Kaku and Kalifa didn't. They had to eat it to find out what abilities it had, and then they would go look for the name. That's how the conversation went. The conversation is in volume 40, by the way. That's it for the Question Corner for volume 45! See you next volume!

Chapter 440:
FIRE FIST VS. BLACKBEARD

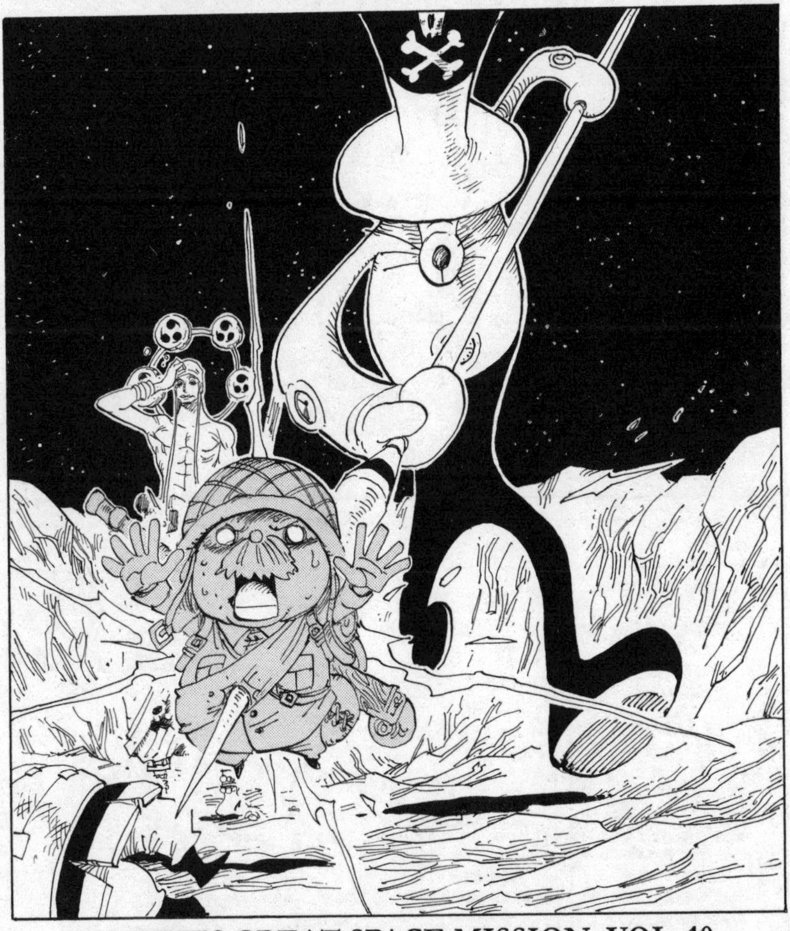

ENERU'S GREAT SPACE MISSION, VOL. 10:
"LIEUTENANT SPACEY IS KILLED BY A SPACE PIRATE"

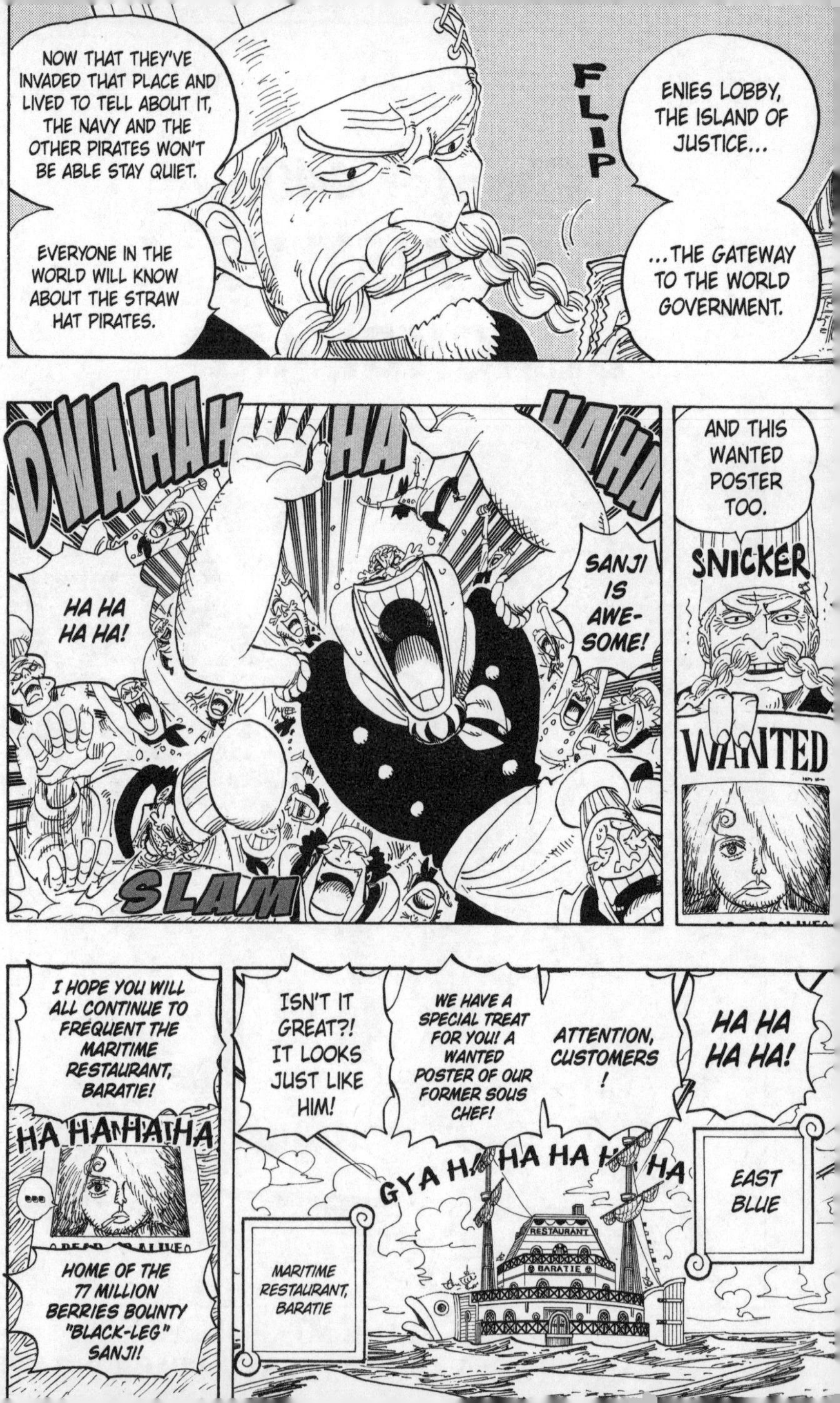
FLIP
ENIES LOBBY, THE ISLAND OF JUSTICE...
...THE GATEWAY TO THE WORLD GOVERNMENT.
NOW THAT THEY'VE INVADED THAT PLACE AND LIVED TO TELL ABOUT IT, THE NAVY AND THE OTHER PIRATES WON'T BE ABLE STAY QUIET.
EVERYONE IN THE WORLD WILL KNOW ABOUT THE STRAW HAT PIRATES.
AND THIS WANTED POSTER TOO.
SNICKER
WANTED
HAHA
SANJI IS AWE-SOME!
DWAHAHAHA HA
HA HA HA HA!
SLAM
HA HA HA HA!
ATTENTION, CUSTOMERS!
WE HAVE A SPECIAL TREAT FOR YOU! A WANTED POSTER OF OUR FORMER SOUS CHEF!
ISN'T IT GREAT?! IT LOOKS JUST LIKE HIM!
EAST BLUE
GYA HA HA HA HA HA HA
RESTAURANT
BARATIE
MARITIME RESTAURANT, BARATIE
I HOPE YOU WILL ALL CONTINUE TO FREQUENT THE MARITIME RESTAURANT, BARATIE!
HA HA HA HA HA
...
HOME OF THE 77 MILLION BERRIES BOUNTY "BLACK-LEG" SANJI!

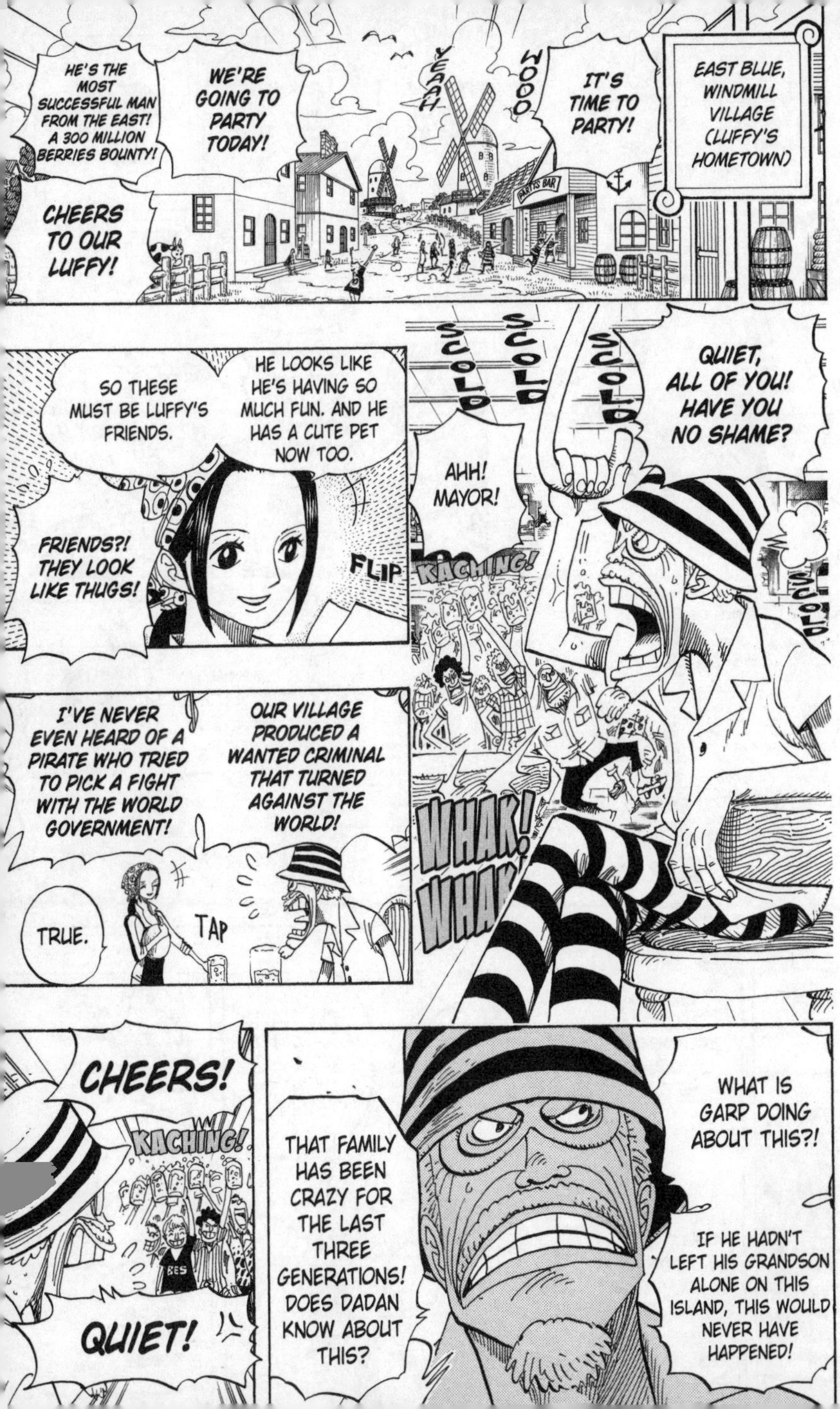
EAST BLUE, WINDMILL VILLAGE (LUFFY'S HOMETOWN)
IT'S TIME TO PARTY!
WOOO
YEAAH
WE'RE GOING TO PARTY TODAY!
HE'S THE MOST SUCCESSFUL MAN FROM THE EAST! A 300 MILLION BERRIES BOUNTY!
CHEERS TO OUR LUFFY!
SCOLD
SCOLD
SCOLD
QUIET, ALL OF YOU! HAVE YOU NO SHAME?
AHH! MAYOR!
KACHING!
SCOLD
WHAK! WHAK
HE LOOKS LIKE HE'S HAVING SO MUCH FUN. AND HE HAS A CUTE PET NOW TOO.
SO THESE MUST BE LUFFY'S FRIENDS.
FLIP
FRIENDS?! THEY LOOK LIKE THUGS!
OUR VILLAGE PRODUCED A WANTED CRIMINAL THAT TURNED AGAINST THE WORLD!
I'VE NEVER EVEN HEARD OF A PIRATE WHO TRIED TO PICK A FIGHT WITH THE WORLD GOVERNMENT!
TAP
TRUE.
WHAT IS GARP DOING ABOUT THIS?!
IF HE HADN'T LEFT HIS GRANDSON ALONE ON THIS ISLAND, THIS WOULD NEVER HAVE HAPPENED!
THAT FAMILY HAS BEEN CRAZY FOR THE LAST THREE GENERATIONS! DOES DADAN KNOW ABOUT THIS?
CHEERS!
KACHING!
QUIET!

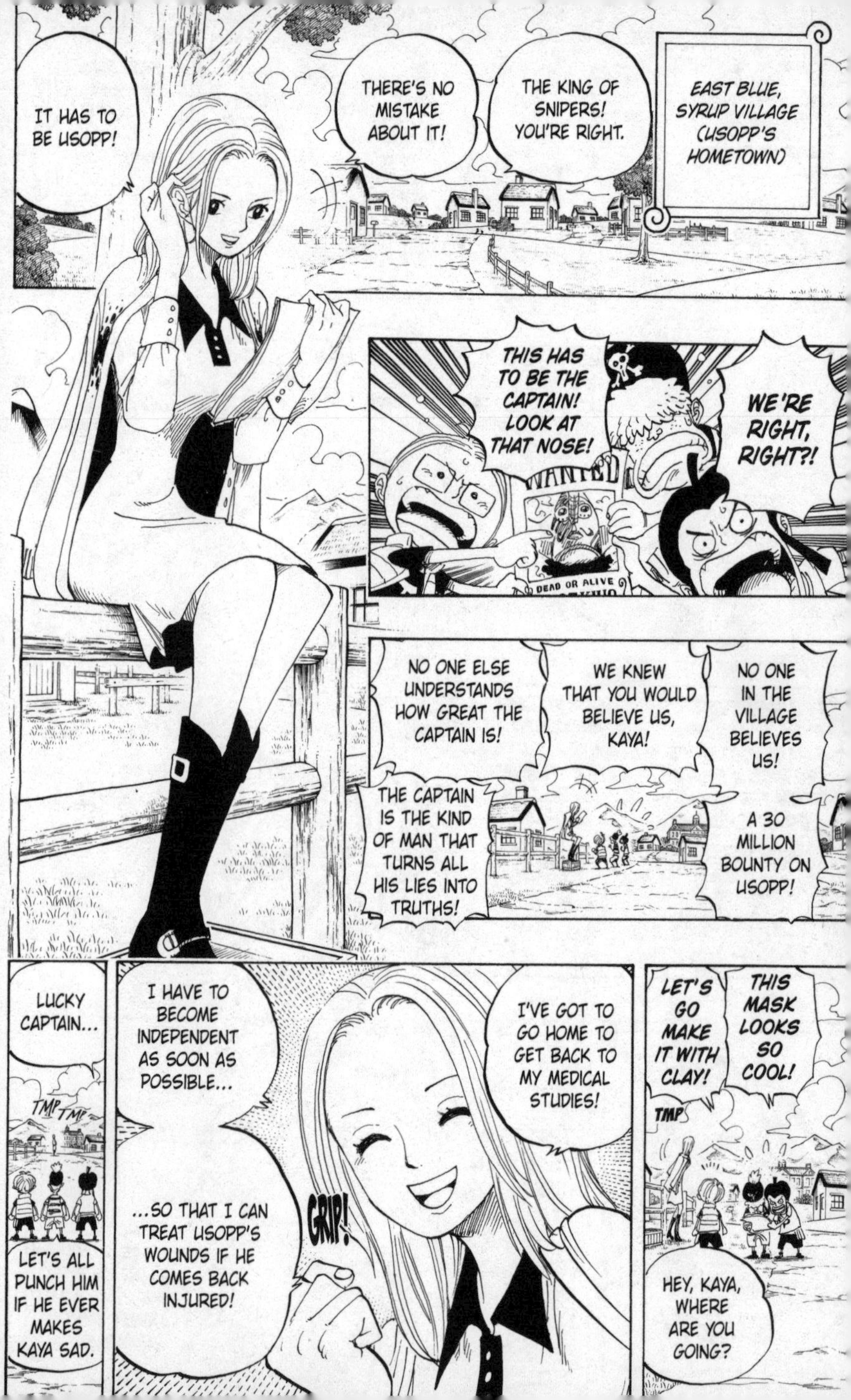
EAST BLUE, SYRUP VILLAGE (USOPP'S HOMETOWN)
THE KING OF SNIPERS! YOU'RE RIGHT.
THERE'S NO MISTAKE ABOUT IT!
IT HAS TO BE USOPP!
WE'RE RIGHT, RIGHT?!
THIS HAS TO BE THE CAPTAIN! LOOK AT THAT NOSE!
WANTED
DEAD OR ALIVE
NO ONE IN THE VILLAGE BELIEVES US!
WE KNEW THAT YOU WOULD BELIEVE US, KAYA!
NO ONE ELSE UNDERSTANDS HOW GREAT THE CAPTAIN IS!
A 30 MILLION BOUNTY ON USOPP!
THE CAPTAIN IS THE KIND OF MAN THAT TURNS ALL HIS LIES INTO TRUTHS!
THIS MASK LOOKS SO COOL!
LET'S GO MAKE IT WITH CLAY!
TMP
HEY, KAYA, WHERE ARE YOU GOING?
I'VE GOT TO GO HOME TO GET BACK TO MY MEDICAL STUDIES!
I HAVE TO BECOME INDEPENDENT AS SOON AS POSSIBLE...
GRIP!
...SO THAT I CAN TREAT USOPP'S WOUNDS IF HE COMES BACK INJURED!
LUCKY CAPTAIN...
TMP TMP
LET'S ALL PUNCH HIM IF HE EVER MAKES KAYA SAD.

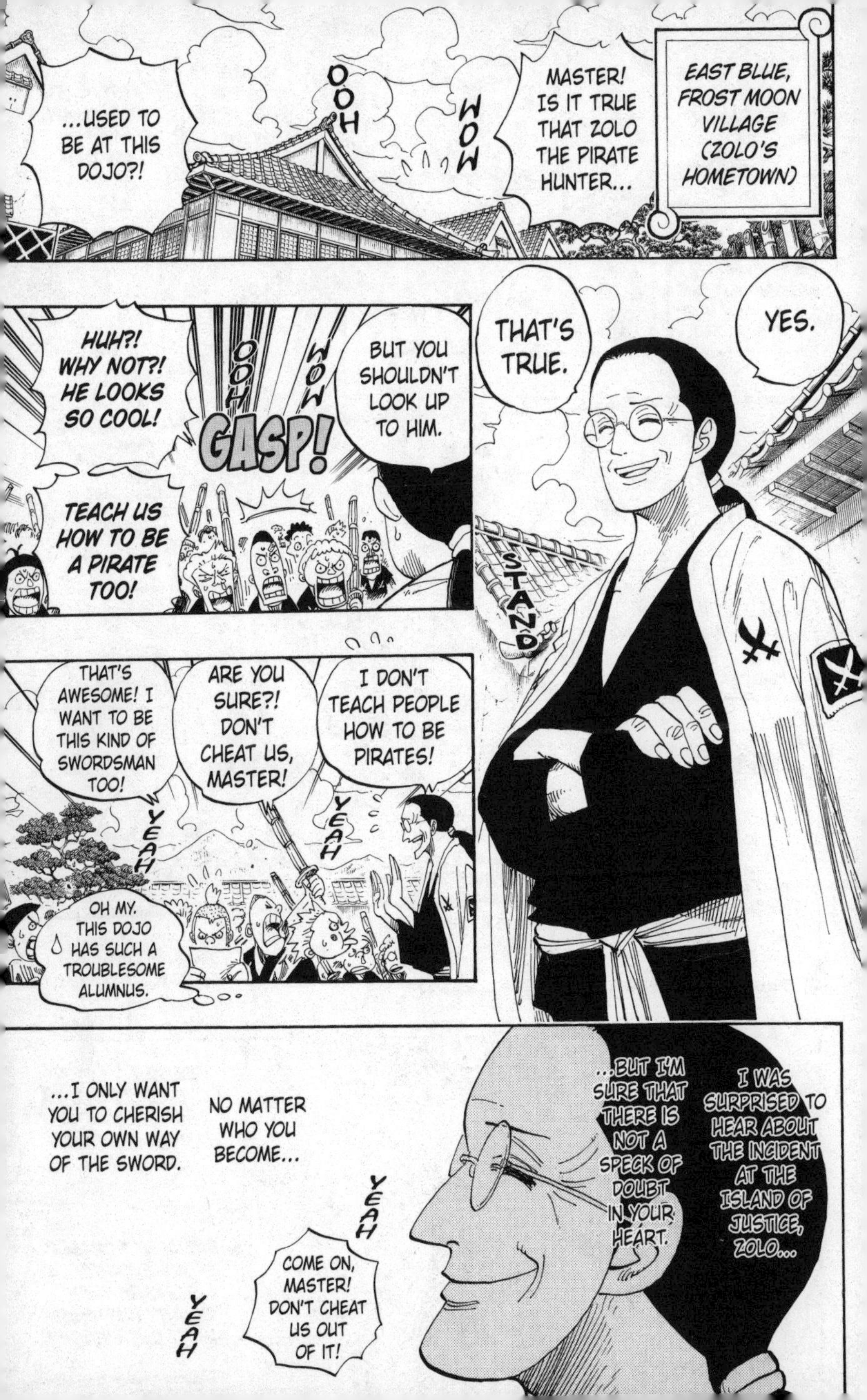
EAST BLUE, FROST MOON VILLAGE (ZOLO'S HOMETOWN)
MASTER! IS IT TRUE THAT ZOLO THE PIRATE HUNTER...
WOW
OOH
...USED TO BE AT THIS DOJO?!
YES.
THAT'S TRUE.
STAND
BUT YOU SHOULDN'T LOOK UP TO HIM.
WOW
OOH
GASP!
HUH?! WHY NOT?! HE LOOKS SO COOL!
TEACH US HOW TO BE A PIRATE TOO!
I DON'T TEACH PEOPLE HOW TO BE PIRATES!
ARE YOU SURE?! DON'T CHEAT US, MASTER!
THAT'S AWESOME! I WANT TO BE THIS KIND OF SWORDSMAN TOO!
YEAH
YEAH
OH MY. THIS DOJO HAS SUCH A TROUBLESOME ALUMNUS.
I WAS SURPRISED TO HEAR ABOUT THE INCIDENT AT THE ISLAND OF JUSTICE, ZOLO...
...BUT I'M SURE THAT THERE IS NOT A SPECK OF DOUBT IN YOUR HEART.
YEAH
NO MATTER WHO YOU BECOME...
...I ONLY WANT YOU TO CHERISH YOUR OWN WAY OF THE SWORD.
COME ON, MASTER! DON'T CHEAT US OUT OF IT!
YEAH

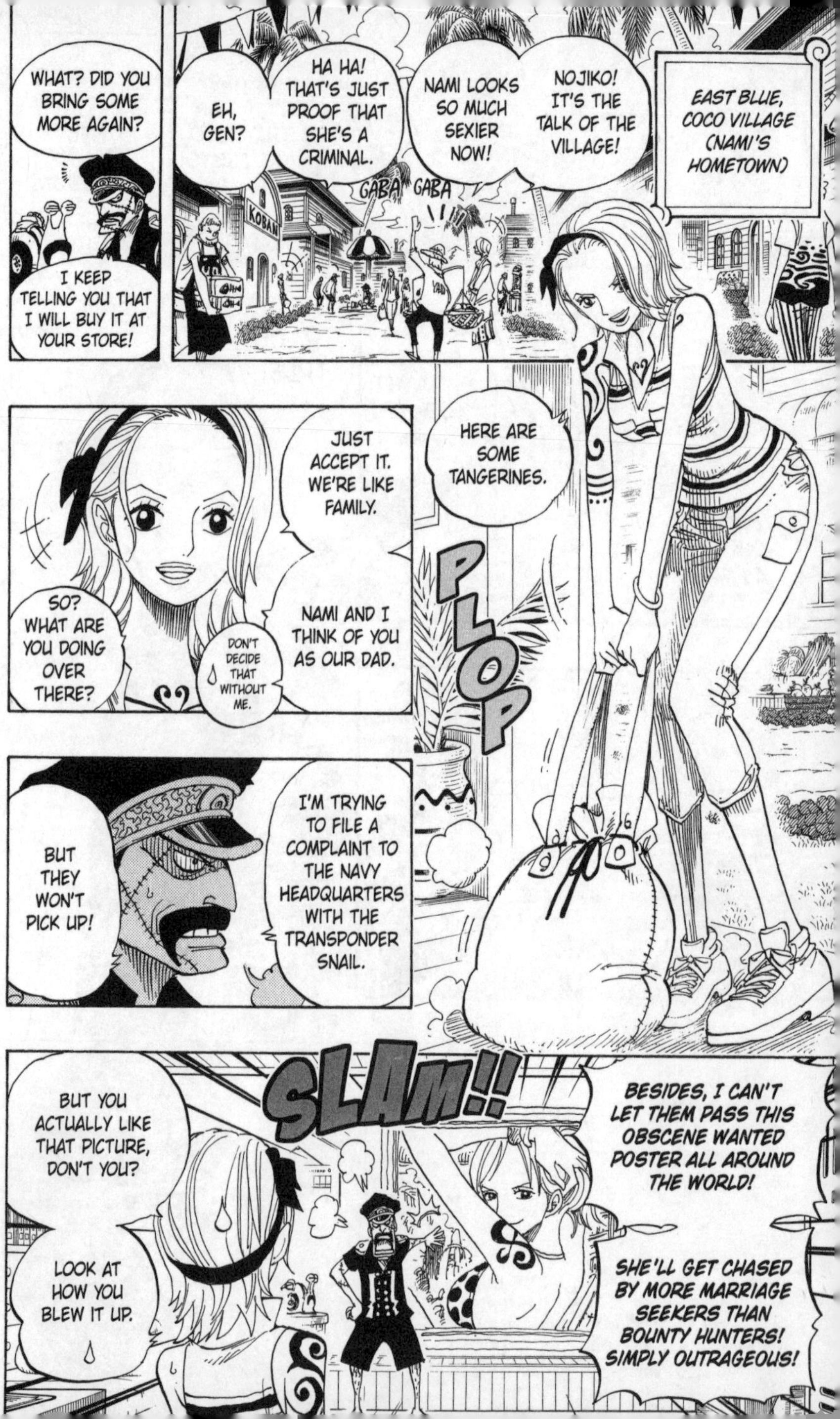
EAST BLUE, COCO VILLAGE (NAMI'S HOMETOWN)
NOJIKO! IT'S THE TALK OF THE VILLAGE!
NAMI LOOKS SO MUCH SEXIER NOW!
GABA GABA
HA HA! THAT'S JUST PROOF THAT SHE'S A CRIMINAL.
EH, GEN?
KOBAN
WHAT? DID YOU BRING SOME MORE AGAIN?
I KEEP TELLING YOU THAT I WILL BUY IT AT YOUR STORE!
HERE ARE SOME TANGERINES.
PLOP
JUST ACCEPT IT. WE'RE LIKE FAMILY.
NAMI AND I THINK OF YOU AS OUR DAD.
DON'T DECIDE THAT WITHOUT ME.
SO? WHAT ARE YOU DOING OVER THERE?
I'M TRYING TO FILE A COMPLAINT TO THE NAVY HEADQUARTERS WITH THE TRANSPONDER SNAIL.
BUT THEY WON'T PICK UP!
SLAM!!
BESIDES, I CAN'T LET THEM PASS THIS OBSCENE WANTED POSTER ALL AROUND THE WORLD!
SHE'LL GET CHASED BY MORE MARRIAGE SEEKERS THAN BOUNTY HUNTERS! SIMPLY OUTRAGEOUS!
BUT YOU ACTUALLY LIKE THAT PICTURE, DON'T YOU?
LOOK AT HOW YOU BLEW IT UP.

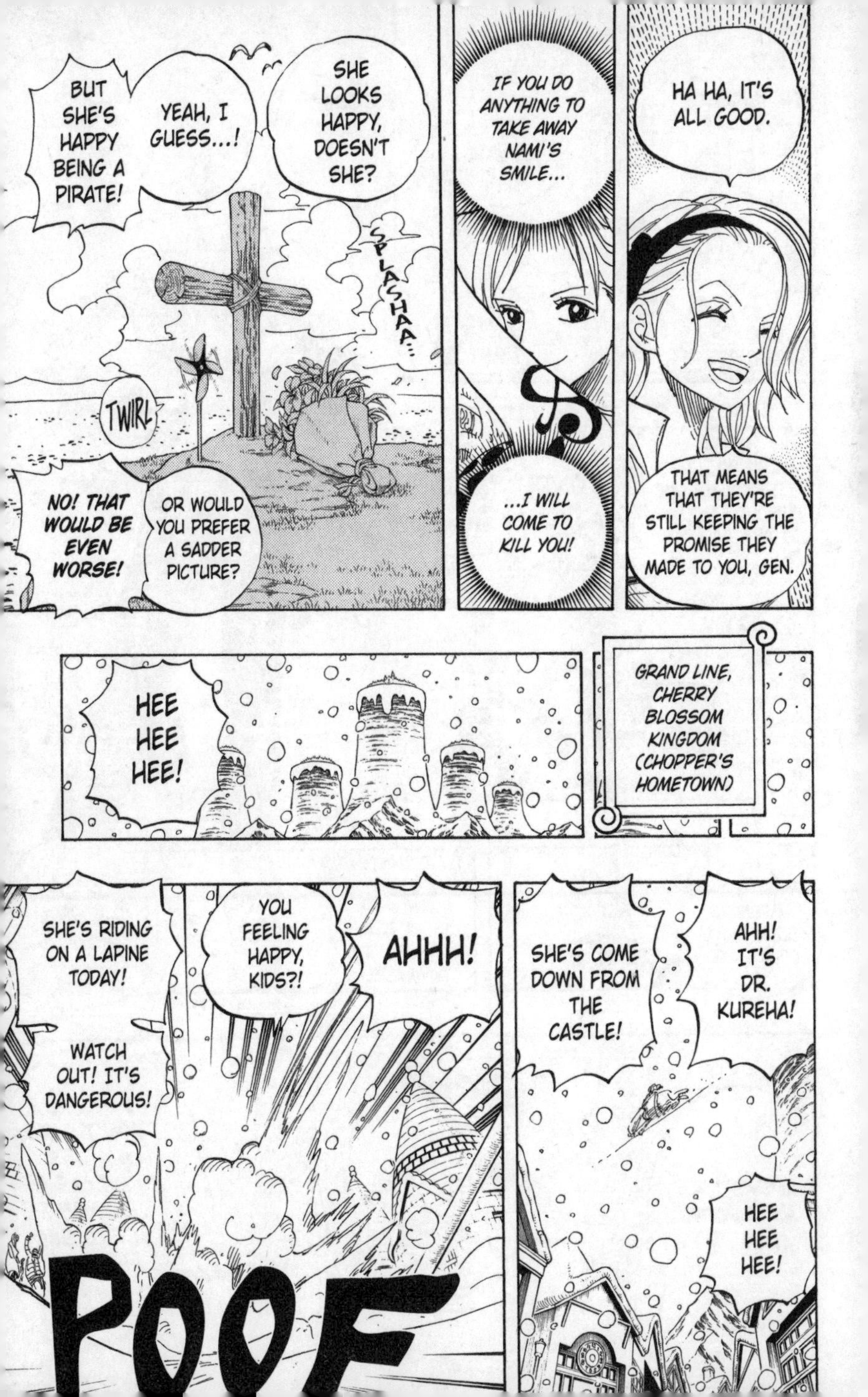
HA HA, IT'S ALL GOOD.
THAT MEANS THAT THEY'RE STILL KEEPING THE PROMISE THEY MADE TO YOU, GEN.
IF YOU DO ANYTHING TO TAKE AWAY NAMI'S SMILE...
...I WILL COME TO KILL YOU!
SHE LOOKS HAPPY, DOESN'T SHE?
YEAH, I GUESS...!
BUT SHE'S HAPPY BEING A PIRATE!
SPLASHAA...
TWIRL
OR WOULD YOU PREFER A SADDER PICTURE?
NO! THAT WOULD BE EVEN WORSE!
GRAND LINE, CHERRY BLOSSOM KINGDOM (CHOPPER'S HOMETOWN)
HEE HEE HEE!
AHH! IT'S DR. KUREHA!
SHE'S COME DOWN FROM THE CASTLE!
HEE HEE HEE!
AHHH!
YOU FEELING HAPPY, KIDS?!
SHE'S RIDING ON A LAPINE TODAY!
WATCH OUT! IT'S DANGEROUS!
POOF

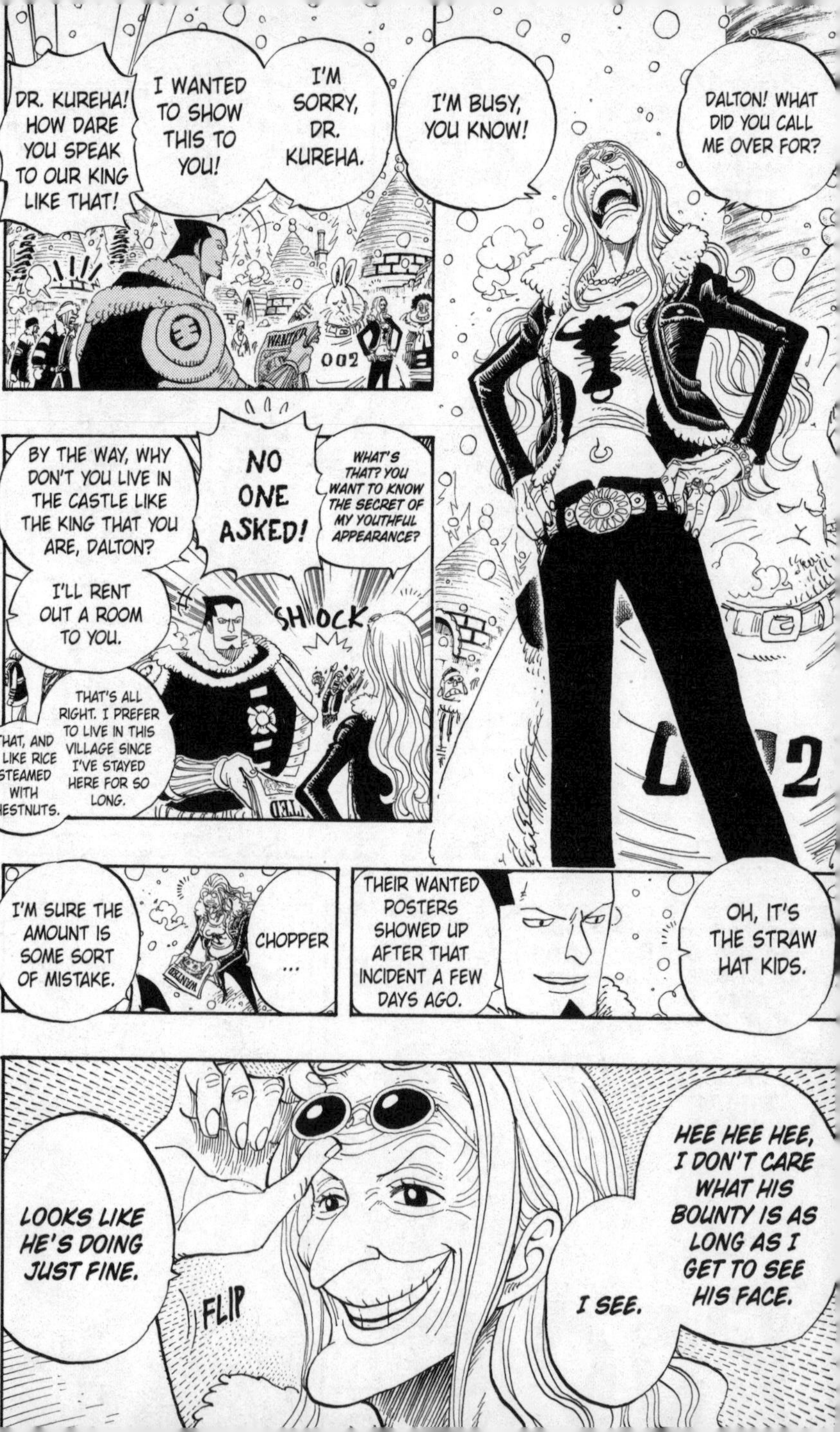
DALTON! WHAT DID YOU CALL ME OVER FOR?
I'M BUSY, YOU KNOW!
I'M SORRY, DR. KUREHA.
I WANTED TO SHOW THIS TO YOU!
DR. KUREHA! HOW DARE YOU SPEAK TO OUR KING LIKE THAT!
WHAT'S THAT? YOU WANT TO KNOW THE SECRET OF MY YOUTHFUL APPEARANCE?
NO ONE ASKED!
SHOCK
BY THE WAY, WHY DON'T YOU LIVE IN THE CASTLE LIKE THE KING THAT YOU ARE, DALTON?
I'LL RENT OUT A ROOM TO YOU.
THAT'S ALL RIGHT. I PREFER TO LIVE IN THIS VILLAGE SINCE I'VE STAYED HERE FOR SO LONG.
THAT, AND I LIKE RICE STEAMED WITH CHESTNUTS.
OH, IT'S THE STRAW HAT KIDS.
THEIR WANTED POSTERS SHOWED UP AFTER THAT INCIDENT A FEW DAYS AGO.
CHOPPER ...
I'M SURE THE AMOUNT IS SOME SORT OF MISTAKE.
HEE HEE HEE, I DON'T CARE WHAT HIS BOUNTY IS AS LONG AS I GET TO SEE HIS FACE.
I SEE.
LOOKS LIKE HE'S DOING JUST FINE.
FLIP

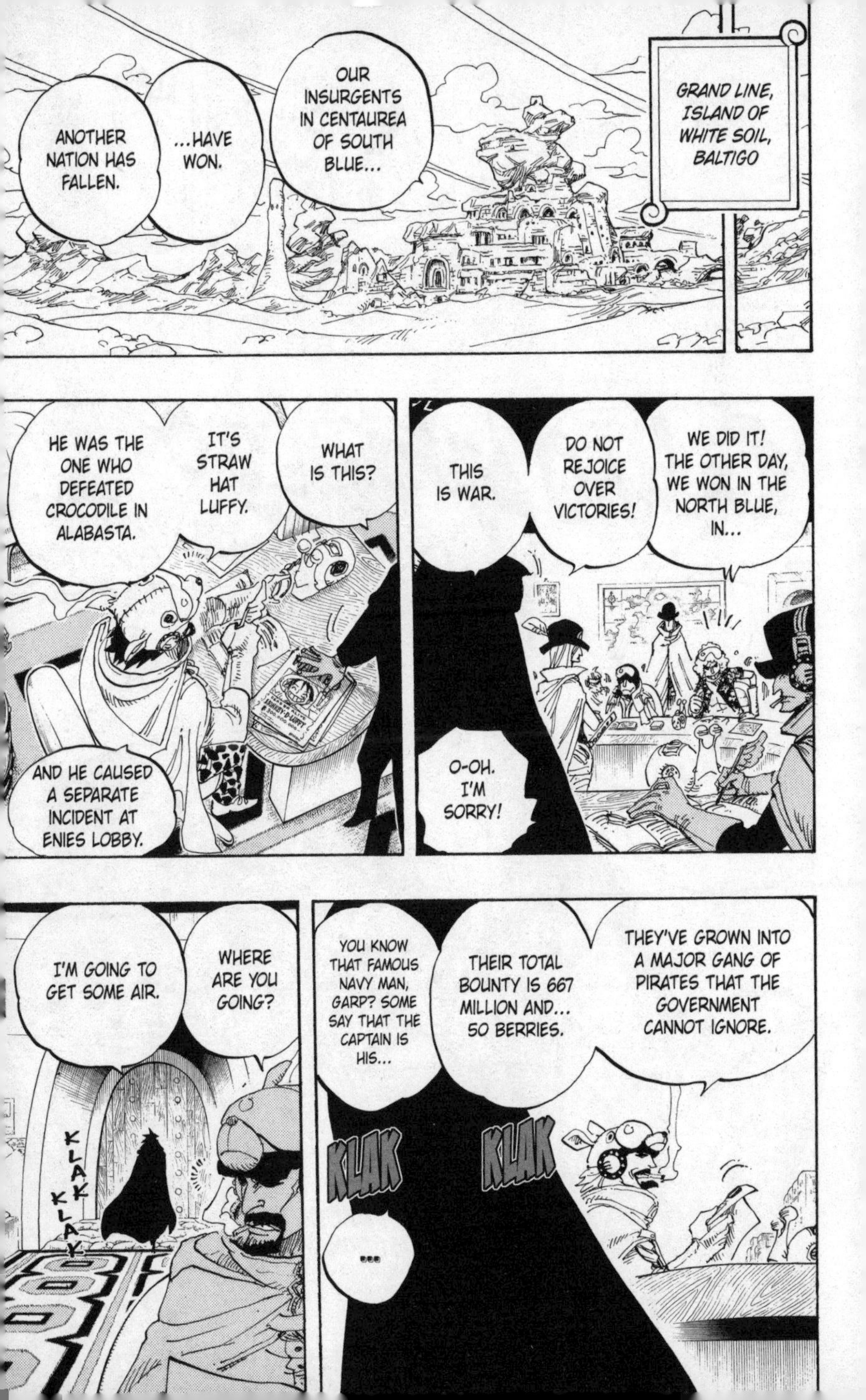
GRAND LINE, ISLAND OF WHITE SOIL, BALTIGO
OUR INSURGENTS IN CENTAUREA OF SOUTH BLUE...
...HAVE WON.
ANOTHER NATION HAS FALLEN.
WE DID IT! THE OTHER DAY, WE WON IN THE NORTH BLUE, IN...
DO NOT REJOICE OVER VICTORIES!
THIS IS WAR.
O-OH. I'M SORRY!
WHAT IS THIS?
IT'S STRAW HAT LUFFY.
HE WAS THE ONE WHO DEFEATED CROCODILE IN ALABASTA.
AND HE CAUSED A SEPARATE INCIDENT AT ENIES LOBBY.
THEY'VE GROWN INTO A MAJOR GANG OF PIRATES THAT THE GOVERNMENT CANNOT IGNORE.
THEIR TOTAL BOUNTY IS 667 MILLION AND... 50 BERRIES.
YOU KNOW THAT FAMOUS NAVY MAN, GARP? SOME SAY THAT THE CAPTAIN IS HIS...
KLAK
KLAK
...
WHERE ARE YOU GOING?
I'M GOING TO GET SOME AIR.
KLAK KLAK

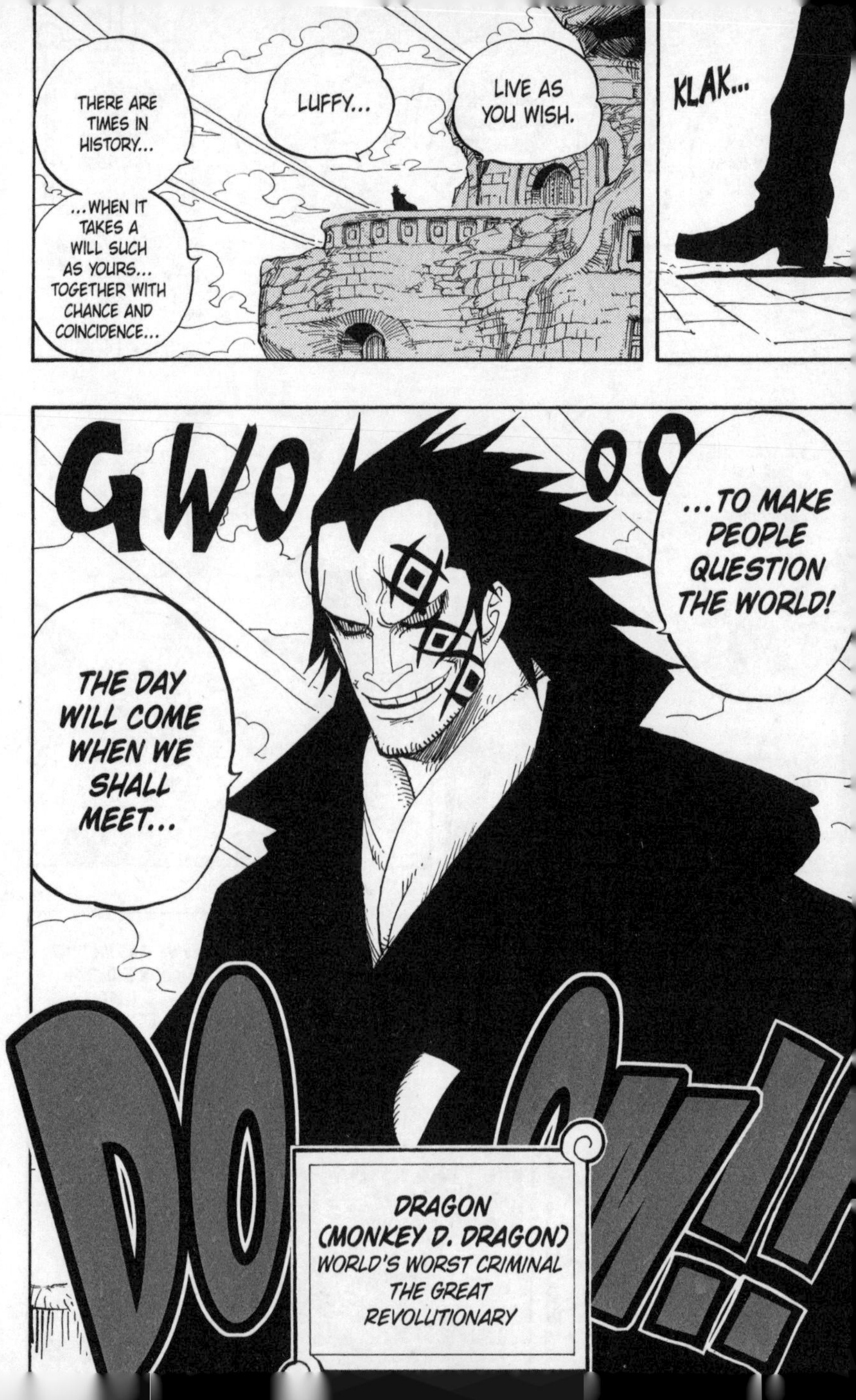
KLAK...
LIVE AS YOU WISH.
LUFFY...
THERE ARE TIMES IN HISTORY...
...WHEN IT TAKES A WILL SUCH AS YOURS... TOGETHER WITH CHANCE AND COINCIDENCE...
GWOOO
...TO MAKE PEOPLE QUESTION THE WORLD!
THE DAY WILL COME WHEN WE SHALL MEET...
DOON!!
DRAGON (MONKEY D. DRAGON) WORLD'S WORST CRIMINAL THE GREAT REVOLUTIONARY

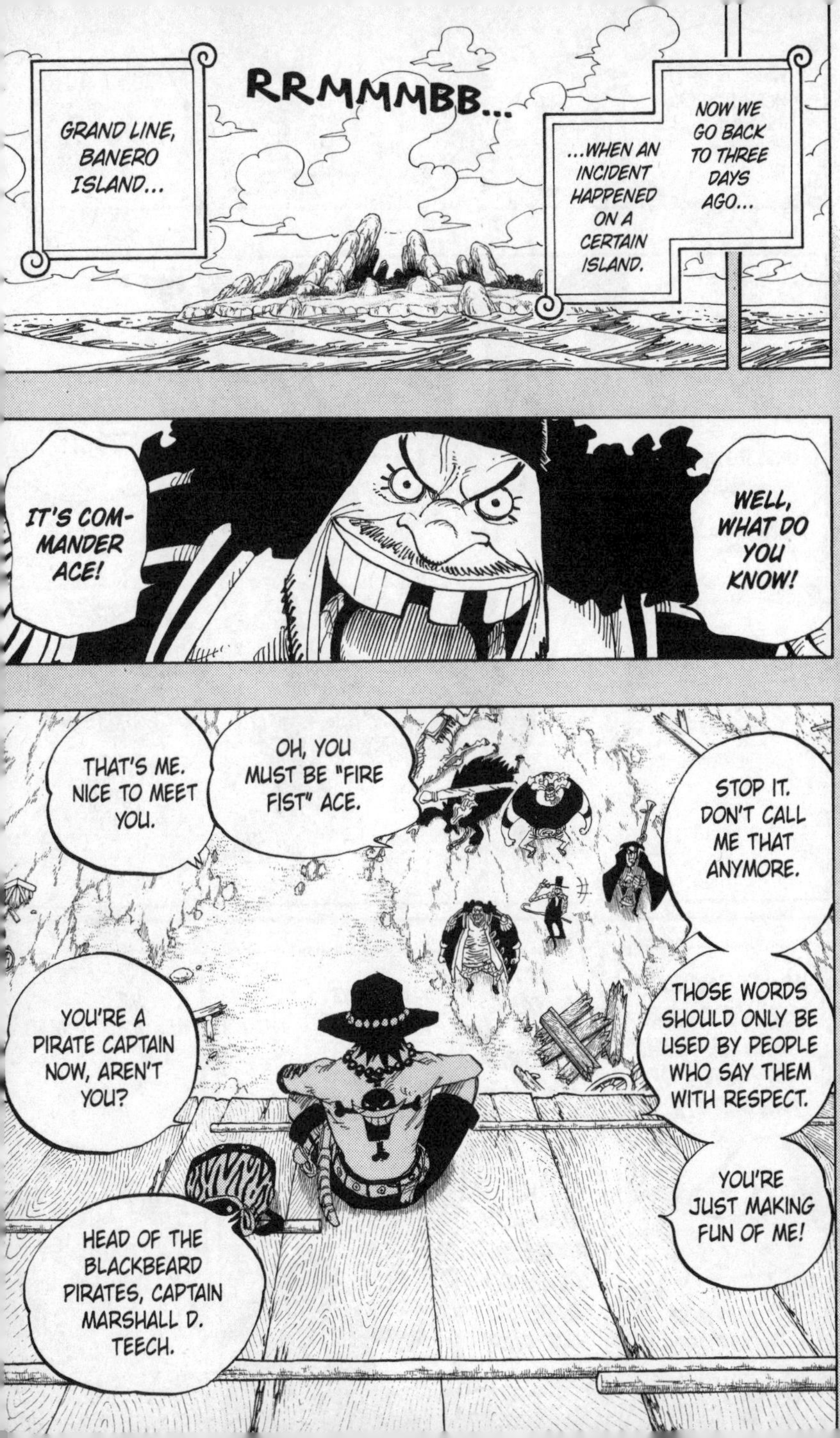
NOW WE GO BACK TO THREE DAYS AGO...
...WHEN AN INCIDENT HAPPENED ON A CERTAIN ISLAND.
RRMMMBB...
GRAND LINE, BANERO ISLAND...
WELL, WHAT DO YOU KNOW!
IT'S COMMANDER ACE!
OH, YOU MUST BE "FIRE FIST" ACE.
THAT'S ME. NICE TO MEET YOU.
YOU'RE A PIRATE CAPTAIN NOW, AREN'T YOU?
HEAD OF THE BLACKBEARD PIRATES, CAPTAIN MARSHALL D. TEECH.
STOP IT. DON'T CALL ME THAT ANYMORE.
THOSE WORDS SHOULD ONLY BE USED BY PEOPLE WHO SAY THEM WITH RESPECT.
YOU'RE JUST MAKING FUN OF ME!

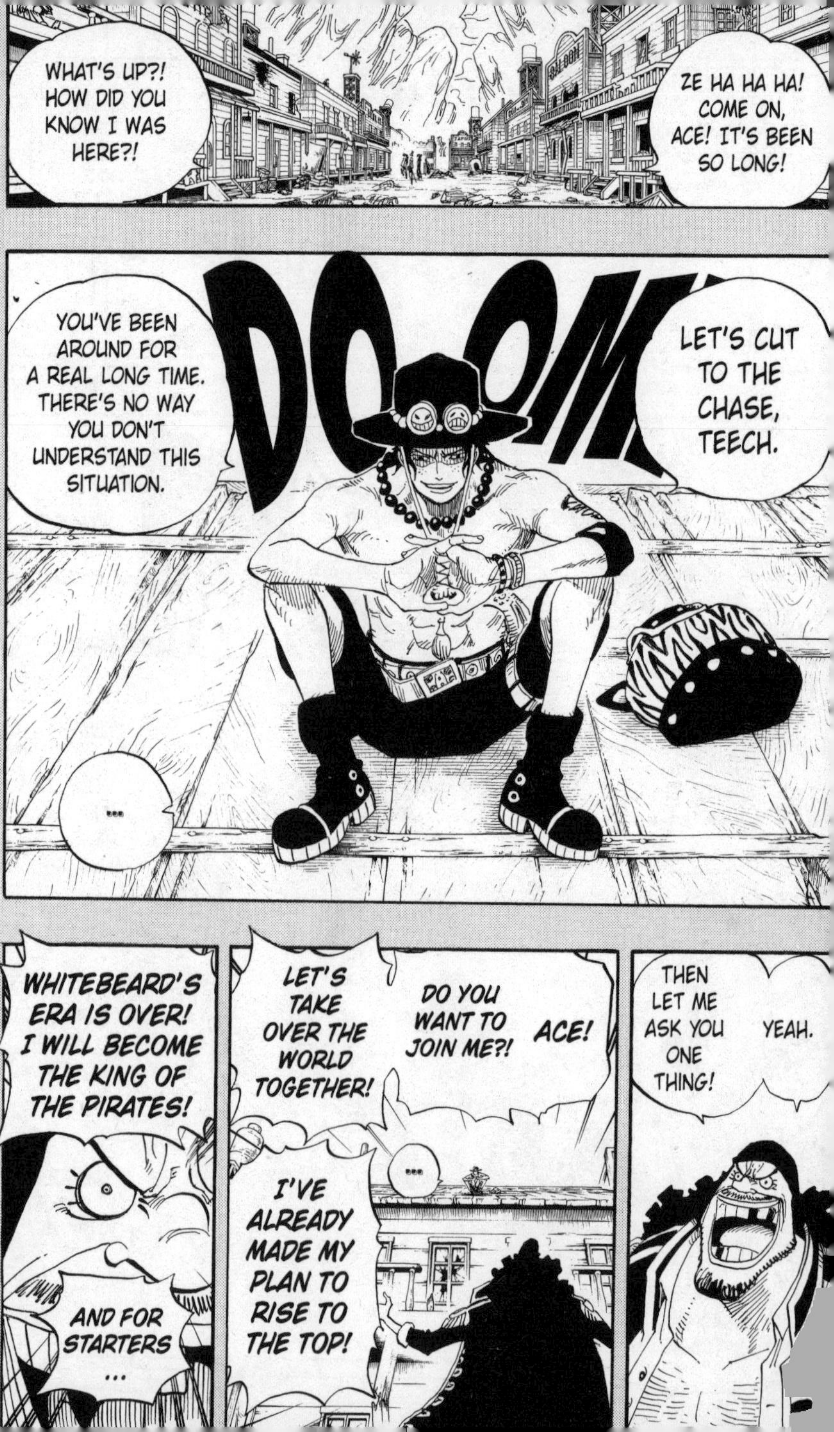
ZE HA HA HA! COME ON, ACE! IT'S BEEN SO LONG!
WHAT'S UP?! HOW DID YOU KNOW I WAS HERE?!
LET'S CUT TO THE CHASE, TEECH.
DOOM
YOU'VE BEEN AROUND FOR A REAL LONG TIME. THERE'S NO WAY YOU DON'T UNDERSTAND THIS SITUATION.
...
YEAH.
THEN LET ME ASK YOU ONE THING!
ACE!
DO YOU WANT TO JOIN ME?!
LET'S TAKE OVER THE WORLD TOGETHER!
...
I'VE ALREADY MADE MY PLAN TO RISE TO THE TOP!
WHITEBEARD'S ERA IS OVER! I WILL BECOME THE KING OF THE PIRATES!
AND FOR STARTERS ...

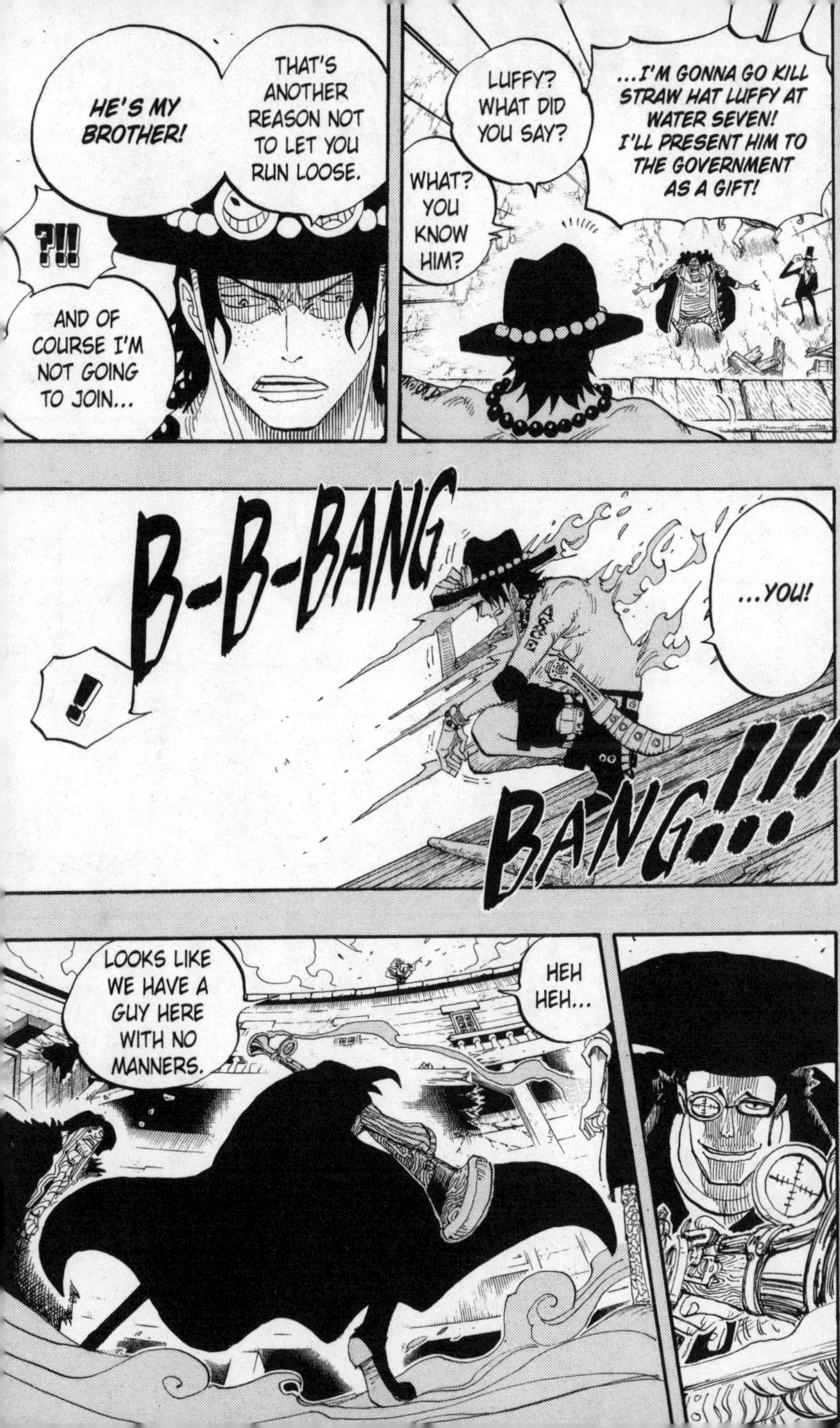
...I'M GONNA GO KILL STRAW HAT LUFFY AT WATER SEVEN! I'LL PRESENT HIM TO THE GOVERNMENT AS A GIFT!
LUFFY? WHAT DID YOU SAY?
WHAT? YOU KNOW HIM?
THAT'S ANOTHER REASON NOT TO LET YOU RUN LOOSE.
HE'S MY BROTHER!
?!!
AND OF COURSE I'M NOT GOING TO JOIN...
...YOU!
B-B-BANG
BANG!!!
!
HEH HEH...
LOOKS LIKE WE HAVE A GUY HERE WITH NO MANNERS.

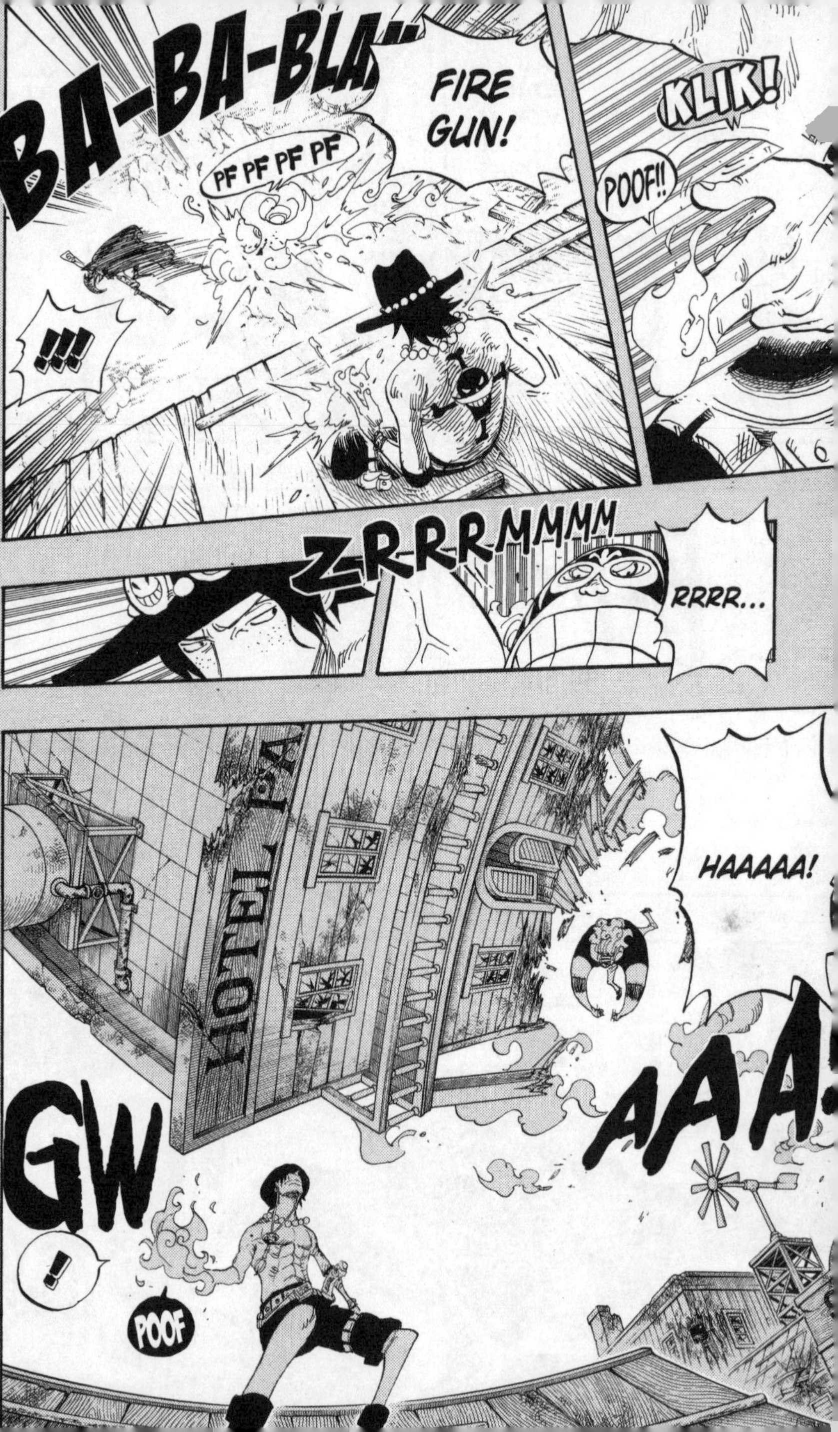
KLIK!
POOF!!
FIRE GUN!
BA-BA-BLA...
PF PF PF PF
!!!
RRRR...
Z-R-R-RMMMM
HAAAAA!
AAA
GW
!
POOF

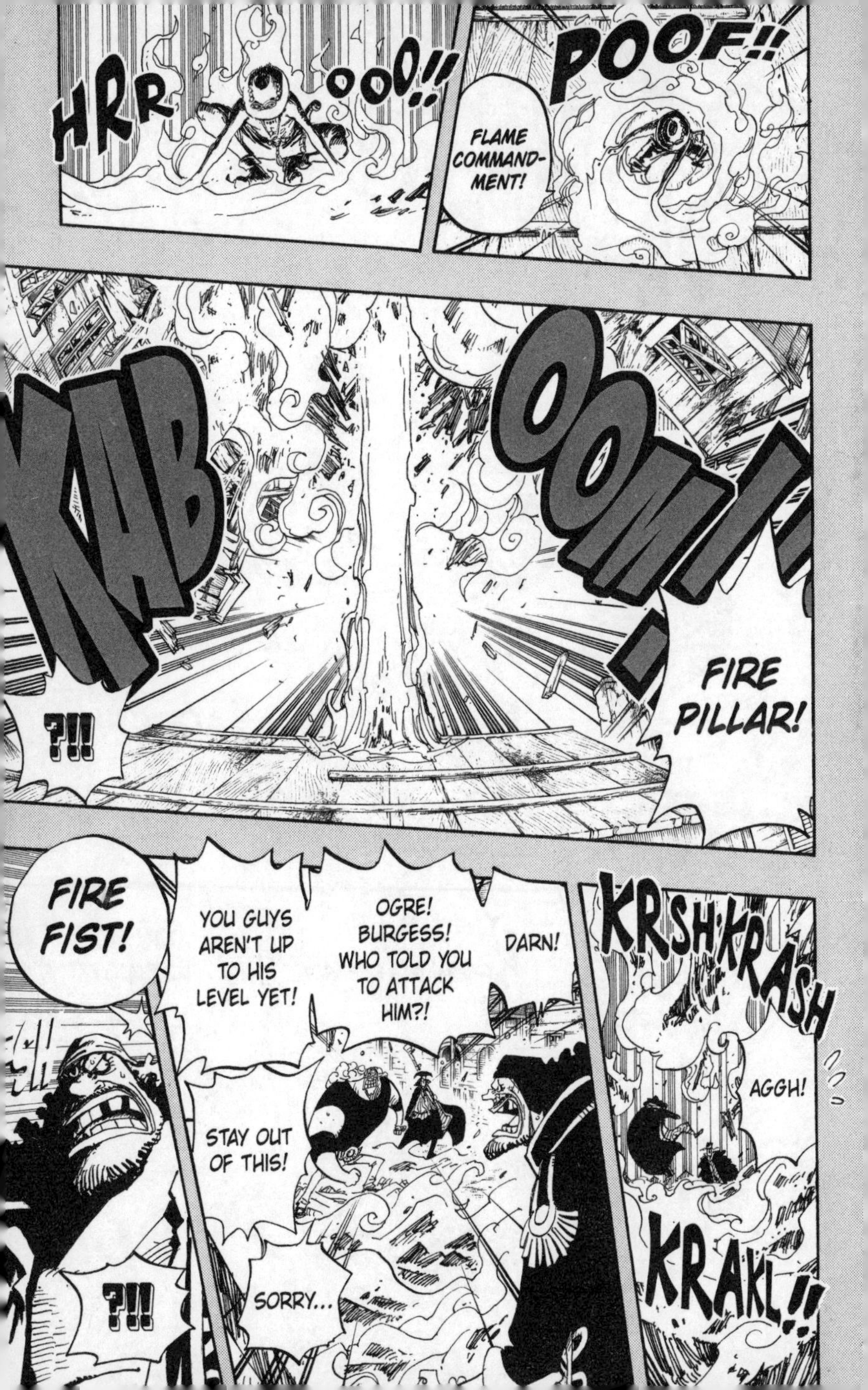
POOF!!
FLAME COMMANDMENT!
HRR OOO!!
KABOOM!!
FIRE PILLAR!
?!!
KRSH KRASH
AGGH!
KRAKL!!
DARN!
OGRE! BURGESS! WHO TOLD YOU TO ATTACK HIM?!
YOU GUYS AREN'T UP TO HIS LEVEL YET!
STAY OUT OF THIS!
SORRY...
FIRE FIST!
?!!

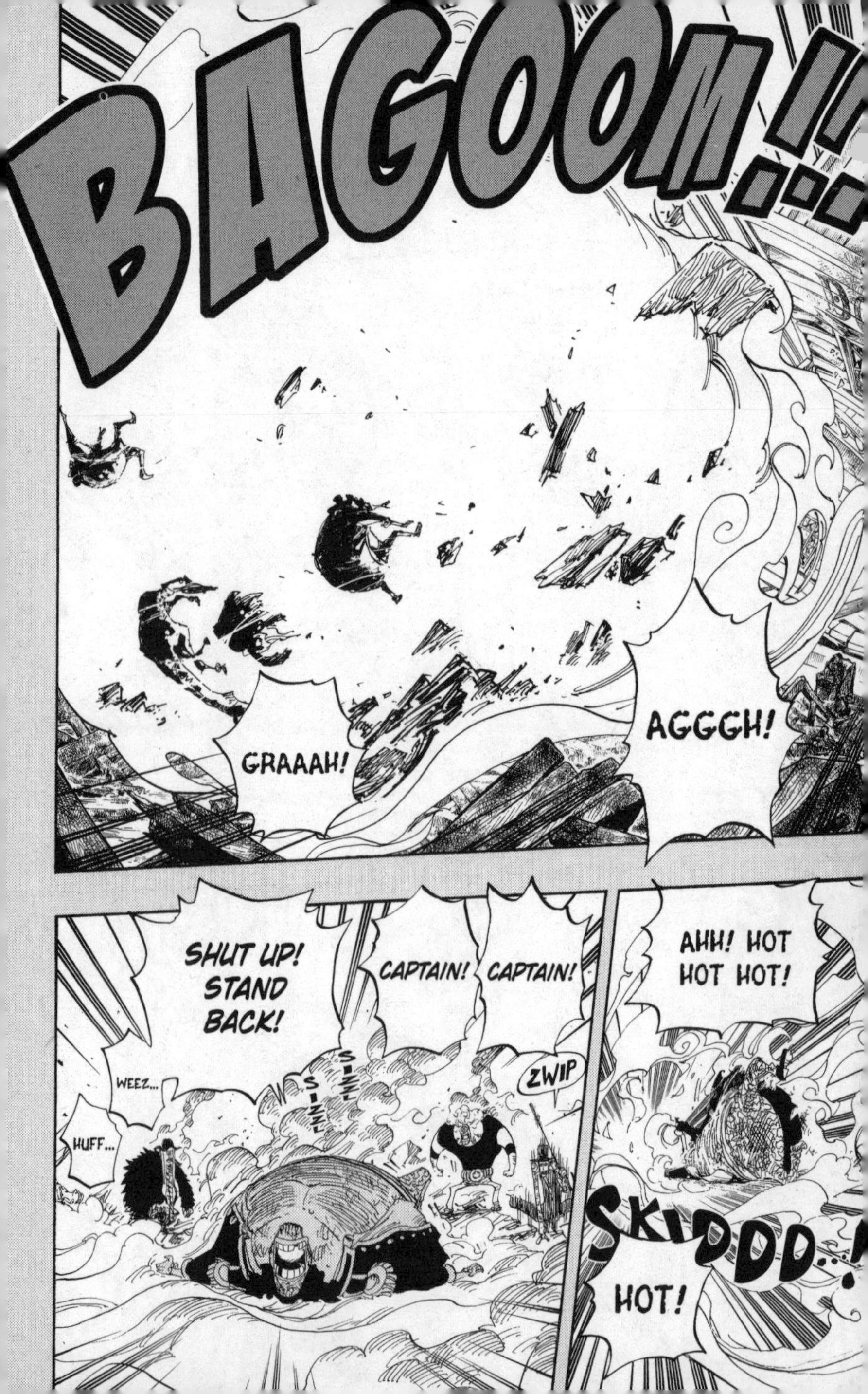
BAGOOM!!
AGGGH!
GRAAAH!
AHH! HOT HOT HOT!
SKIDDD..!!
HOT!
CAPTAIN!
CAPTAIN!
SHUT UP! STAND BACK!
ZWIP
SIZZL
SIZZL
WEEZ...
HUFF...

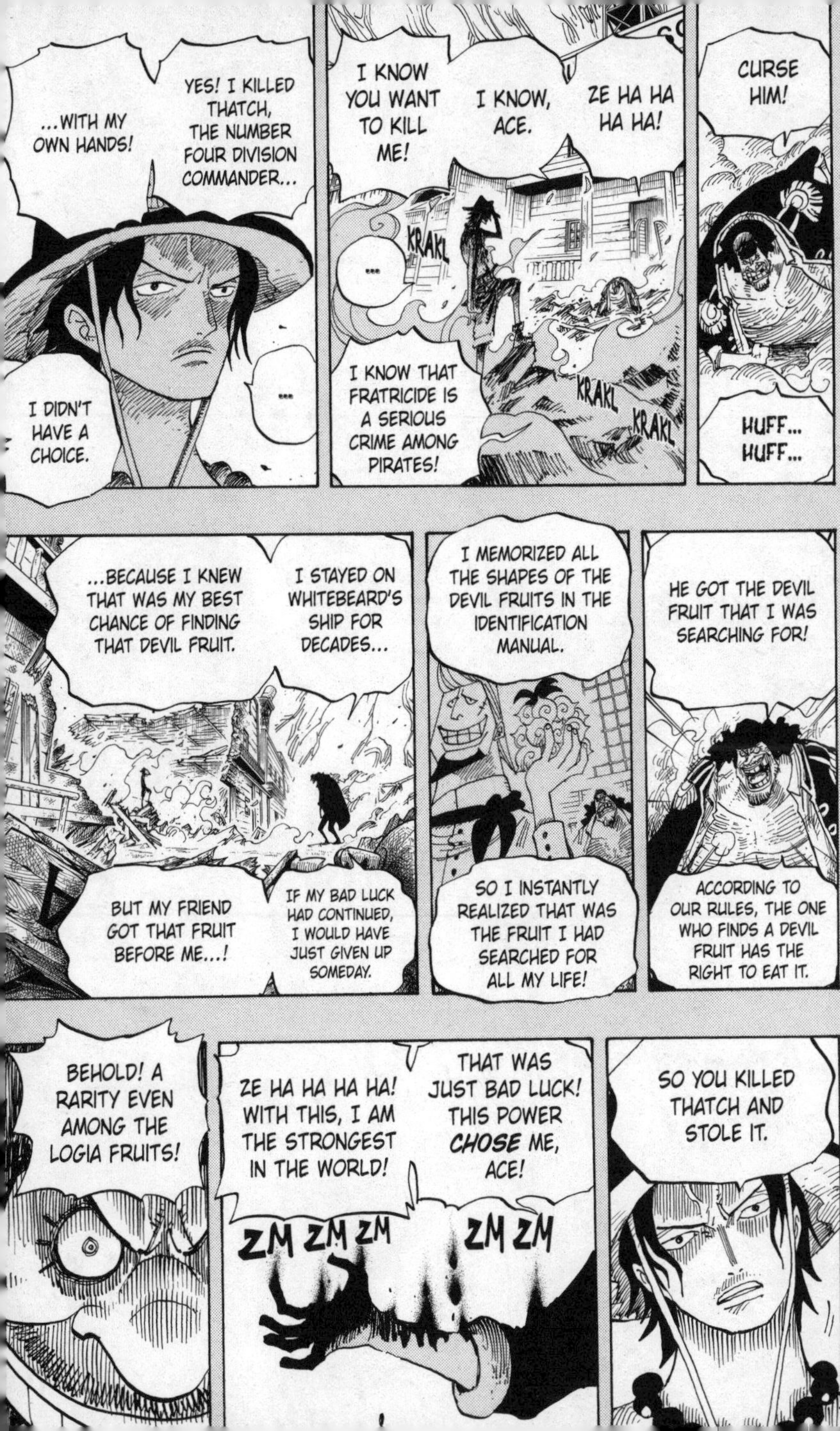
CURSE HIM!
HUFF... HUFF...
ZE HA HA HA HA!
I KNOW, ACE.
I KNOW YOU WANT TO KILL ME!
KRAKL
...
I KNOW THAT FRATRICIDE IS A SERIOUS CRIME AMONG PIRATES!
KRAKL
KRAKL
YES! I KILLED THATCH, THE NUMBER FOUR DIVISION COMMANDER...
...WITH MY OWN HANDS!
...
I DIDN'T HAVE A CHOICE.
HE GOT THE DEVIL FRUIT THAT I WAS SEARCHING FOR!
ACCORDING TO OUR RULES, THE ONE WHO FINDS A DEVIL FRUIT HAS THE RIGHT TO EAT IT.
I MEMORIZED ALL THE SHAPES OF THE DEVIL FRUITS IN THE IDENTIFICATION MANUAL.
SO I INSTANTLY REALIZED THAT WAS THE FRUIT I HAD SEARCHED FOR ALL MY LIFE!
I STAYED ON WHITEBEARD'S SHIP FOR DECADES...
...BECAUSE I KNEW THAT WAS MY BEST CHANCE OF FINDING THAT DEVIL FRUIT.
IF MY BAD LUCK HAD CONTINUED, I WOULD HAVE JUST GIVEN UP SOMEDAY.
BUT MY FRIEND GOT THAT FRUIT BEFORE ME...!
SO YOU KILLED THATCH AND STOLE IT.
THAT WAS JUST BAD LUCK! THIS POWER CHOSE ME, ACE!
ZE HA HA HA HA! WITH THIS, I AM THE STRONGEST IN THE WORLD!
ZM ZM
ZM ZM ZM
BEHOLD! A RARITY EVEN AMONG THE LOGIA FRUITS!

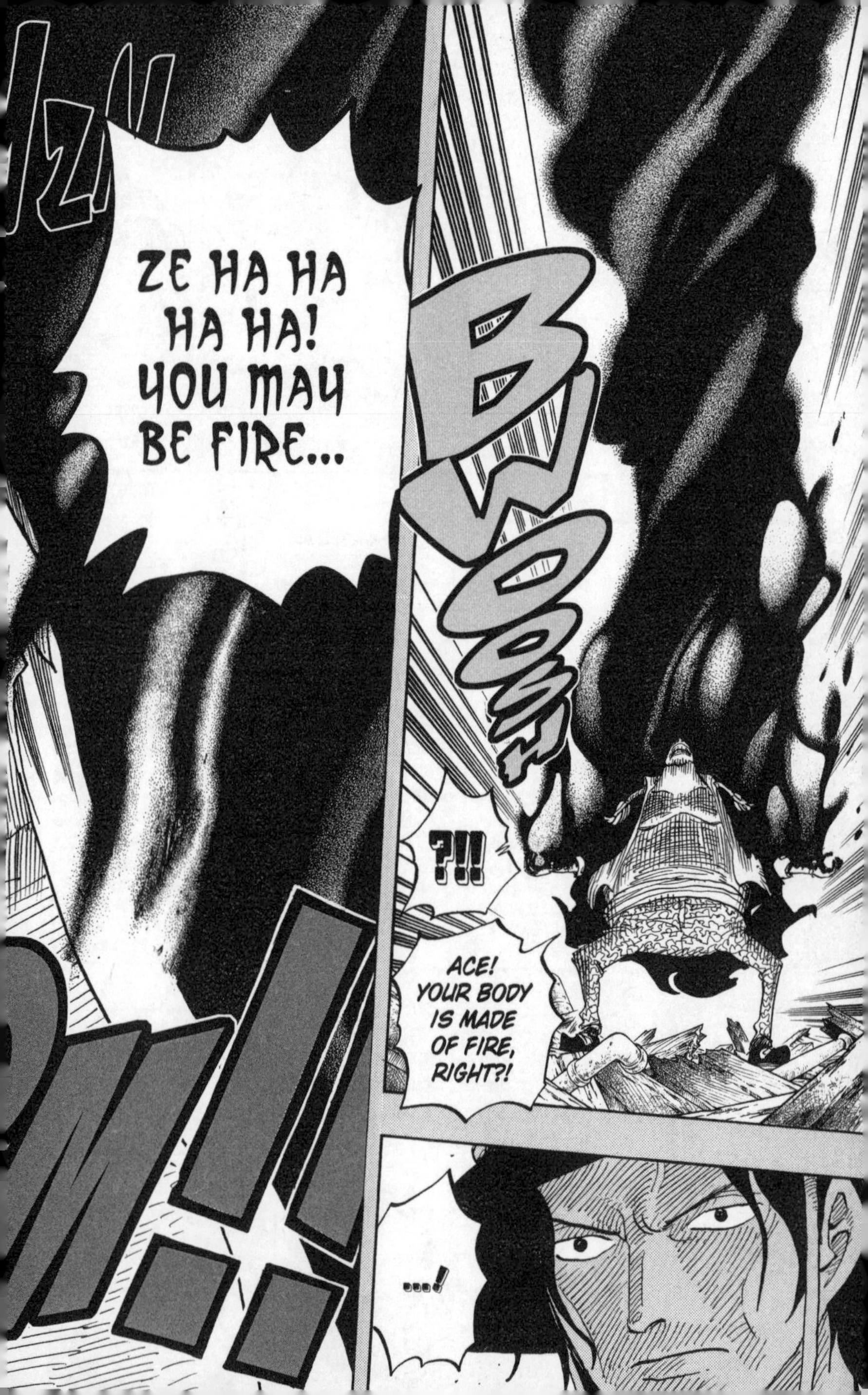
BWOOM!!
?!!
ACE! YOUR BODY IS MADE OF FIRE, RIGHT?!
...!
ZE HA HA HA HA! YOU MAY BE FIRE...

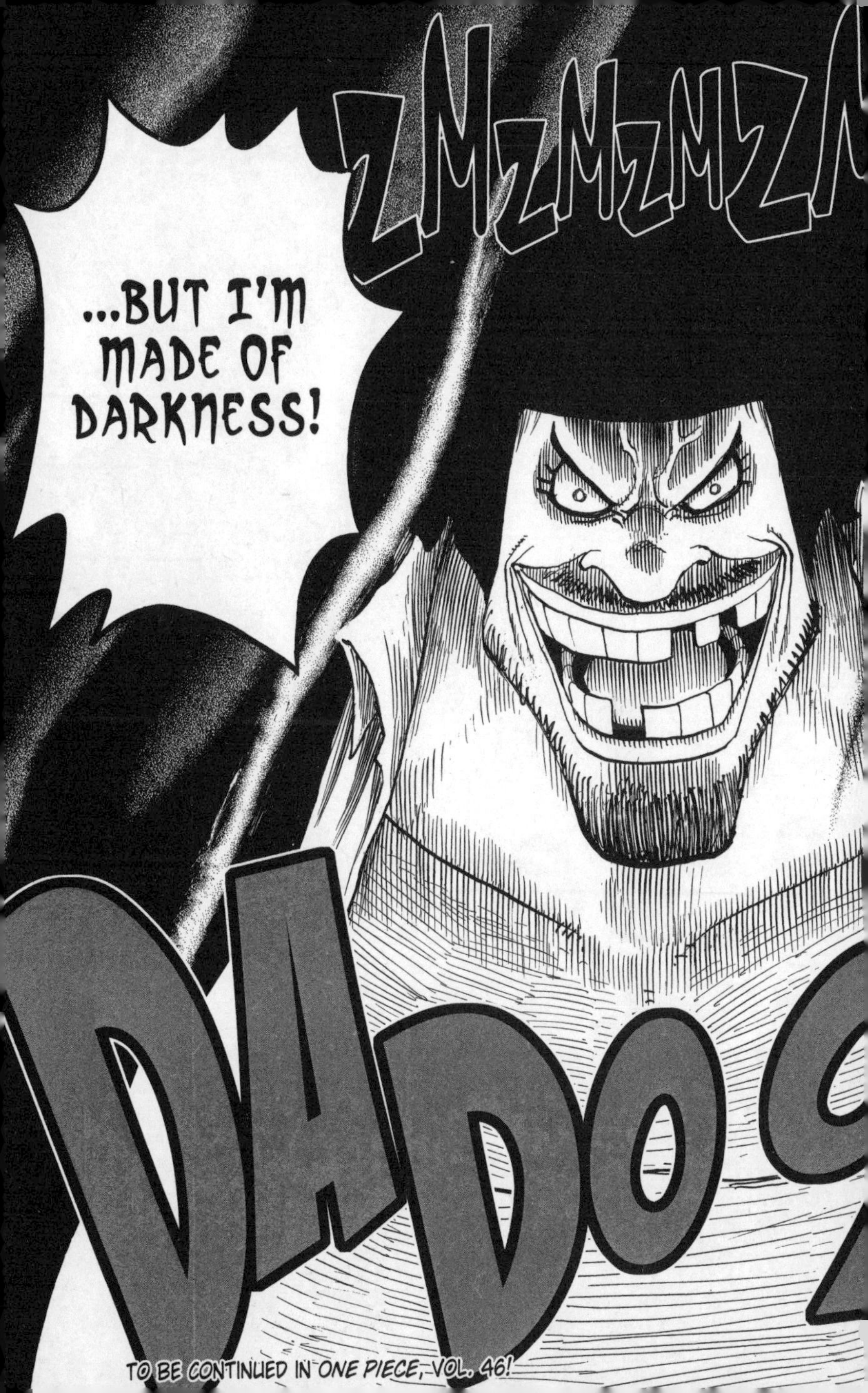
ZMZMZMZMZ
...BUT I'M MADE OF DARKNESS!
DADOO
TO BE CONTINUED IN ONE PIECE, VOL. 46!

COMING NEXT VOLUME:

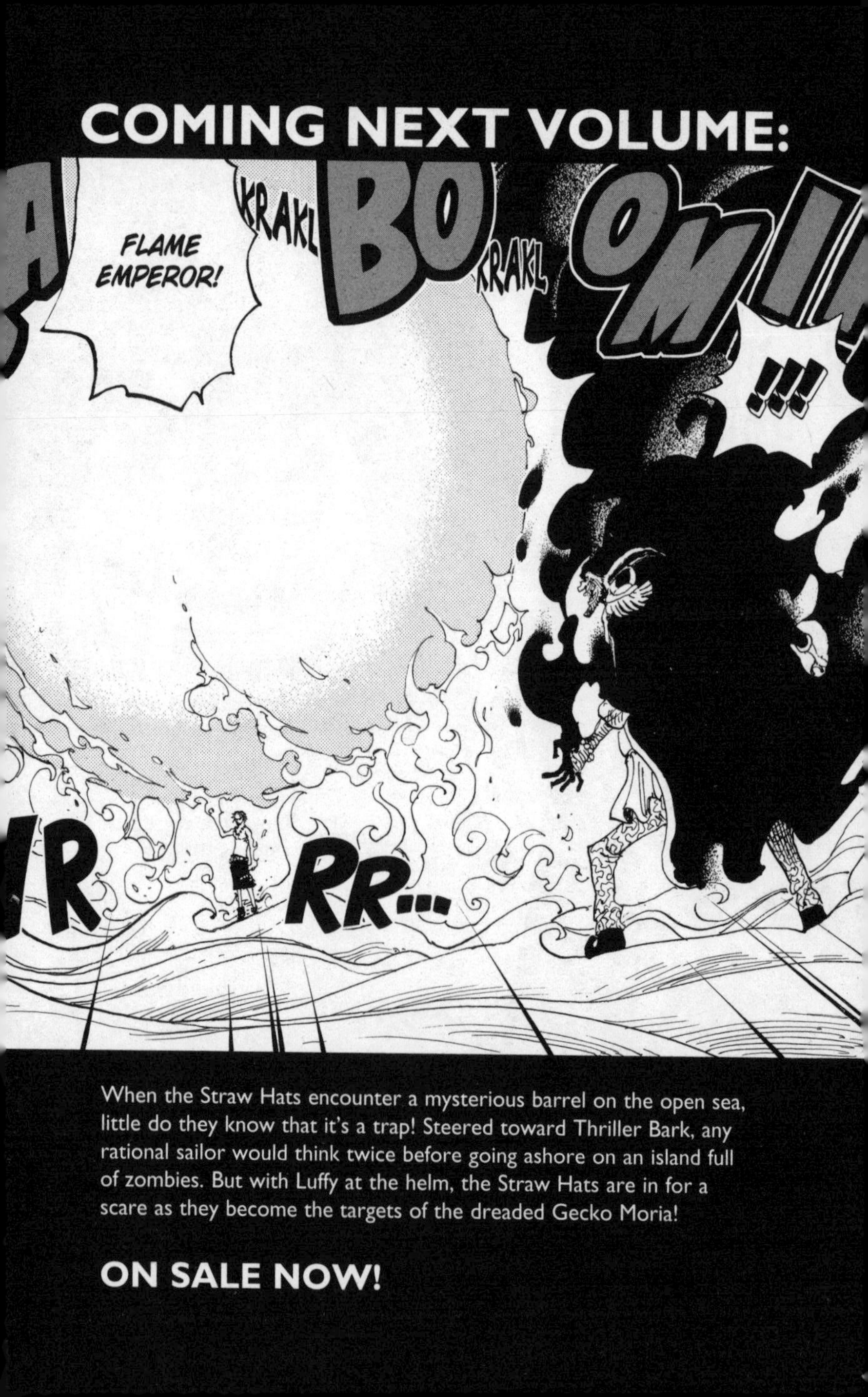
FLAME EMPEROR!
KRAKL
BO
KRAKL
OM
!!!
R
RR...

When the Straw Hats encounter a mysterious barrel on the open sea, little do they know that it's a trap! Steered toward Thriller Bark, any rational sailor would think twice before going ashore on an island full of zombies. But with Luffy at the helm, the Straw Hats are in for a scare as they become the targets of the dreaded Gecko Moria!

ON SALE NOW!

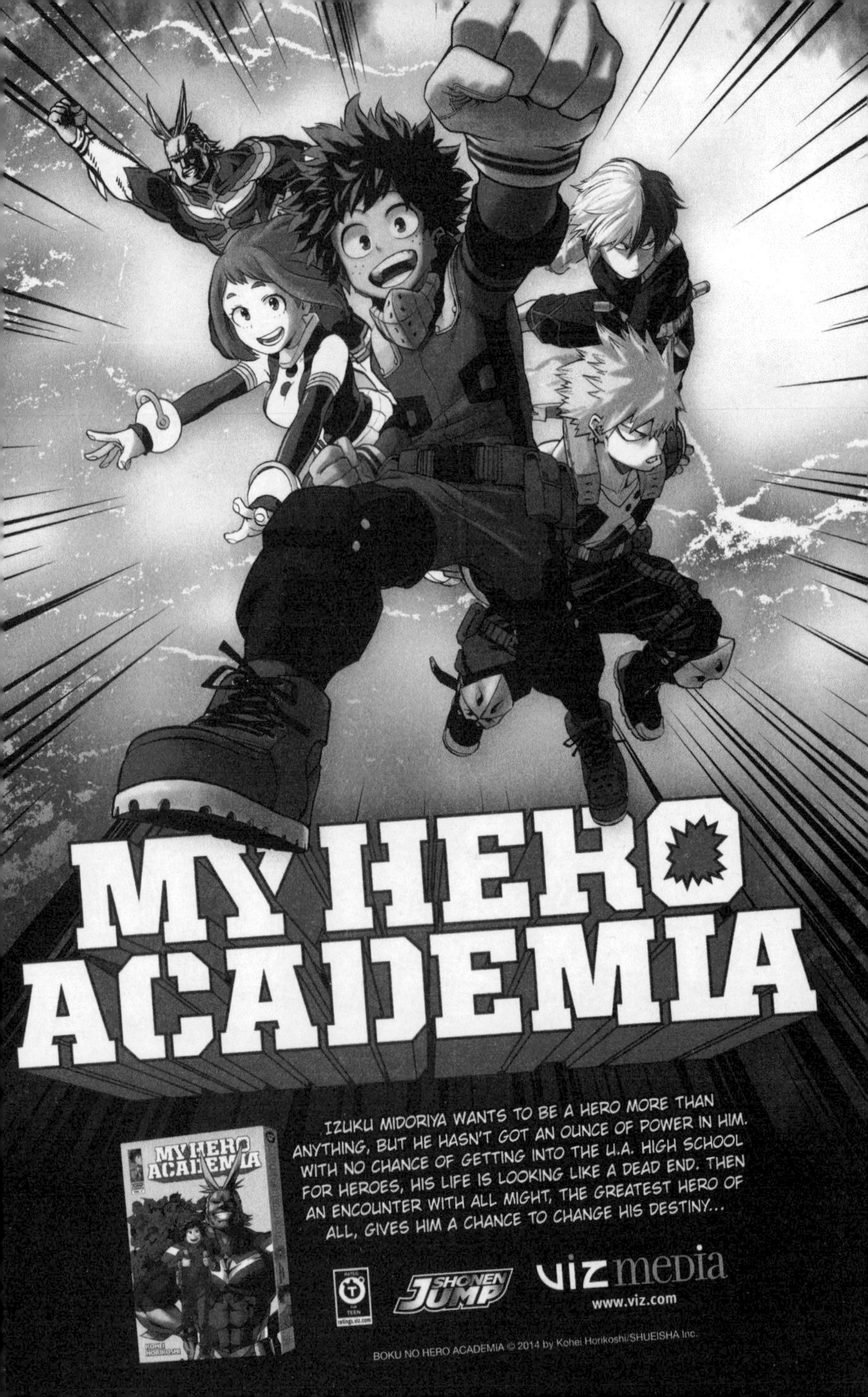
MY HERO ACADEMIA
IZUKU MIDORIYA WANTS TO BE A HERO MORE THAN ANYTHING, BUT HE HASN'T GOT AN OUNCE OF POWER IN HIM. WITH NO CHANCE OF GETTING INTO THE U.A. HIGH SCHOOL FOR HEROES, HIS LIFE IS LOOKING LIKE A DEAD END. THEN AN ENCOUNTER WITH ALL MIGHT, THE GREATEST HERO OF ALL, GIVES HIM A CHANCE TO CHANGE HIS DESTINY...
MY HERO ACADEMIA
KOHEI HORIKOSHI
RATED T TEEN ratings.viz.com
SHONEN JUMP
viz media
www.viz.com
BOKU NO HERO ACADEMIA © 2014 by Kohei Horikoshi/SHUEISHA Inc.

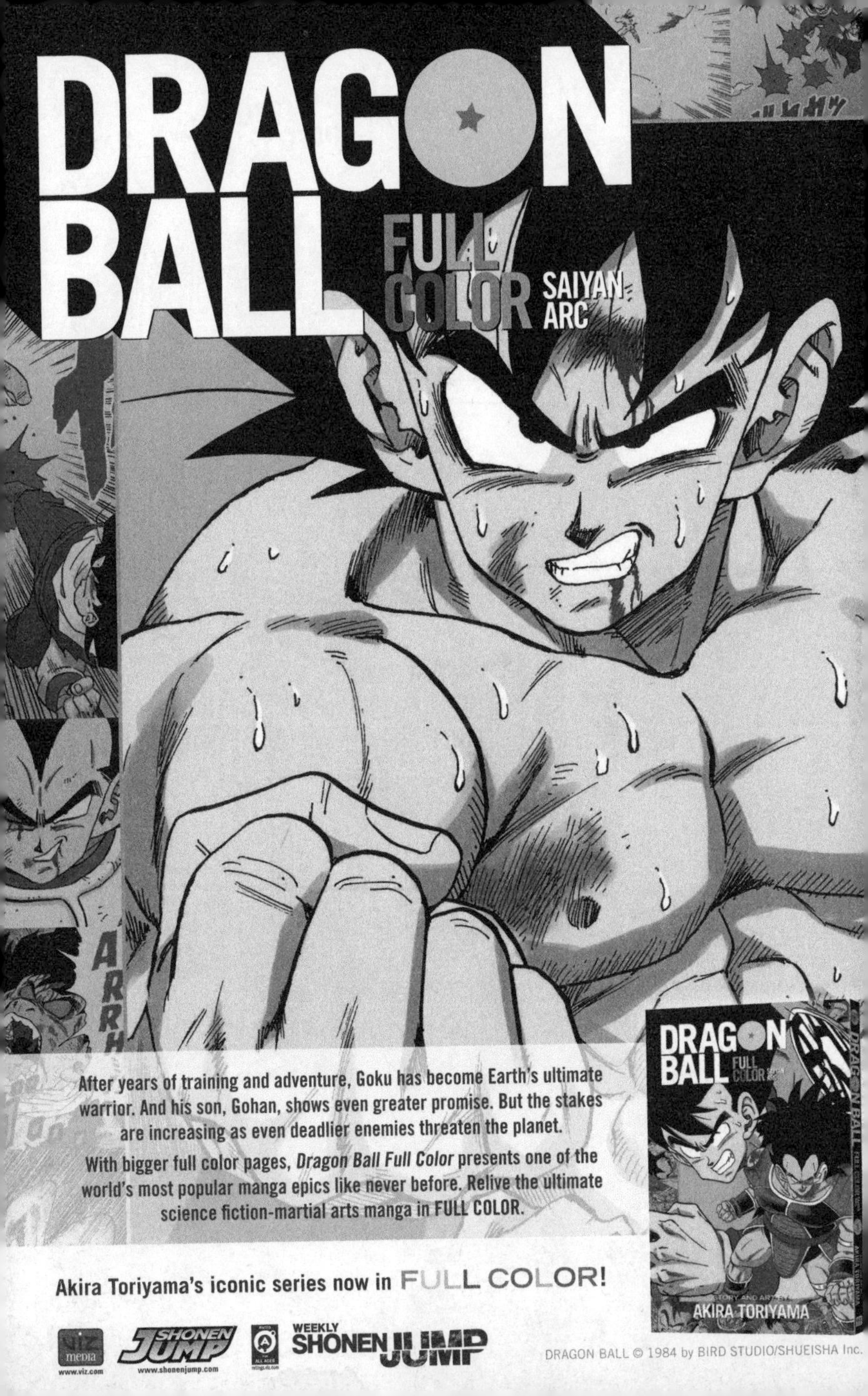
DRAGON BALL
FULL COLOR
SAIYAN ARC
ARRH
After years of training and adventure, Goku has become Earth's ultimate warrior. And his son, Gohan, shows even greater promise. But the stakes are increasing as even deadlier enemies threaten the planet.
With bigger full color pages, *Dragon Ball Full Color* presents one of the world's most popular manga epics like never before. Relive the ultimate science fiction-martial arts manga in FULL COLOR.
DRAGON BALL FULL COLOR
STORY AND ART BY
AKIRA TORIYAMA
Akira Toriyama's iconic series now in FULL COLOR!
viz media
www.viz.com
SHONEN JUMP
www.shonenjump.com
WEEKLY SHONEN JUMP
DRAGON BALL © 1984 by BIRD STUDIO/SHUEISHA Inc.

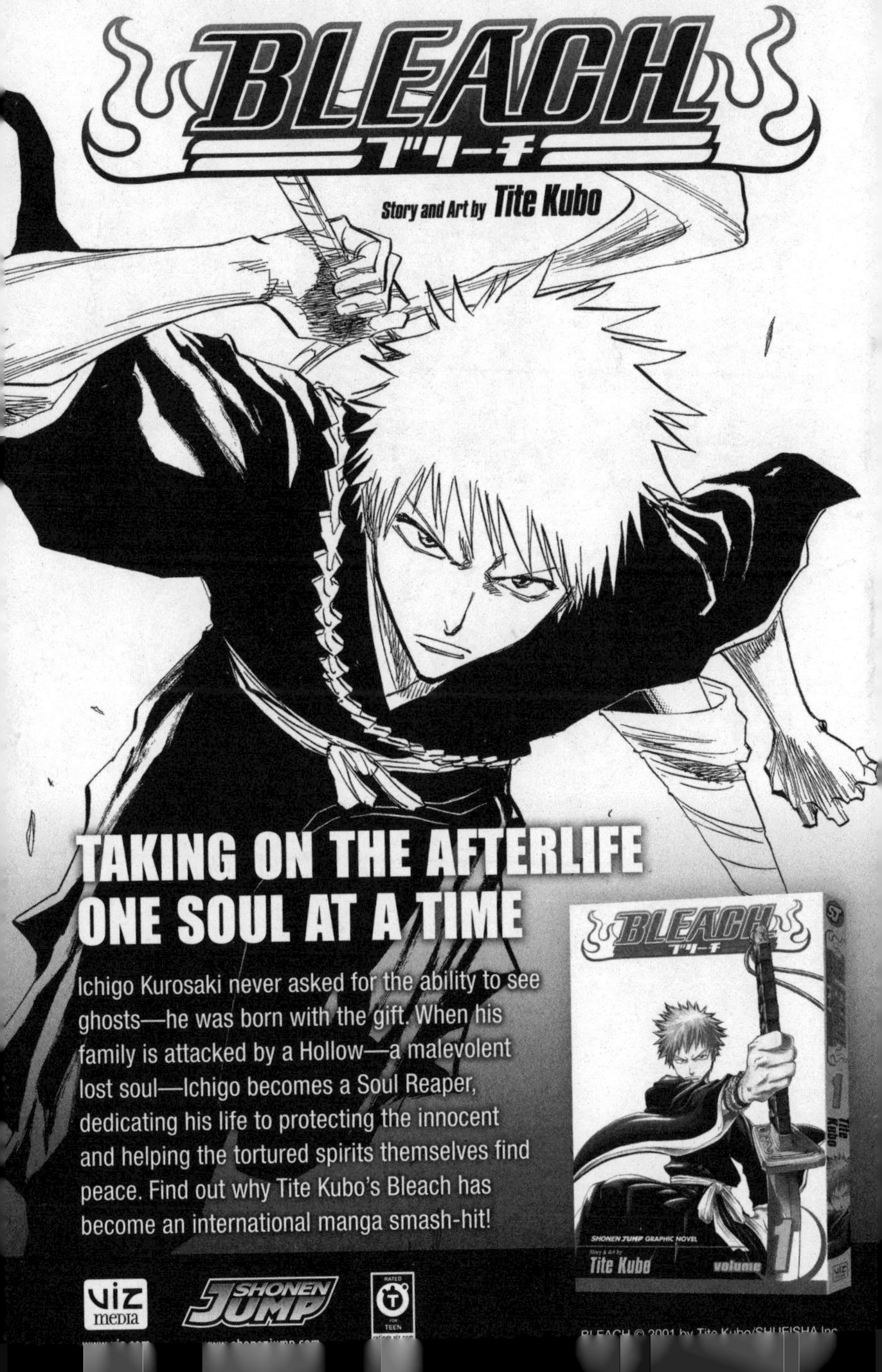
BLEACH
ブリーチ
Story and Art by Tite Kubo
TAKING ON THE AFTERLIFE ONE SOUL AT A TIME
Ichigo Kurosaki never asked for the ability to see ghosts—he was born with the gift. When his family is attacked by a Hollow—a malevolent lost soul—Ichigo becomes a Soul Reaper, dedicating his life to protecting the innocent and helping the tortured spirits themselves find peace. Find out why Tite Kubo's Bleach has become an international manga smash-hit!
BLEACH
ブリーチ
SHONEN JUMP GRAPHIC NOVEL
Story & Art by
Tite Kubo
volume 1
viz media
SHONEN JUMP
RATED T FOR TEEN

NARUTO

the Seventh Hokage and the Scarlet Spring

STORY AND ART BY
MASASHI KISHIMOTO

In the years since the great ninja war, peace has bloomed in the ninja world, and a new generation has begun to take root. Naruto's work as an adult seems to be pretty mundane, but his son, Boruto, is constantly demanding attention. Luckily for Naruto, he can make clones of himself to babysit his son. But Sasuke's daughter, Sarada, could be the target of a mysterious figure who has connections to the Uchiha clan!

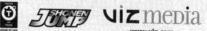

THE ACTION-PACKED SUPERHERO COMEDY ABOUT ONE MAN'S AMBITION TO BE A HERO FOR FUN!
ONE-PUNCH MAN
STORY BY ONE
ART BY YUSUKE MURATA
ONE-PUNCH MAN
01
STORY BY ONE
ART BY YUSUKE MURATA
SHONENJUMP MANGA
Nothing about Saitama passes the eyeball test when it comes to superheroes, from his lifeless expression to his bald head to his unimpressive physique. However, this average-looking guy has a not-so-average problem—he just can't seem to find an opponent strong enough to take on!
Can he finally find an opponent who can go toe-to-toe with him and give his life some meaning? Or is he doomed to a life of superpowered boredom?
RATED T TEEN ratings.viz.com
SHONEN JUMP
VIZ media
www.viz.com
ONE-PUNCH MAN © 2012 by ONE, Yusuke Murata/SHUEISHA Inc.

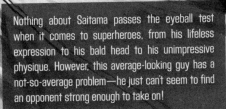

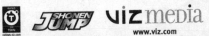

You're Reading in the Wrong Direction!!

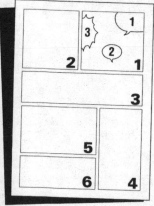

Whoops! Guess what? You're starting at the wrong end of the comic!

...It's true! In keeping with the original Japanese format, **One Piece** is meant to be read from right to left, starting in the upper-right corner.

Unlike English, which is read from left to right, Japanese is read from right to left, meaning that action, sound effects and word-balloon order are completely reversed...something which can make readers unfamiliar with Japanese feel pretty backwards themselves. For this reason, manga or Japanese comics published in the U.S. in English have sometimes been published "flopped"— that is, printed in exact reverse order, as though seen from the other side of a mirror.

By flopping pages, U.S. publishers can avoid confusing readers, but the compromise is not without its downside. For one thing, a character in a flopped manga series who once wore in the original Japanese version a T-shirt emblazoned with "M A Y" (as in "the merry month of") now wears one which reads "Y A M"! Additionally, many manga creators in Japan are themselves unhappy with the process, as some feel the mirror-imaging of their art skews their original intentions.

We are proud to bring you Eiichiro Oda's **One Piece** in the original unflopped format. For now, though, turn to the other side of the book and let the journey begin...!

—Editor